About

William Minter is the edito
(www.africafocus.org). His
*Victories: African Liberation and American Activists over a Half
Century, 1950-2000* (2007), co-edited with Gail Hovey and
Charles Cobb, Jr. Minter's extensive experience of southern
Africa includes teaching at the secondary school of the
Mozambique Liberation Front in Tanzania and
Mozambique in the 1960s and 1970s and work with the
Africa solidarity and anti-apartheid movements in the
United States. He holds a Ph.D. from the University of
Wisconsin (Madison), with a concentration in political
sociology and African studies.

'Minter's book could not be more timely. With the ANC
victory in South Africa, the world is ready to forget
southern Africa, and forgive the near destruction of Angola
and Mozambique in defence of apartheid South Africa.
Minter reminds us of how the wars there were nourished
and largely incited to prevent human liberation. It is a
sobering tale with lessons for the immediate future.'
Immanuel Wallerstein

'Minter handles the extremely fragmentary and
controversial material on the wars in southern Africa in a
remarkably lucid, dispassionate yet committed way. His
book takes account of the many different views and
attempts to weigh the evidence systematically and
judiciously. It should be read by all those with an interest in
contemporary southern Africa, or whatever persuasion.'
Shula Marks

'By far the most comprehensive analysis of racist South
Africa's destabilization campaigns in Angola and
Mozambique.' *Georges Nzongola-Ntalaja*

'All those responsible for the 'contra' subversions in Angola
and Mozambique will be cursed by history for enormous
and terrible crimes, which will long weigh heavily on the
whole of southern Africa. William Minter gives us the
factual and balanced record; it is, for all of us, an
indispensable contribution.' *Basil Davidson*

Books by William Minter

Portuguese Africa and the West (Harmondsworth: Penguin, 1972 and New York: Monthly Review Press, 1973).

Imperial Network and External Dependency: The Case of Angola (Beverly Hills: Sage Professional Papers in International Studies, 1972).

Imperial Brain Trust: The Council on Foreign Relations and United States Foreign Policy (with Laurence Shoup) (New York: Monthly Review Press, 1977).

King Solomon's Mines Revisited: Western Interests and the Burdened History of Southern Africa (New York: Basic Books, 1986).

Operation Timber: Pages from the Savimbi Dossier (Trenton, NJ: Africa World Press, 1988).

No Easy Victories: African Liberation and American Activists over a Half Century, 1950-2000 (edited with Gail Hovey and Charles Cobb Jr.) (Trenton, NJ: Africa World Press, 2007).

Reviews of *King Solomon's Mines Revisited*

'An invaluable work, elegantly organised and written ... I have named it one of my choices for "Books of the Year"' - Nadine Gordimer

'The most challenging of recent books on Southern Africa' - Professor Leonard Thompson, *The New York Review of Books*

'An original, highly readable study ... a very important new book that warrants wide readership' - *Choice*

'Indispensable ... probably the best historical overview yet published' - Victoria Brittain, *Guardian*

'Compulsory reading for anyone seriously interested in South Africa' - Donald Woods, *Third World Quarterly*

'A must for scholars and analysts of South Africa and the U.S. stance towards that country' - *Foreign Affairs*

A rich mine of essential historical information, shrewd political insights and comments' - *The Black Scholar*

'A powerful, wide-ranging and ambitious book' - Professor Shula Marks, *Southern African Review of Books*

'A big, important book, deserving of the attention it has already received. Authoritative in academic terms, it is readily accessible to a general readership' - *International Journal of African Historical Studies*

Apartheid's Contras

An Inquiry into the Roots of War in Angola and Mozambique

WILLIAM MINTER

Originally published in 1994 by
Zed Books and Witwatersrand University Press

2008 reprint by
BookSurge Publishing

Copyright © William Minter, 1994.

Cover designed by Andrew Corbett.
Cover photograph by Carlos Guarita/Reportage.
Maps reproduced from *Africa Recovery* by kind
permission of United Nations, Africa Recovery.

Set in Monotype Baskerville
by Ewan Smith, London E8.

The right of William Minter to be identified as the
author of this work has been asserted by him
according to the Copyright, Designs and Patents Act,
1988.

All rights reserved.

ISBN 1-4392-1618-5

Contents

Acknowledgements

This is not so much a book I chose to write as a book I felt had to be written. I am most grateful to those many individuals who encouraged me, reaffirmed the project's importance, and shared their hospitality and insights. I hope this work contributes to our common concern that simplistic rewriting of history should not exonerate those who bear principal responsibility for massive human suffering.

The names are too many to cite, but a few whose timely encouragement was particularly important must be mentioned: Sven Hamrell, Sten Rylander, and Prexy Nesbitt.

I am grateful for financial support to The Ford Foundation, SIDA in Sweden and NOVIB in the Netherlands.

Many others also contributed indirectly to this book. I drew inspiration from the many committed individuals, Angolans, Mozambicans and foreigners, who have continued working to serve the people as best they could, despite disillusionment and discouragement. I am indebted to the small group of writers who have coped with the many difficulties in doing serious research on Angola and Mozambique, from Basil Davidson's pioneering work to recent investigations by Mozambican and Angolan researchers and journalists. Most will find clues that I have incorporated their insights, however inadequately, and will, I hope, forgive me for only the most cursory of mentions in footnotes.

I particularly wish to thank those who commented on the manuscript at the almost final stage: Merle Bowen, António Matonse, Robert Molteno, Jeanne Penvenne, Otto Roesch, Kathy Sheldon, David Sogge, Catherine Sunshine, and Ken Wilson. News of Otto's death in an automobile accident in Mozambique came just as I was completing these acknowledgements; his committed and careful scholarship will be sorely missed.

I thank my colleagues at the Washington Office on Africa for understanding my need to take time for the book. In bearing with my frustrations while writing it, Cathy managed admirably to keep her sense of humour and Cynthia her 4-year-old energy and enthusiasm unchecked.

William Minter, June 1994

List of Abbreviations

ANC	African National Congress
CIO	Central Intelligence Organization (Rhodesia)
COSATU	Congress of South African Trade Unions
FLEC	Front for the Liberation of the Enclave of Cabinda
FLNC	Congo National Liberation Front
FNLA	National Front for the Liberation of Angola
Frelimo	Mozambique Liberation Front
MNR	Mozambican National Resistance
MPLA	Popular Movement for the Liberation of Angola
OAU	Organization of African Unity
PAIGC	African Party for the Independence of Guinea-Bissau and Cape Verde
Renamo	Mozambican National Resistance
SADCC	South African Development Coordination Conference
SADF	South African Defence Force
SSC	State Security Council (South Africa)
SWAPO	South West African People's Organization
SWATF	South West Africa Territorial Force
UDF	United Democratic Front
UNAMO	Mozambique National Union
Unita	National Union for the Total Independence of Angola
UPA	Union of Peoples of Angola
ZANU	Zimbabwean African National Union
ZAPU	Zimbabwean African People's Union

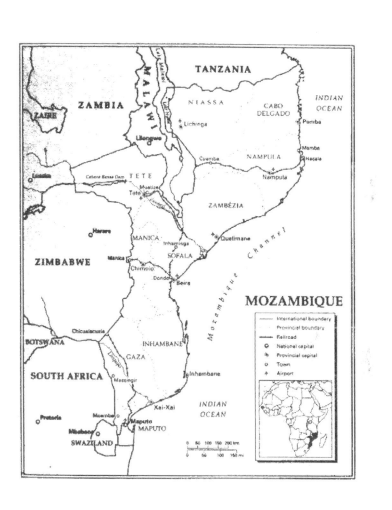

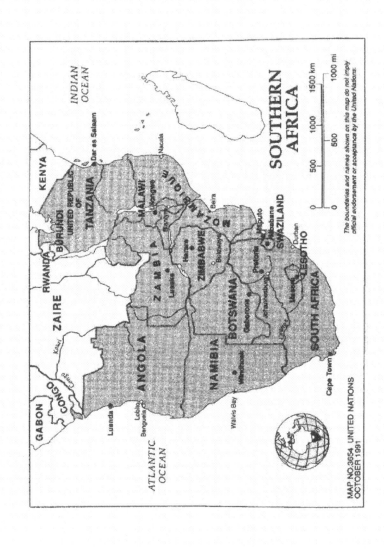

SOUTHERN AFRICA

The boundaries and names shown on this map do not imply
official endorsement or acceptance by the United Nations.

0   500   1000   1500 km
0   500   1000 mi

MAP NO.3654 UNITED NATIONS
OCTOBER 1991

Introduction

Two hidden wars ravaged Angola and Mozambique in the 1980s, with a toll in human suffering that easily rivalled if not surpassed the more publicized conflicts in Nicaragua and Afghanistan. The southern African wars, however, rarely appeared on television screens around the world. South Africa captured media attention mid-decade, but few international observers made the critical connection between the apartheid regime's violence at home and its role in fomenting war in neighbouring countries. On occasion, massacres or famines in Mozambique or Angola won brief mention in the news. But for the most part, the killing went on unremarked.

The aftermath in 1992–93, as Angola was plunged into war again after widely applauded multi-party elections, was even more horrific. Over 100,000 people were killed within a year, rates far exceeding the wars in the former Yugoslavia, as the losing party went on the attack, besieging cities and blocking relief supplies while the world press and the international community paid no more than token attention. The post-election catastrophe, an ominous precedent for other African countries planning for elections, would have been impossible without the systematic build-up of insurgent forces over the previous decade.

Much of the detailed history of these wars may never be recovered. Nevertheless, disentangling the main threads is critical to understanding the legacy of the 1980s at several levels. To start with, flawed interpretations of the past are likely to contribute to future failures to establish stable bases for peace and national reconstruction. Secondly, Angolans and Mozambicans must interpret these tragedies to come to terms with fundamental themes of their national histories. In addition, understanding the dynamics – and counting up the costs – of apartheid's struggle to maintain itself is impossible without including Angola and Mozambique. Finally, these two conflicts are among the prime examples of 'freedom-fighter' insurgencies celebrated by the international right wing in the last decade of the Cold War.

Angola and Mozambique feature a complex interplay of internal,

regional and global factors that refuse to fit simple models of wars
between nation-states or of purely internal civil wars. State and non-
state actors both played active roles. In the post-Cold War era, with
national boundaries being readjusted and a bewildering profusion of
conflicts, sorting out such multi-level interactions of factors is likely to
become even more important.

As a case-study, this book focuses primarily on the particularities of
the two cases. But as a comparative study, it also draws out points of
wider relevance, both for the parallel 'Reagan-doctrine' anti-Marxist
insurgencies of the late Cold War and, more generally, for the kind of
warfare most recently labelled 'low-intensity conflict'.

The term 'low-intensity conflict' distinguishes guerrilla wars and
other unconventional warfare from 'medium- and high-intensity' conventional wars on the scale culminating in nuclear confrontation. But
gauged in terms of human suffering, 'low-intensity' is a monstrous
misnomer for wars such as those in Angola and Mozambique. Large-
scale battlefield encounters, such as those in south-eastern Angola in
the mid-1980s, were indeed exceptional. But the cumulative toll of
violence year-in and year-out, plus the fact that the victims were overwhelmingly civilians, imposed a trauma on these societies comparable
with that of the Second World War on Europe.[1]

The war in Mozambique began soon after the country achieved
independence in 1975 under the leadership of the Mozambique Liberation Front, known by its Portuguese acronym Frelimo. Frelimo
granted refuge to Zimbabwean guerrillas fighting for majority rule in
Rhodesia. The Rhodesian army supplemented raids on Mozambique
against Zimbabwean guerrillas with sponsorship of the Mozambican
National Resistance, known at first as MNR and later as Renamo. When
Zimbabwe achieved independence in 1980, South Africa took over
sponsorship of Renamo and dramatically augmented its military capacity. Despite a 1984 non-aggression pact between Mozambique and
South Africa, Renamo operations continued to escalate. Intermittent
peace talks beginning in 1990 finally led to a ceasefire in October 1992.

For many newspaper readers, the horror of the war in Mozambique
crystallized for the first time in 1987, when news reports highlighted
'the worst atrocity of a savage eleven-year war'.[2] On 18 July Renamo
forces attacked the small town of Homoine in Inhambane province,
killing 424 civilians. Survivors said the victims included pregnant women, children and other patients in the town's clinic. Some were shot
with automatic weapons, others killed with machetes.

Renamo spokesmen in Lisbon and Washington denied that the
organization was responsible for the massacre, instead suggesting that
local militia had clashed with government troops, or that government
forces had disguised themselves as rebels. Senator Jesse Helms, in the

midst of a campaign to win US government support for Renamo, told the Senate Foreign Relations Committee that the charges were a 'set-up'. A US military attaché visiting the site a week later noted sceptically that damage to buildings was limited and that the people 'did not appear to be devestated [*sic*], on edge or very angry as one would expect'.[3]

Scepticism might have prevailed had not there been an American eyewitness, Mennonite agricultural worker Mark Van Koevering. Van Koevering, who hid in a shed outside his hotel to escape the massacre, spoke with survivors in the hours and days following the event. He stated that local residents had no doubt at all that Renamo was responsible. Reporters who interviewed the injured and other residents came to the same conclusion.[4]

The Homoine incident, together with the cumulative impact of reports by journalists, aid workers and diplomats, consolidated an international image of Renamo as brutal and ruthless. A State Department consultant's report in 1988, based on interviews with refugees and displaced persons, held the group responsible for 95 per cent of the abuses of civilians in the war, including the murder of as many as 100,000 civilians.[5]

A United Nations study in 1989 estimated that Mozambique suffered economic losses of approximately $15 billion between 1980 and 1988, five and a half times the 1988 Gross Domestic Product (GDP). By the end of 1988, 978 rural health clinics – almost half the total in the country – had been destroyed or forced to close by Renamo attacks. UNICEF estimated that 494,000 Mozambican children under the age of five died between 1980 and 1988 from war-related causes, both direct deaths and those due to the war's effect of increasing famine and disease.[6]

Despite the consensus on the damages of war, and on Renamo's culpability, many aspects of the war in Mozambique remained mysterious. Eyewitnesses of the Homoine attack noted the new uniforms and boots worn by Renamo troops, and Mozambican officials cited a parachute found in the bush a few weeks before the attack and other signs of recent re-supply by South Africa. But South Africa denied involvement, and Western observers pointed to the lack of recent documentary proof of the connection. As the war ground on, analysts continued to puzzle over Renamo and its motives. To what extent was it still an agent of South Africa's covert special forces, as it clearly had been in the early 1980s? To what extent had it instead become embedded as a pathological growth in Mozambican society itself, fed by the multiple weaknesses of the post-colonial state? The horror was undeniable. But the causes, and thus the responsibility, were elusive.

In Angola the post-colonial conflict began even before independence.

Portugal and three Angolan movements agreed on a plan for peaceful transition in January 1975. But fighting over the next year pitted the National Front for the Liberation of Angola (FNLA) and the National Union for the Total Independence of Angola (Unita) against the Popular Movement for the Liberation of Angola (MPLA). The United States, Zaire and South Africa headed the external forces ranged against the MPLA, while Cuba and the Soviet Union came to its support.

By March 1976 the MPLA had emerged as the government of independent Angola. In subsequent years, while the FNLA faded in importance, Jonas Savimbi of Unita found support for his organization from South Africa and other countries. Angola aided guerrillas seeking the independence of South West Africa (Namibia) from South African rule, while South African troops based in Namibia joined Unita in attacking southern Angola.

In the second half of the 1980s, the CIA again openly joined with South Africa in boosting Unita's military campaign. South African and Cuban involvement officially ceased after implementation of 1988 agreements on the independence of Namibia and withdrawal of South African and Cuban troops from Angola. Unita and the Angolan government signed a ceasefire agreement in May 1991. In September 1992, after a generally uneventful ceasefire, the ruling MPLA won a majority in elections deemed free and fair by international observers. But Savimbi ordered his troops to return to war, reigniting full-scale conflict.

The statistics of destruction in Angola – even before renewed war at the end of 1992 – were as numbing as those from Mozambique. The UN estimated that Angola lost $30 billion from war over 1980–88, six times the 1988 GDP. UNICEF calculated 331,000 children dead of causes directly or indirectly related to the war – a smaller number than in Mozambique, but a larger percentage of the population of 9.7 million. Unita's extensive use of land-mines helped rank Angola with Afghanistan and Cambodia in the number of amputees – conservatively estimated at over 15,000.[7]

In the case of Angola, however, no clear international image crystallized of the human impact of the war, or the responsibility for it. There were few first-hand press reports from inside Angola. A February 1986 massacre of over 100 people by Unita guerrillas in the village of Camabatela went unmentioned in the international press at the time.[8] Journalists and other Westerners visiting the Angolan capital rarely travelled to the interior. Visitors to Unita-controlled areas almost never deviated from their guided tour culminating in an interview with the photogenic guerrilla leader Jonas Savimbi. The Western images of the Angolan war were caricatures, featuring a Marxist government supported by Cuban troops and assailed by anti-communist guerrilla fighters. In Africa, South Africa's military involvement on the side of

Unita produced the contrasting image of an African country under assault from apartheid. But even Angola's allies received little direct information to put a human face on the conflict.

The first outside reports based on systematic interviews with refugees and displaced persons came out only in 1989 and 1991. Africa Watch researcher Jemara Rone documented significant abuses of civilians, particularly the repeated forced displacement of villagers by both parties to the war. She particularly noted Unita's strategies aimed at starving civilians in government-held areas by attacks, kidnappings and planting of land-mines on paths used by peasants. Despite Unita's support on ethnic grounds from many Umbundu-speaking Angolans, Africa Watch reported that civilians of that same group suffered most from Unita attacks.[9]

Particularly revealing of the information gap regarding Angola was the time it took for the outside world to take notice of human rights abuses within Unita. Later reports revealed killings of suspected rivals to Savimbi as early as 1979, and a 1983 incident witnessed by hundreds in which Savimbi presided over burning an entire family to death. Yet these charges first surfaced only in 1988, in the Portuguese press and in Amnesty International reports, echoed the next year by Savimbi biographer Fred Bridgland. Finally, in March 1992, the defection of two top Unita leaders led to public confirmation that former Unita leader Tito Chingunji had been executed the previous year on Savimbi's orders. Even then some Savimbi supporters still dismissed the charges.[10]

The Angolan war was complicated by the juxtaposition of Unita's guerrilla campaign with conventional battles featuring both South African invaders and Cuban troops reinforcing Angolan government forces. In Mozambique, South Africa almost never publicly acknowledged its intervention. South Africa occasionally announced the presence of its troops in Angola, but most often tried to maintain the possibility of denial, using units composed primarily of black soldiers.

Neither in Angola nor in Mozambique was there a conventional war between states. Although both governments saw their primary enemy as the white-minority regime in Pretoria, the combatants on the ground were primarily Angolans and Mozambicans. But the 'civil war' label alone was also misleadingly simplistic. Outside involvement, from Pretoria and elsewhere, was too extensive to dismiss as only secondary. Sorting out the causes of any war is a complex task. In the murky cases which fall in between conventional inter-state war and unconventional internal war, the difficulty is multiplied many times. The question 'why' has too many answers, each with some initial plausibility.

Some saw the wars primarily as ethno-regional or other group-based competition for control over the independent states which succeeded Portuguese colonial rule. The crude version of this, seeing stereotypical 'tribal' hostility as the primary source of conflict, will not stand up under scrutiny. But it is true that both Angola and Mozambique, as modern states, are creations of colonial rule. The societies were only partially integrated as modern nations. Both governments and insurgents sought support across ethnic lines. But Unita's primary base was clearly among Umbundu-speaking Angolans, while Renamo's military leadership was dominated by Ndau-speakers from central Mozambique. In each country, moreover, people from the capital city and its immediate rural hinterland were disproportionately represented in top government ranks. Whether or not such factors were at the root of conflict, they contributed to shaping its course.

Other interpretations focused on the socialist ideological orientation of the ruling parties and the opposition by social forces committed to other models of society, or whose interests were challenged by the new order. People who had benefited from the colonial order included not only hundreds of thousands of Portuguese settlers, the majority resettled in South Africa or Portugal, but also substantial numbers of *mestiços*, Asians and Africans. The unusually conservative Catholic hierarchy resented its loss of privileges as the state church. And there were others, from urban churchgoers to traditionally oriented peasants, who applauded independence but were indifferent or hostile to ambitious plans to build socialism. Stress on this theme, whether by opponents or supporters of the regimes, highlighted internal sources of conflict. Within this logic even external involvement originated, rightly or wrongly, in reaction to the revolutionary policies adopted by Frelimo and the MPLA.

Most analysts acknowledged, however, that external actors were reacting not just to developments inside Angola and Mozambique, but also in terms of regional and global power balances. Neither the logic nor the scope of external intervention can be directly derived from the internal orientation or even the bilateral foreign policies of Luanda and Maputo.

Would tensions around national unity or internal ideological questions, in the absence of intervention by South Africa and other external forces, have produced the wars of the 1980s? This hypothetical question, as important as it is difficult to answer, is one of the fundamental topics of this study. However it is answered, there is no doubt that external intervention had decisive effects in both Angola and Mozambique.

Like it or not, both countries were on the front line in the campaign to rid Africa of white-minority rule. Along with South Africa and Rhodesia, Portugal resisted demands for African independence and majority rule in the 1960s. When Portuguese colonial rule collapsed, after a decade and a half of war, white-minority rule remained intact in Rhodesia. South Africa still defended apartheid at home and in its colony South West Africa (Namibia). Support for liberation in these territories was not confined to ideological radicals: it was the consensus among African states and the majority view in the United Nations as well. In supporting the liberation movements in Zimbabwe, Namibia, and South Africa, African states knew they risked retaliation from the white regimes. Mozambique and Angola received more than their share.

It is well established that Renamo was founded by the Rhodesian Central Intelligence Organization, and transformed from a small group to a potent military machine in the early 1980s under the direct supervision of South African Military Intelligence. Although analysts differ on the factors responsible for its subsequent spread and persistence, there is agreement on the decisive external role in its origins.

The Angolan conflict, in contrast, was under way before intervention by South African forces in August 1975. But Pretoria played direct as well as indirect roles in the fighting in Angola for the next fifteen years. Without such South African involvement, would Unita possibly have given up guerrilla war and made its peace with the Angolan government, as did most of those affiliated with the FNLA, the third contender in the battles at the time of independence?

Answering this question requires considering not only the relative weight of internal factors and South African involvement, but also another external source of conflict. Once the United States opted in January 1975 for intervention, and the Soviet Union decided to follow suit, Angola became a focal point in superpower competition. It was the US government which urged South Africa to send in its troops in 1975, and which sustained Unita's guerrilla campaign after South African supplies dwindled following the independence of Namibia in 1990. The presence of Cuban troops in Angola evoked the bitter antagonism to Havana in Washington policy-making circles. Angola might not have seen peace even without Washington's unrelenting hostility and the military involvement of the Soviet Union and Cuba on the other side. But these factors surely had significant effects on the character and duration of the conflict.

Although Renamo's partisans in Washington failed to get the group on the list of approved Reagan-doctrine insurgencies, Mozambique's war too was significantly influenced by Cold War politics. Reagan's tilt to Pretoria as a Cold War ally encouraged South Africa's hard-line assault against its neighbours, particularly those regarded as ideologically suspect. Even after Mozambique successfully wooed Western support and isolated Renamo diplomatically, far-right groups in Europe and the US took up Renamo's cause as part of their global anti-communist crusade.

All of the above factors made some contribution to conflict in Angola and Mozambique. But what factors were most important, and how did they interrelate? In what measure was all this suffering the toll from apartheid's total strategy or the Reagan doctrine, in what measure the result of ill-conceived efforts at revolution, or of other conflicts disguised in ideological trappings?

The answers to these complex questions relate not just to the past, but also to the future. Interpreting these years of trauma is above all an issue for Mozambicans and Angolans themselves. But they also have wider relevance, because Mozambique and Angola in southern Africa, like Nicaragua in Central America, had and have symbolic power for both friends and enemies around the world. And while the Reagan doctrine may have expired with the Cold War, unconventional conflicts intermingling national and international factors are likely to be just as frequent, if not more so, in the post-Cold War era.

Getting the history right requires making judgements on the relative importance of the different factors involved. Despite the difficulty of obtaining definitive answers, such judgements are implicit in every interpretation, however casual. Catch-phrases in newspaper accounts cite ethnic rivalry in Angola or peasant discontent in Mozambique as fundamental causes of conflict. South African intervention appears either as virtually the only cause or as a merely incidental aggravating factor. Specialized studies of the conflicts tend to focus on one particular aspect, such as diplomatic manoeuvring or the shape of war in a particular rural area, often to the exclusion of other important aspects.

The answers are important in political and moral as well as academic terms. As in any conflict, there is more than enough blame for every party involved. But while there may be no innocents, some should bear a heavier responsibility than others. Inside Angola and Mozambique, those involved have to live with the consequences. The need for reconciliation implies a willingness to forgive, but understanding what happened will continue to be a fundamental theme of national life. Elsewhere, even in close-by South Africa, the tendency now is to relegate what happened to obscurity. It should be no surprise that decision-makers in Pretoria, Washington or Moscow take little time for reflection on dead Africans in the countryside of Angola and Mozambique. But honesty requires a closer look.

The comparative approach of this study is also designed to isolate factors and patterns of interaction between different factors that may apply to other conflicts as well. The other Reagan-doctrine conflicts of the 1980s, such as Nicaragua, Afghanistan and Cambodia, shared a complex interplay among national, regional and global causes, providing many points of comparison with Angola and Mozambique. More broadly, the Angolan and Mozambican cases suggest hypotheses applicable to other 'low-intensity conflicts', both in the Cold War era and in the emerging period of new world disorder. Space precludes detailed consideration of other cases in this book. The potential for wider comparison, however, is discussed particularly in Chapters 3 and 11, and is implicit in the method adopted throughout.

The book begins with a chronological overview. Chapter 1, including a brief review of the pre-independence background, takes the story up to 1980. Chapter 2 continues with the periods of most intense conflict and of peacemaking. This part is intended to serve as an introduction for the reader unfamiliar with the two cases. But it also reflects my conviction that chronology is essential to understanding causality. The dynamics of the beginning of a war are not necessarily the same as the factors that make it continue, or the processes at work after years of conflict. The chronological framework is thus fundamental to the later thematic examination of different aspects.

Chapter 3 lays out theoretical and methodological questions relevant to the investigation of causality in unconventional conflicts such as Angola and Mozambique. Chapter 4 examines the background factors that might have produced conflict regardless of the policies of the post-independence governments or of external intervention. Chapter 5 focuses on the policies and impact of South Africa and other regional powers, while Chapter 6 looks at geopolitics and Washington's Cold War policies in particular. Chapters 7 and 8 examine how the armies of Renamo and Unita functioned in practice.

Chapters 9 and 10 take up the issue of the impact of policies and practices of the post-colonial states in provoking, fuelling or aggravating the conflicts. Chapter 11 sums up the results and reflects on the wider significance of the Angolan and Mozambican experiences.

Notes

1. I am acutely aware that this analytical study does not begin to convey the human reality of this trauma. Those readers with their own personal experience of Angola or Mozambique will fill in this gap from their own memories. Others should try to see one or more of the documentary films which include personal testimony; among the best are Anders Nilsson's *Killing a Dream* (1986), on Mozambique; Toni Strasburg's *Destructive Engagement* (1987) and *Chain of Tears* (1989), both on the region; and Ole Gjerstad's *Riding Out the Storm* (1989), on Mozambique. The numbing statistics are cited in several sources, listed in note 6 below. On Mozambique, among the profusion of publications by journalists and non-governmental organizations, one might highlight Mozambican journalist Lina Magaia's *Dumba Nengue* (1988) and Boothby, Sultan and Upton (1991). On Angola the material is far scarcer, but Kapuściński (1987) vividly portrays the atmosphere of 1975–76. Sogge (1992) portrays the cumulated damage before the return to war after the 1992 elections.

2. *Time*, 3 August 1987.

3. Cable Maputo to Washington, 29 July 1987. The Renamo press release

from Washington representative Luís Serapião is dated 29 July. Senator Helms's statement was reported by Reuters on 24 July.

4. Statement by Mark Van Koevering, Washington, DC, 28 October 1987. Among journalists citing survivors' reports after visiting the scene were Larry Olmstead (*Detroit Free Press*, 3 August) and John Battersby (*New York Times*, 25 July). In September a captured Renamo fighter named Simião Laquene told a press conference in Maputo that he had been at the base when the operation was planned (*AIM Bulletin*, October 1987). Africa Watch researchers cited additional eyewitness accounts from interviews in 1990 and 1991 (Africa Watch, *Conspicuous Destruction* (1992), 50–52).

5. Gersony (1988).

6. See Noormahomed and Cliff (1990); UNICEF (1989); United Nations Inter-Agency Task Force, Africa Recovery Programme (1989). Also Johnson and Martin, *Apartheid Terrorism* (1989).

7. *Ibid.* On land-mines in particular see Africa Watch, *Land Mines in Angola* (1993); Human Rights Watch and Physicians for Human Rights, *Landmines: A Deadly Legacy* (1993). Current estimates rank Angola second to Cambodia in its proportion of amputees due to mines.

8. The incident finally surfaced in the *Washington Post* five months later (29 July 1986), when reporter David Ottaway visited the village and collected numerous eyewitness accounts.

9. Africa Watch, *Angola* (1989) was based on interviews with refugees in Zaire. Africa Watch, *Angola* (1991) was based on interviews inside Angola.

10. The initial articles appeared in *Expresso* (Lisbon, 30 April and 11 May 1988) and in *África* (Lisbon, 11 May 1968). Other articles on the topic include William Minter (*Atlanta Constitution*, 20 June 1988); *Africa News*, 6 February 1989; Fred Bridgland (*Sunday Telegraph*, 12 March 1989); Craig Whitney and Jill Jolliffe (*New York Times*, 11 March 1989); Amnesty International press release, 23 March 1989; Leon Dash (*Washington Post*, 30 September 1990); Fred Bridgland (*Washington Post*, 29 March 1992); interview with Nzau Puna in *Domingo* (Maputo, 10 May 1992).

1

From Colonial Rule
to Liberation

September 7, 1974: In Mozambique angry white settlers occupied the national radio station, protesting Portugal's agreement to independence after ten years of war. The group FICO ('I Stay') and ex-commandos calling themselves 'Dragons of Death' were joined by a handful of black opponents of the Mozambique Liberation Front (Frelimo), which had fought for the country's freedom. The demonstrators said they too wanted an independent Mozambique, just not one ruled by Frelimo. But the flag they waved was Portugal's.

The rebels released imprisoned members of the former political police. White vigilantes cruised the African townships, shooting black civilians. In some areas blacks retaliated with clubs or machetes. Settlers who had earlier fled to Rhodesia or South Africa began returning to support the rebellion. Official figures put the death toll over the next few days at fourteen whites and seventy-seven blacks. Rumour spoke of hundreds or even over a thousand dead.[1]

A week later Portuguese President General António de Spínola convened a secret meeting in Cape Verde to discuss the situation in Angola with Zaire's President Mobutu Sese Seko. Mobutu, like Spínola, wanted to exclude Agostinho Neto's Popular Movement for the Liberation of Angola (MPLA) from power in an independent Angola. Their reported plan was to build a coalition among Neto's opponents, including Mobutu's Angolan protégé Holden Roberto, of the National Front for the Liberation of Angola (FNLA), Jonas Savimbi of the National Union for the Total Independence of Angola (Unita), and Daniel Chipenda, a dissident from Neto's group.

At home Spínola's plans were contested by leftists and centrists. The general, chosen to head the new government after the April military coup against the Portuguese dictatorship, had criticized the colonial wars. But he wanted to preserve as much as possible of the old system. Having conceded independence on the terms of the liberation move-

11

ments in Guinea-Bissau and Mozambique, he was trying to maintain a strong Portuguese presence in Angola, the richest of the colonies and the one with the deepest symbolic significance for Portugal's imperial identity. Neither Portuguese Foreign Minister Mário Soares, a moderate socialist, nor Admiral Rosa Coutinho, the left-wing Portuguese administrator in Angola, was invited to the Mobutu summit.[2]

The right-wing revolt in Mozambique lasted only four days before Portuguese troops restored order with the help of newly arrived Frelimo soldiers. South Africa did not intervene, dooming the rebels to failure. On 20 September Joaquim Chissano of Frelimo took office as the head of a government of transition, to lead the country until independence in June. Spínola's efforts to control the process in Angola also failed. Intriguing to isolate the left in Lisbon, Spínola instead was forced to resign on 30 September. Portugal turned to an Angola policy including Neto as well as Roberto and Savimbi, which succeeded in bringing a momentary unity. In January 1975 the Alvor Accord established a coalition government, with independence set for November 1975.

These brief episodes between the Portuguese coup in April 1974 and independence for Mozambique and Angola the next year have not yet attracted the detailed attention of historians. But one can see in them several features that prefigure the wars that were to come.

Those who opposed Frelimo in the radio takeover had no leaders who rose above obscurity, nor were they united in presenting a political platform. Their fortunes depended on decisions made in Pretoria, reflecting Mozambique's umbilical relationship to South Africa. Yet their action had hidden effects. The polarization they provoked accelerated the exodus of thousands of white settlers whose skills were vital to a future economy, and reinforced Frelimo's conviction that its opponents were traitors tied to the old colonial order and neighbouring white-minority regimes.

The Angolan drama featured a more complex array of internal contenders and external powers. The Spínola plan took shape without Spínola as Washington engineered an anti-MPLA coalition. While South Africa eventually overshadowed Zaire as a sponsor of war in Angola, Mobutu's patrons in Washington kept the anti-MPLA coalition going through many ups and downs. Neto's party, which won the fight to govern independent Angola, found itself the repeated target of conspiracies and assaults from north as well as south.

The wars that harassed newly independent Angola and Mozambique in the late 1970s and laid them to waste in the 1980s were not just a derivative of the past. But the shape of the conflict was decisively influenced by history. This book must therefore begin, if only briefly, with the rise and fall of colonial control.

To the hour of victory

Portuguese presence in the territories now called Mozambique and Angola dates to the first voyages and coastal settlements of the fifteenth and sixteenth centuries. But the common reference to over four centuries of Portuguese colonialism is misleading. Before the end of the nineteenth century, colonial rule was confined to only a few enclaves. At independence in 1975 Portuguese domination was, for the most part, less than a century old, coinciding with the European occupation of the African interior by Britain, France, Belgium and Germany.

On the east coast Portugal claimed a long strip of land stretching more than 1,500 miles from the German (later British) colony of Tanganyika in the north to British-controlled South Africa and Swaziland in the south. To the interior Mozambique bordered on the British-held territories of Southern Rhodesia, Northern Rhodesia and Nyasaland. By the turn of the century most of this territory had been conquered. The Gaza chiefs in the south were finally defeated in 1897. But conquest was only completed with the close of the First World War. A widespread revolt in Zambézia was suppressed only towards the end of 1918.

Portuguese-ruled Mozambique had a population of approximately 10,000 whites, 12,000 *mestiços* (persons of mixed race) and almost 3 million Africans, according to estimates published in 1920.[3] The least developed colonial power, Portugal lacked the capacity to administer, much less develop, the territory. From the 1890s huge portions of the country were handed over to concessionary companies financed by British and other foreign capital.

Mozambique's dependence on other white powers was also reflected in the transport links and labour flows to its neighbours. Before the colonial powers arrived, shared languages had joined the peoples of southern Mozambique to South Africa, central Mozambique to Rhodesia, and northern Mozambique to central and east Africa. The economic bonds forged under colonialism reinforced these east–west axes, leaving north–south links within Mozambique to neglect.

The South African connection made southern Mozambique an economic dependency of the mining economy of the Transvaal and the most developed area within Mozambique. Portugal supplied the mines with migrant workers, while South Africa channelled trade through Lourenço Marques and eventually agreed to remit part of the miners' wages to Mozambique in hard currency.

In central Mozambique, Beira served as the port for Southern Rhodesia. Mozambican migrants went to work in the mines and on white farms across the border, although in smaller numbers than the southern flow to South Africa. Even further north, on a less organized basis, Mozambicans emigrated to find work in Nyasaland, Tanganyika and as far afield as Zanzibar and Kenya. There was a glaring contrast between the economic opportunities available under Portuguese colonialism and in these neighbouring countries.

In most areas, nevertheless, the majority continued to depend on small-scale subsistence agriculture. Their participation in the colonial economy was limited to occasional forced labour on roads or on Portuguese plantations or, later in the century, forced cultivation of cotton and other crops to serve industry in Portugal. Portuguese colonialism was not unique in coercing a labour force to serve the European economy. Its relative underdevelopment, however, meant that market incentives were less significant and force more prevalent than in neighbouring British territories.

According to Portuguese colonial theory, African natives (indígenas) could exempt themselves from forced labour by assimilating Portuguese culture and in effect becoming Portuguese. A small number succeeded in meeting the tests of income, education and life-style to gain this assimilado status. Others, even if not assimilated, were incorporated into the colonial order with relative advantages over other Mozambicans: chiefs used in administration, as overseers on plantations, teachers in mission schools, semi-skilled workers in the ports or administration.

At mid-century, this colonial order appeared to be a stable though backward system. The Salazar regime, which took power in Portugal at the end of the 1920s, had constructed a more integrated Portuguese empire, expanding forced cultivation and encouraging Portuguese settlement. The white population of Mozambique increased from about 18,000 in 1930 to some 85,000 in 1960. Salazar's corporatist ideology excluded dangerously liberal democratic ideas both at home and in Africa. Independence was not an issue, the theory held, because the colonies were an integral part of Portugal. Neither African protest, as in South Africa, nor nationalist stirrings, as in other African colonies, were particularly visible in Mozambique before the 1960s.

Even the assimilado elite, however, who to a certain extent bought into the Portuguese model of culture and politics, rejected its implications of white racial superiority. They also reacted against competition from an increased flow of white immigrants, who were legally assumed to be 'civilized' even if illiterate. Discrimination favoured whites from Portugal not only over Africans, but also over mestiços and even locally-born whites.

Mozambican nationalism emerged first of all among those who had some education, whether or not they were officially assimilados. The numbers were not large – in the late 1950s there were probably not more than a few thousand Africans and a somewhat larger number of mestiços who had completed more than four years of school. The largest cluster of educated Mozambicans was close to the capital, in the south, where Portugal had permitted Protestant missions from the US and Switzerland. Beira and the Zambezi area were other zones of concentration.[4]

The individuals and groups who came together in June 1962 to form Frelimo reflected these diverse origins. The founding congress met in Dar es Salaam, Tanganyika – later to become Tanzania – which had just won independence from Britain. The leaders of Frelimo had the example of the successful independence struggles by Britain's African colonies. The movement's first president, Eduardo Mondlane, had served in the UN Secretariat overseeing independence referenda in West Africa. The contrast with Portugal's refusal even to consider independence was striking. It was clear that the route to independence for Mozambique would pass through war.

In September 1964 Frelimo guerrillas launched attacks in northern Mozambique, beginning the 'armed struggle'. It was, above all, Frelimo's virtually undisputed leadership of this war of national liberation that positioned it as the natural successor when the Portuguese colonial state collapsed a decade later. Tanzania and later Zambia gave Frelimo bases for diplomacy and for the guerrilla war inside Mozambique. Portuguese secret police intrigue, exploiting internal divisions, culminated in the assassination of Frelimo President Mondlane in early 1969. But the leadership which regrouped around top guerrilla commander Samora Machel proved remarkably cohesive. Although rival organizations announced their existence from time to time in various African capitals, none gained significant credibility. Individual rivals to the Frelimo leadership either deserted to the Portuguese or faded into obscurity in exile.

Frelimo sought to create a broad base of international support. It declined to take sides in the Sino-Soviet dispute and won military aid from both China and the Soviet Union. In the West, religious organizations and the Nordic countries provided support for Frelimo's health and education programmes. But efforts to build links with other Western governments or mainstream organizations foundered on vested interests tying the Western bloc to Lisbon.

This pattern of international support, together with the radicalizing effect of guerrilla war, reinforced Marxist ideas within the Frelimo leadership. The emerging Frelimo perspective stressed collective commitment and mobilization of the people for social justice as well as national independence. Those who opposed Mondlane and Machel were seen as opponents of the revolutionary process, as witnessed by their pursuit of individual privilege, their resort to divisive ethnic and racial appeals, and their willingness to be wooed by the colonial authorities.

Portuguese repression ruled out open political action, so Frelimo's activities were played out in exile, in areas of guerrilla operations and in scattered clandestine cells. The war opened up 'liberated areas' in the north in Cabo Delgado, Niassa and Tete. Here the movement set up administration, health services and schools. By 1973 Frelimo forces in these areas, as well as in several other provinces, were stretching the Portuguese military. The Portuguese coup in April 1974 allowed clandestine Frelimo supporters greater freedom to operate. The movement was met with a wave of enthusiasm and applauded for defeating colonialism.

Nevertheless, most areas of Mozambique, including the cities, experienced little impact from the war of liberation. When the independence agreement was signed in September, the movement's organizational structures around the country were at best rudimentary. In this period Frelimo entrusted local organization to *grupos dinamizadores* (dynamizing groups). These were *ad hoc*, self-constituted residential or workplace committees of Frelimo members or sympathizers. While they took their general direction from the national leadership, their membership ranged from long-time supporters to others newly engaged by the excitement of the hour or by the sense that this was the bandwagon to ride. Their activities ranged from political organization to literacy campaigns and cultural programmes. As Portuguese authority receded and settlers left, abandoning or sabotaging their farms and shops, the local *grupo dinamizador* was often called on to pick up the pieces.

One month before independence, Frelimo President Samora Machel left Tanzania for a triumphal tour of Mozambique from north to south. On independence day, 25 June, dance troupes from all ten provinces performed before festive crowds in Lourenço Marques and in each provincial capital, symbolizing national unity. The constitution promised people's power under Frelimo's leadership, solidarity with national liberation movements, and a drive to eliminate underdevelopment and exploitation. Few expected such ambitious goals to be easy, but most were optimistic. Hope was the dominant note, not just of the day, but of the years immediately to follow.

As in Mozambique, the Portuguese only completed their conquest of Angola within the last 100 years. Even areas already conquered saw repeated revolts into the second decade of this century, from the Kongo area in the north through the Luanda hinterland and the Umbundu plateau to the Ovambo areas bordering German Southwest Africa (Namibia). The far interior, bordering on Belgian and British territory, was also finally 'pacified' in the same period.[5]

In contrast to Mozambique, some portions of Angola stayed more consistently under Portuguese occupation. Luanda was a Portuguese-controlled settlement almost continuously for four centuries, from 1576 until independence, and Benguela for only a few decades less. The immediate hinterlands of these cities, and the Kongo kingdom to the north as well, were marked by intimate links to the Portuguese empire. African and *mestiço* families of these coastal settlements were part of Atlantic as well as African cultural worlds.

The slave trade was the central theme of this connection. More sustained and pervasive than that along Mozambique's coast, the Atlantic trade moulded an economy of violence. Along a shifting frontier, some African societies were devastated by the wars the trade provoked, while others at times managed to escape its worst effects and skim some profit for themselves. Even interior peoples who had little direct contact with the Portuguese were affected.

Twentieth-century colonial Angola also differed from Mozambique in its place within the regional and world economies. While Mozambique was firmly encapsulated in the southern African nexus dominated by South Africa and Britain, Angola's regional ties were weaker and more diverse. By the 1920s Angola was linked to the central African mining complex by the Benguela Railway, which served the copper-producing interior of the Belgian Congo and Northern Rhodesia. Some Angolan workers also went to South Africa. But Angola also looked north, to French-speaking Africa; its most important economic ties were to Portugal and other Atlantic powers.

After the Second World War Angolan links to Europe and North America became even more prominent. Coffee, grown primarily on farms owned by Portuguese settlers, became Angola's top export in the 1950s and 1960s. The number of Portuguese jumped from 44,000 in 1940 to almost 300,000 in 1970, about 5 per cent of the total population (as compared to only 2 per cent in Mozambique). Beginning in the 1960s investment in the new oil sector came to dominate the export economy, bringing in American and French companies. Finally, the Congo crisis of the early 1960s made the region a focus of superpower rivalry. Angola was thus positioned in a fracture zone between central and southern Africa, vulnerable to geopolitical tremors from either direction.

The colonial system in Angola was similar to Mozambique's. But the greater weight of Portuguese settlement and different pattern of interaction with neighbouring countries helped determine a distinctive evolution. In comparison with their Mozambican counterparts, Angolan nationalists had a more complex historical legacy and more intractable structural bases for division.

In Luanda, the capital, the tradition of Angolan resistance to colonialism had deep roots. The relatively large number of African *assimilados* and *mestiços* provided the context for a nineteenth-century protest journalism, criticizing Portuguese colonialism and the way in which even educated Africans were shoved aside by new Portuguese settlers. As in other colonial contexts, most Africans with Western education accepted aspects of the colonial system. But Angolan nationalists of the

1950s and 1960s looked back to a literary tradition stressing Angolan identity and protest. It is no accident that the first president of Angola, Agostinho Neto, was also a renowned poet.

The MPLA, led by Neto, grew from this Luanda milieu, coming together as a clandestine organization at the end of 1956. Harassed by police repression, with key leaders in prison or in exile, MPLA supporters launched an armed assault on political prisons in February 1961. In response white vigilantes killed hundreds of Africans in the city's suburbs. The following month an even bloodier conflict erupted in northern Angola. Rebels linked to the Union of Peoples of Angola (UPA) killed hundreds of white settlers in the coffee plantation zone, and targeted mestiços and Africans from other parts of Angola as well. The Portuguese retaliated with vigilantes and troops, inflicting a death toll estimated at up to 50,000.

The Angolan war for independence thus exploded suddenly. It caught both the colonial authorities and the nationalist leaders unprepared. The divisions evident in that initial eruption persisted throughout the thirteen years of struggle against the Portuguese – and beyond.[6]

UPA had been formed in 1957 in the Belgian Congo as the Union of Peoples of Northern Angola. Led by Holden Roberto, it relied primarily on Kikongo-speaking northern Angola and on exiles in the former Belgian Congo. In the early 1960s UPA also recruited student exiles from other areas of Angola, including Jonas Savimbi and his colleagues from the central plateau. The common thread was suspicion of nationalist currents in Luanda, embodied in exile by the MPLA.

For Mozambicans, Tanganyika provided a hospitable refuge within which to construct unity. Angolans had wider gaps to bridge, and most found exile in the Congo, itself beset by internal strife and the first major Cold War confrontation in Africa. By the end of 1963 the MPLA had been totally excluded from Congo (Kinshasa) and had set up a headquarters across the river in the former French Congo (Brazzaville). Congo (Kinshasa) was run by CIA-installed leaders, and Holden Roberto's movement, now called the National Front for the Liberation of Angola (FNLA), was also being subsidized by the CIA. The US aimed to build barriers against Soviet-tied radicalism, by isolating the MPLA in particular.

Disunity and geopolitical manoeuvring thus undermined prospects for a sustained guerrilla offensive against Portuguese rule. The FNLA continued actions in parts of the north, as did pockets of MPLA guerrillas north-east of Luanda. The MPLA opened up a front in Cabinda from its Brazzaville base. Zambia's independence permitted the MPLA to launch an eastern front in 1966, which for some years was the most significant military threat to the Portuguese in Angola.

But there were divisions in the east as well. Breaking with the FNLA in 1964, Jonas Savimbi two years later founded the National Union for the Total Independence of Angola (Unita), appealing primarily to Umbundu-speakers and others from southern and eastern Angola. He installed a small guerrilla operation in eastern Angola, in the same area as the MPLA. Unita failed to win any open support from African states, but boasted of self-reliance and espoused Maoist rhetoric. By 1971, Savimbi and the Portuguese forces secretly agreed to concentrate their military efforts against the MPLA. When the Portuguese coup came in 1974, the MPLA was also suffering internal strife, exacerbated by the difficulties of guerrilla war and of coordination among exiled leaders dispersed among different African capitals.

The scenario that followed in 1974–76 played out both the legacy of Angolan divisions and the Cold War dynamics that had previously focused on the Congo. In January 1975 the three movements and Portugal signed an agreement in Alvor, Portugal, calling for a transition government and elections leading to independence in November 1975. But the agreement could only have worked if all the parties, both Angolans and their external allies, agreed on power sharing and a process of confidence-building, or if some external force were neutral enough and powerful enough to insist on peaceful competition. None of these conditions was met.

With Portuguese authority in Angola tattered, none of the three contenders for power held a decisive advantage. The MPLA had perhaps six thousand troops, mostly recent recruits. The FNLA enjoyed military superiority, with roughly twenty thousand conventional troops and the backing of Zaire. Under Rosa Coutinho, the Portuguese administration helped bolster the MPLA and maintain a balance. He was replaced in January 1975 by a conservative official who was accused of favouring the FNLA, but was in any case incapable of mediating among the contending forces. In Portugal the struggle for political power increasingly focused on domestic issues. The dominant role of leftists in Lisbon in mid-1975, although it heightened anti-communist panic in Washington as well as Portugal, did not carry over into military capability to influence events in Angola.

Politically, the positions of the Angolan movements roughly followed the stereotypes attached to them, although the labels oversimplified a complex and changing reality. The FNLA maintained its political base among Kikongo-speaking Angolans, including exiles in Zaire. It offered a programme that combined populist rhetoric with promises of security for free enterprise, asking that its leadership be accepted into the emerging bourgeoisie along with white Angolans.

The MPLA offered a socialist vision tempered with pragmatism. Its major assets were popular support among the Kimbundu-speaking population of Luanda and its hinterland, along with a policy of non-racialism and non-tribalism that gave good prospects of wider national support. It won loyalty among urban workers, students and middle-level government employees around the country, of all races and linguistic groups. Most whites saw the MPLA as a Marxist nemesis, although the participation of white and *mestiço* leftists in the movement also exposed it to 'black power' critiques from the other two movements.

Unita, characteristically, had a less defined programme. It sought to rally eastern and southern ethnic groups, while appealing to whites on the basis of opposition to the MPLA's radicalism. More than its rivals, it relied on loyalty to a charismatic leader – Jonas Savimbi.

In January, only a few days after the Alvor Agreement, the US decided at White House level to allocate $300,000 to support its client, the FNLA. Two months later, the FNLA launched a military assault on MPLA positions in Luanda, casting the die for a military resolution of the conflict. Popular mobilization and the arrival of Eastern bloc arms enabled MPLA forces to expel the FNLA from the Luanda area in July, after a series of major confrontations. By all accounts the major external involvement in this period was that of Zaire. Mobutu's regime, encouraged by the US, served as patron of the FNLA, supplying funds, arms and even troops. The MPLA had a small number of foreign military advisors, mostly left-wing Portuguese but also a few Cubans.

As the conflict in northern Angola continued into the second half of 1975, a new area of confrontation opened up in the south, bringing in not only Unita but also South African and Cuban troops. Until mid-year Unita had been a bystander in the military confrontation, seeking to consolidate its position in the plateau and south. As the conflict in Luanda intensified in June and July, however, Unita supporters fled the capital, particularly after MPLA troops killed more than fifty Unita recruits in a confrontation. In July and August MPLA leaders tried to draw Unita into an alliance, but the effort failed.[7] Savimbi found it more attractive to join Holden Roberto in receiving CIA support, increased to $14 million for the two movements in July.

The US also encouraged South Africa to join the anti-MPLA military alliance. South African troops went into Angola in August, linking up with forces of MPLA dissident Daniel Chipenda, who had joined the FNLA, and with Unita. In October, South Africans, mercenaries and troops from FNLA and Unita joined in a well-equipped mechanized column of more than three thousand troops to launch a lightning strike aimed at reaching Luanda before the 11 November independence day. Like the US, the South African government hoped to keep its involvement secret.

The decision to escalate and involve the South Africans was opposed by some US diplomats, who doubted it could be kept secret and predicted it would backfire by discrediting the US-backed Angolan groups and provoking further escalation. Indeed, the operation did unravel with amazing rapidity. By independence day, thousands of Cuban troops were arriving in response to Neto's plea for help. The Soviet Union provided arms sufficient to equip the MPLA and the Cubans, and by mid-December the anti-MPLA coalition had lost the military initiative. The FNLA was forced back north of Luanda, and the South African-led forces were blocked to the south.

As the CIA scrambled to revive the flagging fortunes of its allies with infusions of mercenaries and additional arms, the political cover for intervention was collapsing. Revelations of South African involvement tipped African opinion decisively in favour of the MPLA. Key African states such as Nigeria and Tanzania recognized the independent People's Republic of Angola. In the US, congressional opposition to the intervention culminated in a December amendment barring further US covert aid in Angola. New escalation was blocked. Pretoria, feeling betrayed, withdrew its armoured columns in March 1976. In subsequent years the Carnival of Victory, celebrated on 25–27 March recalled the expulsion of the South African invaders, victory in what the MPLA termed the 'Second War of National Liberation'.[8]

Institutionalizing hope

In the years just after independence, Frelimo and the MPLA had good cause to celebrate. Two years earlier, few would have predicted the rapid collapse of Portuguese colonialism. No one would have imagined white South African troops retreating before an African army reinforced by Cubans. Portugal, with Rhodesia and South Africa, had held the line against African freedom for a decade and a half. As Portugal withdrew, black South African students celebrated Mozambique's independence and watched the white government's abortive invasion of Angola. The Soweto student rebellion, only months later, reflected new confidence that white power was vulnerable.

For millions of Angolans and Mozambicans, the end of colonial repression was immediate cause for rejoicing. Forced labour, physical punishment and insults from Portuguese administrators were no more. Africans assumed positions of responsibility at all levels. Health and education services expanded and reached out to rural as well as urban Africans.

There was a sombre side, however, even from the start. Hundreds of thousands of white settlers fled, creating economic turmoil. In Angola, the toll of conventional war included not only destruction in the cities and internal refugees fleeing the fighting, but also bitter feelings between losers and winners in the struggle for power. In Mozambique as well, there were those who did not share in the general rejoicing. Some, nostalgic for the old order, opposed independence as such. Others simply regretted that they were not among the new rulers.

Institutionalizing the hopes of independence was a complicated process with few unambiguous victories. Even these would later be obscured by the ravages of war and by broader institutional failures. But for some time optimism was sustained by some striking successes.

In Mozambique one well-documented case was health. Before independence the country had approximately 500 doctors, overwhelmingly of Portuguese origin. They served primarily the white population and a fraction of urban blacks; most rural communities had little or no access to modern health care. Less than 100 of these doctors stayed on after independence. But after nationalizing health care in July 1975, the new government managed to expand services, stressing preventive medicine and primary health care.

By recruiting foreign health workers from a wide variety of countries, and by training large numbers of nurses and paramedics, the new health system quickly extended rudimentary coverage around the country. A national vaccination campaign in 1976, achieving coverage of 96 per cent, was rated a remarkable success by the World Health Organization (WHO). In 1982, the last year before war became generalized in most of the countryside, a WHO study of randomly selected rural areas found 'extensive contact by mothers and their young children with rural health services'.[9]

The health budget, 3.3 per cent of state expenditures in 1974, increased to an average of over 10 per cent over the 1976–82 period. Mozambique's poverty meant that this added up to only US$5 per capita in 1982, the peak year. Making the most of limited resources, the Health Ministry established a formulary of several hundred basic drugs, requiring competitive bidding from foreign suppliers. The new system reduced costs of imported medicines by 40 per cent, making it possible to provide rural health posts with relatively regular supplies.

Even in 1982, regular preventive measures were reaching less than half the population, and even fewer had access to curative medicine. The majority of doctors were still in the cities, and less than a third were Mozambican. Management, particularly in the hospitals, left much to be desired. But given the starting point and the resources available, Mozambicans rightly took pride in the achievements of their health policies.

Developments in education were also impressive. Just before independence the illiteracy rate, including that of whites, was over 90 per cent. Only one per cent – about 80,000 people – had completed more than four years of school, and most of these were Portuguese settlers. In 1973, only forty of the 3,000 university students were African. By 1980, illiteracy was down to 75 per cent. Primary school enrolment expanded from 666,000 in 1973 to 1.4 million in 1980. Secondary school enrolment went from 33,000 to 91,000 over the same period, an extraordinary pace considering that in 1973 a high proportion were white. New teacher training courses in each province increased the number of primary teachers from 11,000 to 19,000. Double shifts and classes held outdoors or under hastily constructed shelters partially made up for a lack of school buildings.

Even before independence, Frelimo's *grupos dinamizadores* organized adult literacy classes around the country. Between 1978 and 1982 the Ministry of Education organized four national literacy campaigns, with a total enrolment of over a million and 350,000 who successfully passed the final achievement test. Comparing the series of campaigns, however, reveals a significant decline in pass rates in 1981–82. High reliance on popular mobilization and on poorly trained volunteer teachers made it difficult to sustain the programme as initial enthusiasm waned.

These difficulties in institutionalizing the high hopes of the early years would have been pervasive even without the test of war. Frelimo was able to call on the people in mass campaigns organized for specific purposes, such as vaccination, literacy or the well-managed census in 1980. But routine functions of state and economy, on which long-term development depended, were beset by structural weaknesses. The war exacerbated every one.

In Angola too the new government oversaw a dramatic expansion in education, and, to a lesser extent, in health care. In 1973, Angola had 500,000 primary school students (one-third of them Portuguese) and 72,000 secondary school students (80 per cent Portuguese). By 1977, with most of the Portuguese gone, enrolment was up to almost one million primary and 100,000 secondary students. The first national literacy campaign reached 102,000 adults; by 1981, over 700,000 were enrolled in literacy classes. In health care, with less than 100 Angolan doctors and about 400 Cuban doctors, the government restaffed provincial hospitals largely deserted by the Portuguese, and increased health posts staffed by nurses from 133 in 1979 to 1,000 in 1983.[10]

Angolan independence was born not just of guerrilla struggle but of a conventional war. The MPLA's hastily assembled force proved superior to its rivals in 1975, and then with Cuban reinforcements beat back the South Africans as well. It was hardly surprising, therefore, that the new government concentrated with particular urgency on building up FAPLA, the national army. Despite regional divisions within Angola, the new government stressed recruitment of both troops and officers on a national basis, and advancement on merit within the ranks. Building up a conventional army with a national draft produced many reluctant or unwilling recruits, but it also made the military one of the most widely representative institutions in Angolan society.

The new army received systematic Cuban and Soviet training. Top army commanders paid attention to problems of lack of discipline and technical training, ranging from literacy classes for illiterate recruits to selection of candidates for pilot's training. By the mid-1980s, Angola was able to match itself against South Africa in the highly technical realm of air power.

The resources for this achievement came not only from the Soviet bloc but also, ironically, from another major asset: friendly and profitable relations with Western oil companies. Oil became Angola's principal export in 1973, providing 30 per cent of total export earnings that year. Although production dropped off in 1975–76, it expanded rapidly in the 1980s. The government set up a national oil company in 1977. But it was also careful to maintain good relations with foreign companies, negotiating joint production ventures with established companies such as Gulf Oil in Cabinda and seeking a variety of partners for new exploration. Between 1981 and 1985 Angola's oil attracted more than $400 million in new investment a year. Angola negotiated relatively good terms with foreign companies, while building a reputation for professional management.[11]

Despite its troubled birth, post-independence Angolan nationalism was also reflected in peaceful activities. Angolans took pride in a veritable explosion of new literary activity. Under Portuguese rule Angolan writers, often sympathetic to the MPLA, had been censored, exiled or imprisoned. The Angolan Writers Union, founded as war was still raging in December 1975, sponsored publication of previously censored and new writing, including poems, short stories and novels. As many as twenty books a year appeared, with some editions of 20,000 or more selling out in a few weeks.[12] In 1977 alone the Writers Union sold 270,000 books by Angolan authors, an astounding figure in a country just emerging from 90 per cent illiteracy.

Like Mozambique, however, post-independence Angola faced serious structural weaknesses, some left by colonialism, others inherent in the divided nationalist legacy. In comparison with Mozambique, Angola had the advantages of oil wealth. But it also had a more deeply entrenched gap between city and countryside. In both countries, even discounting war, those trying to build sustainable new societies faced formidable obstacles.

The post-independence governments took charge of economies in a state of collapse. Bright spots such as the Angolan oil industry were few. In the previous decade, the colonial economies had achieved significant growth in traditional exports and services and in small-scale industrial production. But this development spurt was based on expanding Portuguese settlement and coercion of the rural African labour force. With independence, both these supports of the colonial economy fell away, leaving space the new states proved unable to fill.

In both countries virtually all skilled positions were occupied by Portuguese before independence. The peasant cash economy depended on Portuguese wholesalers and shopkeepers whose trucks and stores ensured the exchange of crops for tools, clothes and a few other goods. The exodus of at least 90 per cent of the Portuguese between 1973 and 1976 had a traumatic impact.

Both governments in principle welcomed whites of Portuguese origin who were willing to identify themselves as Angolans or Mozambicans, including private businessmen. Some who retained Portuguese citizenship also stayed on. In Angola at least, most of those who left fled primarily the chaos and uncertainty of war rather than specific government actions or policies. Many Mozambican settlers fled before independence; others left after post-independence government decisions to nationalize health care and rental housing. Undoubtedly a high proportion simply refused to accept living under independent governments which allowed them no special privileges for being white. But no one has analysed the exodus in detail to probe how many might have stayed if there had been greater efforts to allay their fears.

Neither Angola nor Mozambique had a policy of nationalizing factories, farms or shops that were functioning enterprises. But in practice most of the modern commercial sector fell to state control. In large part, it consisted of enterprises abandoned by their owners or run down when foreign investors withdrew their capital. In both countries, the transition period was marked by abrupt economic decline. Mozambique's aggregate production fell by 21 per cent between 1973 and 1975.[13] Angolan coffee output dropped by more than two-thirds. Factory production declined precipitously. Without adequate transport or a retail network, agricultural marketing was crippled.

After independence there was limited economic recovery. Mozambique's aggregate production, for example, increased by 5.5 per cent from 1975 to 1977, and by 11.6 per cent from 1977 to 1981. Diamond production and some industrial sectors in Angola also chalked up increases. But again, with the exception of oil in Angola, no economic sector in either country showed a robust recovery, even before the escalation of war in the 1980s. Mozambique had traditionally relied for foreign exchange on the service and transport sector which served neighbouring countries. That too was slashed, when Rhodesian trade was cut off by Mozambique's decision to adhere to UN sanctions.

Frelimo and the MPLA declared themselves Marxist-Leninist parties in 1977 and laid out the goal of developing their countries along socialist lines. The economic base for their ambitious plans, however, was extraordinarily fragile. Ideological declarations masked the fact that the nascent states were taking on state sectors far larger than they could manage, including many enterprises that were already bankrupt.

Ideology and over-optimism joined with an apparent lack of other options to keep enterprises alive, despite persistent failures to produce adequate returns.

The political model was a hybrid of African nationalist and revolutionary themes. The rulers' credentials consisted in having taken the lead in struggling against Portuguese colonialism and, in the case of Angola, against the South Africans as well. Their future legitimacy, according to the model, depended on mobilizing and leading the majority of workers and peasants in developing the nation's material wealth and human resources for the benefit of the majority. The party itself would play an organizing role, helping the majority to articulate their interests and guiding the state in implementing socialist policies. Legislative assemblies from local to national levels would provide another avenue for the people to evaluate policies and monitor state performance. The party would see to it that workers and peasants, not just those with education or other privileges, played key roles in party and legislative bodies.

For Angola and Mozambique, as for other African countries, the pre-independence model of political authority was the colonial administrative hierarchy, hostile even in theory to participation by its subjects. In contrast to English or French territories, moreover, the ex-Portuguese countries had no tradition of political democracy even among their European masters. The most prominent 'Western democracies' had sided with Portugal in the conflicts leading to independence. It is not surprising, therefore, that Frelimo and the MPLA opted for models of government based on the Marxist traditions of most of the countries and movements which had supported them.

At its best, this model provided real opportunities for grass-roots participation and new voices for a wide range of citizens. Not only party leaders and the somewhat better-educated persons who occupied the jobs and houses of the departing Portuguese, but also urban workers, peasants, women and youth were encouraged to speak out and participate.

In Mozambique in particular, the party fostered such participation in a variety of local contexts. People's Assembly elections at local levels in 1977 and 1980 provided the opportunity for voters to accept or reject party-proposed candidates (10 per cent were rejected in 1977, 11 per cent in 1980), and were the basis for indirect elections to provincial and national assemblies.[14] Periodic party congresses were also used to encourage criticism and public debate. In practice, the functioning of these representative bodies and other local groups such as *grupos dinamizadores*, party committees and workers councils varied widely. Many functioned only in formal terms, while many others declined after an initial period of enthusiasm or when key leaders were transferred or dropped out.

In Angola, in contrast to Mozambique, the early development of both party and assembly structures was curtailed by the war atmosphere at the time of independence, and then by an abortive coup within the MPLA government which deepened the atmosphere of distrust. In May 1977 a mixed bag of self-styled radicals within both the party and the army, led by Nito Alves, tried to overthrow the Neto government. They failed, but several prominent MPLA leaders were killed before the group was defeated. The MPLA's subsequent efforts to build party structures and representative assemblies reflected strong concern with loyalty and security. The first People's Assemblies at provincial and national level were only elected in 1980.[15]

Regardless of the effectiveness of popular participation, an equally critical issue was policy implementation. In comparison with other African states, often labelled by political scientists as 'weak states', Angola and Mozambique faced even more daunting difficulties in putting policies into practice. The Portuguese colonial state was exceptionally bureaucratic and inefficient. In most sectors it was this colonial legacy, more than socialist ideology, that provided the practical model for the state's operations. It was, moreover, a model implemented by functionaries with levels of education drastically lower than the departed Portuguese.

Popular enthusiasm or concentration on specific projects by top leaders produced some successes. But the structural weaknesses of the state were profound. Its capacity to provide what the leadership and the people wanted was limited. While clashes of armies and ideologies were more widely publicized, this vulnerability was the ever-present backdrop to the wars to come.

Cross-border operations, 1976–79

In the late 1970s, the spectre of war for Mozambique and Angola was real, but it appeared manageable. Portugal was concerned with its own internal problems; *retornados* from the colonies who might dream of revenge were no real military threat. Mozambique adopted pragmatic policies towards South Africa; it confined its practical support for guerrilla warfare to the struggle against white-ruled Rhodesia, which was smaller and diplomatically isolated. Retaliation was predictable, but it seemed containable. Angola, facing a more multi-faceted threat, tried persistently to patch up relations with Zaire. Although Angola gave sanctuary to guerrillas fighting against the South African occupation of Namibia, it seemed plausible that Pretoria's retaliation could be confined to the far south. Unita guerrillas too were on the defensive after their defeat in 1976.

South Africa was caught up in a messy political transition from Prime

Minister Vorster to his successor P. W. Botha. It was also confronted with the Soweto revolt and smarting from US failure to follow through on the joint Angolan intervention. The US was still under the influence of the Vietnam syndrome, apparently uninterested in resuming an interventionist role in Africa. The prestige and economic fortunes of Zaire's Mobutu were at a low point. The Soviet Union was willing to pledge security support for both Angola and Mozambique, and the Cuban troops in Angola were a backstop even if they soon removed themselves from direct combat roles.

Luanda and Maputo expected limited 'cross-border operations' in reprisal. But it seemed that guerrilla war and negotiations could soon lead to independence for Namibia and Zimbabwe. The sacrifice seemed a necessary and acceptable price for the next steps in African freedom.

Angola (northern front)

When FNLA and Zairian troops were driven back from Luanda by MPLA and Cuban forces in December 1975, the rout was decisive. Last-minute CIA efforts to stiffen the resistance with mercenaries proved an embarrassing failure. Presidents Neto and Mobutu met in late February 1976 in Brazzaville, seeking a quick diplomatic *détente*. China, which had earlier backed the FNLA, had already withdrawn its advisors in November. Other African states recognized the new People's Republic of Angola, and Congress cut off US aid for military operations in Angola. Mobutu, too, seemed ready to accept the *fait accompli*.

Before 1974, as many as 400,000 Angolan refugees, nominally supporters of the FNLA, were living in Zaire. After the defeat, many returned to government-held areas in Angola, seeking land in their home villages or gathering in the towns of northern Angola.[16] Pockets of staunch FNLA supporters sought refuge in isolated bush areas or stayed in Zaire. But the FNLA never again became a serious contender for power.

The promise of peace with Zaire was illusory. Mobutu continued to provide sanctuary for military operations against Angola by the FNLA and by the Front for the Liberation of the Enclave of Cabinda (FLEC), a group seeking independence for the oil-rich Angolan province of Cabinda. The FLEC and FNLA attacks, though small, served to maintain an atmosphere of tension. Kinshasa also served as the hub for plotting by exiles and intelligence agencies contemplating *coups* in Angola. The plots were sometimes fantastic, but still an ongoing worry for Luanda. Although the CIA was barred by Congress from covert intervention in Angola, US hostility was unabated. And there were others – French, Belgian, South African, or unidentified – willing to dabble in intrigue.

Tension between Angola and Zaire escalated when a rebellion broke out in Zaire's Shaba province (formerly Katanga) in March 1977.[17] The insurgent Congo National Liberation Front (FLNC) was built on a force of Katangan gendarmes who had been in exile in Angola since the 1960s. In 1975 they had sided with the MPLA and helped secure north-western Angola for Luanda. It is unclear whether the Angolan government could have restrained them, but in any case Neto had no incentive to help Mobutu. The FLNC took control of much of Shaba and called for a national revolt against Mobutu.

Mobutu put down the revolt with the aid of Moroccan troops airlifted in by France. The pressures against the Angolan government grew rather than diminished. Plotters in the internal coup attempt in Luanda in May sought support from both East and West with contradictory stories. They promised Soviet diplomats that they would be more loyal allies than the independent-minded Neto while offering Western contacts new oil concessions, a share of power for everyone but Neto's supporters, and a break in ties with the Soviet Union.[18]

Although the coup failed, it sharply accentuated Luanda's insecurity. Mobutu facilitated transit facilities for Savimbi. Flying from Namibia to Kinshasa and then on to the Ivory Coast, Senegal and Morocco in October 1977, Savimbi made arrangements with Morocco's King Hassan for officer training and other military support. France and the US, Morocco's two most important allies, encouraged Hassan's decision. Within the US administration, National Security Adviser Zbigniew Brzezinski and others lobbied for repeal of the Clark amendment and for new assistance to Unita.[19] He was opposed by UN Ambassador Andrew Young and Secretary of State Cyrus Vance, who advocated defusing tensions with Angola.

The debate intensified after the FLNC launched a second rebellion in Zaire's Shaba province in May 1978. This time the Western response was even more massive, with French and Belgian paratroops and US military transport. Washington launched a major propaganda blitz charging Cuban complicity in Shaba, although officials later admitted the evidence was flimsy. The incident heightened anti-Angolan sentiment in Washington, but also provided an opening for diplomacy. Continuing to destabilize Angola through Zaire might backfire by sparking yet another outbreak in Zaire itself. While Mobutu had put down the Shaba II rebellion, disruption to the key copper-mining industry was devastating to Zaire's hard-pressed economy; a Shaba III might be fatal.

Encouraged by US diplomats, Mobutu and Neto agreed to restrain each other's exiled opponents. Angola then imposed strong controls on the FLNC; Mobutu also took action, albeit less consistent, to curb Angolan exiles. Joint planning began for reopening of the Benguela

Railway across Angola, the best route to the sea for Zaire's copper. During the second half of 1978 Angola exchanged ambassadors with France, which bet its business interests on better ties with Luanda. A June 1978 summit between Neto and Portuguese President Ramalho Eanes was another sign of improved relations with Western countries. Contacts with Washington never matured into reconciliation, as Brzezinski's Cold War faction gained ascendancy over Africa policy. But with Mobutu chastened, the northern front was for some years only a minor threat to Angolan security.

Angola (southern front)

The threat in the south eventually proved more dangerous by far. But it took some time for this to be apparent. In principle, South Africa's occupation of Namibia was illegal, and Angola's support for Namibian guerrillas was in line with the international consensus at the United Nations. A deal with South Africa such as that with Mobutu was not plausible without Pretoria's acceptance of independence for Namibia. But the guerrilla threat to Namibia was not large enough to require large-scale South African retaliation. The areas bordering Namibia were remote from Luanda, and South Africa was cautious at first in its forays across the border. Its support for Unita was limited.

The South West African People's Organization (SWAPO) began its guerrilla struggle in 1966, the same year the UN General Assembly legally terminated South African authority over Namibia. Before Angolan independence SWAPO guerrillas infiltrated through Portuguese-controlled Angola, with occasional help from Unita. As Unita sided with South Africa in 1975, SWAPO developed closer ties with the MPLA. In 1976 SWAPO opened exile offices in Luanda, and was granted access for refugee camps, military training bases and transit facilities. For the first time SWAPO guerrillas posed a significant security problem for South Africa in northern Namibia.

South Africa cleared free-fire zones along the border with Angola and expanded counterinsurgency forces. After the 1975–76 fiasco, South African Prime Minister Vorster was at first reluctant to authorize retaliatory raids by regular South African troops. But elite special forces regularly mounted small-scale operations inside Angola. The several-thousand-strong 32 Battalion fought primarily in Angola, attacking both SWAPO guerrillas and Angolan civilians.[20]

In late 1977 Vorster decided to allow larger conventional raids into Angola. The most dramatic was a May 1978 air and paratroop attack against a SWAPO camp near the mining town of Cassinga. Although South Africa claimed the camp was purely a military target, the majority of the over 600 killed were civilian Namibian refugees, including many

women and children. Coming just as Western powers were pressing
negotiations for an independence agreement for Namibia, the military
action over 150 miles inside Angola underscored South African determination to hang on to Namibia. South African military sources claimed
that the Cassinga raid, together with coordinated actions along the
border, had dealt a crippling blow to SWAPO's guerrilla campaign.[21]

Parallel and overlapping the border war was South Africa's clandestine assistance to Unita. Unlike 32 Battalion, Unita retained its
separate organizational structure. South Africa supplied access to Namibia, along with arms and training, but on a limited scale until late
1978.[22] Most of the Unita army and its civilian supporters were dispersed
in the Angolan countryside, concerned primarily with the struggle to
survive. Just across the Angolan border from Namibia's Ovamboland,
Unita guerrillas under António Vakulakuta were active from 1976, retreating back into Namibia when under attack. Vakulakuta, who had
support among Cuanhama-speaking people of the border area, later
died in Unita custody after challenging Savimbi. But for several years
his forces gave Unita a military presence in south-western Angola.

The principal supply route for Unita, however, was through Namibia's Kavango area into the sparsely populated Cuando Cubango province of south-eastern Angola. The eastern border with Zambia, by
virtue of its geographical isolation, was virtually a no-man's land,
through which Unita could even bring in an occasional foreign visitor.
In the north-east, there was also access to Zaire's Shaba province. These
lands 'at the end of the earth', as the Portuguese had called them, were
remote from Angola's more developed coastal and central zones. Even
large groups of Unita supporters travelling through the bush country
easily avoided the scattered government outposts. But by the same token,
activities in these outlying areas were little threat to the central government.

In 1976 and 1977 Unita units in the interior regrouped, and some
mounted attacks against strategic targets. The Benguela Railway's 1,300
kilometres of track, for example, passed both through the central plateau
– where Unita retained significant support – and through the sparsely
populated east. It was an easy target: Unita caused thirteen derailments
in 1976, seven in 1977 and sixteen in 1978. Occasional ambushes or
mines laid for road traffic also made travel insecure in outlying areas
of the plateau as well as further east.[23]

Several hundred thousand civilians followed Unita into the bush
voluntarily in the face of the MPLA/Cuban advance. Others were
forced out of government areas by Unita attacks, or compelled under
threat to go with Unita. Those suspected of loyalty to the government
were forced more deeply into the bush so that they could not easily
return. In the 1976 retreat from the towns, moreover, many MPLA

supporters, including Umbundu-speakers regarded by Unita as traitors, were reportedly massacred. The next few years saw indiscriminate reprisals on both sides.

By 1979–80, however, the government could claim some success in establishing security over wider areas. A significant proportion of those who had fled with Unita returned to government-controlled zones, weary of privation in the bush and no longer convinced of Unita's claim that they would be slaughtered by government forces. Savimbi himself reportedly escaped capture in late 1978 only by calling in a South African helicopter. Early in 1979 Unita abandoned its headquarters on the edge of the central plateau and relocated to Jamba, near the south-eastern border with Namibia. The Benguela Railway opened briefly to international traffic in 1979, carrying several cargoes from Zambia and Zaire.

Mozambique (Rhodesian front)

Mozambique at independence was engaged in no open conflict. But its indirect involvement in the guerrilla war in white-ruled Rhodesia was already several years old. In the early 1970s, guerrillas of the Zimbabwe African National Union (ZANU) gained access to eastern Rhodesia through Frelimo guerrilla zones in Mozambique. Rhodesian troops operated in Mozambique in coordination with the Portuguese. After independence both Rhodesia and Mozambique expected the conflict to escalate.

Frelimo regarded its commitment to Zimbabwean liberation as unavoidable. Participating in South African-Zambian 'détente' talks, the Mozambican government went along with a ban on the Zimbabwean guerrilla campaign during 1975. But when it became clear that the white-minority regime would hang on, Mozambique provided the rear base for escalating guerrilla war.

Mozambique also chose, in March 1976, to implement United Nations sanctions against Rhodesia. Rhodesia had evaded the mandatory sanctions, imposed a decade earlier at British request, by using trade routes through South Africa and Portuguese-controlled Mozambique. By closing its border to Rhodesia, Mozambique took the decisive step towards making these international measures effective. Since the action was in line with official Western policy as well as African demands, Maputo hoped for international support for the costs involved.

The combination of guerrilla warfare and sanctions proved effective, bringing an independence settlement for Zimbabwe less than four years later. But Mozambique paid a high price. The cost of sanctions over four years was estimated at over $500 million, more than double Mozambique's annual exports during these years. The economy of

central Mozambique was crippled. Mozambique had no secure source
of foreign exchange, and could ill afford defence budgets which mounted
to over $100 million a year by 1979.[24] The international community
provided only token amounts to offset these losses.

Rhodesian raids also wreaked extensive damage in Tete, Manica
and Gaza provinces. They ranged from small border clashes to large-
scale attacks on guerrilla bases, refugees and Mozambican economic
targets. At Nyadzonia in June 1976 and again at Chimoio in 1979, the
Rhodesians killed hundreds of civilian refugees as well as ZANU
guerrillas. In September 1979, they targeted agricultural zones in the
Limpopo valley, killing at least fifty Mozambican civilians and causing
material damage of some $37 million, despite loss of one helicopter to
the Mozambican defenders. The Rhodesians failed to check ZANU
infiltration and met with stronger Mozambican resistance as the war
went on. But when peace came in 1979, Mozambique's economic and
military resources had been tightly stretched.

Rhodesian attacks were supplemented by a group called the Mozambican National Resistance (MNR), in this period only a sideshow to the
main conflict. The MNR, which grew from a few hundred in 1976 to
as many as 2,000 by late 1979, incorporated several components: intelligence agents recruited by Rhodesia's Central Intelligence Organization
(CIO) since the early 1970s, Africans and a few others who had served
in Portuguese counterinsurgency units or secret police networks, and
deserters from the Frelimo army both before and after independence.
They were welded into a fighting unit by the Rhodesian CIO and elite
Special Air Services (SAS) commandos, and their ranks were swelled by
recruits kidnapped in the border area. Their first commander was André
Matsangaissa, who fled to Rhodesia in October 1976, after he had
briefly served as a quartermaster in the Frelimo army and been arrested
for corruption.

The MNR broadcast anti-Mozambican propaganda over the Voice
of Free Africa from Rhodesia. In addition to acting as spies for Rhodesian attacks, the MNR accompanied Rhodesian commandos in some
sabotage missions and carried out others on their own. In their first
major action, against the Mozambican town of Gorongosa in October
1979, Matsangaissa was killed. The next day Rhodesian helicopters flew
Afonso Dhlakama into Mozambique to replace him.

Mozambique sought to keep the conflict with Rhodesia distinct from
relations with South Africa, adopting pragmatic policies on economic
ties with Pretoria. South Africa also refrained during this period from
direct attacks on Mozambique. South African liaison officers were involved with Rhodesia's MNR operation, however, and South Africa
provided military hardware and personnel for the Rhodesian war, including the attacks on Mozambique.

South Africa also added to the pressure on Mozambique by cutting back economic ties. The number of Mozambican miners working in South Africa was cut from 100,000 a year in the early 1970s to 45,000 a year in the second half of the decade. In April 1978 South Africa unilaterally terminated long-standing arrangements for payment of part of the miners' wages in gold at official prices, which had financed balance of payments deficits for colonial Mozambique. Traffic through Maputo port was cut by 27 per cent between 1974 and 1979.

When the Rhodesian war ended, however, the Mozambican government still hoped for a *modus vivendi* with South Africa. It had no intention of providing support for guerrilla warfare in South Africa as it had in Rhodesia.

Military outlook on the eve of the 1980s

At the turn of the decade, the prospect for Mozambique looked bright. Mozambique played an important role in fostering the Lancaster House agreement on Zimbabwean independence. The overwhelming victory of Mugabe's ZANU in the February 1980 elections ensured a friendly government that felt deep obligation to Frelimo. The MNR was on the run. For the first time, it seemed, the country could focus on peacetime tasks.

For Angola, the picture was more ambiguous. Relations with Zaire were relatively good. Despite foreign commentators' predictions of contention, the transition to President José Eduardo dos Santos after President Neto died in September 1979 was smoothly managed. Border attacks in the south continued, as did Unita guerrilla actions farther afield. But in most areas road travel was relatively secure. Namibia was not independent, but negotiations were continuing. Many observers held out hopes that South Africa would follow through on its commitment in principle to an international solution.

The groundwork was being laid, however, for conflict of a higher order of magnitude. Unita's headquarters retreat placed them farther from the central plateau, but close to South African supplies. Most of the MNR fled Mozambique or were kept on the run by government troops, but their sponsorship was handed over wholesale to South African Military Intelligence and special forces. Black and white veterans of the Rhodesian army also moved south, many to join up with South African special forces and to be assigned to Namibia, Angola or Mozambique.

South Africa, moreover, was reorienting its military strategy from the *ad-hoc* policies of the 1970s to what was termed a 'total strategy'. When former Defence Minister P.W. Botha became prime minister in September 1978, the new thrust took top priority. Among its components was massive escalation in the use of special forces, covert operations and proxy armies.

Notes

1. In the case of Mozambique there are a few first-hand accounts of this period by participants in the white revolt, such as de Saavedra (1975) and Mesquitela (1976), but no subsequent historical study. Most standard sources skip quickly over this period, but for general context, see particularly Maxwell (1982) and Antunes (1980).

2. On Angola, there is very little published which concentrates on this critical period in September 1974. The most informative memoir by a participant so far is Pezarat Correia (1991). The most important general source, in addition to those mentioned in note 1, is Heimer, *Entkoloniesierungskonflikt* (1979) (a shortened version in English is *Decolonization Conflict* (1979)).

3. Pélissier (1987), I:195.

4. For references on education in the colonial period, see Johnston (1984), as well Mondlane (1969), 58–69.

5. Angola's European population, according to a survey in 1846, numbered only 1830, with 1,600 of them in Luanda. The same survey counted as under Portuguese control 6,000 *mestiços* and 386,000 blacks, including 86,000 slaves. By 1920, Portuguese statistics enumerated some 21,000 whites, 7,500 *mestiços* and 4.3 million blacks. Most of the white population was still concentrated in the coastal cities of Luanda, Benguela and Moçamedes. Bender (1978), 64ff. on 1846, subsequent statistics on p. 20.

6. The classic reference work on Angolan nationalism is Marcum (1969, 1978). For references to other sources see my bibliographical essay (Minter, 1992).

7. Stockwell (1978), 193; Pezarat Correia (1991), 146; Heimer, *Entkoloniesierungskonflikt* (1979), 199–200.

8. Historian David Birmingham describes the Carnival in Birmingham (1992), 89-95, relating it to the history and structure of Angolan society.

9. Hanlon (1984), 58. Other sources on health in this period include Barker (1985). On education see Marshall (1990) and Lind (1988).

10. *AfricaAsia*, February 1984, 31–32; Somerville (1986), 154ff.; Wolfers and Bergerol (1983), 111ff.

11. Hodges (1987), Chapter 5: Oil and Energy.

12. Riaúzova (1986), 12. Among the abundant sources (mostly in Portuguese) on Angolan literature, one might cite particularly Ferreira (1986) and Hamilton (1975).

13. People's Republic of Mozambique (1984), 13.

14. Egerö (1990), 120ff.

15. For summary data on the political system, party and state see Wolfers and Bergerol (1983), 158-90 and Somerville (1986), 78-130.

16. *AfriqueAsie*, 10 January 1977; *Marchés Tropicaux*, 13 May 1977, in *Facts and Reports*, 13 July 1977.

17. In early 1977 President Neto denounced a plot allegedly linking Mobutu, FLEC, the FNLA, Unita and right-wing Portuguese in plans for a coordinated

invasion of Angola; *The Observer*, 17 April 1977. For a summary view of Shaba I (1977) and II (1978) see Zartman (1989), 143–69.

18. See the well-informed account of the coup attempt in *AfriqueAsie*, 11 July 1977, as well as Wolfers and Bergerol (1083), 85-100, and Birmingham (1978), 554–64.

19. *Washington Post*, 19 May 1978; Minter (1986), 296–7 and sources cited there.

20. Also known as the Buffalo Battalion, this unit was primarily composed of FNLA troops who had accompanied the South African invading column in 1975 and retreated with it to Namibia. For several years even the existence of this unit was denied, until a British mercenary deserted in 1981: *Guardian*, 29 January 1981, 2 February 1981; *Africa News*, 23 March 1981.

21. The Cassinga raid is described from the South African military point of view in Steenkamp (1983), 47–144. For eyewitness accounts see International Defense and Aid Fund (1981) and Africa Watch, *Accountability in Namibia* (1992), 27–32.

22. Steenkamp (1989), 68.

23. *Benguela Railways* (1987), 127.

24. People's Republic of Mozambique (1984), 30; Johnson and Martin, *Apartheid Terrorism* (1989), 43.

2

Total War and its Aftermath,
1980–93

For South Africa's rulers, the 1970s were frustrating. First Portugal abandoned Angola and Mozambique. The *détente* initiative collapsed in Rhodesia. Then they gambled unsuccessfully on military intervention in Angola. A few months later youth in Soweto erupted in protest, to be put down only with embarrassingly bloody repression. South Africa killed protest leader Steve Biko, but failed to block the first mandatory United Nations sanctions – the arms embargo of November 1977. Guerrillas threatened seriously for the first time in Rhodesia and in Namibia, while what South Africa saw as dangerously liberal governments in Washington and London pressed for negotiations for independence in those two countries.

There was as yet no guerrilla threat in South Africa itself. Nor were Western governments even considering serious sanctions against the apartheid regime. But South Africa's strategists saw peril everywhere. They attributed it to a 'total onslaught' orchestrated by the Soviet Union, involving South African exiles, internal demonstrators, African states, and their collaborators among Western churches, lobbies and even governments.

The policies of Prime Minister John Vorster, in office since 1966, seemed both incoherent and unsuccessful. If South Africa was to gear up for survival, his internal critics charged, the National Party needed more decisive leadership, men with a plan and with strong management skills.

South Africa's total strategy

The military establishment had such a vision: a 'total strategy', they said, to counter the 'total onslaught'. And they had their candidate, P. W. Botha, a party politician who had served as Defence Minister since 1965. In 1973 Botha had warned parliament that 'for a long time already we have been engaged in a war of low intensity'.[1] The 1977 Defence

White Paper summed it up: all government policy must be subordinated to a 'Total National Strategy' to defend the non-negotiable 'principle of the right of self-determination of the White nation'.[2]

The slogan, from French counterinsurgency theorist André Beaufre, stressed flexibility and coordination of political, diplomatic, economic and military actions. The Botha coalition included not just military men but also businessmen and politicians on the *verligte* (reform) wing of the National Party. Botha was elected in September 1978 with the support of Roelof ('Pik') Botha, a rival who then served as Foreign Minister throughout the Botha era.

Total strategy was a framework for putting together a mix of reform and repression, both internally and in foreign policy. Implementation varied, depending both on circumstances and on policy debates. There were no real doves – officials agreed that any means were justified against Pretoria's enemies. But there were often differences on the balance between violence and other measures, not only between the military and the Foreign Ministry, but also within the military itself and among civilian officials.

Initially there was no obvious contrast between Botha and his predecessor. But after defeat in Angola the South African military built up a massive capacity for open and covert action in the region. As Prime Minister, Botha continued the trend and stiffened the regime's will to use its expanded capacity for destruction. The defence budget spiralled upward. Covert operations, previously focused on espionage and political manipulation under the aegis of the Bureau of State Security, burgeoned within the military. The Department of Military Intelligence became the premier intelligence agency. Special commando forces grew rapidly, incorporating black as well as white recruits. By 1980 South Africa had an enormous conventional military edge over its neighbours and virtually unchallenged air power. It also had units capable of functioning in lightning raids or in long-term covert direction of proxy forces.

In 1979 South African military actions still seemed related primarily to the conflicts in Namibia and Rhodesia. But the next year saw the beginning of 'total onslaught' on Angola and Mozambique. This shift followed Robert Mugabe's landslide victory in the February 1980 election in Zimbabwe, which made nonsense of South African expectations that they could successfully manipulate black politics simply with cash and intrigue. Zimbabwe became the centrepiece of the Southern African Development Coordination Conference (SADCC), which brought together nine states in pursuit of greater economic independence from South Africa. Angola, Botswana, Mozambique, Tanzania, Zambia and Zimbabwe also formed a six-state Frontline group pledged to coordinate diplomatic policy on liberation of the subcontinent.

South Africa's protective shield of friendly states, now virtually non-existent, could not be reconstructed. But South Africa had the military might to make its neighbours pay dearly for any aid given to the anti-apartheid cause.

Unleashing the dogs of war, 1980–82

In part the threat the South Africans saw was real. After Soweto thousands of students fled the country, many to seek guerrilla training with the African National Congress (ANC). The ANC had its headquarters in Zambia and training camps in Tanzania and northern Angola. Significantly, none of these facilities was in countries bordering on South Africa, which were too vulnerable to South African attack. For getting recruits out of South Africa, and infiltrating trained guerrillas or arms, the ANC depended on clandestine networks passing through Botswana, Zimbabwe, Mozambique, Swaziland and Lesotho. These networks functioned sometimes with the help of officials who looked the other way, and sometimes despite police who cooperated with the South Africans. But none of these countries considered giving the same kind of sanctuary that Mozambique gave Zimbabwean guerrillas or that Angola was giving to SWAPO.

The ANC's guerrilla struggle was thus low-key and limited in military terms. Its primary significance was as a symbolic aid to political anti-apartheid campaigns. Each ANC success inside South Africa provided new incentive for military retaliation in neighbouring states. But inside South Africa, these attacks served to enhance the group's prestige among blacks.

The independence of Zimbabwe helped spur a new surge of political resistance inside South Africa. A school boycott by Coloured and Indian students showed that the younger generation in these communities identified with black protest. On 1 June 1980, the ANC carried out its first successful large-scale guerrilla action, against coal-to-oil plants near Johannesburg. In retaliation South Africa bombed two houses in Swaziland, killing a South African exile and a Swazi child.

Just the month before, in response to increased SWAPO attacks in northern Namibia, South Africa launched Operation Sceptic (Smokeshell), described as the largest South African infantry assault since the Second World War. Some 2,000 South African troops attacked SWAPO bases more than 100 miles inside Angola, and targeted Angolan troops and civilians as well. Throughout 1980 South Africa also carried out numerous smaller military operations in the same area. South African commandos sabotaged oil installations in Lobito harbour, an operation claimed by Unita. In close coordination with the South African offensive, Unita occupied sections of Cuando Cubango province. The border town of Cuangar fell in February 1980, Luengue in June, and

Mavinga in September. According to its former commander Jan Breytenbach, 32 Battalion played a key role in this campaign, but all public
credit was given to Unita.[3]

While Angola was facing this new conventional assault, Mozambique
was celebrating the independence of Zimbabwe and chalking up military victories against the remnants of the MNR. In February the MNR
was expelled from its base in the Gorongosa mountains north of the
Beira–Zimbabwe corridor; in June Mozambican forces ousted the MNR
from a new base at Sitatonga, near the South African border. Helicopter
landing pads and captured supplies revealed that South African forces
were actively involved.

In April, just before Zimbabwe's independence, the MNR command
and as many as 250 troops were transferred from eastern Zimbabwe to
South Africa, with perhaps 1,000 left inside Mozambique. South Africa's
'Operation Mila' then moved into full swing, with training camps in
South Africa, air supplies, and special forces units in and out of Mozambique by helicopter. But attacks were still small-scale, and largely limited
to remote areas of Manica and Sofala provinces.

On 30 January 1981 South African commandos raided ANC houses
in a suburb of Maputo, killing thirteen ANC members and a Portuguese
bystander. The raid, allegedly in retaliation for an ANC attack eight
months earlier, came only days after new US Secretary of State Alexander Haig spoke of the need to retaliate against 'rampant international
terrorism'. It also benefited from precise intelligence and apparently
the cooperation of some Mozambican officers.[4]

Whether or not South African and CIA-linked spy rings provided
intelligence for the attack, there is no doubt that the changing Cold
War political climate encouraged South Africa. By the second half of
Carter's term, National Security Advisor Zbigniew Brzezinski's stress
on countering the Soviets had largely eclipsed hesitant anti-apartheid
impulses in Washington. Two relatively liberal US policy-makers,
Andrew Young and Cyrus Vance, left the Carter administration during
the same period. On the global stage the Shah of Iran fell at the
beginning of 1979; Soviet troops moved into Afghanistan at the end of
the year. In the Horn of Africa superpower rivalry intensified as the
Ethiopian government sought Soviet and Cuban support.

The incoming Reagan team was even more heedless of African
concerns and sympathetic to the South African vision of a threat from
Soviet-allied forces. Angola, with Cuban troops and no diplomatic
relations with Washington, would receive no sympathy at all. Mozambique, which expelled six US diplomats accused of espionage in March
1981, could expect little more. Internationally, South Africa felt it had
a green light for the use of force.

In 1981, MNR military activity expanded gradually. In addition to

Manica and Sofala, MNR detachments penetrated northern Inhambane, just south of the Save river, and western Gaza province across from the Kruger National Park in South Africa. South Africa shipped supplies by sea to Inhambane and Sofala as well as continuing air drops. South African commandos attacked two key bridges near Beira, Mozambique, and the marker buoys in Beira harbor. But in December 1981 Mozambican troops took a large MNR base at Garágua, in southern Manica province.

In Angola in August 1981 South Africa launched Operation Protea, a conventional invasion of Cunene province with over 10,000 troops, five times the previous year's number. South Africa occupied much of Cunene province, including the provincial capital Ngiva. As in previous years, Cuban troops remained in rear positions and did not participate in active combat. Unita meanwhile fended off Angolan attempts to retake Mavinga and captured several small towns in southern Moxico province. South African commandos attacked the oil refinery in Luanda in November, causing $12.5 million of damage. Unita claimed the operation.

The following year South African forces, still occupying part of Cunene province, also launched attacks further north. Unita, which held its 5th Congress at Mavinga in mid-year, picked off the outpost of Lumbala in Moxico province, and stepped up guerrilla actions in many areas, including the central plateau. Unita warned foreign workers to get out of Angola, and attacked targets such as the Red Cross clinic in Huambo, which fitted injured people with artificial limbs.

Unita released fifteen foreign hostages in September 1982, including a Swiss nurse captured in May. This episode marked the beginning of a systematic campaign of hostage-taking, in which the captives were generally marched south to the Jamba area and eventually released in a burst of publicity. Unita also adopted a strategy of planting massive numbers of land-mines in government-held areas, and attacking civilian as well as military traffic on the roads.[5] Such actions escalated significantly in 1981–82 and succeeded in their purpose of creating a climate of insecurity.

The MNR also began taking hostages, beginning with the kidnapping of a British zoologist and several Portuguese at the end of 1981. Although the MNR lacked Unita's skill at reaping propaganda advantage when it released its captives, the actions had a similar effect in hampering rural development. Systematic MNR attacks extended to several more provinces, including Zambézia, Tete, Inhambane, Gaza, and Niassa. According to MNR sources, its ranks had grown to some 10,000 armed men. South African supplies began flowing freely through Malawi and over land from South Africa, as well as arriving by helicopters, DC-3s and from the sea. To stress its Mozambican identity, the group dropped the English-based acronym MNR; by 1983 the Portuguese-based acronym Renamo was in general use.

Between 1980 and 1982, in sum, military pressure against Angola and Mozambique grew from low-level harassment to massive sustained assault. With the exception of the far south of Angola, where South African conventional forces as well as Unita operated, Unita and Renamo concentrated on attacking dispersed targets. In both countries South African commandos carried out special operations, such as the late 1982 attacks on the Giraul bridge in southern Angola and fuel depots in Beira. Government forces could launch successful attacks on guerrilla bases, but could not be everywhere at once. There was little effective defence which could cope with tactics designed to create terror and insecurity among civilians in the rural areas.

Talk, talk, fight, fight, 1983–84

Over the next two years diplomatic efforts to reduce the violence led to South African agreements with Angola in February 1984 and Mozambique in March 1984. But the agreements provided no resolution of the conflicts, nor did South Africa make a serious effort to implement them. The wars continued with scarcely a pause.

These negotiations did not directly involve either the insurgent movements opposing South Africa (SWAPO and the ANC), on the one hand, or Unita and Renamo on the other. They were concerned with the more limited objectives of curtailing government involvement in what were termed 'cross-border operations'.

There was a superficial parallel between the two sides. SWAPO and the ANC operated against South Africa with support from the Frontline States; Unita and Renamo attacked Angola and Mozambique with support from South Africa. But the parallelism concealed profound differences. Troops from Angola or Mozambique never launched operations into South African-controlled territory; by contrast, South African troops repeatedly raided and invaded neighbouring countries. SWAPO and ANC guerrilla operations were small-scale, caused only limited casualties, and avoided indiscriminate attacks on civilians. Unita and Renamo operations were explicitly designed to destroy the economies and spread terror among civilians.

These differences reflected the vast material imbalance in military means between the South African regime and its opponents, as well as a contrast in political and moral values. Pretoria showed total disregard for the deaths of black civilians. Although civilians also died at the hands of anti-apartheid forces, leaders generally succeeded in mandating a policy of restraint. The resultant disparity in deaths and suffering recalled the common pattern of earlier colonial combats: the white regime and its African allies killed hundreds for each death caused by their opponents.

Unlike in the late nineteenth century, however, even such destruction could not provide security for white rule in Namibia and South Africa. SWAPO and the ANC could not be blocked entirely, even if neighbouring states should refrain from giving them any assistance. South Africa was universally condemned, giving the campaigns against the regime international legitimacy that South African direct or proxy attacks on Angola or Mozambique could never achieve.

South Africa's maximum objective was to create a southern African region in which all other states accepted South Africa's legitimacy and hegemony, and cooperated actively in policing opposition to the apartheid regime. But that level of control was impossible, even over such small and totally dependent states as Lesotho or Swaziland. More specific maximalist objectives included installing Unita in Luanda and Renamo in Maputo. But that would require large-scale overt South African invasions. Even if they won, the South Africans would have to defend those regimes. The net gain for South African security would be doubtful.

Alternatively, Pretoria might seek specific limits on Angolan and Mozambican actions, hoping at least to cripple SWAPO and ANC guerrilla campaigns. But these could not destroy the support for SWAPO and the ANC inside Namibia and South Africa, or in the international arena. Since guerrilla action was only a small part of their strategy, and low levels could be maintained without significant support from the Frontline States, such agreements could not eliminate the perceived threat to South Africa. This created a recurrent temptation for Pretoria to transfer the conflict to the military arena, where South Africa still enjoyed enormous advantages.

Within the South African government there was no clear consensus on the practical regional objectives. Until 1988, the potential gains from diplomacy were never so decisive that they outweighed the military momentum. South Africa paid no significant penalty for military escalation, nor were the human costs counted at all by Pretoria's total strategists.

Nevertheless, changes in 1983 and 1984 increased the pressure for diplomatic solutions. The Reagan administration was being criticized by Congress and by its European allies for its excessive tilt to Pretoria. Some administration policy-makers felt that South Africa's destabilization policies were getting out of hand. With the end of Reagan's first term approaching, there was a demand for results from constructive engagement. At the same time, Angola and Mozambique were stepping up their defences. A comprehensive defence was not possible. But they could and did increase the cost to South Africa of military action.

South Africa continued its occupation in southern Angola during 1983, with sporadic raids further afield. Unita extended its actions into new areas. Commandos sabotaged a crucial hydroelectric dam at Lomaum; Unita captured sixty-six Czech technicians at a paper factory at Alto Catumbela. But the Angolan government reorganized its forces in mid-year and began counter-offensives. In August Unita had to call on South African reinforcements in a battle at Cangamba, in Moxico province. The Soviet Union warned South Africa in November against further escalation. In late 1983 and early 1984, 'Operation Askari' met with a response from Angolan forces that South African General Constand Viljoen called unexpectedly fierce.

In the wake of Operation Askari, Angolan and South African negotiators met in Lusaka, Zambia, in February 1984, and agreed to the withdrawal of South African troops from Angola in exchange for limits on SWAPO guerrilla presence in the border area. The Angolans hoped the agreement would be followed by progress on long-stalled negotiations for Namibian independence. But the South Africans balked even at implementing the withdrawal, leaving their troops in Angola throughout 1984. South Africa signalled its ongoing support for Unita when Jonas Savimbi attended P.W. Botha's inauguration as State President in September 1984. Military supplies for Unita increased in both 1983 and 1984. Unita attacks extended to major targets as far afield as Sumbe in Kwanza Sul province and a diamond mine in Lunda, where Unita captured sixteen British, forty Portuguese and fifty Filipino hostages.

In Mozambique Renamo attacks also escalated in 1983. Only Cabo Delgado province in the far north-east was spared. The stepped-up fighting between 1981 and 1983, which devastated social services and transport links, coincided with the most extended drought in over fifty years, affecting particularly Tete, Gaza and Inhambane provinces. In drought-stricken areas Renamo attacked food relief convoys. Some estimates put the death toll from famine during this period at over 100,000. South Africa launched another open commando raid on Maputo in May 1983, killing five Mozambicans and one South African refugee.

Zimbabwean troops went into Mozambique by late 1982, to aid in defending transport corridors critical for Zimbabwe's trade and oil supplies. A reorganized Mozambican army gained some successes, particularly in Inhambane province. But the ruling Frelimo party also decided on a diplomatic offensive to reduce the South African military assault. The aim was to convince South Africa's Western allies that Mozambique was genuinely non-aligned, and that it was South Africa that was responsible for the instability in the region. Mozambique sought a military *détente* with South Africa, while refusing to abandon its political support for the ANC.

After a meeting between Mozambican Foreign Minister Joaquim Chissano and US Secretary of State George Shultz in October 1982, Washington openly criticized South African support for Renamo. Mozambican and South African negotiators met in December 1982 and May 1983, but only in December 1983 did the South Africans seem ready to negotiate seriously. The Nkomati Accord, signed in March 1984, provided that neither South Africa nor Mozambique would allow any support for armed action against the other from its territory. Mozambique kept its side of the bargain by restricting ANC presence in Mozambique to a small diplomatic office. The agreement was strongly criticized elsewhere in southern Africa as Mozambican capitulation to South Africa, although some critics said the pressures Mozambique was under made the move understandable.

The South African regime gained diplomatic credit with the West for the Nkomati and Lusaka agreements. But it was the image rather than the content of the agreements that favoured South Africa. If implemented in good faith, they would have imposed greater restrictions on the South African regime than on its opponents.

None of the insurgent groups on either side was directly involved in the 1984 agreements. But Unita and South African operations in Angola depended on large-scale involvement of air power and conventional troops in part of the country; in Mozambique Renamo operations depended on consistent South African involvement in logistics and communications. In contrast, the smaller-scale guerrilla operations of SWAPO and ANC, with their linkages to political organizations and legitimacy inside their countries, could continue with less resources.

South Africa found it useful to sign the agreements. And some officials may have argued that it was useful to keep them. But South African military operations continued against both Angola and Mozambique. The promise of a pause for diplomatic celebration proved illusory.

Stoking the flames of violence, 1985-87

While South Africa's total strategists argued that they could control events if only the outside world let them alone, their most critical vulnerability was at home. The reform side of Botha's strategy culminated in a trilateral parliament in 1984, where Indians and Coloureds were given token representation along with whites. A strengthened executive presidency cleared the way for the regime to control the pace of change, with the aim of allowing African representation through the homelands and through councils for an elite of urban Africans. But the scheme had so little credibility that it helped ignite a new wave of black protest, rooted in community organizations and unions and closely allied with the ANC. Even the ANC's guerrilla actions, despite greater difficulties in transit through Mozambique, were on the increase again in 1985.

In Namibia, likewise, the internal coalition of white and black groups which South Africa put together to run the country failed to gain any legitimacy. SWAPO managed to win new political support inside the country. Although South Africa announced with each strike into Angola that SWAPO's guerrilla capacity had been destroyed, the movement continued to infiltrate guerrillas and to maintain its base in populous northern Namibia.

South Africa had gained diplomatic points with Western governments from the peace gestures of 1984. Now, however, the new internal resistance triggered higher levels of popular anti-apartheid organization in the US and in Europe. Diplomacy had not produced the promised breathing spell for apartheid. Neither had the military actions against Angola, Mozambique and other neighbouring states. But with the escalating threat inside South Africa, the hawks argued successfully for hitting the ANC and its allies wherever they might be. ANC guerrillas still had training bases in northern Angola, and Mozambique still pledged moral support if nothing more. The campaigns against Angola and Mozambique might not be the most effective response to the ANC's growing political strength inside South Africa. But they were easy, and clearly damaged those whom the South African hawks saw as part of the Soviet conspiracy against them.

In the US, meanwhile, President Ronald Reagan was re-elected by a landslide in late 1984, and proclaimed the 'Reagan doctrine' of US support for anti-communist 'freedom fighters'. The international community condemned escalating attacks against Angola and Mozambique, and US diplomats cautioned South Africa to be more moderate. But powerful Washington ideologues praised South Africa's strong military action against Soviet allies, especially Angola.

The Mozambican government, encouraged by US mediation, still hoped that South Africa would live up to the Nkomati Accord. The South African Foreign Ministry hosted indirect talks between the Mozambican government and Renamo in October, and a deal involving Renamo recognition of the Mozambican government was apparently in the works. But Renamo backed out, and it was later revealed that South African Military Intelligence had been working to sabotage the talks. Just before Nkomati, moreover, South Africa had stepped up arms supplies, and top generals pledged to maintain support for Renamo. Arms shipments were resumed in mid-year. Renamo attacks continued and even hit previously secure areas, such as the road from Maputo to Swaziland.

The US administration, which congratulated itself on helping to broker the treaty, made no vigorous attempt to restrain South Africa from violating it. As Mozambique sought Western support in pressuring South Africa, the State Department instead tried to fend off public and congressional demands to sanction South Africa for its internal apartheid system. The US far right lobbied for including Renamo as a Reagan doctrine client, along with the Nicaraguan Contras and Unita. Advocates of diplomatic rapprochement with Mozambique blocked these efforts, and President Samora Machel was received by President Reagan on a state visit in 1985.

Machel brought new proofs of South African violations of Nkomati, captured in an attack on the Renamo central base. South African Foreign Minister Pik Botha was embarrassed, but admitted only 'technical violations' of the treaty. Over the next two years South African military support for Renamo continued, and apparently escalated, supplemented by growing involvement of a tangled network of right-wing groups, entrepreneurs and intelligence agencies in other countries.

Escalation of Renamo attacks culminated in an offensive from Malawi in October 1986 against the provinces of Tete, Zambézia and Sofala. South African commandos participated in the assaults, which succeeded in capturing a number of district capitals. Mozambican and Zimbabwean troops finally blocked the offensive before it could achieve its apparent objective of splitting Mozambique with a Renamo-controlled corridor to the sea.

After a land-mine exploded in South Africa near the Mozambican border, South African Defence Minister Magnus Malan threatened retaliation. A few days later, President Samora Machel's personal airplane crashed just inside the South African border while returning to Mozambique from a Frontline summit in Zambia. The Mozambican president and thirty-three others were killed. South Africa claimed it was an accident caused by pilot error, but evidence indicated the pilots had been led astray by a decoy radio beacon that was never explained.[6]

In the wake of the 1986 offensive, the new Mozambican president, Joaquim Chissano, renewed efforts with other Frontline States to persuade Malawi to reduce support for Renamo. Tanzanian as well as Zimbabwean troops helped Mozambique recover control of much of the affected provinces. In July 1987 publicity from the Homoíne massacre dealt a serious blow to pro-Renamo campaigners in Washington. President Chissano visited Washington in October, renewing requests for the US to put pressure on Pretoria. But South African material support for Renamo's guerrilla actions continued unabated.

In Angola as well, 1985 and 1986 were years of escalating conflict. Unita continued its guerrilla warfare in most of the countryside. Angolan counter-attacks against Unita base areas brought larger South African forces into conventional battles inside Angola. In May 1985 a South African commando unit was stopped on a sabotage mission against Gulf Oil installations in Cabinda, and one man captured, leading to tension between Pretoria and Washington.

Nevertheless, the right-wing bandwagon for US support of Savimbi gathered steam. Congress repealed the Clark Amendment barring covert intervention in Angola in mid-1985, and within months Reagan decided to grant new covert aid to Unita. The estimated $15 million in 1986 was only a token, in comparison to South African involvement. But it encouraged the aggressive South African stance. When Angolan troops threatened Mavinga in late 1985, South African air and artillery units helped rescue Savimbi's forces. In 1986 South Africa joined in shelling the Angolan base of Cuito Cuanavale, as well as continuing to raid south-western Angola.

Unita also continued its guerrilla attacks. In several incidents, such as at Camabatela in February 1986 and at a village in Huambo province in January 1987, Unita killed large numbers of civilians. Unita captured another 200 foreign workers in early 1986. But the most damaging tactics were still the planting of land-mines and the interruption of transport routes.

International pressure for sanctions against South Africa meanwhile continued to escalate. South Africa responded belligerently, launching raids on Botswana, Zimbabwe and Zambia in May 1986, just as a Commonwealth Eminent Persons Group was visiting South Africa to explore grounds for negotiations. Later that year, a number of Western countries imposed partial economic sanctions on South Africa. In the US, Congress passed the Comprehensive Anti-Apartheid Act of 1986 over President Reagan's veto. The sanctions eventually helped to force South Africa into a more conciliatory posture. But in the short run they probably reinforced South African intransigence. In any case Western public opinion paid little attention to South Africa's regional military actions.

The wars escalated significantly in both countries in 1987. In Angola the primary focus was another round of fighting in Cuando Cubango province, between Cuito Cuanavale and Mavinga, beginning in September. The battles, which saw the most massive involvement of South African and of Cuban forces ever, eventually resulted in a major setback for South Africa and Unita. But at the end of 1987 Savimbi was claiming major victories, such as the recapture of Munhango on the Benguela Railway. Overall, the conventional military confrontation was at a stalemate.

In Mozambique, 1987 saw not only the massacre at Homoíne, but the death of almost 400 civilians in three ambushes on convoys in southern Mozambique in October and November. Another fifty people were killed and the tea plantations of Guruè destroyed in Zambézia province. Eyewitnesses reported that two whites led the attack on Guruè;

parachutes and other evidence of new South African supplies were linked to the attacks in the south. Smaller-scale attacks around the country were rampant.

Winding down the conventional war:
war and negotiations, 1988-89

By 1988, the wars in both Angola and Mozambique reached peak intensity. War-weariness was pervasive. This period saw the beginning of serious negotiations. But the results came only piecemeal: first independence for Namibia, then an Angolan ceasefire two years later. In late 1992, as Mozambique was finally celebrating a ceasefire, resumed war in Angola revealed fundamental flaws in the regional peace process. For five years, however, the theme was de-escalation.

The first issues to be resolved were Namibian independence and the parallel conventional war in southern Angola. In 1988 the price was rising for all parties involved. The previous year Angolan forces with Soviet encouragement and new supplies had overextended themselves in south-eastern Angola and were driven back to Cuito Cuanavale by South African reinforcements. Then the South African forces in turn found themselves losing their previous air superiority. Maintaining the siege was costly and threatened a politically unacceptable rise in white casualties. Crack Cuban reinforcements arriving in November 1987 bolstered the Angolans at Cuito Cuanavale and joined with SWAPO as well as Angolan forces to advance towards the Namibian border in the south-west. For the first time, South African troops in northern Namibia were vulnerable.

These military developments coincided with other factors conducive to rethinking. International sanctions against South Africa were beginning to bite. Political resistance inside Namibia, through student and worker strikes, was on the rise. At the global level, Soviet and American diplomats were increasingly in accord on the need for settlements of 'regional conflicts'. The US was willing for the first time to include Cuba in the negotiations. A complex series of new rounds of talks began in May 1988, culminating in December in two parallel agreements. The first, signed by Cuba, Angola and South Africa, set the timetable for United Nations-supervised elections in Namibia by the end of 1989, to be followed shortly by independence. The second, between Cuba and Angola, specified a timetable for staged withdrawal of Cuban troops from Angola, with 50 per cent leaving before the Namibian elections in November 1989, and the remainder by mid-1991. The US and the Soviet Union participated as observers rather than as signatories.[7]

The accords included a South African commitment to cease military support for Unita, together with Angolan agreement to require the

ANC to transfer its guerrilla bases to another country. There were no commitments, however, on US military aid to Unita, or on Soviet support for the Angolan government.

Meanwhile, in Mozambique Renamo's attacks continued unabated. The lack of conventional combat or of superpower diplomatic concentration contributed to the war's obscurity. The campaign in Washington to win official support for Renamo suffered a major setback, however, when a State Department-sponsored report released in April 1988 charged Renamo with large-scale and systematic atrocities. The Mozambican government and press continued to cite South African responsibility for supplying arms to Renamo. President Botha met with President Chissano in September, reaffirming South Africa's willingness to pursue peaceful economic ties. He denied any continuing support for Renamo. But no evidence emerged that the new declaration was being implemented any more seriously than was the Nkomati agreement.

Early in 1989, President Botha suffered a mild stroke, and was replaced as National Party chairman by F.W. de Klerk. After an uneasy interregnum, Botha also lost the presidency to de Klerk in August. The transition apparently had little immediate effect on regional policy. Angola and Mozambique both started new peace initiatives in 1989. But neither bore fruit, despite an abortive summit in Zaire which was briefly heralded as a breakthrough.

Despite covert South African efforts to manipulate the Namibian election, which decreased SWAPO's election margin, a high level of international involvement facilitated the relatively smooth implementation of the 1988 accords. South African troops withdrew from southern Angola and Namibia on schedule. SWAPO fell short of the two-thirds majority necessary to adopt a constitution on its own, but was in any case committed to a conciliatory approach in the constitutional assembly. Namibia became independent on 21 March 1990.

International monitoring, with the participation of Angola, Cuba, South Africa, the US, the Soviet Union and the United Nations, also verified the smooth implementation of Cuban troop withdrawal from Angola. South Africa could no longer provide large-scale supplies over land to south-eastern Angola. But monitors did not look too closely at the continued presence of South African advisers with Unita, at small-scale movements across the border, or at air flights from South Africa to Jamba. The US helped to make up for the reduction in South African supplies, both by airlifts to the Jamba area and by supporting Unita's increasingly vigorous military campaign in northern Angola. This northern campaign, supplied over the land border with Zaire, directly threatened the Angolan capital Luanda.

Immediately following the New York agreements, in early 1989 the Angolan government proposed an internal peace settlement based on incorporation of Unita members and leaders into government structures, including cabinet posts, while reserving a dominant role for the existing government. It also included the 'temporary and voluntary retirement' (not exile as often reported) of Savimbi from Angolan political life. The diplomatic strategy focused on building up pressure from African heads of state, including Mobutu Sese Seko of Zaire, whose country had become Unita's most important military rear base. The first part of 1989 saw a complex African tug-of-war as Angola tried to build a coalition of African states to support its plan, while Unita and its supporters sought to block it, holding out for equal status with the Angolan government.

The State Department's Africa Bureau at this point was in transition. Eight-year veteran Chester Crocker was turning over leadership to Herman Cohen, while Unita's lobbyists and congressional allies watched closely for any sign of disloyalty to the Unita crusade. Crocker's 1988 hints that Angola would be rewarded for its flexibility in signing the New York accord were not fulfilled, as the US refused to follow through with plans for a US interest section in Luanda and an Angolan interest section in Washington. CIA aid to Unita increased from an estimated $30–$45 million in 1988 to $50–$60 million in 1989.

In June 1989 President Mobutu hosted a meeting at his palace in Gbadolite, Zaire, attended by eighteen African heads of state, with the presence of both President dos Santos and Jonas Savimbi. According to most of those present, and to the declaration of a later summit in Harare, Savimbi agreed to a ceasefire and settlement which largely corresponded to the Angolan government plan. Dos Santos and Savimbi embraced in the presence of the heads of state, and the ceasefire was scheduled to take effect within days. But the key details were agreed only in oral understandings (or misunderstandings). Savimbi denied he had agreed to anything more than the general communiqué and continued discussions. Mobutu was subsequently accused of having deceived both sides into thinking the other had agreed to their conditions.

While ordinary Angolans on both sides rejoiced, the ceasefire lasted only a few days. Then Unita troops received orders to resume guerrilla attacks. President dos Santos and the Angolan military came under internal criticism for having accepted Savimbi's word and let down their guard. Mobutu's mediator role was fatally discredited. The war continued. Formal negotiations did not resume until after the independence of Namibia in March 1990.

President Chissano of Mozambique took a similar approach in 1989, appealing to Presidents Moi of Kenya and Mugabe of Zimbabwe to serve as mediators. In a July news conference, soon after the Zaire summit, Chissano laid out the government's principles for peace, including a willingness to discuss further modifications in the constitution. The public offer had been preceded by government encouragement of private contacts by Mozambican church leaders with Renamo. The same week Chissano met with National Party leader de Klerk of South Africa, who gave new pledges of South African support for peace.

But peace was not imminent in either Mozambique or Angola. The Kenyan government, picked as a mediator because of its ties with Renamo, instead became more deeply involved in supporting the group. Renamo attacks continued unabated, with supplies and support from South Africa, from Malawi and now from Kenya as well. In Angola the Gbadolite fiasco provoked tension between Savimbi and Mobutu, and for several months CIA supply flights from Zaire's Kamina base to Jamba were suspended. Unita concentrated on stepping up attacks in vulnerable north-western Angola. Jamba was supplied with flights from South Africa, in violation of the New York agreements. Following the successful completion of the elections in Namibia, the Angolan government launched a new conventional offensive against Unita base areas in late December. Angolan troops succeeded in driving Unita out of the key town of Mavinga, but renewed US supplies enabled Unita to hold out. The government was eventually forced to reallocate military resources to meet Unita's intensified attack in the north. The military stalemate continued.

Promises of peace: war, negotiations and war, 1990-93

When Namibia finally became independent in March 1990, the time was ripe for another attempt at negotiations in Angola. After the inconclusive results of the last round of conventional fighting, it was clear to all parties that major new shifts in the military balance were unlikely. In April, talks between the Angolan government and Unita began, with Portuguese Secretary of State for Foreign Affairs Durão Barroso as mediator. US and Soviet representatives followed the process closely, although they did not become directly engaged until late in the year.

For the Angolan government the key sticking points were acceptance of competitive multi-party elections rather than simply incorporation of Unita into the government, and agreement that the future national army would be recruited equally from government and Unita forces. President dos Santos won agreement within the party for these principles early in the year. But getting a consensus on details was slowed by intense suspicions that Unita and the US would use any concessions as an opening for the overthrow of the government. By the end of 1990, however, the MPLA party congress accepted a multi-party constitution; the party officially abandoned Marxism-Leninism in favour of democratic socialism in April 1991. Unita, for its part, was even more reluctant to accept the legitimacy of the Angolan government, even on an interim basis preceding elections, and sought to guarantee the separate existence of the two armies and zones of control until after elections.

Both the government and Unita faced potential loss of international patronage. Soviet interest in withdrawal from regional conflicts was strong, bolstering dos Santos's arguments within the party for further compromises. Unita, with strong backing in Washington, initially had less incentive to compromise. In October, however, the US House of Representatives narrowly passed an amendment that would suspend covert lethal aid to Unita if the Angolan government agreed to a ceasefire and a 'reasonable' election timetable. Although the legislation containing the amendment was vetoed by President Bush on other grounds, it was a signal to Savimbi that his superpower assets were also waning.

In November, at the suggestion of Soviet Foreign Minister Shevardnadze, the US and the Soviet Union became more actively involved in the negotiations, building consensus around a set of concepts to guide discussion of ceasefire and election timing. Unita argued for a maximum of twelve months between ceasefire and elections. The Angolan government initially proposed thirty-six months, reduced to twenty-four months in early 1991, as the time needed to implement the ceasefire, establish a neutral national army, remove mines from the roads and set up other conditions for holding an election. The final agreement set the election for fifteen to eighteen months after the 15 May ceasefire.

In Mozambique, the transition to a multi-party system advanced rapidly in 1990 and 1991, but negotiations with Renamo made little progress. Having officially dropped Marxism-Leninism as the party's ideology at the party congress in July 1989, Frelimo in early 1990 initiated a nationwide popular debate on a new constitution, with a multi-party system being presented as an option for discussion. Although the majority, particularly in rural areas, spoke for retaining a one-party model, the party decided that minority support for a multi-party constitution was large enough to mandate its adoption. The new constitution went into effect at the end of 1990. Over the next two years, many small opposition parties made their appearance.

Although the changes in Mozambique pleased its Western allies, and apparently satisfied all the demands of Renamo propaganda over the years, they had little effect on the war. Nor did they put ceasefire negotiations on the fast track. President de Klerk, astonishing the world with the release of Nelson Mandela and the beginning of negotiations with the ANC, took no effective action to block military support for Renamo from South Africa. Nor did the shadowy figures involved in Renamo supply networks in Malawi and Kenya as well as South Africa show any signs of opting for peace rather than war.

Mediation efforts featuring Kenya and Zimbabwe, with Malawi as a host for potential direct talks, culminated in a fiasco in June 1990 when Renamo representatives refused to show up. The Mozambican government then persuaded the Roman Catholic order of Santo Egidio, together with the Italian government, to host talks in Rome. The first round took place in July.

The prolonged negotiations, delayed repeatedly by Renamo hesitation and backtracking, produced in November 1990 a limited agreement on a ceasefire for the Limpopo and Beira corridors, with restriction of Zimbabwean troops to these areas. In May 1991, when Angolans signed a peace accord, mediators in Rome had only succeeded in gaining Renamo's consent to an agenda. As the talks stretched out, over seemingly minor points, most observers and diplomats agreed with the Mozambican government's diagnosis: Renamo was afraid of peace, because its chances of winning support in peaceful political competition were so low and because its leaders had become accustomed to war as a way of life. Nor did their obscure backers, in South Africa or elsewhere, have a clear vision of their bottom-line requirements for peace. Through successive rounds of talks followed in Rome, the war ground on, through 1990 and 1991 and 1992.

In October 1992 a ceasefire agreement was finally signed, providing for demobilization, a new national army, and elections within a year. The UN Security Council voted support for a mission to help implement the accord. In the following months the ceasefire generally held, refuting doubts about Renamo's control over its dispersed troops. But every other provision of the accord was delayed, by slow arrival of international personnel, by Renamo's on-off participation in the commissions set up for implementation, and by a series of new Renamo demands.

In Angola the May 1991 ceasefire was implemented with remarkably few violent breaches. Small opposition parties proliferated. But the United Nations mission charged with monitoring the ceasefire and the planned elections was woefully short-staffed and poorly funded – less than one-fourth the amount allocated to Namibia in 1989, for a country with ten times the population and a war-ravaged infrastructure. Unita kept a tight rein on the local population in areas it controlled. The provision for demobilization of the two armies and creation of a new national army was not implemented, with Unita in particular maintaining its command structure and arms caches virtually intact. The US, Russia and Portugal, charged with monitoring the agreement's implementation, were reluctant to act against Unita or to allow any delay in the schedule for elections.

The elections, held on 29–30 September 1992, produced a turnout of over 90 per cent. They proceeded in a peaceful and orderly manner which won praise from international observers. The United Nations observer mission judged the process generally free and fair, as did other non-governmental and diplomatic observers. The MPLA won 54 per cent of the legislative seats, as compared with 34 per cent for Unita. President dos Santos fell just short of 50 per cent in the presidential race, compared with 40 per cent for Unita leader Savimbi.

Savimbi refused to accept the results, choosing instead to return to war. With the aid of supplies from South Africa and Zaire, Unita launched a series of offensives around the country. In late October the government responded, expelling Unita from the capital. By early 1993, the country was at war again, on a scale exceeding that of the entire previous period.

Notes

1. International Defence and Aid Fund (1980), 3.

2. Cawthra (1986), 29. Like Cawthra (1986), a systematic compilation of data, most studies on the southern African wars came out in the mid-1980s. Although specific references will be cited in chapters to come, the reader seeking an overview might consult the following major sources: Coker (1987); Hanlon (1986); Jaster (1989); Legum (1988); Johnson and Martin (1988). A useful survey, despite its brevity, is Jaster et al. (1992). For a focus on strategy and the institutions of the South African military, see Cock and Nathan (1989), Frankel (1984), and Grundy (1986). More specifically military details, from perspectives sympathetic to the South African military, can be found in Heitman (1985); Steenkamp (1989) and Moorcraft (1990). On diplomacy, 1981–88, Crocker (1992) is self-serving and highly selective, but provides a useful chronological framework and insights into US perspectives. Of the many studies of Renamo, the one with the most careful attention to detail and useful guide to earlier sources is Vines (1991). There is nothing comparable on UNITA, but two volumes by UNITA partisans, with chronological framework and much detail, are Bridgland (1987) and James (1992).

3. See Breytenbach (1990), Chapters 8 and 9.

4. Mutemba (1982).

5. Africa Watch, *Land Mines in Angola* (1993).

6. The full transcript of the agreed joint international report of Soviet, South African and Mozambican representatives can be found (in Portuguese translation) in Marques (1987). The South African government also conducted a unilateral inquiry, with international observers chosen by Pretoria, which decided the cause was exclusively pilot error, particularly in failing to respond to ground proximity warnings. The radio beacon which led the plane to home in on Swaziland rather than Maputo, however, was never explained.

7. The text of the agreements can be found in Jaster et al. (1992), 167–73. The negotiations are presented, from the US State Department point of view, in Crocker (1992). Among analytical articles appearing so far, see Berridge (1989), McFaul (1989, 1990), Jaster (1990) and Wood (1991).

3

Explanations – Theories, Facts and Arguments

'Of all the insurgencies against pro-Soviet regimes anywhere in the world, Renamo's is closest to victory', trumpeted the Heritage Foundation in 1986, describing Renamo as 'an anti-communist, popularly supported resistance'. Renamo lobbyist Tom Schaaf told the *Washington Times* that South Africa had abandoned Renamo, implying that its military achievements were based on internal support.[1] Three years later, London-based academic Gervase Clarence-Smith announced a 'paradigm shift' in analyses of the Mozambican crisis. 'Frelimo has dug its own grave in the face of an apparently derisory opponent', he wrote, heralding a shift in emphasis from 'Pretoria's policies and actions' to 'why Frelimo's agrarian policies went so disastrously wrong'.[2]

To these commentators, South Africa's involvement with Renamo was a peripheral factor in what was fundamentally a civil war. Blaming the apartheid regime was seen as a convenient diversion from examining the true roots of the conflict. Critics countered that whatever Frelimo's faults, the war was still primarily the responsibility of the covert South African war machine.

The Mozambican crisis produced a multitude of studies with emphases ranging widely along the 'civil war/war of destabilization' spectrum. Only a few stressed exclusively one factor, but explicitly or implicitly each highlighted some factors over others. The scholarly literature on Angola was much less extensive. But alternative perspectives were implicit even in short newspaper articles. In September 1987, for example, as battles raged around Cuito Cuanavale, a *Washington Post* article headlined 'Angola, Savimbi Forces Clash Anew' made no mention of the South African military.[3] Later South African accounts, placing their forces at the front the month before, described the battles as essentially a contest between the South African Defence Force and the Angolan army, with Unita in an auxiliary role.[4]

How does one decide among such drastically different emphases? In retrospect particular details may be confirmed: that a raid attributed to Unita, for example, was carried out by South African commandos, that South African supplies to Renamo continued after the Nkomati Accord, that some Angolans regarded the Cuban presence as foreign occupation, or that some peasants in a particular Mozambican district joined Renamo because of government hostility to their traditional cultures. But wars are complicated processes. It is likely that some evidence can be found that almost any hypothesized factor 'contributed to' if not 'caused' a conflict. It is easy to reject the most grossly propagandistic accounts, and to say that no single-factor explanation can be adequate. But working out what factors were most important is complicated not just by information gaps, but also by issues of theory, methodology, political commitment and moral judgement.

Each reader will bring his or her own perspectives to such an enquiry, based on personal involvement with Angola or Mozambique, or on views derived from other social, political or academic contexts. Answers depend to a great extent on how questions are asked, and it is therefore important to try to put the questions clearly. That is the purpose of this chapter.

Why explanations matter

During a war, explaining the causes of conflict is connected with very practical concerns – how to end the war and on what terms. Different analyses of what factors caused the conflict, and what factors keep it going, reflect different preferences for the outcome and imply distinct prescriptions for peace. When Mozambican President Machel spoke of dealing with the organ-grinder rather than the monkey, he was not just making a rhetorical point. He was expressing his government's view that the war was directed by South Africa for South African objectives, and that serious negotiations must first address Pretoria. When critics stressed internal roots of the conflict, the implicit agenda was to argue for dealing with Renamo's concerns, or, alternatively, for policies that might reduce Renamo's support within the country.

Once a peace settlement has been reached, the issue remains of whether the factors promoting conflict have been resolved or simply temporarily assuaged. Granted, new conflicts may emerge for different reasons. But if underlying structural tensions were responsible, conflict is particularly likely to resume once one of the parties recovers from war-weariness or sees new possibilities of gaining an advantage by the force of arms.

Even if conflict is not reignited, a war that is lost or that ends inconclusively must lead to reflection on responsibility for the suffering involved. Victors can easily evade the issue; the fruits of victory are

taken to justify the sacrifices of the winners, and the plight of the losers
is attributed to their own account. Losers have a more urgent imperative
for historical reflection: was the war a fundamental error to start with,
were they betrayed by incompetent or treasonous leaders, or simply
overwhelmed by circumstances beyond their control? In wars with no
clear winners, the cost in human suffering stands out, with few offsetting
accomplishments. The question of blame is inescapable – and divisive.
In wars such as those in Angola and Mozambique – not only inconclusive but also civil in the sense of dividing Angolans and Mozambicans, even if not primarily internal in origin – it touches fundamental
questions of historical identity as well as political credibility.

Of the wider conflicts with which these wars were intertwined, the
anti-apartheid struggle also failed to gain a clear-cut victory. As of 1993,
the white minority regime in South Africa was still manoeuvring for
maximum power in the post-apartheid order. The covert security forces
involved in regional warfare were still largely intact; some in their ranks
were implicated in internal violence. Whatever the shape of the transition, it was clear that reconciliation and compromise had to take priority
over any parallel to de-Nazification after the Second World War. On
the global level, the Cold War ended with the collapse of the Soviet
Union and its allies. It was easy for the victors to fit regional conflicts
into a standard model of the failure of Soviet-allied regimes.

In the early 1990s, many attributed the tragic destruction in Angola
and Mozambique primarily to internal division and failed efforts to
impose Marxist socialism, with the responsibility of Pretoria or Washington relegated to an occasional perfunctory mention. Such interpretations
easily rationalized post-war neglect by the international community. If,
on the contrary, the lion's share of the blame fell on the South African
regime and the Reagan administration's policies, then they would have
a moral debt to the peoples of Angola and Mozambique. Such debts
are rarely honoured in practical political terms. But historical honesty
requires that they not be forgotten.

Individuals and groups experienced these wars not only on different
sides but in different geographical and social locations. For most individuals and local communities, the war came from the outside, a
reality to cope with rather than a drama entered into voluntarily. Many
combatants also found themselves at war rather than decided to go to
war. Victims of Renamo attacks often lamented to visitors that they just
didn't understand: 'In a war soldiers fight soldiers. But they are attacking
us. And we don't know why.' The why of a war may be just as mysterious for participants as for distant observers. In so far as people
made sense of their participation, however, there were many different
collective stories to choose from.

At the local level, any war may intersect with local hostilities and disputes. At the least, the atmosphere of violence and confusion gives the opportunity for settling unrelated grievances. In other cases, pre-existing local factions opt for different sides, intertwining the dynamics of their own conflict with that of the wider war. Such realities are likely to have a decisive influence on how rural communities experience conflict. But they are not necessarily primary in understanding the reasons for the war's origin and continuation.

At the national level, these wars directly followed the wars of in-dependence. In both countries, the movements coming to power saw their history as virtually identical with that of the creation of the nation, and their opponents as foreign enemies or internal traitors collaborating with them. These images had elements of myth and propaganda. But they were firmly believed by large numbers of politically conscious Mozambicans and Angolans, and had justification in the historical record. Frelimo was the undisputed leader of the independence struggle. In Angola, despite nationalist fragmentation, the MPLA was the move-ment that aimed most consciously and successfully at national support. Unita, on the other hand, deliberately shaped a regional appeal, and had collaborated militarily with the Portuguese army during the war of independence.

The insurgents also claimed nationalist credentials, with varying degrees of success and historical accuracy. Unita denied the charges of collaboration with the Portuguese military, and claimed to represent the numerically predominant peoples of central and southern Angola. Not only supporters of Renamo and Unita, but also other critics, noted the presence in the ruling parties of whites and *mestiços*, and the prominent role played by people from the capital city area. Unita and Renamo propaganda stressed that they, not the ruling parties, were more exclusively black, more deeply rooted in rural African culture, and consequently more genuine African nationalists.

This claim clashed discordantly with the regional line-up. The An-golan and Mozambican governments stood for freeing Africa from white minority domination, while Unita and Renamo sought excuses for their participation in South Africa's war machine. For those actively opposed to apartheid, Unita and Renamo were definitively discredited, whatever might be the flaws of the governments they attacked. Whether they were puppets of Pretoria, or independent agents seeking Pretoria's aid out of perceived necessity, they were seen as traitors to African freedom.

Supporters of the apartheid regime, who saw it as victimized by a total onslaught of Moscow-aligned Marxists and their dupes, correspond-ingly saw Unita and Renamo as defenders of African freedom from Marxist domination. By the 1980s there were few, even within the South African regime, who explicitly defended racial superiority as a doctrine. Instead they placed regional conflicts in a global ideological context. In this vision, former supporters of colonialism and apartheid together with their victims and critics should unite, white and black, against foreign-inspired Marxist threats to private property, religion and tradition.

Such a view, in competition with claims of national loyalty or of African liberation, appealed to some Angolans and Mozambicans. But ideological alienation from the ruling parties was by no means the same as willingness to join South Africa, Renamo or Unita in violence directed against civilians as much as against the regimes. Internal ideological and other divisions among Angolans and Mozambicans are relevant to understanding the wars, but an accurate picture must also take account of the many ways people sought to limit commitment to, or involvement with, either side.

Outside southern Africa, involvement of governments, groups or individuals with these wars was most often a function of their position in the international conflicts over racial injustice in southern Africa or over Third World revolution. There were exceptions. The pragmatic ties of Gulf Oil (later Chevron) with the Angolan government were based on specific interests in Angola's petroleum. Portuguese politics was influenced not only by over half a million returned settlers, but also by specific business interests and by the complex networks of personal ties built up over the colonial period. Many individuals who spent time in Mozambique or in Angola relied on personal knowledge. But for the most part, the non-African policy-makers and publics who paid some attention to these wars had only the most general ideas of the relevant social reality or historical background. Their decisions and attitudes, nevertheless, sometimes had profound effects.

Descriptions of a war can focus on one aspect without much explicit justification beyond the particular experiences or interests of the author. Attempts to weigh the relative importance of different factors require more precise specification of just what is being explained.

Many studies of Angola or Mozambique, whether sympathetic or hostile to the socialist project, have focused on explaining its failure, or, in other words, explaining the catastrophic crises in which the countries now find themselves. In such a model the war appears as one possible cause for crisis, along with other structural weaknesses or fundamental failures of policy-making or implementation. In the absence of war, could Frelimo and the MPLA have made good their promises? Or was failure inherent in a flawed vision which would have collapsed on its own or provoked war out of its own contradictions? What happened to the hopes of the mid-1970s, and why? Were the failures in Angola and Mozambique distinctive in origin, or did they replicate disillusionment with other African states, whether they espoused leftist or rightist ideologies or none at all?

These essential questions overlap significantly with the themes of this study. But the topic here is different. Rather than focusing on the contribution of the wars and other factors to the crises, the present study analyses the impact of various factors on originating and prolonging the wars. In the discussion of agricultural policies in Chapter 10, for example, the focus is not on the success or failure of these policies as such (a topic worth many books in its own right), but on the degree to which these policies were in fact responsible for provoking or exacerbating the conflict. Policies may fail, as they have in African states of all ideological descriptions. To what extent the policy failure provokes or contributes to a war is another question.

In searching for causes of a conventional inter-state war, the focus is most often on the beginning: who and what provoked the war? What diplomatic steps might have avoided it? The subsequent course of a war is most often considered by military historians, who assess the balance of forces, military strategy and tactics. Students of diplomacy come in again in considering how wars end. The primary focus is most frequently on state actors, although economic capacity and home-front morale also appear as contributing factors.

In unconventional wars, the interaction of state and society takes on a higher profile throughout. One must not only analyse the interactions of the opposing parties but also figure out who the relevant actors are. In searching for explanations of the wars in Angola and Mozambique, therefore, one is asking a series of related but distinct questions. Why did the wars begin? Why did the wars continue? In what respect are the wars different from other wars, and from each other, and why? Who were the state or non-state actors who were active decision-makers or participants in the fighting? Why did the different participants become involved, and what factors shaped their participation?

Are there theories which might help untangle the causal nexus in these two cases? There are, in fact, far too many with some possible relevance, from general studies of the causes of war to the voluminous literature on revolution and its causes. I have chosen three sets of literature which seem most pertinent: 1) theories of state, nation and ethnicity as they may illuminate the concept of 'civil war'; 2) theories of revolution, particularly those few which give some attention to the concept of counter-revolution; and 3) writings on unconventional warfare as well as the related concepts of guerrilla war and low-intensity conflict.[5]

State, nation, ethnicity and race and the boundaries of 'civil war'

Wars pitting fellow citizens against each other are not necessarily connected to ethnic or regional divisions. Conflict may focus around factional rivalries or ideological divisions. It may be initiated by a foreign power but played out on national soil, confronting citizens with painful decisions over whether to collaborate or to resist. But in societies divided by cultural characteristics, such divisions are likely to interact with the war even if they are not its source. Loyalties are tested; the strength of national sentiment and competing claims to represent the nation are under strain.

Even whether a conflict is termed a 'civil war' is part of the dispute over loyalties. Long after their defeat, for many in the southern US, the Civil War was the 'War between the States', a term rejecting the implication of national unity. A successful secessionist movement claims victory in a war of independence or national liberation, not a 'civil war'. Supporters of the governments in Angola and Mozambique who rejected the term 'civil war' were not denying that citizens were involved on both sides, but rather claiming that the source of war was primarily external.

What is loyalty to the 'nation' or to some subnational group, and how do these loyalties provoke, or relate, to conflict? Commonly, current hostilities are read back into unchanging 'age-old' rivalries based on national, ethnic or 'tribal' distinctions. Yet most scholars now argue that such identities and commitments, however potent, are far from unchanging. Although national and ethnic identities build on prior cultural legacies, the world's nations and ethnic groups almost all crystallized as such during the last two hundred years. In Africa the territorial units which are today's nations are almost all little more than one hundred years old. The current ethnic groupings labelled tribes by the European conquerors largely date from the eras of conquest and colonial rule.[6]

It is widely recognized that the boundaries of African states were imposed by European conquest in disregard of previous social and cultural divisions. The state framework thus preceded the formation of a 'nation' identified with that particular territory. Recent studies of nationalism, however, show that this is not as different from other historical experiences as commonly presumed. The nineteenth- and twentieth-century myth of the nation-state, in which cultural boundaries and state boundaries coincide, is the exception rather than the rule in historical reality. E.J. Hobsbawm, for example, notes that in 1789 only half the population of France spoke French. Most nations of Latin America, whose nationalism Benedict Anderson argues preceded most European nationalisms, were built on the administrative divisions left by the Spanish empire. The turmoil in the former Yugoslavia and the former Soviet Union makes it clear that precise correspondences between 'nation' and 'state' are illusory abstractions from messy historical reality.[7]

The common elements in modern nations are a state which sets the parameters of social advance, particularly in terms of language and education, and historical myths which project into the past the legitimacy of the nation associated with the state. Nationalism implies either an existing state recognized as sovereign by the international community, or the aspiration to establish such a state. In myth each nation corresponds to one culture, but in practice, the cultural variety within a recognized nation may be enormous. The boundaries of cultural and political units almost never correspond precisely. Despite the proliferation of states in recent years, they still number less than two hundred, as compared to the ten thousand or more groups that could be enumerated on the basis of linguistic or other cultural distinctions.

Thus national loyalty may coexist with loyalties to subnational groups, which may be labelled in ethnic, tribal, linguistic, religious or regional terms. These subgroups too, however powerful the sentiment attached to them, change over time. Their boundaries and their meanings shift, and their significance for political rivalry or war cannot be simply derived from the magnitude of the cultural distinctions. The term 'tribe' is particularly misleading. It conveys an unrealistic image of similar small-scale primitive communities rather than groups as various in their histories and internal make-up as the 'nations' and 'ethnic groups' of other continents.

Attachment to the local community is a characteristic of rural peoples everywhere, not only in Africa. But the boundaries of that community – village or group of villages – rarely correspond to 'tribes' or 'ethnic groups'. Those are identities which may derive in part from pre-colonial states or cultural commonalities, but also from people who are grouped together for administration by the colonial state or linguistically by the creation of a written language. Oral language is fluid; dialect distinctions may fade imperceptibly into distinctions between different languages. But written language imposes uniformity. So does the use of a language in state administration, or as a lingua franca by migrants to an urban or other multi-ethnic work environment. Just as recent research on the history of nationalism gives much weight to the use of written language in state and school, so recent research on ethnic identities in modern Africa highlights similar factors, related as much to the opportunities in the national society as to the 'traditional' backgrounds people bring to it.

Such general considerations serve as a caution to pay attention not just to cultural diversity but to the particular historical factors making some subnational identities more prominent than others. Only a few of the possible separate identities come to channel political competition; even fewer serve as rationales for claiming dominance within a state or establishing a separate state.

In contrast to European experience, few of Africa's ethnic groups spawned nationalist ideologies. Among the few exceptions were Somali nationalism, aiming to unite Somalis dispersed under different colonial administrations, and Baganda separatism in Uganda. Following African independence, there were only a handful of secessionist civil wars. They were generally based on colonial administrative divisions rather than ethnic boundaries (eastern Nigeria, southern Sudan, Katanga). The Eritrean and Western Saharan nationalist movements were based on colonial territories incorporated forcibly by larger neighbours.

Other forms of civil strife, including *coups* and other violent conflicts, often pitted Africans within a country against each other along ethnic lines. But the issue was most commonly power within a state, not the demand for a new state. The new African states emerged from colonial rule with regional and ethnic disparities in education, economic status, and position in key sectors such as the military. Virtually every national policy decision, from building roads to recruitment for political leadership, had potential for reinforcing or ameliorating these disparities. Either peaceful competition or violent conflict could be structured along ethnic lines. But only rarely, to date, have there been explicit demands to exclude citizens on the basis of their ethnic origin.

Nationhood defined by the colonial borders emerged both from the experience of alien rule and from struggle against it. Within that framework the pre-colonial histories of those incorporated appeared as strands of one history: local or regional episodes of resistance to colonial conquest took their places within one national story. So did the roles of different communities in the movement for national independence. When the nationalist movement was forced to turn to violence to achieve its aims, as in Algeria, Kenya and most of southern Africa, the stands taken in the period of war had a significant impact on the consciousness of nationhood.[8]

Colonial experience also made for a common 'African' nationalism extending beyond territorial boundaries, and for transnational identities cutting across geographical and ethnic divisions. Africa was pre-eminently the continent of European conquest. Almost everywhere, the whites were the rulers or former rulers. Throughout the continent, but particularly in the southern third, the right to rule was defined in racial terms. Anti-colonial national consciousness therefore implied, to a greater or lesser degree, consciousness of the continent-wide struggle.

This should not be understood simplistically as an automatic identification of all Africans with the struggles in southern Africa. The extent of knowledge or identification varied with physical distance and access to communications networks as well as political options. But in southern Africa the alliance of Pretoria, Salisbury and Lisbon implied corresponding links among the forces for liberation. While distant states might pay little more than lip service to the Organization of African Unity's Liberation Committee, for states and movements in the region a transnational perspective was a practical as well as an ideological imperative.

Race, a cultural identity defined internationally, reflected the Eurocentric hierarchy established by commercial expansion and conquest on a global scale.[9] It intersected the conflicts in southern Africa at multiple levels and with sometimes surprisingly divergent effects. Both regionally and within each country, some saw the anti-colonial and anti-apartheid struggles as anti-white, and looked with suspicion at intermediate groups of mixed race or Asian origin. Other resistance forces, most prominently the ANC of South Africa as well as Frelimo and the MPLA, stressed their opposition to the criterion of race as such. They welcomed fellow citizens of non-African ancestry into their ranks, their leadership and their definition of the nation.

With so many varying identities and loyalties at play, it would be misleading to look only for conflict between groups well-defined by age-old boundaries. Conflict also extends to the choice by individuals and groups of what labels are politically significant. Any analysis of the possible impact of national and ethnic loyalties in promoting or channelling conflict, accordingly, must look both to the historical roots of these identities and to the changes thrown up by the conflict situation and its immediate antecedents. Chapter 4 will focus on these elements.

State, revolution and counter-revolution

Theories of revolution cover different sets of cases, depending on the definition used by the theorist. Highly general definitions include virtually every violent change of government, including unsuccessful attempts, and sometimes even peaceful changes, that seem profound enough to warrant the term. At the other extreme, many scholars restrict the term to successful violent political upheavals accompanied by profound social transformation. For our purposes, several concepts associated with general theories, identifying factors such as weaknesses of the state and the mobilization of contenders for power, serve as helpful pointers. Each can be specified by considering both characteristics particular to African states and the special circumstances of 'counter-revolutionary' insurgencies.

Charles Tilly defines a 'revolutionary situation' as one of multiple sovereignty, in which more than one power bloc effectively claims sovereignty over some portion of a territory previously ruled by only one sovereign government. A 'successful' revolution is defined by the victory of the challenging power bloc as the exclusive effective claimant to sovereignty.[10] This builds on Max Weber's classic definition of the state as 'a human community which successfully claims the monopoly of the legitimate use of physical force within a given territory'[11] and on Trotsky's description of dual power prior to a revolution. Tilly de-emphasizes the criterion of legitimacy and defines an effective claim in terms of the subject population's behaviour: paying taxes, expressing verbal loyalty, and obeying other orders of those asserting authority. In this conceptual framework, the revolutionary contender is by definition the insurgent, regardless of ideological orientation.

Tilly distinguishes between causes of a revolutionary situation and causes of a revolutionary outcome. A revolutionary situation requires: 1) the emergence of contenders to power; 2) significant *de facto* support for the contenders from a significant portion of the subject population; and 3) inability of the state incumbents to carry out effective repression. Evaluating the chances of a revolutionary outcome requires weighing the balance of forces between the insurgent coalition and the coalition which includes the incumbent power-holders.

Tilly's framework provides a useful classification of causal factors. But for our purposes it can be strengthened by distinguishing between revolution and counter-revolution rather than treating revolutionary and insurgent as identical. Few scholars have focused on counter-revolution, and its meaning is rarely specified beyond the general notion of some kind of opposition to revolution. As used here, the concept of counter-revolution identifies processes that closely follow revolutions that are not fully consolidated. Counter-revolution implies opposition to the new revolutionary regime. It does not necessarily imply the objective of restoring the old regime or explicitly right-wing ideological goals, although those objectives are likely to be prominent.

Counter-revolution in this sense is distinct from counter-insurgency, which is the military response by an incumbent regime to insurgency. In Tilly's general framework, a counter-revolutionary insurgency would be a contradiction in terms. Here it is used to specify an insurgency against an incumbent regime that itself was the result of a revolution. Within each set of possible causes for insurgency, this special circumstance has specific implications.

The weakness of the state, in Tilly's terms the inability to repress successfully, is also identified by other recent theorists as a key precondition of revolution or insurgency. Skocpol, for example, stresses the internal political crises and external pressures on the old-regime states as essential preconditions for the classic revolutions of France, Russia and China. Goldstone singles out fiscal distress and elite conflict as two fundamental conditions for a broader range of revolutions, from the early modern period to the present. It has long been a truism that revolutionary upheavals are facilitated by inter-state wars which weaken and stretch the resources of contending states, as witnessed by the aftermath of the First and Second World Wars. The possible reasons for state weakness are many, and it is unlikely that one general theory can encompass them all.[12]

For an incumbent regime that is itself the product of a recent revolution, however, certain weak points are normal. A new revolutionary government lacks the stability due to the habit of obedience which established regimes acquire simply by the passage of time. All ex-colonial African states, even if they achieved independence peacefully, shared this initial vulnerability of newness. In the case of a revolution, the destruction involved in the conquest of power and the loss of some citizens to exile generally depletes economic resources. Popular aspirations for improvements are likely to be high, while the resources for satisfying them are correspondingly thin. In short, an infant revolutionary regime is inherently likely to be vulnerable to challenge.

The breakdown of the monopoly of violence also requires the emergence of an alternative power bloc, with its own leadership and the capacity to mobilize military resources. Possible sources of such division include the ethnic and regional cleavages discussed previously. General theories of revolution, however, call attention to classes, elites or other hierarchically defined social groups. Such divisions, reflecting the position of different groups under the social system defended by the incumbent regime, are taken to determine the likely origin of contenders for power and the likely response by different social groups to their claims.

Some theories focus more on the revolutionary leadership, others on the followers who are mobilized or rise up spontaneously. Students of the classic revolutions often note that revolutionary leaders are rarely recruited among the most oppressed groups, but come rather from marginalized sectors of strata with some assets within the system: military skills, intellectual or organizational assets, or economic resources. If violent conflicts over government power occur within such groups without any changes in structure, of course, it is likely to be labelled a *coup* or factional strife rather than a revolution. But most analysts identify some degree of defection from those within a system as a significant source of revolutionary leadership. While classic Marxist theory gave little attention to these considerations, these and related issues are at the heart of Leninist reflections on the role of the vanguard party and Gramscian discussion of the role of 'organic intellectuals' in revolution.

In the late colonial and early post-colonial African context, one group provides most leadership for both incumbent power blocs and potential challengers: the group defined by access to secondary and post-secondary education. In class terms this group has most often been labelled the petty bourgeoisie, but the family ties of individuals within the group may still reflect close links to the rural peasantry, to urban workers, or to pre-colonial traditional elites. The category is very broad, from mid-level employees up to the military officer corps as well as political, administrative and commercial elites. While some scholars have discerned within the group more well-defined classes such as a 'bureaucratic bourgeoisie' or a 'commercial bourgeoisie', which have succeeded in accumulating capital and in distinguishing themselves from other groups, the lack of consensus on terminology reflects the uncertain boundaries of such class distinctions.

In the immediate aftermath of decolonization, at least, flux rather than stable class consolidation seems to have been the rule. Access for Africans to resources that might define a privileged class position – education, capital, state power – was certainly not equally distributed. But it was generally new, and the results for individuals and families were highly uncertain.

In terms of a general model of revolution, it is to marginalized sectors of this broadly defined group with access to education that one should look for potential challengers to the state. Marginalization may be structural or result from the play of events. The specific concept of counter-revolution, however, points to a specific source of potential challengers. In the immediate aftermath of revolutionary victory, the losers of the former regime have almost never suffered a complete defeat. Many may have transferred themselves and a large part of their assets into exile. They have the experience and the habit of leadership, personal contacts and intimate knowledge of the society, the residual loyalty of many within the country, deeply felt grievances and nostalgia. Some kind of challenge to the new order, effective or ineffective, is almost inevitable.

The chances of finding leaders for a counter-revolutionary challenge are enhanced by two other normal features of a revolutionary process. First, there is almost always strife within the revolution's own ranks, whether provoked by the numerous agents of the old regime, by debates over military strategies or social policies, or by personal, factional or ideological rivalries in the chaotic context of war. Losers from these battles may join in counter-revolution or oppose the revolutionary regime with the claim that it has been betrayed.

Secondly, revolutions almost always have an international component, which carries over into the stage of possible counter-revolution. Neighbouring countries with similar social regimes, former allies of the old regime, and powers with claims to regional or international hegemony, all may have been involved in opposing the revolutionaries prior to the overthrow. They may have specific interests within the country, which they fear to lose. They may fear the domino effect, or seek revenge for damage to their international prestige. Even in classic cases such as Russia and China, international reaction was a significant component of counter-revolutionary war after the revolution. Revolutions in small highly dependent countries logically expect an even greater foreign component in counter-revolution.

But the existence of malcontents eager to overthrow a regime is not a sufficient condition for upsetting the monopoly of violence by incumbents. The challengers must also mobilize sufficient resources to overcome routine repression. Any extensive challenge that is not purely an international war must involve mobilizing support, willing or unwilling, among some segment of the national population. Many theories focus on the variable susceptibility of subject groups to revolt, stressing either government failure to meet popular expectations or the imposition of new unpopular demands such as increased taxation.[13] Some theories consider these factors in aggregate terms, without breaking down the population into classes or other subgroups. But others, taking a general orientation from Marxist perspectives, focus the explanation of revolution on the changing class structure and organization of class struggle. Thus the English revolution of the seventeenth century and the French revolution of the eighteenth are characterized as 'bourgeois' revolutions, while twentieth-century revolutions are analysed in terms of the role of the working class and/or the peasantry.

Explanations of successful revolutions or large-scale revolts in the global South, such as the classic studies by Eric Wolf and Jeffery Paige, have tended to focus on rural class patterns likely to lead to revolt. In the African context, similar concerns have informed studies of early resistance to colonial conquest, with newly imposed taxes a common spark for resistance.[14] Among modern instances, the case of Mau Mau in Kenya has produced a significant body of literature probing the class roots of revolt, and several recent studies have appeared on Zimbabwe. Ironically, while the revolutions against Portuguese colonialism inspired much general comment on peasant revolution, the empirical research on the impact of rural social structure on these wars has barely begun.[15]

While counter-revolutionary insurgency opposing a new regime finds its place in the national histories of France, Russia and Spain as well as contemporary Nicaragua and Mozambique, there has been little explicitly theoretical consideration of the social bases of such insurgency. Among the few scholars who have focused on the social base of counter-revolution are Charles Tilly and diplomatic historian Arno Mayer.[16] While the specific contexts they examine are far from southern Africa, each provides some concepts of possible relevance. Tilly's sociological study of western France tries to isolate reasons why in some areas local dominant classes as well as peasants and artisans joined the revolt against the revolutionary government, while in other areas they did not. He finds the guiding thread in the differential penetration of the urban economy, resulting for example in greater resistance by the clergy to displacement from power and in greater willingness of the rural community to follow traditional leaders in opposition to the demands of the revolutionary regime.

Mayer, whose detailed studies centred on the interaction of domestic and international factors in the diplomacy surrounding the First World War, finds the social roots of the followers of counter-revolution in intermediate class segments threatened with loss of status by social turmoil, particularly the petty bourgeoisie. In contrast to Tilly, the focus is not on those embedded in tradition but on those who are socially dislocated. Mayer repeats suggestions of Marx that this group may align itself with a revolution in an early stage, but be particularly vulnerable to bribery or defection under the pressure of revolutionary crisis. Whether or not this hypothesis is verified by empirical class analysis, it is relevant to the Angolan and Mozambican cases because of its currency in Marxist circles as a ready-made explanation.

Mayer also stresses that both revolutions and counter-revolutions must be understood in international rather than purely national terms, particularly in small countries. Whether it takes the form of aid or intervention, he argues, 'this external entanglement is central to the international civil war of an historical era that is as counter-revolutionary as it is revolutionary'.[17]

For a revolutionary situation, in Tilly's sense of *de facto* multiple sovereignties, each of the three conditions (state weakness, the presence of challengers with a rival claim, and some support or acquiescence among the citizenry) must reach some minimum threshold. The outcome of the process then becomes dependent on a test of strength between incumbents and challengers. This balance of forces, in turn, depends on a wide range of factors, from military skill, matériel and morale to the reactions of internal groups and foreign states. The continuation of conflict, or the victory by one side, depends not only on the direct contenders but also on broader coalitions.

The rival coalitions may consist of groups with diverse interests and with distinct roles in the conflicts. While the intensity of conflict may force individuals and groups to choose sides, many may prefer and actively seek ways to remain neutral or uninvolved. The balance of forces in a particular conflict is thus intrinsically dependent on multiple factors, coming together with different weights and dependent in turn on variables which may be external to the conflict itself.

Theory and practice of unconventional warfare

A third body of literature, overlapping but distinct from historical and theoretical studies of revolution, consists of reflections on unconventional warfare by military men, policy-makers and policy-oriented intellectuals.

These works tend to reflect the practical concerns of revolutionaries or counterinsurgency officials. Most focus on prominent cases: the Chinese and Vietnamese revolutions, guerrilla struggles in Latin America, the successful counterinsurgency campaigns in Malaya and the Philippines, the war in Algeria. The best-known revolutionary strategists spoke from an Asian or Latin American context, while counterinsurgency doctrine was developed primarily out of French, British and US experience in Asia and Latin America, with occasional reference to Algeria or Kenya.

Recent US military doctrine has adopted the rubric of 'low-intensity conflict'. But the term, used by British counterinsurgency strategist Frank Kitson two decades ago, is less conceptual innovation than the packaging of old ideas in a new label for public relations and lobbying purposes. While 'counterinsurgency' was discredited by the failed experience of Vietnam, the new label provided a neutral-sounding cover to justify US involvement in a variety of conflicts. The one major innovation was the prominent inclusion of 'pro-insurgency', US backing for insurgencies against regimes seen as hostile. Even this, however, has numerous precedents, from the Bay of Pigs invasion of Cuba to the brief support of Kurdish rebels against Iran.[18]

The fundamental components of unconventional warfare, guerrilla and counter-guerrilla operations, are premised on asymmetry between insurgents and defending forces. Guerrillas, lacking the strength for prolonged confrontation in conventional battle, seek to compensate by mobility, surprise and lack of attachment to permanent positions which they must stand and defend. An incumbent regime must allocate significant forces to defend fixed targets. Cities cannot be moved; nor can rail lines, roads, factories, mines or plantations. To the extent that this asymmetry does not apply, when insurgent forces capture and seek to hold fixed installations, the conflict moves into conventional rather than guerrilla warfare.

Geographical factors – such as distance, terrain, dispersion of resources, population density, transportation networks – are therefore as fundamental to guerrilla conflict as to conventional wars. But while these factors affect opposing conventional forces in roughly similar ways, the implications for guerrilla and counter-guerrilla forces are fundamentally different.

Guerrilla attacks are facilitated by the availability of numerous fixed targets. The defensive government forces must either spread out their forces to try to defend all the targets, thus making each concentration vulnerable to guerrillas brought together in larger groups for the attack, or concentrate on defending essential installations, leaving much of the country unprotected. Since the guerrillas do not have fixed bases they must defend, but can change location rapidly, they do not have the same defensive problem. This is the basic reason for the counterinsurgency maxim that requires the government to have a substantial superiority in force over the guerrillas (Maxwell Taylor estimated in 1965 that a superiority of 25 to 1 was essential in Vietnam).[19]

Similarly, the government is responsible for managing the economy. Destruction of fixed economic assets drains the government's strength; the guerrillas, in contrast, have few fixed and costly assets that can be easily destroyed. Since the guerrillas may be no match at conventional battles, and a full military victory is impossible without transition to conventional warfare or a total collapse of the target regime, the classic guerrilla strategy is based on attrition. If the guerrilla force can maintain its destructive capability at a high enough level, in theory the government will eventually be forced to come to terms.

The material inferiority of the guerrilla force, and its reliance on surprise and mobility, imply lower requirements for logistics than a conventional army. Small units may extract their basic supplies by force or persuasion from the local population, while relying on light weaponry that does not require massive supply lines. The skilful guerrilla fighter is presumed to be able to carry his supplies on his back, perhaps with some assistance from unarmed porters recruited locally. In contrast the conventional army must get not only its weapons but also its food from central stocks.

The stereotype of the totally self-reliant guerrilla force, however, is found more often in propaganda and myth than in reality. While guerrilla forces have more modest supply needs than conventional armies, the cases of sustained insurgencies that are totally cut off from outside supplies are few. Rear-base access for supplies is almost always a central concern for guerrilla commanders, and cutting off that access a corresponding priority of counterinsurgency planners. Outside sanctuaries, providing the possibility of retreat from counterinsurgency forces, almost always feature in guerrilla conflicts, although in large countries the sanctuary may be in a remote area of the same country rather than across national borders.

Another frequently noted consequence of guerrilla material inferiority, and of the dispersion of guerrilla units, is the requirement for high morale and personal commitment. While conventional armies may rely in large part on conscription and on the effect of large numbers, disciplined by military routine, guerrillas are often presumed to be strongly motivated. With the difficulties of control by a central command over dispersed units, it is assumed that guerrillas will find it easier to desert than the rank-and-file of a conventional force.

Similarly, guerrillas are presumed to rely to a large extent on local rural communities for food and information. While this may to some extent be extracted by force and terror, the vulnerability of the guerrilla force presumably implies greater reliance on persuasion. Counterinsurgency doctrine also calls for winning hearts and minds, but an incumbent regime's access to the machinery of repression means that the temptation to rely primarily on force is very powerful. Overwhelming force in counterinsurgency may also be effective, imposing itself without consent by civilians. For guerrillas that option is presumably ruled out by military weakness.

These characteristics of guerrilla warfare are all derived from the balance of forces between the various parties: guerrillas and conventional counterinsurgency troops, commanders and soldiers within each kind of army, civilians and guerrillas, civilians and armies. Judging a particular case, therefore, requires asking whether the forces involved correspond to the standard model. In addition, in guerrilla warfare, as in other kinds of war, these balances may well shift with changes in the technologies of transport, communications and weaponry. This topic is relatively unexplored in the literature, but the questions are extremely pertinent. In what ways is a guerrilla with a high-powered automatic weapon, easy radio communications with headquarters, and access to resupply by airdrop comparable to his counterpart of earlier generations? And to what extent do these factors alter the guerrillas' potential relationships to counterinsurgency forces or civilians?

Moving beyond the battlefield, rubrics such as 'low-intensity conflict' and 'total strategy' recall the classic maxim that war is the continuation of politics by other means. They emphasize the orchestration of diplomacy, economic pressure, propaganda and other government policies together with military force. Insurgents, without a state at their command, have limited means to manage such coordination. But theories of revolutionary strategy consist in large part of reflection on how to take advantage of if not to manage and provoke such parallel non-military challenges to authority. To cite only one example, the ANC regarded the international sanctions campaign and protest inside South Africa as pillars of the struggle along with guerrilla actions.

When there is significant international involvement, these broader factors are particularly relevant to the military balances. Whatever might be the internal factors at work, a guerrilla force that operates with the support of a powerful neighbouring state also targeting the incumbent regime with other pressures is in a fundamentally different position from one that functions with only weak or distant outside support. Similarly, the extent of outside military support for an incumbent regime, and the resources of those outside supporters, have multiple effects inside the country.

In a romantic view of guerrilla war, the only 'real war' is out in the bush, where the soldiers and the political organizers of the guerrillas and the regime fight it out for control over the rural population. Practitioners on both sides know that the 'real war' is everywhere: it may be won or lost not only in the bush but also by political or economic decisions elsewhere, in the capital or in distant foreign cities.

Logics of comparison and historical explanation

Comparative social science scholars have different reasons for comparing countries. Some aim to elaborate, illustrate or confirm general theories. Others use comparison to illuminate the features of particular cases.[20] This study is primarily of the second kind. By placing the Angolan and Mozambican wars in joint focus, I seek to highlight features of each that might be missed in a study confined to one case. I also seek to identify common features, both those specific to the historical and geographical contexts they share and others that may apply more widely.

Other cases are not discussed in any depth in this book, although the concluding chapter advances several more general hypotheses. The theoretical discussion of this chapter sets up comparisons with simplified models derived from a wide range of other cases. I rejected, however, the option of elaborating in detail on other cases, in favour of exploring the processes in Angola and Mozambique in greater depth.

This decision implies that the study is ill-suited for confirming or elaborating general theories. It does, however, have potential consequences for such theories. Even one contrary case can refute a general hypothesis: if, for example, a general theory holds that guerrilla forces are always predominantly volunteers driven by strong ideological or ethnic motives, that theory may be disproved (as, to anticipate, the evidence in Chapter 7 strongly suggests). This may suggest, but not confirm, another general hypothesis, such as that guerrilla forces with secure access to outside resources and modern communications may be largely recruited by force just as conventional armies rely in large part on conscription.

Comparative studies oriented primarily to theory, rather than to understanding particular cases, tend to feature a limited number of factors (variables) whose relevance is tested by standard social science procedures of causal inference. Thus Paige's study of agrarian revolts identifies four types of landholding patterns, each expected to lead to a specific form of agrarian social movement. Taking correlations of 135 export sectors in seventy developing nations between 1948 and 1970, as well as case studies of Peru, Angola (1961) and Vietnam, he concludes that revolutionary revolts are most likely in cases of decentralized share-cropping or settler estates.[21] In another influential study, Skocpol compares the revolutions of France, Russia and China with the contrasting cases of Prussia, Japan and England. Isolating the conditions present in the positive cases, she argues that: 1) state organizations susceptible to administrative and military collapse, and 2) agrarian sociopolitical structures that facilitated widespread peasant revolts, were the sufficient distinctive causes of social revolution in the three countries.[22]

Although the above authors elaborate their theories with narrative detail, the factors identified as theoretically significant are applied to the cases as a whole or to geographical subunits. The procedure involves abstraction from the particular sequences of events within a process. Characteristics that applied before the historical event to be explained are compared with the presence or absence of the expected result. Pre-existing conditions found to be common to all cases of the result are considered as possible causes. The absence of a particular condition, combined with the absence of the result, adds greater confidence that it is indeed a cause.[23]

The theorist thus abstracts from factors presumed to be specific to particular cases. The non-theoretically inclined historian of a single case may focus on narrative without troubling to identify separate 'factors' of varying importance, leaving such judgements implicit in choices of what to include or what to stress. This study, concerned primarily with particular cases but also with making judgements about the relative importance of different factors, walks a delicate line between the two perspectives.

There are more than enough common factors that might explain the beginning and/or continuation of war: the heritage of Portuguese colonialism leading to vulnerable post-independence states, large geographical area and underdeveloped transport making control difficult, military weakness *vis-à-vis* powerful South Africa, the existence of ethnic diversity in new nations, the adoption of Marxist-Leninist one-party state systems, the configuration of the Cold War in the 1980s, and more.

The multivariate social science remedy for sorting out such complexity is to find more cases, to determine which generalizations are most widely established and therefore presumably causal rather than just accidental. Yet this procedure takes one ever further away from the causal connections in the particular cases. This study moves instead towards the explanatory logic of historical narrative, by specifying time sequences more precisely and outlining plausible mid-level mechanisms connecting the presumed causal factors and the results. Comparisons between the two cases, and implicitly with other cases, are used primarily as guides to what to look for in the sequence of events. And it is assumed that the impact of different factors may be different at different stages within the extended process that is summed up by the word 'war'.

The relevant time divisions may be different for different processes. Thus, in discussing the presumed impact of the policy of communal villages on the war, one must ask when and where the policy was implemented, as compared to when and where the war began or was intensified. If dispersed peasants were not forced into villages in a particular area, or if this followed rather than preceded the beginning of war, then its status as a 'cause' of the war in that area is doubtful. To determine the impact of South African military involvement in the war in Mozambique, one has first to judge how long it continued at significant levels. It makes a profound difference whether one assumes that it stopped or was reduced to insignificant levels after 1985, or, alternatively, accepts the evidence that it continued throughout Botha's presidency and even into the 1990s.

While more specific timing is relevant for specific topics, broader periods are useful for an overview. Taking into account regional and global trends as well as developments in Angola and Mozambique, the five-year periods 1976–80, 1981–85 and 1986–90, together with the current period beginning in 1991, represent clearly distinguishable phases of the wars in both countries. In the first period conflict was limited, and in the second there was massive escalation. By the third there was stalemate at a high level of conflict, coinciding with escalation of the internal struggle in South Africa, the apex of the international anti-apartheid movement, and the Gorbachev era in the Soviet Union. By the beginning of the 1990s Mandela's release and a climate of negotiation again set a radically different context.

The chapters that follow, therefore, in examining the possible impact of different factors on the wars, will explore both the how and the when of presumed connecting mechanisms. Thus while ethnic diversity is indeed present in both societies, determining its possible connection to the war requires specifying how and when hostilities along ethnic lines either led to the outbreak of conflict or were exacerbated by it.

When one goes beyond describing such mechanisms to judge how important (in causal terms) a particular factor was, the implicit logic is a thought experiment.[24] If, for example, Henry Kissinger in 1975 had accepted the professional diplomats' advice not to intervene militarily in Angola, would the Soviet Union and Cuba still have stepped in to aid the MPLA? Would Angolan internal rivalries still have led to war, and if so would it have ended sooner, or differently? Or, at a somewhat more general level, if Mozambique's agricultural policies had been as successful as its policies in health and education, would it have been able to block South Africa's build-up of Renamo in the early 1980s? Such thought experiments cannot provide answers as can experiments in the laboratory, because the hypothetical road not taken is no longer available. Historical explanations are subject to repeated reinterpretation. But asking the questions can help clarify what is being claimed by a particular interpretation.

Combining time periods, factors and levels of explanation gives a complex matrix. Three kinds of factors (national/ethnic identities; class, state and ideology; and military and diplomatic) and four geographical levels of analysis (internal local/provincial; internal national; international regional and international global) combine with four distinct time periods to give forty-eight possible cells. It would be too cumbersome to follow the matrix precisely in the chapters to follow, and investigation of all the possible cells would be a task for many books. But the distinctions should serve as a reminder of the main features of the tangled web we are trying to untangle.

Piecing together the evidence

Analysing any significant historical development is complex, even with abundant data. The difficulties multiply when, as in the present study, information gaps loom far larger than the fragments of confirmed information. As compared with other African countries, there is little background research on Portuguese-speaking Africa. In Mozambique, since independence, there has been significant research by both foreigners and Mozambicans that is beginning to fill the virtual vacuum left by the Portuguese. But on Angola virtually the only topic which has been explored by more than a handful of scholars is pre-nineteenth-century history.

Investigating wars in which covert operations played such a central role, and which are ongoing or only recently terminated, implies that published information is both sketchy and open to significant doubts. Memoirs by key participants are few and not very revealing. Some of the parties involved (for example, the South African security leadership) have remained virtually free from defection or leaks that might give clues to their deliberations. Only a handful of journalists followed the wars closely enough and long enough to have a historical perspective, and of those few, none was intimately acquainted with both sides of the wars. A high proportion of what was published, moreover, was written by journalists or scholars who knew neither Portuguese nor any local African language in Mozambique or Angola.

Given this situation, an analyst has several options. One is to choose a small part of the picture and examine it in depth, bringing new information to light with primary research. New insights in the long run depend on this kind of work.[35] But it cannot address the issue of the relative importance of different factors to the overall picture. Or one might abandon the idea of a synthetic analysis for now, taking up the topic one or two decades hence with the benefit of new monographs, memoirs and the other advantages of hindsight. I have opted, however, to essay a tentative overview now, with the intention of contributing to a debate which will continue as more information and different perspectives emerge.

My strategy for coping with contradictory or missing information involves several principles: 1) be clear in indicating information gaps when they exist; 2) make the best assessment possible by collecting the maximum range of sources and giving greater confidence to those points on which divergent sources agree; and 3) evaluate the credibility of sources on the basis of their access to the information they claim to know and their previous record of truthfulness and accuracy.

My research has included a wide range of published material, both scholarly and journalistic, in English, Portuguese and other relevant European languages. In my own interviews and conversations on extended visits to Angola, Mozambique and other southern African countries, I have spoken with direct participants in the conflicts as well as with observers in the capital cities. I have not travelled in Unita- or Renamo-held territory, but I have talked with many who have, and I have systematically examined virtually all published reports from such visits.

The third point brings in two additional guidelines. An account gains credibility by being a first-hand description of something the witness was really in a position to observe. And it gains or loses credibility according to past evidence of the witness's reliability. In contested claims about, for example, the extent of South African military involvement at a particular time, evidence which may have emerged about an earlier period is highly relevant, although not decisive.

This is because South African strategy was to conceal or minimize the connections, in order to enhance the legitimacy of their clients and provide deniability for charges of external aggression. By and large, Western media and academic accounts tended to give the benefit of the doubt to the South Africans. Accusations by the Frontline States were frequently rhetorical and general, and were often dismissed as self-interested propaganda. Even when detailed evidence was presented, it was most often oral testimony by peasants or combatants. This rarely received the attention or the credence it deserved, due both to time delays and to the biases of media outlets.

In the period following the 1984 Nkomati Accord, for example, South Africa routinely denied it was continuing to supply arms to Renamo. The documents captured at Gorongosa in August 1985 showed that although deliveries stopped for several months after the Nkomati Accord, extra supplies had been dropped just before the signing, and air shipments were resumed in August 1984. In this case South African denials were shown to be without foundation. In subsequent years, scattered but cumulatively abundant evidence turned up of continued South African military involvement, until the 1992 ceasefire.[26] But deniability worked: the dominant tendency among Western observers was still to give new South African denials the benefit of the doubt against oral testimony from Mozambican eyewitnesses.

As mentioned earlier in this chapter, similar success in perception management marked the decisive battles in southern Angola in 1987–88. These two cases suggest rankings for the credibility of sources different from the conventional equal weight for South Africa and its critics; they cast doubt on the tendency to regard a Western journalist or diplomat as a more reliable source than an African peasant. While no possibly relevant information should be accepted or rejected simply because of its source, every investigator makes judgements of reliability, acknowledged or unacknowledged. Acknowledging the possibility of exceptional cases, I regard journalists or scholars without knowledge of Portuguese or long-term residence in Angola or Mozambique as less likely sources of reliable information than those who have an intimate acquaintance with the countries. All official statements about the conflicts by officials of any involved government (or insurgent group) require some kind of outside confirmation for credibility, but those involved in large-scale covert operations which depended on concealing their role (i.e., notably South Africa and the US) have particularly low credibility.

Such judgements on credibility of sources inevitably have some role in weighing up the evidence. But since these judgements are likely to vary widely according to the backgrounds of authors or readers, the most important criterion is still that of finding independent confirmation from distinct sources, identifying consistencies and inconsistencies, and seeing what holds up when one tries to put all the evidence together. This procedure, analogous to triangulation in surveying, is the fundamental approach I have taken in this study.

Notes

1. Heritage Foundation, *National Security Record* (No. 92, June 1986); *Washington Times*, 2 June 1986.

2. Clarence-Smith (1989), 10.

3. *Washington Post*, 11 September 1987.

4. See Minter, 'Glimpses of the War in Angola' (1992).

5. The point of discussing these theories is not to test their general validity, which would require a more extensive range of cases. Rather it is to find concepts and insights that may apply to wars involving a complex interaction of internal and external factors. The following references are not comprehensive, but provide major sources to provide an entry into the literature for the interested reader.

6. Major sources on this topic include Young (1976, 1986), and Vail (1989).

7. Hobsbawm (1990), 60. Anderson (1991). Another seminal work with emphasis on the recent character of nationalist identity is Gellner (1983). In contrast,

Smith (1986) emphasizes the antiquity of the identities incorporated into modern nationalisms.

8. Thirty years after the decade of independence, in the face of the crisis of the post-colonial African state, much of this history is now being subjected to searching re-examination, as, for example, Davidson (1992). The re-examination, however, lays even more emphasis on the variability and changes in consciousness of identity.

9. See, among many other sources, Wallerstein (1989).

10. Tilly (1978), 191.

11. Gerth and Mills (1946), 78.

12. Among major recent works dealing with this issue are Skocpol (1979), Goldstone (1991) and Wickham-Crowley (1991).

13. See Tilly (1978), 204 ff., and sources cited there.

14. Wolf (1969), Paige (1975). Among many other sources on African resistance, see Ránger (1977).

15. On Mau Mau the Library of Congress lists almost forty books between 1965 and 1993, including eight since 1989. On Zimbabwe see particularly Ranger (1985), Lan (1985), Kriger (1992), and Maxwell (1993). For sources on the revolts against Portugal see Minter, 'Lusophone Africa' (1992). One area on which there is a variety of significant work, by Allen Isaacman, Edward Alpers and research teams of the Oficina da História in Maputo, is Cabo Delgado province in Mozambique. Notable among recent primary research making use of new sources are Adam (1988) on Cabo Delgado, Borges Coelho (1989) on Tete province in Mozambique, and Dhada (1993) on Guinea-Bissau.

16. Tilly (1964), Mayer (1971).

17. Mayer (1971), 84.

18. Of the abundant recent literature on low-intensity warfare, see Klare and Kornbluh (1988), Shultz et al. (1989), and earlier, Kitson (1971). Among guides to the classic literature one may cite Laqueur (1976), Chaliand (1982), and Rice (1988). See also the more extensive references in Chapter 7.

19. Laquer (1976), 275.

20. See Skocpol and Somers (1980), Ragin (1987), Tilly (1984).

21. Paige (1975).

22. Skocpol (1979).

23. For a summary description of these methods, based on John Stuart Mill's canons of induction, see Ragin (1987), 36 ff.

24. See Weber (1949), 180.

25. References to this kind of work, particularly on Mozambique, appear primarily in Chapters 7 to 10. Among scholars who have published such research on the wars, I am particularly indebted to the work of Christian Geffray, Otto Roesch, and Ken Wilson, for their local and regional studies, and Alex Vines, for his detailed research on Renamo's internal organization and external sponsors. My own efforts in primary research include investigation of the documents published in Minter (1988) and interviews published in reports in Minter (1989) and Minter (1990).

26. See the discussion of this topic in Chapter 7.

4

Nationalism, Ethnicity and Decolonization

One of the Angolan refugees I interviewed on the Namibian border in 1991 was a Methodist who grew up near Luanda speaking Kimbundu. With this background he would most likely support the MPLA. Another was Umbundu-speaking, and therefore presumably sympathetic to Unita. In fact both were loyal to the FNLA, generally pictured as an organization of Kikongo-speaking northern Angolans.

The stereotypes were not wrong, but they were half-truths. One of the refugees chose the FNLA in 1975 because he considered the group realistic in advocating a continuation of the capitalist system followed by the Portuguese. The other, a supporter of MPLA guerrilla leader Daniel Chipenda, followed him into the FNLA when Chipenda split with Agostinho Neto in 1974. He stayed loyal to the FNLA even when Chipenda rejoined the government in Luanda. During the same visit, a local Namibian with Angolan relatives told me that many people from the border area privately supported the Angolan government rather than the FNLA or Unita, but had no choice but to make their peace with the South African-sponsored groups.

A year earlier in Luanda two top government officials told me how they had resisted pressures to join Unita in the mid-1970s. One, who grew up on the central plateau, told how he had to flee for his life to escape Unita's attacks on Umbundu-speaking young people, considered traitors for not supporting Savimbi. The other, from the far south, spoke of Unita's calls to him to desert the MPLA because Unita was 'the natural movement for southerners'.

The conversations were apt reminders that linkages between ethnic identities and political loyalties are far from simple. Stereotypes both reflect social reality and help mould it, as individuals are pressured to conform. But a host of other factors, including personal choice and circumstance, also affect the political line-up.

The contrast between Angola and Mozambique poses the issue at another level. Nationalist division into three separate organizations in Angola, versus Frelimo's hegemony in Mozambique, had profound effects. Yet ethnic diversity and regional disparities were present in both cases. In each, economic opportunities and social mobility varied widely with geographical divisions, which correlated with potential ethnic divides. What factors then produced the different outcomes?

Historical roots of ethno-regional distinctions

Colonial Angola and Mozambique each brought under a common administration a wide range of previously unintegrated communities. Yet no attempt to identify a list of 'tribes' or ethnic groups – divided up neatly from each other by language, culture or politics at some particular date – could possibly succeed. The vast majority of Angolans and Mozambicans speak one or another Bantu language, but even this phrasing implies clear language boundaries that do not necessarily exist. As Ranger put it for Zimbabwe's Shona-speaking peoples, 'each village spoke the "same" language as its neighbor, across the whole territory, but there was nevertheless gradual lexical and idiomatic change so that by the time a man from the extreme western edge reached the extreme eastern edge, he encountered significant differences.'[1] The same applied for many linguistic distinctions in Angola and Mozambique.

By and large, the pre-colonial units of political and cultural allegiance were either too small (the village or group of villages) or too large (states with subjects of a variety of languages and cultures) to correspond precisely to groups identified today as 'tribes' or ethnic groups. The boundaries of political allegiance, cultural similarity and personal loyalties rarely fitted neatly into the sharp lines drawn between 'tribes' by European ethnographers. And, contrary to the image of a static pre-colonial past, the boundaries shifted with conquests, peaceful cultural influence, and migrations.[2] Captives, conquerors and other immigrants were assimilated into and influenced host societies, their relatively quick adoption or imposition of a new language facilitated by the similarity of related Bantu tongues. Before the late nineteenth century, even Europeans as well as Arabs and Indians were sometimes assimilated into African societies, especially along the Mozambican coast and the Zambezi Valley. Multilingualism, most often in African languages but also including Portuguese, was a common phenomenon in earlier centuries as it is today.

Of the multitude of pre-colonial states in the two countries, only one (the Kongo kingdom) served in modern times as a focus for an ethnically conscious restorationist movement. But despite its historical prominence, and a line of kings from the sixteenth-century monarchs who adopted Christianity from the Portuguese, the project's viability was undercut by dispersion of Kikongo-speakers under French, Belgian and Portuguese rule. It never became a serious political option. While the history of the Mwenemutapa and other Shona-speaking rulers served as a source of pride for Mozambicans as well as Zimbabweans, it never became the focus of a Shona unification or independence movement. The wars of resistance fought by peoples from all regions of Angola and Mozambique found their way into stories of national resistance, rather than being appropriated by one linguistic group. In any case, there were resisters and collaborators in every area; some revolts were clearly multi-ethnic in composition.[3]

According to a rough linguistic division, the population incorporated into Mozambique included Tsonga speakers in the south; Shona speakers in the centre, north of the Save River; a variety of intermixed groups along the Zambezi River; the related Lomwe and Macua cluster north of the Zambezi; and Yao and Makonde spilling over in the north to neighbouring countries. Angola encompassed Kikongo speakers in the north; Kimbundu in Luanda and its hinterland; Umbundu on the central plateau; Nyaneka and Cuanhama (Ovambo) in the far south; Chokwe and numerous small groups labelled Ngangela in the sparsely populated east.

The largest language cluster in Angola was Umbundu, spoken by approximately 36 per cent, followed by Kimbundu (approximately 26 per cent) and Kikongo (approximately 13 per cent). In Mozambique speakers of Macua and Lomwe made up roughly 36 per cent of the population, with speakers of Tsonga some 22 per cent and Shona about 7 per cent.[4] None of these groups corresponded precisely with pre-colonial political units, nor did the labels necessarily match what the people called themselves. But the linguistic zones roughly corresponded with geographical divisions, and consequently, with different experiences of colonial conquest, of incorporation into the colonial economy and of Christian missions. These factors, in turn, affected to what extent particular ethnic or regional distinctions would become politically salient and what roles people of different origins would play in the nationalist movement.

In the Portuguese colonial state, administration, white settlers, commerce and social services were highly concentrated in the capital city. Its African population, therefore, had disproportional access to what Heimer termed the 'central society', as compared to those in other cities or rural areas.[5] This was a factor both for Luanda and its Kimbundu-speaking hinterland, and for Maputo (Lourenço Marques) and Tsonga-speaking southern Mozambique. While Portuguese assimilation policies presumed the abandonment of African culture for the small minority who acquired such status, even those who demanded racial equality within the terms of assimilation had roots in the popular culture of the capital and its hinterland. Those who came to Lourenço Marques, if they did not already know Portuguese or Tsonga, had to learn at least one of the two. To make one's way in Luanda required either Portuguese or Kimbundu.

Maputo and Luanda shared these primary city characteristics. The social and political self-consciousness associated with access to this society was not precisely 'ethnic' in character, nor was it exclusively 'urban', since most urban Africans retained close ties to the countryside. But it did imply the potential for condescending attitudes towards provincial outsiders. In Portuguese colonial society, only white Portuguese born in Portugal were truly first-class citizens. The social hierarchy then descended by steps first to locally-born whites, then to *mestiços* and Asians, to assimilated Africans, and to other Africans with access to the urban society. Independence brought new opportunities most immediately for those Africans with their feet already on the ladder because of their proximity to the capital city – particularly those with some previous education.

The urban and peri-urban culture was far more deeply implanted in Luanda, with its history of several centuries of Afro-European 'creole' societal links, than in Maputo, which became a significant urban centre only in the late nineteenth century. Early Portuguese presence in Mozambique was most intense along the northern coast and in the Zambezi valley; by the nineteenth century the primary focus had shifted south.

While political power under Portuguese colonialism centred on the capital, the economic structure showed sharp regional differentiation, in which the network converging on the capital ran parallel to networks focusing on other provincial centres or corridors. Even today a railway map of Angola or Mozambique clearly outlines these distinctions. Southern Mozambique served not only as hinterland to Lourenço Marques, but also as a labour reservoir for South Africa. The trip to Johannesburg as well as the trip to the Mozambican capital defined a common experience. Beira in the centre defined a hinterland with its primary pole in Southern Rhodesia (Zimbabwe) and a secondary link to Nyasaland. North of the Zambezi the rails from Quelimane and Nacala linked to hinterlands within Mozambique (the Nacala line did not reach Malawi until 1970).

The Angolan pattern tied the port of Benguela to the copperbelt of central Africa, traversing the central plateau. Luanda-Malanje in the north and Moçamedes-Sá de Bandeira (Namibe-Lubango) in the south anchored two distinct railway corridors. Unlike the Benguela line, both stopped long before reaching Angola's interior borders. While the rail lines did not define all the zones of economic importance (neither Uíge's coffee nor Cabinda's oil were included), they indicated the major areas of interest in the colonial economy before the Second World War.[6]

Portuguese settlement also fell into regional clusters. In 1970, more than half the Portuguese in Angola were in the zone from Luanda to Malanje, 20 per cent were in the Benguela–Huambo corridor and another 12 per cent in Huíla (Sá de Bandeira) or Moçamedes. In Mozambique more than half the Portuguese lived in Maputo province, with another 20 per cent in the central region of Manica e Sofala. Zambézia and Nampula provinces, most populous overall, together had only about 14 per cent of whites.[7]

The regional dispersion of economic activities, combined with the restriction of most skilled work to Portuguese settlers, meant that in general few African workers in the modern economy found themselves competing with their counterparts from other linguistic zones. The pattern was most consistent in Mozambique. Southern Mozambicans went to South Africa or Maputo; those in the centre of the country to Zimbabwe or to Beira; those in the north stayed in their own areas or emigrated to Malawi or Tanzania. People from different areas were distinct but not in competition for the same economic opportunities. Among the exceptions were Umbundu-speaking contract workers, who provided a significant part of the labour force on the coffee plantations of northern Angola and made up as much as 10 per cent of the African population of Luanda by 1970.

Capital city primacy set the stage for possible tension between geographically favoured groups and others. Distinct economic regions created the potential for rival groupings. But possibly the most influential factor in determining which ethnic identities became politically salient was the distribution of Protestant missions which fostered literacy in African languages.

Ranger, Vail and others have sketched out for other southern African countries the influence of missions in defining 'standard' languages, which then become vehicles for the educational advancement of a particular group. People speaking non-written languages may be assimilated. Missionaries, anthropologists, government officials and, most importantly, their converts and informants, construct visions of ethnic history which serve as identity references.[8]

In British-ruled areas, indirect rule reinforced 'tribal' identities using traditional authorities (and creating them where they did not exist). Portugal's more direct administration and ideology of assimilation gave less impetus to ethnic identities beyond the local community. Portuguese officials discouraged literacy in African languages, while Portuguese Catholic missions gave less emphasis to fostering written languages than Catholic missionaries in other territories. Where Protestant missions did establish a significant base, therefore, their educational and linguistic initiatives stood out by contrast. This held even though Protestant schools were required by law to give priority to Portuguese over African languages.

In Angola, American Methodist missionaries fostered literacy in Kimbundu. British Baptists educated generations of Kikongo-speaking converts. Congregationalist missionaries from the US and Canada built a large educational infrastructure in the Umbundu-speaking heartland of Angola. Leading scholars of Angolan nationalism, such as Marcum, Heimer and Henderson, have called attention to the resulting correspondence among ethnic identity, religious allegiance and the tripartite division of Angolan nationalism. The religious factor, through its influence on literacy and ethnic consciousness, seems to have had a particularly formative impact.

Other Angolan linguistic groups had little or no Protestant mission presence, with consequent lags in language standardization and access to education. Accordingly, they showed less tendency to coalesce as coherent groups with a cultural or political agenda. In Mozambique, where the Portuguese barred significant penetration of Protestant missions north of the Save River, only the Tsonga-speaking south produced many Africans with literacy in their own language.[9] Although there were undoubtedly other reasons why the numerically prominent Macua-Lomwe of northern Mozambique did not show a politically significant group-wide consciousness parallel to the Umbundu in Angola, the absence of a standardized written language was certainly of major significance. In Zimbabwe, the Shona subgroup Ndau was associated with the Congregational Church. But that church's outreach in Mozambique was small and fragmented between south and centre, contributing little to a strong Shona or Ndau identity within Mozambique.[10]

Thus in Mozambique the one African linguistic cluster with significant literacy in its own language was also the group with access to the capital. In Angola, in contrast, there were two other potential foci for regional or provincial loyalties. In each country, modern political leadership emerged from a small group of educated Africans. Within that group in Angola, however, there was a critical mass with the potential for subnational as well as national loyalties.

Inventing the nation

In Angola and Mozambique, organized nationalist movements are even more recent than in other African countries. Portuguese repression and restriction of education for Africans helped ensure that until the early 1960s there were virtually no visible signs of nationalism. One can note many examples of anti-colonial resistance, as chronicled, for example, in the painstaking accounts compiled by René Pélissier for both countries.[11] A few scholars have probed the consciousness of oppression under the Portuguese, reflected in popular song and other informal resistance. But there are few hints as to when these anti-colonial currents began to reflect also the consciousness of being part of nations called Angola and Mozambique. What we can see, crystallizing in organized movements in the 1960s and preceded by fragments of literature, is but a small part of the picture.

The official perspective imposed by the Portuguese colonial state clearly denied any alternative identity. Portugal was mythologized as a multicontinental nation. In this 'nation' only culture derived from Portugal counted as civilization; inferior African cultures were destined to disappear. The vast majority of Africans, categorized as *indígenas* (natives), were subjects considered irrelevant to the identity of the nation. Assimilation for the small fraction who advanced to civilized status implied total replacement of African customs and identities by Portuguese ones.

In contrast to Anglo-Saxon or Afrikaner racial theories, which stressed separation, Portuguese 'lusotropicalism' exalted racial mixture as one of the means of spreading civilization. In practice, neither *mestiços* nor *assimilados* were more than a small minority in either country. Nor were they in fact accepted in colonial society as equal with whites. But Portuguese colonialism was sufficiently distinctive to ensure that the milieu within which explicit national sentiment and organization emerged was multiracial rather than exclusively black.

In Mozambique in 1950, out of a total population of 5 million, there were approximately 27,000 whites, 16,000 *mestiços*, 10,000 Asians, and almost 5,000 *assimilados*. In Angola that same year, out of 4.1 million total, there were 79,000 whites, 30,000 *mestiços* and 30,000 *assimilados*, a significantly higher proportion than in Mozambique. At mid-century, *indígenas* formed 97 per cent of the population in Angola and 99 per cent in Mozambique. Some *indígenas*, but certainly fewer than 5 per cent, had some education in Portuguese and thus presumably the potential for assimilation.

In both countries nationalist leadership emerged primarily among *mestiços* and Africans with achieved or potential *assimilado* status. Their position was inherently ambivalent: relative privilege and presumed equal status with the colonists contrasted with their experience of *de facto* discrimination and white attitudes of racial superiority. As with early nationalists elsewhere in Africa, the first expressions of resistance stressed demands for equality within the system rather than the seemingly unthinkable demand for national independence.[12] Only after the Second World War did more explicit expressions of national sentiment emerge.

Nationalism developed on broadly parallel lines in the two countries. Waves of Portuguese settlement, in the early twentieth century and then in greater numbers after the Second World War, raised new obstacles to the advancement of local Africans, *mestiços* and even African-born whites. In each country, the nationalist identity found expression in poetry, particularly in the 1950s, before it could take political form. *Angolanidade* ('Angolan-ness') and *Moçambicanidade* ('Mozambican-ness') were discussed as identities that might be assumed by some whites as well as by *mestiços* and Africans. In each, the few who went to Portugal or other countries for higher education played critical roles in consolidating ideas of national unity. In each case, nationalists of the 1960s and 1970s were keenly aware that they were not just fighting for national independence but were also still creating a national identity that was not yet accepted as natural by much of the population.

Several important differences, however, helped set the stage for distinct scenarios. First of all, there was the significantly greater historical depth of the 'national' social formation in Angola. The importance of urban strata in the social base of the MPLA, often noted by analysts, reflects differences preceding the formation of nationalist organizations. This was reflected, for example, in the development of Angolan literature, and in the number of local whites who participated in both literary and political expressions of nationalism. Only a minority of whites in either country took this path instead of identifying themselves as Portuguese, but that minority was more visible in Angola than in Mozambique. More generally, Angola was the pacesetter among the nationalist movements in the Portuguese colonies: the first literary figures, the first clandestine nationalist organization, the first to begin guerrilla war in the 1960s. Earlier development, however, had its price. Luanda was also a potential pole of repulsion for those from the provinces who felt excluded. When the liberation wars against the Portuguese began in the 1960s, lines between the capital city and the provinces were already more sharply drawn in Angola than in Mozambique.

The borders with other colonial territories also significantly influenced the concept of nation in both countries, by distinguishing the colonial experiences of Angolans and Mozambicans from their neighbours, and by determining the flows of labour migration and later of political exile. Migration to neighbouring countries was fundamental to Mozambique's political economy. Those who went, unless they became permanently integrated in the host countries, gained a consciousness of being Mozambicans, as distinguished from South Africans, Rhodesians, Nyasalanders or Tanganyikans. In almost every part of Mozambique, but particularly the south and centre, a high proportion of male Mozambicans had this experience. In Angola the experience of migrant labour across borders or emigration was much less common. Only small numbers went south to the mines in South Africa or to the central African copperbelt. Only with the Belgian Congo to the northwest was there significant cross-border movement, and even there most were refugees in the early 1960s, after the outbreak of war in northern Angola.

Neither in Angola nor in Mozambique was it possible for nationalist groups to function openly, and the exile milieu was therefore particularly important for emerging nationalist ideas. Significantly, Mozambicans were exposed to the political currents of English-speaking Africa, from South Africa's African National Congress to Commonwealth African politicians such as Julius Nyerere and Kenneth Kaunda. Angolans, in contrast, had closer links to Portugal, and to the Francophone intellectual and political world. These differences, reflected in the contrasting political histories of Tanzania and Zaire, had profound effects on the movements.

Organization and hegemony in the nationalist movement

With open political expression barred, communication difficult within each country, and regular contact of exiles with those at home practically impossible, it should be no surprise that nationalist networks were fragmented geographically. This was true not only in Angola, as Marcum has traced out in his classic work, but also in Mozambique, where Mozambicans in Rhodesia, East Africa and Malawi formed separate groups, while nationalists in Lourenço Marques had only a student group as an organizational presence. At the beginning of the 1960s, neither Angolans nor Mozambicans had any organization which could claim national political representation.

The fact that fifteen years later a clearly hegemonic Frelimo presided over independence, while the fragile Alvor Accord required three Angolan signatories, only to collapse into war, may have in part been predictable from the greater divisive potential in Angola. But neither outcome was preordained. The specific events and contingent conditions of the wars for independence also had identifiable influences which tipped the balance one way in Mozambique and another in Angola.

The two countries differed, first, in how the wars began. In Angola, two separate and largely spontaneous revolts erupted in February and March 1961, first in Luanda and then in the coffee country of northern Angola. MPLA militants played active roles in Luanda and in the Dembos coffee-growing area, while the FNLA (then the União das Populações de Angola – UPA) was involved in the majority of the coffee-growing districts, where Kikongo speakers predominated. The minimally prepared rebels met savage reprisals from the Portuguese, who slaughtered hundreds in the slums of Luanda and tens of thousands in the rural north. In theory repression might have served to consolidate national unity. But it also virtually eliminated the possibility of contacts among nationalist leaders divided among prison, exile, the bush, and clandestine concealment in the city. The UPA-sponsored revolt built additional barriers, as the rebels killed not only white settlers but also *mestiços, assimilados* and Africans from other areas of the country. This racially and ethnically oriented violence strikingly contrasted with the MPLA's call for Angolan anti-colonial unity across ethnic and even racial lines.

Mozambican nationalists, on the other hand, were able to talk about unity in exile before the conflict turned to violence. A greater proportion of the potential leadership was able to escape the country, and they did not carry the burden of blood already separating the FNLA and MPLA constituencies. Aware from the Angolan precedent that any quick revolt would be suppressed while the international community limited itself to token condemnation of the Portuguese, Mozambicans could take time to prepare.

Distinct exile environments also influenced the prospects for unity. Mozambican nationalists found in Dar es Salaam a congenial locale for coordinating their activities, later supplemented by Lusaka. The close ties between President Nyerere and President Kaunda facilitated discussion between the host governments and with Frelimo, which was formed in Dar es Salaam in 1962. In contrast, Angolan nationalist leaders were scattered among Kinshasa, Brazzaville, Lusaka, Dar es Salaam, and, in the early years, even distant Conakry. These sites were not only linguistically but politically diverse. The country best placed to influence Angolan nationalism was Zaire (then Congo), itself beset by division and Cold War intervention.

By mid-1961 the FNLA's Holden Roberto had joined his Congolese friends on the CIA payroll. For two years, the MPLA also had offices in Kinshasa, winning some support even among Kikongo-speaking Angolan refugees. But its efforts to supply guerrillas inside Angola were blocked by the FNLA, which controlled the border area and at least twice executed MPLA members passing through. In 1963, the MPLA was expelled from Kinshasa, retreating across the river to Congo (Brazzaville). Unity with the FNLA would have been difficult in any case, but was definitively ruled out by Cold War imperatives of CIA patronage. The guidelines mandated excluding any possible leftist influences, such as the MPLA, rather than building national unity. With the Congo crisis, actively combating any possible Soviet influence became the top US priority in Africa. Angola, so close to the epicenter of that conflict, could not possibly be insulated.

Another possible location for building national allegiance was in the guerrilla war zones. Although in each area local recruits came from local groups, the middle- and high-level guerrilla leadership was almost always ethnically diverse. Even the FNLA, in the early years, had prominent leaders from elsewhere in Angola. As for Mozambique, Frelimo in particular was keenly conscious that this was the arena for tribalism to die so that the nation might live. The stress on national unity in Frelimo speeches of this era, sometimes taken as underestimating the extent of ethnic diversity, in fact affirmed the recognition that national unity could not be taken for granted but was still to be built. The camaraderie of the guerrilla front, a direct experience for relatively small numbers, nevertheless shaped the consciousness of the core of the nationalist movement.

Angolans were denied this crucible of unity, save in fragmentary form. By the mid-1960s almost all the non-Kikongo within the FNLA were gone, amid charges of killings and discrimination under Holden Roberto's leadership. Unita's leadership included Angolans from Cabinda and eastern Angola as well as Savimbi's fellow Umbundu-speakers, but its guerrilla operations, never large, deteriorated into military collaboration with the Portuguese. The MPLA exhibited the widest diversity among its leadership, and sustained guerrilla operations in three separate zones: north of Luanda, in Cabinda, and in eastern Angola.[13] But communication among the guerrilla fronts, and among exile offices in Brazzaville, Lusaka and Dar es Salaam, was a logistical nightmare.

In both countries the real threat of fragmentation was exploited by the Portuguese, for whom infiltration and attempts to promote disunity were a fundamental strand of counterinsurgency strategy. But the sentiment of national unity was real as well. Despite Portuguese efforts, such as fostering hopes of an independent 'Rombézia' for northern Mozambique, no significant group, either in Mozambique or in Angola, adopted a separatist programme. Even political competition, however bitter, reinforced the idea of Angola and Mozambique as nations, rather than substituting ethnic or regional identities with claims to nationhood.

The outcomes were different, partly because of the structural factors already mentioned and partly because of the harder-to-generalize impact of personalities and micropolitics. But there are also some structural commonalities, which provide some possibility of integrating the complex mix of ethnic, national, class and ideological factors into a common framework.

In the crisis in Frelimo in 1966–69, those who opposed the leadership of Eduardo Mondlane and Samora Machel were disproportionately nonsoutherners. Many were resentful of the prominence of southerners and *mestiços* among Frelimo leadership, and suspicious of the presence of whites. The group whose interpretation prevailed regarded such appeals as opportunistic, divisive, and calculated to undermine anti-colonial unity. They were aware of Portuguese efforts to manipulate such sentiment, and with some empirical evidence regarded vulnerability to ethnic or racial appeals as the first step on the road to possible desertion to the Portuguese. In contrast they stressed political commitment rather than racial or regional origin. This non-racial ideological perspective also justified appeals for solidarity to non-African progressive forces around the world.

The perspective implied integration within the movement of Mozambicans of all ethnic and racial origins, as well as blocking the formation of possible ethnic cliques within the leadership. It also meant de-emphasizing the *de facto* disproportionate role in top leadership played by Mozambicans from social sectors with historical advantages in education and access to the central society. Ethnic balancing was forbidden in theory, although of necessity it affected practical judgements. The Frelimo leadership which emerged from the crisis saw the choice as stark: either national unity together with commitment to social transformation along socialist lines, or counter-revolutionary appeals to racial and ethnic divisions aimed at substituting black faces for white without changing the structures of exploitation. Making the revolution implied making political conduct rather than ethnic origin the guiding orientation.[14]

For the opposing tendency, particularistic identities tended to be more salient than broader frameworks of national or ideological unity. Differences of background or status within the nationalist movement were central preoccupations. There was by no means an exact correspondence between ethnic origin and the position taken in these debates. But the Portuguese rulers, seeing the nationalist challenge as led by people from the next level of society (southerners, *mestiços*), sought possible allies among those placed even lower on the colonial hierarchy.

If Presidents Nyerere and Kaunda had not supported unity around Mondlane and Machel in the mid-1960s, the outcome for Mozambique might have more closely resembled that in Angola, with one or more ethnically or regionally focused nationalist organizations rivalling that linked with the nationalist network of the capital. Instead, Frelimo incorporated Mozambicans of all backgrounds, while the dissidents never achieved any organizational coherence. Some deserted to the Portuguese, while others went into exile. This history, and the geography of the war, ensured that geographical representation in the core of Frelimo leadership was not proportional. The Macua-Lomwe-speaking peoples of Nampula and Zambézia were particularly under-represented, and central Mozambique was less prominent than Beira's second-city status might suggest.

In Angola similar distinctions were accentuated by early crystallization into separate organizations, as well as by greater gaps between the central and provincial milieus. But the themes showed significant parallelism. The 'provincial' organizations FNLA and Unita more strongly emphasized particularistic identities, ethnic or racial, and built on the grievances of outsiders *vis-à-vis* the more racially mixed and more urban nationalist culture of the capital city. As in Mozambique, the Portuguese cultivated the divisions, particularly wooing those opposed to the MPLA, which they saw as the principal danger because of its national orientation and revolutionary ideology. In Mozambique the Portuguese built up stereotypes of the Macua as loyal, as opposed to the 'fierce' Makonde guerrillas of Frelimo; this was paralleled in Angola by the stereotype of Umbundu loyalty and Kongo hostility. In each case the more 'sophisticated' Africans were seen as the most formidable threat. These stereotypes had some basis in social reality. But they were also propaganda, designed to block the nationalist project of constructing unity. Individuals did not conform to or deviate from the stereotypes by some automatic process, but out of a complex mix of backgrounds, circumstances, struggles and personal decisions.[15]

The role of the individual in history is an oft-disputed and never-resolved debating point. Such analysis would require detailed biographical and organizational studies. But, in addition to the nameless individuals making hard choices about identities and loyalties, particular leaders certainly had significant effects. Mondlane's unifying style of work, supported by Nyerere's similar orientation, had a continuing impact after his death. Roberto's non-cooperative leadership style was notorious, raising the question whether other FNLA leaders might have been more receptive to reconciliation with the MPLA. Savimbi's mono-maniacal quest for the top position and undying resentment of Luanda society, as well as his skill at ingratiating himself with different constituencies and sponsors, arguably played decisive roles in leading Unita into alliances with the Portuguese military, South Africa and other external sponsors. Neto's poetic sensibility and personal dedication, which even won recognition from most opponents, were coupled with an introverted leadership style which hampered communication with internal and external opponents.

The unity that emerged in the Mozambican independence movement could easily have failed, given different leadership and a different exile environment. It seems unlikely, however, that even drastically different leadership configurations could have overcome the many factors promoting disunity within Angolan nationalism. To envisage another historical outcome requires a giant leap of imagination, perhaps to a Congo under Lumumba rather than Mobutu, joining with Kaunda and Nyerere in urging unity while providing strong support to the guerrilla actions of a united movement. Even then conflict might still have persisted, but resembling in scale that in Zimbabwe rather than the all-out strife which decolonization precipitated in Angola.

Decolonization scenarios

Portuguese decolonization differed significantly not only from the hand-overs by Britain and France, but also from the negotiated ends to armed struggle in Algeria, Zimbabwe and Namibia. The April 1974 *coup*, in significant part a result of the colonial wars, began a period of internal strife, in which various factions contested the basic shape of Portuguese society and government. There was no broad consensus in Portugal on how to decolonize; many still regarded the very idea of African independence as treason. The shifting Portuguese governments had neither the power nor the will to chart a coherent transition policy, which might have provided continuity and legitimacy. The swift release of the colonies, completed less than two years after the *coup*, paralleled the quick independence of the Belgian Congo fifteen years earlier.

Although the scenarios contrasted dramatically in Angola and Mo-zambique, several commonalities made both societies particularly vulnerable to the conflicts of the 1980s. Portugal's pre-*coup* colonial policy had totally excluded the option of independence, and there was accordingly less preparation than in any other colonial context. Education for Africans had been expanded in the 1960s and early 1970s, but the number of educated Africans was still minuscule. The middle ranks of administration or economic enterprises were filled by whites, with *mestiços* or Indians in second place. Only a minority of whites were born in Africa, and even smaller numbers had begun to accept that they were Angolans or Mozambicans rather than Portuguese. With the white exodus of 1974-76, a high proportion of the leadership positions were vacated. This discontinuity gave an opportunity for creating new revolutionary institutions rather than just adapting colonial ones. But it also ensured that those new institutions would be fragile.

The movements that came to power had – irrespective of their level of popularity – only fragmentary structures of national-level coordination. And their legitimacy was not confirmed by referenda or elections. The colonial power in British, Belgian and French decolonization supervised such exercises, even in Algeria; the international community helped oversee electoral transitions in Zimbabwe and Namibia. In Angola and Mozambique the claim to legitimacy rested instead on the record of anti-colonial struggle and on the ideological promise to defend the interests of the masses. Once the initial enthusiasm wore off, support would depend on fulfilment of the promises.

To what extent could these factors have turned out otherwise, given the history up to 1974? What were the critical decisions or interventions that tipped the balance towards war rather than elections in Angola? How much could Angolans and Mozambicans have done to induce more whites to stay, without giving up the dream of building new independent societies? Would elections or other gestures of conciliation have led opponents to accept the legitimacy of the new order, or only opened new avenues for subversion? How much would any of these options, if they could have been taken, have lessened the likelihood of or vulnerability to the conflicts of the 1980s? The questions are too large and speculative for more than suggestive responses. But one can highlight what happened and where, just possibly, it could have been different.

In what is still the best informed and nuanced account of the 1974–76 conflict in Angola, F.W. Heimer notes that 'hypothetically, the conflict could have been avoided had the FNLA and Unita accepted an early proposal by the MPLA to present common lists and a common programme at the planned elections for a Constituent Assembly', thus substituting an interim attempt at power-sharing for all-out electoral competition.[16] That option, however, was precluded by the deep social and personal as well as political divisions separating the leadership of the three groups. In such an arrangement, FNLA and Unita leaders feared, the 'MPLA's quantitative and qualitative superiority in political and administrative *cadres* would become preponderant'.[17]

The period of electoral competition in early 1975 deepened these divisions, as non-aligned Angolans were pressured into making choices. Had an election occurred, expectations were that there would be no decisive winner; estimates were that Unita might gain a plurality of 40 per cent to 45 per cent, closely followed by the MPLA with 35 per cent to 40 per cent, with the FNLA trailing with less than 20 per cent.[18] The MPLA feared that the other two would form a coalition against it, and, given its past experience with its rivals, anticipated that this would lead to total exclusion from power and likely physical repression.

The historical record leaves little doubt that the initiative for military confrontation came from the FNLA, which had the dimmest electoral prospects and, at the time, the best conventional military position. The FNLA was encouraged by its backing from President Mobutu of Zaire. For most of 1974, while the Soviets had suspended military support for the MPLA, due to its internal divisions, China and the US worked with Zaire to build up the FNLA military. Scholars disagree on the relative importance of Chinese, US and Zairian military patronage of the FNLA, and the extent to which they were coordinated or simply parallel.[19] By early 1975, however, China had decided to disengage. The US, at Kissinger's insistence, opted for escalation. Without this external backing, it is likely that the FNLA would have been forced to consider the MPLA offer of power-sharing.

Instead, polarization was accentuated. Rivalry was reinforced by linguistic distance between the partly French-speaking FNLA leadership and the Luanda-centred MPLA. The conservative ideological cast of the FNLA contrasted with the Marxist-oriented MPLA leadership mobilizing 'popular power' among the urban masses. Kissinger's strategy of crafting an anti-Soviet Sino-American partnership meshed with the internal cleavages and locked them into place in the international Cold War line-up.

Until mid-1975, as the FNLA–MPLA confrontation mounted, Unita had the options of playing a balancing role or choosing one or the other side. On grounds of ethno-regional differences or historical rivalry, Unita had reason for conflict with the FNLA as well as with the MPLA. In the electoral arena, particularly appealing to Unita given its military weakness, an eventual coalition against the MPLA was an attractive prospect, but no final decision needed to come until after the election. Once full-scale military confrontation between the other two groups was under way, however, a choice seemed unavoidable. Despite MPLA feelers for a power-sharing arrangement, many factors pushed Unita to choose the other side.

The level of distrust between the MPLA and Unita was high given the recent history of fighting on the eastern guerrilla front, and the secret military pact between the Portuguese and the Unita leadership. MPLA leaders were also convinced, although the historical proofs are inconclusive on this point, that the Portuguese secret police had been involved in the formation of Unita from the start. Certainly, Savimbi's secret police contacts paid off in 1974, as he sought financial support from the settler community.

Unlike the FNLA, the MPLA was contesting Unita's own constituency, since a significant minority of Umbundu speakers were opting for the MPLA instead of their 'natural' ethnic home. Savimbi's personal resentments of MPLA-dominated urban society reflected and partly moulded widely-held views in Unita's constituency. Some observers have argued that Unita's socialist ideology should have brought it closer to the MPLA than to the FNLA. But the 'black power' and Maoist over-tones of Unita rhetoric resonated with the anti-Soviet partnership of Beijing and Washington. And, perhaps the deciding element, Savimbi was above all an opportunist, seeking a winning constellation in which he could be pre-eminent. Savimbi had received small amounts of aid from South Africa as early as October 1974, and Prime Minister Vorster authorized 20 million Rands for arms to Unita in mid-July.[20] Simul-taneously, the National Security Council ordered the CIA to aid Unita as well as the FNLA. At this time, as Heimer notes, no one foresaw the dramatic increase of Soviet and Cuban aid to the MPLA.[21]

The subsequent course of the war in 1975–76 is an oft-told story, and needs no repetition here. But one particularly significant result needs to be stressed. Some whites in Angola entertained brief hopes in 1974 of a white settler-dominated independence, an option ruled out by the Alvor Agreement. Of those remaining in 1975, the majority supported the FNLA or Unita. As the war escalated, an exodus began which eventually included almost 90 per cent of the white population, leaving a remnant composed of MPLA supporters and others with individual motives for staying.

The war was the immediate reason for most departures. But the Mozambican parallel raises the possibility that even a peaceful transition would not have kept most of the whites in the country. The MPLA, like Frelimo, was committed both to non-racial policies and to radical changes that would in fact challenge white privilege. Unita and the FNLA combined more conservative views with greater willingness to mobilize racial hostility for political gain. Negotiated conciliation with guarantees of white settler interests, as in the later Zimbabwean and Namibian settlements, was ruled out by the Portuguese army's unwillingness to fight for those interests. Nor did the nationalists see a pressing need to reach out to those whites – still numerically predominant – who showed little sign of accepting the legitimacy of African dignity and independence.

Mozambique escaped the initial strife to which Angola was subjected. But Frelimo was determined to mould a new revolutionary society in discontinuity with the colonial social hierarchy. Most whites were unwilling to live under African rule. These factors, together with the limited violence that did occur, resulted in as drastic if not so sudden an exodus as in Angola.

In the six months preceding agreement on Mozambican independence, political power in Portugal was uneasily shared between the young officers of the Armed Forces Movement and General Spinola, who accepted the need to end the wars but also sought to maintain *de facto* Portuguese dominance. Settler leader Jorge Jardim and others identified with the colonial order were trying to block a Frelimo-led independence government in favour of a more conservative alternative. Frelimo saw these efforts as a continuation of Portuguese counterinsurgency stratagems of divide-and-rule. And they were a real threat, because at the national level Frelimo had popular enthusiasm but as yet few other levers of political power. The miscellany of parties that sprang up in 1974 were seen as not only opposed to Frelimo but also disloyal to the Mozambican nation.

The abortive rebellion of September 1974, described in Chapter 1, confirmed the polarization. The parties and individuals who rallied to the rebels, including the small number of black opponents of Frelimo, identified themselves with right-wing opponents of Mozambican independence. Frelimo saw conciliation of these forces as equivalent to betrayal of the national cause. Many whites panicked at the prospect of being ruled by people they saw as 'terrorists'. While Frelimo preached and practised non-racial openness to all Mozambicans, its revolutionary stance was threatening to anyone who had found the old order comfortable or acceptable.

From hindsight in the 1990s, when the multi-party system is applauded as the key component of democracy, it is natural to ask why Frelimo did not ratify its overwhelming popularity with a competitive contest. In part it was because there was little prospect of an impartial administration to oversee such a poll. The Portuguese state was internally contested; the only part of the army that wanted to stay in Africa was the most opposed to independence. But it was also because the Frelimo leadership saw the key to democracy as participation by the masses within movement structures. Frelimo accordingly favoured *poder popular* as modelled on the experience of the liberated guerrilla zones, rather than parliamentary competition which would exclude the illiterate and poorly educated in favour of those with the economic resources to run elections and use the colonial patronage systems to manipulate votes. Frelimo's victory would not have been in doubt. But that was not their conception of how to build democracy.

Chapter 9 will discuss how implementation of this perspective may have contributed to the subsequent wars. What is relevant now is to note that while the transition in Mozambique was indeed peaceful, in contrast to Angola, neither involved negotiated concessions to those with vested interests in the colonial order. Nor did either involve the formal ratification of the new state by election or referendum. Leaving aside for the moment the practical possibility of electoral transitions, or their desirability on other grounds, would such alternatives have provided protection against the subsequent outbreak of conflict? Was the absence of multi-party institutions a decisive determinant in leading to and prolonging war in the two countries? Did Angola's birth in the midst of war inevitably lead to the protracted conflict of the 1980s?

The history of other African states makes it clear that these are not automatic conclusions. Electoral competition under a British-fostered constitutional system was not a secure guarantee of peace: witness Nigeria or Uganda. Nor did the one-party state necessarily lead to war. The one-party state in post-independence Africa, whether conservative, moderate or radical in orientation, has rightly been criticized for its failure to accommodate criticism and open up genuine political participation. But many such states have remained at peace; notable examples include Mozambique's neighbour Tanzania and the smaller Portuguese colonies of Cape Verde and Guinea-Bissau. Even the Angolan war of 1975–76 need not have led to lasting conflict. Nigeria's civil war was just as bitter and even included a bid for secession, but was followed by reconciliation.

Angola and Mozambique are exceptional in the extent of collapse of the colonial order, with the disappearance of a high proportion of those who ran it. Almost certainly this heritage, along with other emergent problems, would have led to disillusionment with the post-colonial state, as in virtually all other African countries.

But were these legacies so severe that they would have necessarily led to the continuation of war in one country and the outbreak of war in the other, with no new external intervention? The most likely answer is a qualified no. Without the ongoing conflict over white-minority rule in the region, and without Washington's unrelenting hostility to Angola, Angola's problems in the 1990s might more closely resemble those of Nigeria, and Mozambique's those of Tanzania.

These factors are better characterized as weakening the capacity to respond to the externally fuelled conflicts rather than as the primary reasons for the wars. The full argument for this conclusion depends on topics discussed in later chapters. But it is also supported by tracing the subsequent impact of the factors present as colonialism departed.

The *ancien régime* and other losers

Between 1973 and 1980, more than half a million Portuguese departed Angola and Mozambique, over 90 per cent returning to Portugal and most of the rest opting for South Africa. A substantial minority, perhaps as many as 80,000 of the adults, had been born in Africa.[22] In comparison, those who stayed in Angola or Mozambique probably numbered less than 40,000. On the face of it, those who left had ample motives to seek to overthrow the post-colonial states or at least to punish them in revenge.

Individuals and groups from this social category played prominent roles in the wars against both Angola and Mozambique. But given the potential of their numbers, those involved were comparatively few. They were rarely the initiators, and their efforts alone would probably have been confined to a succession of futile plots and complaining.

Of the 300,000 *retornados* from Angola and 164,000 *retornados* from Mozambique in Portugal, large numbers sympathized with Unita. A smaller number openly applauded Renamo. Organizations of *retornados* who had abandoned property lobbied for compensation. Resentment over the loss of empire was a potent theme in the political repertory of the far right and much of the centre. Much to the annoyance of Luanda and Maputo, Unita and Renamo offices functioned openly in the Portuguese capital, serving as outlets for Unita's effective propaganda as well as Renamo's ineffective efforts. Lisbon served as a transit point for arms smuggling to South Africa, including shipments for Unita, and as a link in Unita's diamond-smuggling operation. Portugal's military intelligence agency maintained close links with Unita, Renamo and the South Africans.

None of this, however, was sufficient to make Portugal the organizing centre of the post-colonial African wars. Most *retornados* concentrated their economic or political energies on survival in a Portugal oriented to Europe, not Africa. Across the political spectrum, the trend was towards marginalization of Africa. As African countries rather than Portuguese possessions, Angola and Mozambique, even if under different, more conservative, regimes, could be objects of nostalgia or of business opportunities. But the prospects for economic mobility or political power that might attract large numbers of Portuguese were no longer on the historical agenda.

For the short time of their dominance, the radical wing of the Armed Forces Movement, along with the Communist Party, fostered the hope of ties to Angola and Mozambique based on common revolutionary principles. By 1978, the dominant influences on Portugal's Africa policy were the Socialist Party under Mário Soares, along with centrist and conservative politicians who sought pragmatic protection for Portuguese economic ties in Africa. Soares was particularly sympathetic to Unita and hostile to the Angolan government. But by and large pragmatism prevailed in Lisbon. Successive Portuguese governments, despite frequent minor disputes with the former colonies, stopped well short of backing insurgency in Africa.[23]

More significant support for Unita and Renamo came from the Portuguese community in South Africa. The 1980 South African census identified some 57,000 people as Portuguese-speaking, but published estimates in the mid-1980s ranged up to 500,000 or more. Even so, the majority were economic immigrants from European Portugal (including the island of Madeira). Former settlers from Angola or Mozambique probably numbered less than 20,000.[24] While the majority were sympathetic to the apartheid policies of South Africa and strongly opposed the governments of Angola and Mozambique, most concentrated their efforts on economic survival rather than politics.

The most decisive intervention of a former settler was probably that of Orlando Cristina, secretary-general of Renamo until his death in 1983. But even he took second place to the Rhodesian and South African controllers. Other former settlers played key roles as members of the South African armed forces. And yet others ran front companies supporting SADF covert operations. After the Nkomati Accord, some observers highlighted the 'Portuguese factor' in the support for Renamo. But this shadowy network of businessmen, ex-soldiers and intelligence operatives, sometimes referred to as 'white Renamo', never surfaced as an openly organized force. The extent of its later independence from the South African covert network that had fostered it, and how much weight it had on its own in the late 1980s and early 1990s, remained mysterious to the last. But it is highly unlikely that these forces would have been more than a minor nuisance had not the Rhodesian and then the South African regime given them material support.

The former Portuguese settlers probably affected the wars most significantly not by their involvement but by their absence, which added to the vulnerability of new economic and political structures. Those vulnerabilities are the focus of Chapters 9 and 10.

Among other losers in the decolonization process, the most prominent were the FNLA and Unita. Both carried the legacy of hostility to the winning MPLA from pre-independence rivalries. The open conflict of 1975–76 added much bitterness. Whatever the precise balance of war atrocities, or the level of responsibility of top leaders, there were many indiscriminate reprisal killings on all sides during those years. Yet they did not exceed those of the Nigerian civil war a few years earlier, which was followed by reconciliation. There is, moreover, a dramatic contrast in the subsequent roles of the FNLA and Unita, although they suffered equally bitter defeat in 1976.

Within a few years, a significant number of FNLA soldiers accepted amnesty from the Angolan government, and many even joined the government army. Other FNLA supporters stayed in exile in Zaire or overseas, minimizing political involvements. Some were persuaded to join Unita's army and others fought in South Africa's 32 Battalion. Holden Roberto kept a shell of the group going in exile. But by the late 1980s several top FNLA leaders had even taken high positions in the Angolan government. The earlier hostilities were not forgotten, but they did not foster an ongoing FNLA-led military campaign against Luanda.

Unita, obviously, was another story. But to what extent was the difference determined by Angolan divisions as they stood in 1976, and to what extent was it rather a result of external factors and the historical contingencies of the 1980s? Significant numbers of Unita supporters returned to areas of government control in the late 1970s, but despite government offers of amnesty, there were almost no defections among the Unita middle-level leadership, and none at the top, during the war. Defection of government supporters to Unita was also rare. The choices made in 1974–76 proved durable. Even during the 1991–92 ceasefire, when parties proliferated, including dissidents from both Unita and the MPLA, there were only a few cross-overs from one camp to the other.

The reasons are many. Unlike the FNLA, Unita had a plausible claim to support from the numerically significant south. A majority of educated Umbundu speakers had rallied to Unita in 1974, and their loyalty was confirmed by the traumatic events of 1975–76. A significant number of educated youth followed Savimbi on his retreat into the bush or into Namibia in 1976. Yet these factors might well have been insufficient to sustain a united organization, much less a long-term guerrilla war, without the unique role of Jonas Savimbi on the one hand and the availability of South African as well as other outside patrons on the other. These ensured, as will be explored in Chapter 8, that Unita was able to maintain an extraordinarily closed society which curbed any sign of disloyalty by force as well as persuasion. The FNLA, by contrast, had neither strong leadership nor easy access to South Africa. Its immediate patron, Mobutu, was inconsistent in his support, and most FNLA followers had the possibility of seeking non-political options in exile.

The hypothetical question of what might have happened without Savimbi, or without South African intervention, is better postponed to the concluding chapter. But the contrast between the FNLA and Unita does show that the hostilities of 1975–76 are not a sufficient explanation of the Angolan conflict of the 1980s.

Some supporters of Renamo also attribute its war to the aspirations of Mozambican nationalists excluded by Frelimo. Renamo propaganda even lays claim to the heritage of Frelimo founder Eduardo Mondlane, and some scholars have pointed to the presence of former Frelimo soldiers among Renamo commanders. The *Africa Livre* group in Malawi, which merged with Renamo in 1982, can be traced back to rivals to Frelimo in the 1960s. The Renamo exile networks in Kenya and the US included students who had split from Frelimo in the 1960s. Yet what is striking is not the presence of a few such individuals, but that they were so few. Even among Mozambican exiles opposed to Frelimo, most preferred to keep their distance from Renamo.[25]

The African political figures who joined the abortive white-settler revolt in September 1974 included former Frelimo officials who had defected to the Portuguese or been implicated in the assassination of Eduardo Mondlane (notably Lázaro Kavandame and Uria Simango). Held in detention in post-independence Mozambique, this group was apparently the object of a Renamo plan to rescue them in 1983. In an incident which has not yet been discussed in detail by the Mozambican government, they were reportedly executed while in detention.[26] It is plausible to speculate that the followers of some of these figures might have joined Renamo out of resentment. But if so, it is notable that not even supporters of Renamo have provided evidence of this.

Finally, one may cite the response by other social forces threatened by the revolutionary policies of Frelimo and the MPLA: the Catholic Church with its close ties to the colonial order, other religious groups upset with Marxist dogmas, traditional chiefs whose authority was undermined, potential entrepreneurs or small farmers frustrated by socialist planning or bureaucracy. Although these tensions were present in embryo at independence, they are better considered in the context of policy and practice over time, and will be taken up in Chapters 9 and 10.

Ethnicity and regionalism in the
post-colonial wars

Given the historical regional and ethnic disparities described earlier, it would be surprising to find no impact at all of these factors on the post-colonial conflicts. In the Angolan case it is common to portray Unita as 'representing' the Umbundu-speaking population. The prominence of Ndau speakers among the Renamo leadership indicates that ethnicity may be one of the factors in the Mozambican conflict as well. Yet when contrasted to 'ethnic' conflicts in many European societies, or in English-speaking African countries such as Nigeria, Uganda, or South Africa, what is striking is the relative lack of ethnic separatism. There was no counterpart to the 'ethnic cleansing' of disintegrating Yugoslavia, to the stress on Igbo identity in separatist Biafra, or to the chauvinistic Zulu nationalism of Chief Buthelezi's Inkatha. Both government and insurgent forces, in both Angola and Mozambique, defined their objectives in centralizing national terms, rather than in terms of ethnic or local patronage networks.

The stress on revolutionary legitimacy and national unity was not just rhetorical, for either the MPLA or Frelimo. While the historical educational advantages of the capital city area continued to influence the distribution of jobs at higher levels of the government, efforts to expand educational opportunities had the potential for redressing some of that disparity. Recruitment for party and state institutions was national in scope. So was conscription for the armed forces. Umbundu-speaking youth were recruited for officer and jet-pilot training, as were Angolans from elsewhere, according to their educational qualifications.

At the very top, the historical patterns of disproportion prevailed, with Umbundu speakers absent until 1990 from the MPLA Political Bureau, and Macua-Lomwe speakers absent from the Frelimo Political Bureau until 1989. But even there ethnic and regional diversity was substantial. At the next level down (Central Committee in the party, cabinet level in the government, officer ranks within the military), virtually no regional or ethnic group was absent in either country. By the end of the 1980s, some of the leaders from under-represented groups had moved up to the top levels of party leadership. The secretary-general of the MPLA was Marcolino Moco, of Umbundu origin; Feliciano Gundana, from central Mozambique, was secretary-general of Frelimo.

Thus individuals of any ethnic origin could advance within party and state structures. The centralization of authority, however, combined with taboos on the use of ethnic divisions as the basis for patronage or affirmative action, meant that under-represented groups could not openly mobilize patronage networks to advance their ethnic cohorts. Such networks undoubtedly existed, but they were not the basis of political advance, as, for example, in Kenya or Nigeria.

Of the contending parties, Unita probably came closest to resembling an 'ethnic' party. By their numerical weight and educational advantages, Umbundu speakers overwhelmingly dominated the Unita officer corps. Unita's base area and leadership ranks were far more homogeneous than the Angolan government side. Still, its subnational appeals were more often couched in regional than in ethnic terms. The top leadership included several key figures from elsewhere in Angola, and Unita considered the peoples of the south and east as well as of the central plateau its natural constituency. Its guerrilla actions, particularly in the late 1980s, penetrated northern areas where it had no claims to support on ethnic grounds. Despite its strong ethnic base, Unita aspired to national leadership rather than to ethnic separatism.

Renamo's Ndau connection was much less pervasive than the Umbundu presence in Unita. The 1980 census showed only 7 per cent of Mozambicans to be Shona speakers; Ndau, a Shona sub-group, probably accounted for not more than 4 per cent. Ndau speakers were, however, geographically accessible to the Rhodesian recruiters, and are consistently reported to have predominated among veteran Renamo commanders. To a significant extent, Ndau became the *lingua franca* of the Renamo army, although other languages were more used in units with only a few Ndau commanders, and Portuguese was still used for written messages and reports.

The Ndau predominance undoubtedly affected both relationships within Renamo and behaviour towards civilians. A 1987 split of Zambézia-based UNAMO from Renamo probably reflected ethnic rivalry at the leadership level. The ethnic divide was probably most significant in Renamo actions in the south, which were particularly brutal against non-Ndau southerners and which played on the Ndau reputation for magical powers to inspire fear. Renamo most consistently maintained control over Ndau-speaking areas of Manica and Sofala province.[27]

Despite this *de facto* Ndau prominence, Renamo's leadership and its army included people from all regions and ethnic groups in Mozambique, just as did the government side. The bulk of its army was not of Ndau origin, but was recruited by kidnapping wherever combat took place. Non-Ndau speakers were prominent among Renamo's political leadership, and advanced in the military hierarchy as well. It was relatively easy for non-Ndau, especially speakers of other Shona dialects, to assimilate by learning the language. Renamo was eclectic in making use of local traditional magic and religion whatever its origin. The Ndau cultural connection did not imply a conflict defined primarily in ethnic terms.

Would 'ethnic tensions' alone have led to war in Mozambique or to the continuation of war in Angola? The most likely answer is no, given the relatively low correlations between ethnic identity and the politico-military line-up, as well as the relatively low salience of specifically ethnic appeals on either side. The pattern of military action reflected the requirements of military logistics more closely than any ethnic pattern. Ethnic and regional disparities fed into the wars, affecting how individuals and communities experienced the conflict. The wars in turn had consequences for such societal divisions, which, ironically, may become even more salient under conditions of peace and multi-party competition.

By cutting transport links and by devastating rural infrastructure and social services, the wars of the 1980s frustrated most efforts the post-independence states made to remedy regional disparities. Nevertheless, the educational progress of the years since independence resulted in unprecedented numbers of educated Angolans and Mozambicans from virtually every geographic area within each country. In the future, desperate economic circumstances and electoral and free-market competition are likely to increase the prominence of ethnic or regional patronage networks. Renewed conflict may take on accentuated ethnic overtones. But as before, choices of identities and political allegiances will be a complex mix of national, regional and ethnic components.

Voting patterns in the Angolan election in 1992 provide a helpful reminder that ethnicity, however important, is only part of the picture. Savimbi gained large majorities of 81 per cent in Huambo and 84 per cent in Bié, the core Umbundu-speaking provinces. President dos Santos won 82 per cent in Kuanza-North and 71 per cent in Luanda. But in both the presidential and legislative races, each party won at least a significant minority of voters in every province, including their opponents' ethnic home ground.

In Angola, particularly during the return to war after the election, Unita made frequent appeals to regional loyalty. In Mozambique, too, regional inequalities were high on the political agenda as the ceasefire and election process began. Many of the emerging new parties stressed federalism or decentralization. Notably, however, the vigorous and sometimes abusive political debates in both countries were still primarily couched in terms of national issues. The vast majority of Angolans and Mozambicans of all backgrounds, profoundly weary of war, strongly endorsed national unity and reconciliation. Within each ethnic group, people opted for a variety of political viewpoints.

Notes

1. Ranger (1989), 127.

2. See, for example, the description of the peoples of Angola in Miller (1988), 17–39.

3. See Isaacman and Isaacman (1976).

4. For Mozambique the percentages are from the 1980 census, compiled from provincial-level data in *Os Distritos em Números* (Maputo: Conselho Coordenador do Recenseamento, 1983). The last data on linguistic divisions in Angola is from the 1950 census; the percentages given are those generally cited based on that year.

5. Heimer, *Entkolonisierungskonflikt* (1979), 37–56; Heimer, *Decolonization* (1979), 5–16.

6. For a summary of Angolan political economy in the late colonial period, see Castro (1978), or, in English, Herrick et al. (1967).

7. Calculated from 1970 census data.

8. See particularly the chapters in Vail (1989) as well as Young's summary essay (1986) and Maré (1993).

9. On the role of the Swiss missions in linguistic and ethnic identity see Harries (1988).

10. It is interesting to note that prominent nationalist dissidents Ndabaningi Sithole, in Zimbabwe, and Uria Simango, in Mozambique, were both pastors associated with this mission.

11. Pélissier, *Angola* (1986), *Moçambique* (1987).

12. On Mozambique see especially Penvenne (1989), and the introduction by Allen Isaacman to Honwana (1988); on Angola Dias (1984).

13. A vivid picture of the problems and the internal tensions within the MPLA appears in Pepetela (1983). Among the many sources on the history of Angolan nationalism, Marcum (1969, 1978) is a fundamental source. Davidson (1973) combines extensive historical background with first-hand reporting and analysis of the war of liberation. The documentation on Savimbi's collaboration with the Portuguese military can be found in Minter (1988).

14. Sources on the history of Frelimo, and this period in particular, Munslow (1983, 1985) and Christie (1988). An alternate approach to Frelimo's internal conflicts, based on interviews with exiles in Kenya, is taken by Opello (1975). Bragança and Depelchin (1988) have called for new research on the period, but so far little new work has been published.

15. See Pepetela (1983) and for a novel by someone growing up within Unita, see Jamba (1990).

16. Heimer, *Decolonization* (1979), 60; *Entkolonisierungskonflikt* (1979), 15.

17. Heimer, *Decolonization* (1979), 61.

18. These estimates, versions of which appear in many accounts of the period, were not based on surveys or even on detailed projections by province, but on extrapolations of ethnic divisions in the 1950 census and the best guesses of local observers.

19. For a review of the roles of different parties to the conflict, see Klinghoffer (1980), as well as Legum and Hodges (1976).

20. Pezarat Correia (1991), 152, citing a SADF report by F. J. du Toit Spies.

21. Heimer, *Decolonization* (1979), 74.

22. Pires et al. (1984).

23. See Antunes (1990), 109–136, and Gaspar (1988).

24. On the disputed statistics on the Portuguese in South Africa, see Rosa and Trigo (1986), 85–94.

25. The most extensive discussion, including a listing of individuals, is in Vines (1991).

26. Africa Watch, *Conspicuous Destruction* (1992), 158.

27. For discussion of this topic see particularly Vines (1991), 84–5; Minter (1989); and Roesch, 'Renamo and the Peasantry in Southern Mozambique' (1992) and 'Peasants, War and "Tradition" in Central Mozambique' (1993). See also further discussion in Chapter 8.

5

Revolution and Counter-Revolution in Regional Perspective

When Presidents P.W. Botha and Samora Machel met on the South Africa/Mozambique border to sign the Nkomati Accord of 16 March 1984, the pledges on both sides evoked a new era of peace. Neither country would support any form of armed action against the other. They agreed to disagree on South Africa's apartheid policy and Mozambique's moral and diplomatic support for the ANC, but violence would not be allowed to disturb their necessary *modus vivendi*.

Machel proclaimed a victory, seeing in the accord an end to South African support for Renamo's war. Frelimo's leaders had long argued that Pretoria's overwhelming military strength ruled out guerrilla war in South Africa on the Mozambican or Zimbabwean models; they felt that denying the ANC the limited transit facilities it had enjoyed was a necessary concession. The ANC's real strength, they argued, was its political support inside South Africa.

The dominant view of observers, however, was that African liberation had suffered a decisive setback. While Pretoria's friends applauded the accord and anti-apartheid forces lamented it, both tended to see it as the sign of a 'Pax Pretoriana' ratifying South African military hegemony. Commentators fitted the limited disengagement accord between Angola and South Africa into the same pattern. 'Southern Africa is calm because all know who's boss', read a typical headline.[1]

Both views proved wrong. Mozambican leaders did not get the peace they hoped for; South Africa continued the war through Renamo despite strict Mozambican compliance in limiting the ANC to a small diplomatic presence in Maputo. But South Africa's violations of the treaty, and its parallel failure to disengage in Angola, showed that Pretoria had not achieved the security it sought. Celebration of the Pax Pretoriana quickly faded. Botha's peacemaker image lasted barely long enough to give him a friendly reception on a European trip in June.

Without doubt the South African military, directly or through proxies, could impose enormous destruction on its neighbours. In that sense its supremacy was never at issue. But it could not restore a stable order favourable to continued white-minority rule. Even when suffering military defeats, SWAPO and the ANC heightened their legitimacy in Namibia, South Africa and internationally. Since the threat continued, so did the rationale for escalating South African assaults on the easiest targets: the vulnerable societies of Mozambique and Angola.

The persistence of South African involvement, and the cumulative destruction, reflect a more complex pattern than the straightforward application of military power. The distinctive character of the wars in Mozambique and Angola is directly linked to this dilemma of the South African regime: military capacity to inflict enormous pain on neighbouring societies, coupled with inability to translate this force into internal stability or into a new regional constellation of client states.

Initial responses to insecurity

Before 1974, South Africa enjoyed a *cordon sanitaire* of white-ruled states. With the Portuguese keeping guerrillas at bay in the farther reaches of Angola and Mozambique, Ian Smith defending white-ruled Rhodesia, and South West Africa (Namibia) virtually a fifth province of South Africa, anti-apartheid forces had great difficulty keeping up links with the outside world. The regime crushed early guerrilla actions and repressed a generation of black resistance. Although Pretoria's security budget expanded significantly in the 1960s and early 1970s, involvement beyond South Africa's borders was small. No threat to the white state seemed to warrant much alarm.

The collapse of the Portuguese empire fundamentally changed the strategic outlook. For the first time Namibia and Rhodesia (Zimbabwe) were seriously vulnerable to guerrillas. It was not practical to patrol the long Angola/Namibia and Mozambique/Zimbabwe borders. Southern Mozambique bordered South Africa. Even if Mozambique refrained from harbouring South African guerrillas, a liberation movement in power so close to Pretoria was a symbolic threat. With increased ease of contact between internal resistance and exiles, the momentum of the freedom struggle was renewed. South Africa could check the flow, but it could not rebuild the dam.

The responses as Mozambique and Angola moved to independence revealed, in distinct ways, the outer limits of South African power. In Mozambique, the decision not to intervene in support of the abortive September 1974 anti-Frelimo *coup* ruled out what some thought a militarily feasible option. In Angola, the contrary decision in 1975 – to join in trying to block the MPLA from coming to power – proved an embarrassing failure. Notably, despite subsequent invasions, raids, economic pressures and proxy wars, South Africa never again launched a direct military drive to install a client government in the region.

In September 1974, Prime Minister John Vorster reportedly quashed the military's plan to aid the *coup*-makers in Maputo. Although there is no public record of his reasoning, the context provided abundant grounds for caution. In physical terms the operation would not have been difficult. The Mozambican capital is only 90 km. by road from South Africa. The demoralized Portuguese army probably would not have reacted forcefully, and Frelimo's forces were not even close to the capital. But South African intervention would have been impossible to conceal. South Africa cited the principle of non-intervention to counter calls for international action against apartheid. Going into Mozambique would set a precedent that could be used against it.

Despite the presence of black opponents of Frelimo with the white rebels, South Africa had little chance of creating a plausible political cover. Defending a regime with little legitimacy against renewed guerrilla action was a recipe not for security but for insecurity. It was likely, moreover, that any Mozambican government, whatever its ideology, would seek a *modus vivendi* with South Africa. Mozambique adjoined friendly African countries only in the far north -- Rhodesia was still under white control, Malawi an ally of Pretoria and Swaziland ruled by a conservative monarch. Mozambique's economic dependence on South Africa was profound, accounting for almost half of foreign exchange earnings. Even the electricity for Mozambique's capital came from South Africa. Frelimo leaders knew political choices could not undo these inherited bonds.

Finally, intervention on behalf of a white settler revolt in Mozambique would have clashed with Pretoria's strategy in Rhodesia. Despite white solidarity, South African leaders regarded Smith's regime in Rhodesia as expendable. After the Portuguese *coup*, Vorster accepted the implication that a constitutional settlement – and thus some kind of power-sharing with acceptable black politicians – was required. A South African-Zambian '*détente* scenario' included South African support for Zimbabwean independence and a reciprocal commitment to bar insurgent activities against South Africa from Zambia, Mozambique, Botswana or Zimbabwe. Overt intervention in Mozambique would have killed this initiative at its inception.

Although this *détente* exercise proved abortive, it revealed that South Africa was hoping to manage the transition in Rhodesia rather than defend whites-only power in that country to the bitter end. Pretoria's desired regional configuration had shifted from the tripartite white alliance of the 1960s to a 'constellation' of black or power-sharing governments looking to Pretoria for guidance. This concept, formulated by Vorster in 1974 and elaborated under Botha in 1979, implied a primarily diplomatic approach to guaranteeing security. It would incorporate Botswana, Lesotho, Swaziland, Rhodesia, Namibia, South Africa and independent South African homelands, perhaps Zambia as well and maybe even Mozambique.[2] Whether Mozambique was inside or outside a formal constellation, its economic links would ensure its vulnerability to South African pressure.

After the Portuguese *coup* the South African regime also reversed its previous approach of fully incorporating South West Africa (Namibia). Instead it developed the idea of an independent South West African state incorporating blacks as well as whites into its leadership. As in Rhodesia, South Africa aimed at building credibility for selected local leaders, thus damping down both guerrilla war and international pressure. But the regional configuration in the west was significantly different than with Rhodesia and Mozambique in the east.

In South West Africa, racial power-sharing would require sacrificing South Africa's direct political authority, not that of a separate group of settlers. Angola depended on oil and had few economic links to the south. Like Mozambique, Angola derived revenue from rail links to the interior, but to Zaire and Zambia, on the edge of the sphere of South African influence. South Africa thus had little economic leverage over Angola.

South Africa adopted a wait-and-see policy in Angola until mid-1975. The decision to intervene directly with military force later that year resulted not only from the perceived threat of an MPLA victory, but from the opportunity to do so with the political cover of involvement by others. Ironically, South African intervention served to legitimate Soviet and Cuban assistance to the MPLA and to undermine African and international support for Pretoria's favourites. It thus served as a negative object lesson for direct South African military intervention.

The most detailed reconstruction to date of South African decision-making in the Angolan intervention attributes the initiative to Defence Minister P.W. Botha.[3] Foreign Affairs officials were relatively uninvolved. The Bureau of State Security was also reportedly sidelined, despite its previous explorations of arm's-length covert aid to the MPLA's opponents. The involvement was incremental, from a military contingency plan in June to the October blitz by South African-led columns. Prime Minister Vorster approved the plans at each stage, however, and the decision to withdraw in January 1976 was based on political as well as military considerations.

Although influenced by internal bureaucratic politics, the choices depended above all on external conditions. Intervention appeared promising because the FNLA and Unita proved responsive to South Africa in preliminary contacts. Additional points in favour were the active involvement of Zaire and tacit acquiescence of Zambia. Most decisively, the US was taking the lead in the anti-MPLA crusade. South Africa thus thought it could both gain credit with the West and avoid drawing too much attention to its own involvement.[4]

Although Soviet and Cuban military presence undoubtedly heightened South Africa's perception of threat, this was probably of less significance than Western encouragement in determining the timing and extent of involvement. Before South Africa's first major attack, 150 km. inside Angola in August, there were only a handful of Cuban military advisers with the MPLA. By the time South African troops withdrew there were more than ten thousand Cuban troops engaged. The threat was greater. But the possibility of a cheap South African military presence, playing a relatively inconspicuous role secondary to Western and African allies, had disappeared.

The South African initiative, starting with advisers to quickly assembled units of the FNLA, Unita and assorted mercenaries, was designed to be covert. Armoured reinforcements were added hastily, but the military was under pressure to minimize white South African casualties, which could not be easily concealed. Victory thus depended on South Africa's allies. The FNLA/Zairian drive on Luanda proved a military disappointment and US covert involvement was restricted by Congress. Diplomatic support for the MPLA, meanwhile, was galvanized by revelations of the South African role. The costs of continuing the campaign rose dramatically.

Analysts have often noted that the Angolan débâcle promoted Botha's suspicion of American reliability. The concomitant less-noted lesson was that direct South African military intervention to install a client government was a costly venture with uncertain prospects. This strengthened the demand to build up military capacity, but simultaneously reinforced arguments for caution in high-profile military ventures.

In both the Mozambican and Angolan cases, therefore, South Africa had reasons to hesitate at overt military action. The reasons were different: Mozambique was too close and Angola too far. In each the risks outweighed the possible benefits. Conventional military models were inadequate. Thus there were strong incentives to develop new strategies which could minimize negative international reactions as well as potential South African casualties. Two complementary options took on prominence: the quick-strike cross-border raid, and the use of proxy forces.

The cross-border option

Once the outcomes in Angola and Mozambique were clear, South African planners had to expect the two to provide rear bases for guerrillas in Zimbabwe and Namibia. The potential for guerrilla warfare inside South Africa was less immediate. Cross-border raids by counter-insurgency forces were used extensively in four cases: Zimbabwe/Mozambique (1976–79), South Africa/Mozambique (1980–90), and Namibia/Angola in two separate time periods (1976–79 and 1980–88). The results varied in detail. But they all produced some military success while failing to check growing political support for insurgents.

From small-scale beginnings in the mid-1960s, guerrillas opened the first sustained campaign against Rhodesia in the early 1970s. After negotiations with the Smith regime collapsed in 1975, the Frontline States supported renewed guerrilla action. The war entered its most intense phase. The Zimbabwe African National Union (ZANU) operated openly from Mozambique, the Zimbabwe African People's Union (ZAPU) from Zambia and through Botswana.

In response Rhodesian forces targeted guerrilla bases, refugees and transport infrastructure in Zambia, Botswana and, most persistently, Mozambique. Well-trained Rhodesian commando units were air-dropped or infiltrated by road in disguise, relying on superior air power, lack of anti-aircraft defences, and surprise. Destroying ammunition dumps, buildings and bridges, they also tried to kill as many insurgents or potential insurgents as possible before withdrawing. To minimize international response, they counted on quick in-and-out action, on control of the reporting, and on Western indifference to the death of blacks.

As isolated operations, most raids were military successes. Sometimes they had extraordinary kill statistics, such as 675 'terrorists' killed at Nyadzonia in Mozambique with no casualties among the attacking Selous Scouts who drove into the camp disguised in Mozambican uniforms. Most of the dead were unarmed refugees waiting for training as guerrilla recruits. But as a Rhodesian African soldier later remarked, 'We were told ... it would be easier if we went in and wiped them out while they were unarmed and before they were trained rather than waiting for the possibility of them being trained and sent back into Rhodesia'.[5] The attacks also inflicted massive damage on Mozambique's fragile transport system. Although the majority of the dead were Zimbabweans, significant numbers of Mozambican troops and civilians also were killed.

The raids, nevertheless, failed to check escalation of the war inside Zimbabwe. The Rhodesian regime eventually was forced to concede majority rule. One major reason for this failure was the steady flow of new guerrilla recruits. Despite high casualties in external raids, matched by similarly brutal action against guerrillas and civilians inside Zimbabwe – and in part because of these actions – political support from Zimbabwean Africans for the guerrilla cause continued to rise. Secondly,

ZANU and the Mozambican forces improved their defences, particularly by dispersing camps and infiltration routes. External sanctions limited Rhodesia's capacity to expand the attacks. Aircraft were in short supply, and external raids took resources from internal counterinsurgency efforts. South Africa covertly supplied aircraft and military personnel. But Pretoria's commitment was not unconditional, and it was ready at times to press concessions on the Smith regime.

In sum, the double squeeze of war and sanctions put pressure on the Smith regime, even while Rhodesian raids hampered guerrilla operations and made Mozambique and other Frontline States eager to reach a settlement. The Lancaster House agreement of 1979 transferred the conflict to the political arena, resulting in an overwhelming electoral victory for ZANU, the most significant guerrilla force. The lesson for South Africa was that cross-border raids were not necessarily enough to remove a guerrilla threat.

The same lesson was implicit in the initial counterinsurgency experience in Namibia. For the Namibian liberation movement SWAPO, the collapse of Portuguese control in Angola made it possible to expand the guerrilla war begun in 1966. Instead of small-scale infiltration from Zambia, over 700 miles of border were now available, remote from white population centres and much of it adjacent to densely-populated Ovamboland. SWAPO supporters could cross into Angola with relative ease. In early 1976 South Africa declared quasi-emergency rule in most of the north. By 1977 a South African spokesman cited as many as 100 clashes a month with SWAPO guerrillas.

Although regular South African troops withdrew from Angola in March 1976, the SADF established regular air surveillance over both sides of the border and carried out frequent small-scale patrols and raids into Angola, as well as occasional ventures into Zambia. The targets included SWAPO guerrillas, Angolan border posts and villages. Before 1980, most such actions were unannounced, but Angola recorded almost 200 separate South African attacks in the years 1976–79, with over 300 Angolan civilians killed in 1979.

The one large operation in the Rhodesian pattern was the May 1978 attack on the SWAPO refugee and guerrilla recruiting camp at Cassinga, 250 km. inside Angola. In an airborne commando and bombing attack, South African forces killed over 600 SWAPO supporters. In a close parallel to the Rhodesian raids in Mozambique, almost all the dead at Cassinga were unarmed recruits or civilian refugees – only twelve were armed guerrillas. The attackers suffered three dead. A South African military historian says that the operation 'inflicted a well-nigh mortal blow on SWAPO's military capability'.[6] But despite high kill statistics, neither this high-profile raid nor the unpublicized smaller ones stopped the guerrilla campaign. Four years later, in 1982, South

African estimates put the number of trained SWAPO guerrillas at 6,000, almost double their 1977 estimate.[7]

SWAPO's guerrilla war admittedly was not as effective as ZANU's in Zimbabwe, but not because of superior effectiveness of South African cross-border actions. Almost all of Rhodesia was within 300 km. of a border friendly to African guerrillas; white farmland and African reserves were interlocked in a patchwork pattern. In South West Africa the north was remote from the more developed centre and south; much of the intervening terrain was desert. Western countries consistently refused to adopt sanctions against South Africa over its illegal occupation, and Pretoria could accordingly afford for years to pay the costs of military occupation.

The fact that the conflict continued was proof that, as in Rhodesia, internal counterinsurgency plus cross-border raids were insufficient to eliminate the guerrilla threat. Since the white regime failed to establish political credibility, its kills among guerrillas, guerrilla recruits and suspect civilians were compensated by new recruits. Brutality, despite its apparent military efficiency, served to undermine the regime's legitimacy among its victims.

Beginning in 1980, South Africa went beyond short-term raids to 'incursions' that turned into long-term occupation. The primary purpose was to force SWAPO's rear bases to the north, lengthening the infiltration routes that the guerrillas had to cover on foot. In the occupied areas, South Africa adopted a scorched-earth policy, destroying villages and small towns as well as military installations. The invasions involved direct confrontations with Angolan troops, but not with Cuban forces, which were stationed 500 km. north, along the line of the Namibe–Lubango railway. South Africa occupied much of Cunene province continuously from 1981 to 1984, simultaneously assisting Unita in the south-east.

Aggressive cross-border operations depended on the assurance that Western countries would continue to veto sanctions voted by UN majorities. But they also required heavy investments in conventional military hardware, to match Soviet and Cuban support for Angola. The potential costs in military hardware, white casualties and international reaction were always too great for South Africa to consider a conventional attack on the Namibe–Lubango–Menongue corridor, the southernmost target of major economic and strategic importance in Angola.

In 1980, South Africa was determined never to permit a SWAPO government in Windhoek. Until 1988 the SADF had virtual free rein in the border area. Nevertheless, the guerrilla campaign continued in northern Namibia. South Africa failed to develop a credible alternative to SWAPO. Later Western sanctions against South Africa – adopted in

1986 not because of Namibia but because of apartheid and the brutal suppression of township uprisings – began to bite, raising war costs. South Africa lost its decisive air superiority, and the scene was set for an independence settlement.

South Africa faced a different threat from the ANC guerrilla campaign. Zimbabwe and Namibia fitted more or less classic guerrilla war patterns: rural insurgencies with adjacent sanctuary borders over which recruits could flee and trained guerrillas and arms supplies return. South Africa was a far more urbanized society, and there were few rural areas which could sustain insurgency. The regime was strong enough to wipe out large-scale bases in any country near its borders.

The ANC's strategy for armed struggle thus faced enormous difficulties. After the banning of the liberation movements in 1960, armed struggle became one of the three basic strands of the anti-apartheid cause, along with international pressure and internal political mobilization. But the security police crushed the early sabotage campaigns. The buffer of white-ruled states largely frustrated communication between exiles and internal supporters. Then the fall of Portuguese colonialism reduced the geographical barriers and helped spur the revival of black political resistance inside South Africa. Thousands of activists fleeing repression after the Soweto uprising in 1976 left South Africa and joined Umkhonto we Sizwe, the military wing of the ANC.

They soon began trickling back. Small-scale sabotage incidents became more frequent; there were a few larger attacks on police stations or other government targets. In mid-1980 ANC guerrillas hit the state-owned coal-to-oil refinery, causing over $5 million damage. Throughout the 1980s the ANC sustained this pattern of dispersed small-scale attacks, punctuated by an occasional higher-profile action. With few exceptions, the guerrillas followed the ANC policy of avoiding attacks on civilian targets.[8]

Unlike the Zimbabwean or Namibian pattern, the attacks as well as the communications and support routes for the guerrillas were dispersed rather than concentrated. ANC bases with large numbers of people were located in countries distant from South Africa, primarily Tanzania, Zambia and Angola. South Africa's immediate neighbours were for the ANC not rear bases, but 'forward areas' for transfer of personnel and for maintaining communications between the internal underground and ANC exiles scattered not only in Africa but around the world.

South African 'cross-border' actions against the ANC between 1979 and 1989 included air bombing raids (in Angola, Zambia, Botswana and Mozambique), openly acknowledged commando attacks (in Mozambique, Zambia, Botswana and Lesotho), and unacknowledged assassinations (in Zimbabwe, Angola, Mozambique, Swaziland, Zambia, Botswana, Lesotho, and France). These attacks targeted not only guerrillas, but also prominent non-military leaders of the ANC, and the casualties often included non-South African civilians.

The only guarantee against attack for South Africa's neighbours would have been to bar all refugees who might possibly support the ANC, and to cooperate fully with South Africa in detecting any who might pass through their countries clandestinely. No country conformed so closely to South African desires, although Swazi police often co-operated with the South Africans, Mozambique strictly limited the ANC presence after Nkomati, and several other countries required refugees to leave after South African threats.

South Africa's actions helped prevent the ANC's armed struggle from becoming a serious military threat. But they failed to eliminate it and even multiplied its political impact. As political resistance escalated inside South Africa, black support for the ANC grew apace, both among those in direct contact with the organization and among others who saw how frantically the regime was trying to destroy it. Cross-border raids were powerless to block the symbolic reinforcement the armed struggle gave to internal black resistance and to the international campaign for sanctions.

The option of military conquest had been ruled out after the fiasco in Angola, and limited military action against guerrilla sanctuaries was inadequate. Regional diplomacy, too, had only limited potential to reduce South Africa's isolation.

The regional line-up

In the 1960s, South Africa feared – and the opponents of apartheid hoped – that the spirit of African freedom would prove instantly contagious. But as long as the Portuguese and Rhodesians held firm, the regional line-up was not that unfavourable to Pretoria. The African challenge to apartheid was significant but largely symbolic. An anti-apartheid consensus was consolidated in the Organization of African Unity (OAU), and confirmed in majority sentiment in the UN General Assembly. But Africa was powerless to overcome Western vetoes in the Security Council.

The most prominent African spokespersons on the issue were Presidents Julius Nyerere of Tanzania and Kenneth Kaunda of Zambia, who played key roles in regional summit conferences of East and Central Africa between 1966 and 1972. The 1969 summit's Lusaka Manifesto expressed a preference for peaceful liberation but added: 'while peaceful progress is blocked by those at present in power in the States of Southern Africa, we have no choice but to give to the peoples of those territories all the support of which we are capable in their struggle against the oppressors.'[9]

Twelve states signed the manifesto, but only four adjoined white-ruled territories: Congo (Brazzaville) and Congo (Kinshasa) bordered Angola, Tanzania bordered Mozambique, and Zambia faced Rhodesia as well as both Portuguese-ruled countries. Botswana, Lesotho and Swaziland, although members of the OAU, kept a low profile on apartheid, and did not attend the summits. Malawi attended but declined to sign – President Banda's contrary stance was emphasized by an exchange of state visits with South Africa in 1970–71.

The countries at these summits did not form a cohesive bloc, nor did those which served as guerrilla sanctuaries. The Nyerere–Kaunda tie served to coordinate policy on Mozambique and Rhodesia even when disagreements emerged. But divergence was more common than accord when African states dealt with Angola. While African reaction in the Angolan crisis of 1975-76 disappointed South Africa, it also showed deep divisions among African states (a key Organization of African Unity vote on recognition of Angola split 22–22 in January 1976). It was not unreasonable for Pretoria to hope that more subtle diplomacy could succeed with divide-and-rule tactics.

The constellation concept, however, was fundamentally flawed. Pretoria declared Transkei independent in 1976, followed by Bophuthatswana (1977), Venda (1979) and Ciskei (1981). But not even Western countries, much less African states, were willing to give diplomatic recognition to such obvious dependencies of the white regime. A similar contradiction bedevilled South African efforts to promote its clients in Namibia, as successive internal rearrangements failed to gain credibility. The fatal blow to constellation came with Robert Mugabe's stunning electoral victory in Zimbabwe in February 1980. South Africa had the choice of supporting a last-ditch *coup* attempt – with no international legitimacy – or accepting the disagreeable outcome.

Despite its material advantages, South Africa was unable to mobilize a friendly coalition of black states. It could play on the vulnerabilities of each state. All, with the exception of distant Tanzania, had to make accommodations to Pretoria's demands. But only diplomatic isolates Zaire and Malawi joined South Africa's destabilization projects.

African countries in the region, in contrast, despite material vulnerabilities and differences among themselves, sustained a general anti-apartheid consensus and cooperation on diplomatic, economic and even military issues. Their institutions were not strong enough to prevail against South Africa's superior economic and military force. In the diplomatic arena they could not match the US or even Britain. But they barred the consolidation of South African hegemony, and partially offset weaknesses that would have been even greater without mutual support.

In 1974, the leaders of Zambia, Tanzania, Botswana and not-yet-independent Mozambique began regular meetings to coordinate policy for negotiations on Zimbabwean independence. In April 1975, the Front-line States, as they came to be called, won recognition as an *ad-hoc* committee of the OAU to focus on liberation of southern Africa. Joined in 1976 by Angola, and in 1980 by Zimbabwe, the group met regularly both at summit level and in working sessions of other officials.

Frontline membership was defined both by geography and by over-lapping networks of political affinity and personal trust – the leaders of Botswana, Zambia and Tanzania in the tradition of populist Common-wealth African leaders, the MPLA and Frelimo long-time allies, Mozam-bicans conscious of the support they had received from Tanzania and Zambia, the Zimbabwean leadership grateful in turn for Mozambican support. Leaders of the liberation movements in Namibia and South Africa regularly participated as observers.

The Frontline States formed the core of a broader grouping with the goals of promoting common economic development and reducing de-pendence on South Africa. The Southern African Development Co-ordination Conference (SADCC) added Lesotho, Swaziland and even Malawi. By focusing on practical economic cooperation, and coordin-ating appeals to donors for assistance in specific sectors, SADCC won praise as a relatively effective international organization.

Within each organization, the potential for economic or political independence from South Africa differed enormously. Lesotho, sur-rounded by South Africa, had the fewest economic options. Its leader Chief Jonathan, who had stayed in power with South African aid in the 1960s, moved in the 1970s to criticize Pretoria and grant relatively free access to the ANC. He eventually fell victim to a military *coup*, a result of South African pressures. Other cases, however, constituted more significant weaknesses for the region. Swaziland and Malawi, as well as Lesotho, were not asked to join the Frontline States. Zaire was invited into neither body. Swaziland and Malawi adjoined Mozambique, and Zaire bordered Angola. Malawi and Zaire were ideally located to com-plement South African military pressures on Mozambique and Angola. Their tacit cooperation with Pretoria was a critical albeit generally underestimated factor in the regional power balance.

South Africa could not break the regional African consensus in principle on support for SWAPO and the ANC. But both ideology and geography made Angola and Mozambique special targets. Together the two coastal countries provided the most important alternate routes to the sea for the interior. Attacking Angola and Mozambique ensured continued dependence on South African ports for Zaire, Zambia, Malawi, Zimbabwe, Botswana and Swaziland. Communication barriers helped ensure that the outside world would pay little attention to attacks on these Portuguese-speaking countries. In short, to weaken the region as a potential threat, targeting Angola and Mozambique offered both high payoffs and low costs.

These factors weighed unevenly. Angola was the most isolated from predominantly English-speaking southern Africa. Even if the Benguela railway were functioning, Angola was unlikely to form a cohesive bloc with Zaire and Zambia. Angola gained relatively little protection from regional solidarity; for the same reason, attacking Angola had only limited repercussions for the other Frontline States. Mozambique, in contrast, had long ties with English-speaking neighbours. It could call on Zimbabwean and Tanzanian troops as the threat escalated. But it was also a more attractive target for South Africa. By attacking Mozambique, Pretoria weakened Zimbabwe and Zambia without incurring blame for direct attacks on Commonwealth members, and increased its leverage over Malawi and Swaziland as well.

South African officials, with all their potential leverage over unfriendly states, were still frustrated at the region's intractability to their designs. They were convinced that the security of the white regime required finding new resources and new ways to orchestrate a co-ordinated strategy.

Institutional instruments of total strategy

Under P.W. Botha, the State Security Council (SSC) became the key decision-making body, the apex of a 'national security management system' which penetrated all levels of the state. Even the best descriptions to date have not penetrated its strict secrecy. There is evidence of different tendencies – most commonly labelled 'hawks' and 'doves' – but no reliable account of who took which positions in key debates. For obvious reasons foreign affairs officials were more likely to stress diplomacy, and military officials to stress force, but there is no evidence of dissent from the consensus that both were legitimate and useful strategies for South Africa. Nor can one discount differences of opinion within the ranks of diplomats or military men.[10]

Without knowing what went on inside the SSC, however, one can look at the results: the policies applied in Angola and Mozambique, and the growth of state resources. Such an analysis shows that while in theory total strategy was to be 80 per cent political and only 20 per cent military, in practice the proportion was reversed.

South Africa's diplomacy in the 1980s faced a fundamental difficulty. Secure settlements required abandoning or successfully disguising white-minority control. Yet the white state was unwilling to abandon control, and disguises quickly proved transparent. Failure to install a client regime in Zimbabwe in 1980 discouraged taking similar risks in Namibia. Negotiations on South Africa's internal future were not even contemplated until the end of the decade. No grand scheme emerged to replace the constellation mirage. Apart from buying time in Namibia, the regime's regional goals seemed reduced to erecting barriers to the ANC in neighbouring countries by pressing for non-aggression pacts. Internationally South Africa fought a defensive battle against sanctions.

Despite the turn to the right in 1979–80, following the Thatcher and Reagan electoral victories, it was impossible to reverse the international trend denying legitimacy to white-minority rule. Instead South Africa's diplomats tried to change the subject to Soviet penetration of the region, arguing that Angola, Mozambique, SWAPO and the ANC were links in a conspiracy centred in Moscow. The argument appealed to ideologues in Washington. But even conservatives knowledgeable about the region were aware that the anti-apartheid cause brought in not only radicals but also a wide range of nationalists and human rights supporters.

On Namibia the international position was clear: South African occupation was illegal. International opinion on South Africa itself was primarily determined not by diplomacy but by internal developments in South Africa. The Soweto uprising in 1976 and the killing of Steve Biko in 1977 helped provoke the first mandatory arms embargo. The resurgence of internal resistance in the 1980s finally inspired serious, if still partial, economic sanctions.

In the region, only Swaziland and Mozambique signed non-aggression pacts, despite the physical vulnerability of Botswana and Lesotho as well. Even these purported diplomatic victories quickly revealed how little they resolved. The Nkomati Accord did not prevent the rapid growth of ANC support in South Africa. The Swazi agreement – signed secretly in 1982 in exchange for a South African pledge to cede the KaNgwane (Swazi-speaking) homeland to Swaziland – backfired. It may have produced marginally more active cooperation between Swazi and South African police, but it also provoked opposition from white South African farmers as well as blacks.

One potential weapon to supplement diplomacy was South Africa's regional economic weight, which dwarfed the SADCC countries individually or collectively. South Africa applied economic pressure on several occasions, but it was a clumsy tool with several disadvantages. The most notable success was a prolonged slowdown at border posts with Lesotho, which helped provoke an army *coup* and the expulsion of South African refugees. Even so, the military government did not hand over ANC members among the refugees to South Africa, nor did it sign a security pact with Pretoria.

Open use of economic pressures would have undermined South Africa's argument against economic sanctions. Furthermore, extensive pressures against Botswana, Zimbabwe or Zambia would cut South

Africa's trade and transport income, and alienate South African and British business interests which predominated in these countries. The head of South African Transport Services sat on the SSC and undoubtedly acquiesced in such measures as slowing up railway traffic to put pressure on Zimbabwe. But 'transport diplomacy' was primarily devoted to developing long-term ties of dependence as a carrot rather than employing existing links as short-term sticks.

Economic pressures were most feasible politically in the case of Angola. South Africa's own economic interests there were minimal, and US hostility to Angola ensured little reaction even when Western investments were hurt. But with little South African economic leverage, attacking Angola's economy required military means.

Mozambique was the most vulnerable. Cutbacks in South African trade and import of migrant labour could – and did – help cripple the Mozambican economy. The concomitant damage to some South African and Western business interests provided reasons for caution in Pretoria. But Mozambique was not rich enough, or friendly enough to Western countries, for this to be a major bar to South African economic arm-twisting. More significant was Pretoria's need not to be seen openly setting a precedent for sanctions. Little if any restraint was shown in the military destruction of Mozambican economic targets, when the link to South Africa could be obscured.

Diplomacy and economic influence, in short, had inherent limitations. Nor was there any obvious way to enhance their effectiveness. Intangibles such as the white state's lack of legitimacy could not be remedied by hiring more diplomats or logging more time in negotiating sessions. The barrier to more effective use of economic power was not quantitative lack of leverage but negative side-effects. Military force also had limitations, but the military solution had a tempting simplicity: add more and better guns, more and better soldiers, and hit the enemy harder.

The indicators of South African military expansion are familiar. The military budget rose from approximately R257 million in 1970–71 to R2,300 million in 1980–81 and R4,800 million in 1985–86. Active troop strength rose from under 50,000 in 1970 to 150,000 in 1980 and almost 200,000 in 1985. The conscription period for white men increased to two years, followed by twelve years of annual mobilization in three- or one-month camps. The government invested at least half the military budget in capital development, much of it for domestic manufacturing or for high-cost deals to import aircraft and other equipment it could not manufacture. In cooperation with Israel, South Africa established a nuclear weapons capacity.

The nuclear programme was probably unusable save as a vague threat.[11] And most of the SADF's resources were invested in preparation for the improbable scenario of a conventional land invasion. Even with

Cuban troops in the region, South Africa's neighbours never approached the capacity for such action, nor did they plan for it. Although South African forces repeatedly violated their borders, the Frontline States never retaliated in kind.

The military buildup, more than adequate to bar any invasion, also provided hardware for action beyond South Africa's borders. In 1975–76 South African forces in Angola had been challenged by the superior range of Soviet-supplied artillery. They repaired this deficiency with the G-5 cannon, manufactured from prototypes acquired from the US/ Canadian Space Research Corporation in 1976–78. South Africa's air superiority was essential for commando raids and supplies to proxy forces throughout the region, and to support ground operations in Angola. It was not effectively challenged until 1987–88, and then only in Angola.

The most significant gap was manpower. There were never enough white soldiers to cover all the fronts, particularly when troops were used in black townships. South African society was very sensitive to white casualties, as shown already by murmurings following the deaths of less than fifty white soldiers in the 1975–76 Angolan invasion. Military strategy accordingly aimed at reducing the risks to white soldiers. While special forces frequently used black paint to disguise their race during operations, this tactic had its limits. The involvement of large numbers of whites in covert operations would inevitably erode deniability.

The South African military in the late 1970s thus changed complexion dramatically. The army that fought the 'total war' included not only white South Africans, but also black South Africans, white veterans of the Portuguese and Rhodesian armies, and blacks from every country in the region. They were incorporated into a variety of new military units, from 'homeland' armies to elite special forces. On the covert edge it was not always clear, even to the participants themselves, who they were working for.[12]

Despite concern with violating the myth of a white South African military, the need for manpower won the day. Systematic recruitment of blacks by the SADF began in 1974. The SADF supplied officers for armies in the homelands. Beginning with the 'Bushman' Battalion in 1974, the SADF began 'Namibianizing' the war in Namibia – the South West Africa Territorial Force (SWATF) was formed in 1980. The police in both South Africa and Namibia, which already included large numbers of blacks, further expanded black recruitment.

The use of black soldiers to fight for white rule had substantial historical precedent. Afrikaner and British settlers, as well as British and Portuguese colonial armies, repeatedly sought black allies and recruits in the period of conquest. Black troops were essential to the counterinsurgency campaigns by the British in Kenya in the 1950s, and by the Rhodesians and the Portuguese in the 1960s and 1970s. African troops significantly outnumbered whites in the Kenyan colonial forces; 524 Africans among them died fighting Mau Mau, as compared to only sixty-three whites.[13] More than two-thirds of the Rhodesian security forces were black, including many in the elite Selous Scouts.[14] Over 40 per cent of the colonial army in Angola in the 1970s were locally recruited, and over 50 per cent in Mozambique. Some local recruits were white, but the majority were black conscripts.[15]

It was sometimes a political choice for an African to join a colonial or settler army, but often the reason was prosaic – being drafted, being in the wrong place at the wrong time, or the lack of other job opportunities. Particularly useful recruits came from 'turning' insurgents, a practice which became a systematic feature of the southern African wars. British intelligence officer Frank Kitson, who pioneered this technique in Kenya, later reflected that the combination of carrots (employment, loot), sticks (execution) and a plausible rationale (cooperating with a powerful government is wiser than terrorism) could frequently bring a captive around within a few hours.[16] Such recruits were used in another tactic Kitson pioneered: 'pseudo-gangs' of blackfaced whites and Africans disguised as guerrillas for collecting intelligence, attacking guerrillas, and carrying out atrocities against civilians to be blamed on the guerrillas.

The Kenyan example had a direct effect on Rhodesian strategy. The first team of 'pseudo' insurgents was formed in 1973, consisting of two African police and four former insurgents. The technique was developed by the Selous Scouts, which grew to some 1,800 strong and claimed the highest 'kill ratio' in the Rhodesian army. The elite Special Air Service remained a white unit, but used African soldiers from other units in similar operations, as well as handling Renamo recruits.[17]

Black troops in the Portuguese army also played a major role in counterinsurgency. In addition to regular local recruits, there were special units which were primarily black except at officer level. The *flechas* ('arrows') were local militia recruited by the secret police, developed in Angola and extended to Mozambique. In the later stages of the war in Mozambique commando units played important front-line roles. While the regular army primarily relied on conventional conscripts, the special units used many 'turned' insurgents.

While theorists of counterinsurgency often focus on political loyalty, the practitioners concentrated on practical motives – survival, discipline, economic incentives, and the other carrots and sticks of daily life within a fighting unit. The motives for fighting (or simply for not deserting, for once in a military unit fighting was a matter of following orders) undoubtedly varied. But experience brought confidence that men of the most diverse origins could be moulded into fighting units serving the South African state.

The first South African special forces unit was 1 Reconnaissance Commando (1 Recce), formed in 1972. This was expanded into five reconnaissance regiments, which in turn spawned assassination squads such as the Civilian Cooperation Bureau. The Recces were the principal operational resource available to military intelligence planners, who ran the cross-border insurgencies. Although the Recces began as an elite within the white army, active recruitment of blacks made them a thoroughly multiracial and multinational unit by the mid-1980s.

Jan Breytenbach, founder of the Recces, also pioneered the first mixed-race elite unit. In August 1975 he was given command of a unit of FNLA soldiers in Angola. According to Breytenbach, he had long dreamed of imitating US Special Forces in Indochina, by leading 'indigenous guerrilla forces to fight in unfriendly African countries'.[18] When his unit withdrew to Namibia in 1976, he persuaded the army command to allow him to keep it intact. Using US Special Forces training manuals and his own vision, Breytenbach concentrated on weeding out unsuitables, providing intensive training and discipline, and building *esprit de corps*. He aimed to replicate the French Foreign Legion, making the military unit the 'new tribe'.[19]

Two examples show how Africans were incorporated into these forces and deployed on different fronts. An Angolan of mixed race whom I interviewed in prison in Mozambique in 1988 told me how, as a teenage refugee from the fighting in Angola in 1975, he was told by the South African officers in charge of the refugee camp that his job prospects were limited, and that he should choose to join either Unita or 32 Battalion. After four years in 32 Battalion, he was chosen for Recce training. After the two-year course in Durban, he was posted first to Namibia, and then in 1985 to 5 Recce in the Transvaal, rotating in and out of Mozambique with small units supporting Renamo. At the end of 1986 he was transferred to a special unit targeted at ANC exiles, and was arrested in Mozambique in early 1987 when a bomb he had concealed went off prematurely. His self-image was of a military professional, on a career track within South African society.[20]

Another 5 Recce member, Felix Ndimene, was a teacher in the Mozambican border town of Namaacha, taken in a South African raid in 1982. After a month of interrogation and torture, he was offered the choice of joining 5 Recce or being killed. After training, he was sent to the Namibian/Angolan front. After a failed attempt to escape in 1984, he was punished with seventy-five lashes. Transferred back to Phalaborwa in late 1986, he was involved in kidnapping a Swiss couple in Swaziland. In 1987–88, stationed in Pretoria, his unit raided anti-apartheid activists; in 1989 he was in Namibia again for anti-SWAPO operations. Back at Phalaborwa, he fled 5 Recce in 1991.[21]

As of this writing, the history of South African special forces, probably numbering only a few thousand men in all, is still concealed behind official secrecy. But the data does clearly indicate that this multinational, multiracial group was a central tool in the 'total war' of the 1980s.

Proxies, clients or allies?

South African special forces trained and went on operations with Unita and Renamo. So much is not in dispute. But its significance was – and still is – hotly disputed, while many details remain obscure. One view is that Unita and Renamo were so subordinated to South Africa that they served in practice as its proxies. The other extreme perspective is reflected in Savimbi's repeated citation of the proverb about a drowning man falling in a river and being willing to deal with the devil himself if offered a stick to get out.[22] In this version the relationship with South Africa is an arm's-length alliance between parties with highly distinct goals and internal dynamics.

South African strategy was to conceal or minimize the connections, to enhance the legitimacy of their clients and refute charges of aggression. As noted in Chapter 3, Western accounts probably erred on the side of underestimating South African involvement.[23] It is easy to say that neither this nor the mirror image of South Africa as the omnipresent hidden hand accurately reflects the historical reality. But it is not so easy to specify precisely what the relationships were. The South African regime played a dominant role in determining how wide a war to invest in, in deciding when and where to supply matériel and military personnel, and in negotiating over the heads of its clients. But neither Unita nor Renamo was without resources for pursuing their own agendas.

The image of 'patron/client' – rather than the overly mechanical 'proxy' or the misleadingly distant 'ally' – leaves room for variations in the client role, between the two cases and at different times. Whatever their own reasons, Unita and Renamo were fighting in South Africa's battles. Their capacity to pursue goals distinct from their patron's depended on the extent of their organizational autonomy and access to alternate resources for waging war. The information available, despite its shortcomings, justifies some comparative conclusions on these factors.

Savimbi's dominance and his core of loyalists gave Unita an organizational coherence that is well-documented. Access to external support aided Savimbi in suppressing potential rivals by force. But Savimbi and his lieutenants managed both Unita's military operations inside Angola and the Unita delegations in Western countries. South Africa, and other external backers, had to deal with Unita through them.

Renamo, in contrast, was – at least until Nkomati – incorporated within the Rhodesian and then the South African military structure.

Individual leaders undoubtedly had ambitions, but there was no co-hesive leadership group to manage these goals. Although Dhlakama established his leadership over Renamo's military apparatus later in the 1980s, the organization's external representation was noted for frac-tiousness. The loyal core of Dhlakama aides provided an extremely small base for organizational independence.

Nevertheless, the South African imperative to maintain public dis-tance also provided Renamo with potential autonomy. The war in Mozambique required far less external support than that in Angola. While support for Unita was handled explicitly at the highest levels in Pretoria, it seems that after Nkomati disagreements within the SSC left the link with Renamo in official limbo. Support continued without explicit decisions on objectives. With conflicting signals from different representatives of its patron, Renamo was almost forced into a more autonomous stance. Operationally, its links were to sections of the state with little interest in moderating the war.

In material terms, as will be described in Chapter 7, both Unita and Renamo military operations depended on critical support from South Africa and, to a lesser extent, other external sources. Compared with Renamo, Unita had more access to resources other than the South African military. But Unita also needed far more to sustain its op-erations. The result was probably a roughly equivalent proportion of material dependence on Pretoria.

Both relied primarily on taxation in kind and on raids to get food for their soldiers. But outside supplies were also needed, particularly for Unita's base area and conventional troops in south-eastern Angola. Both relied to some extent on trade, largely through private channels linked with South Africa's intelligence network. Ivory was the common de-nominator, as elephant herds in the Angolan and Mozambican bush were ravaged. Renamo added loot from Mozambique's roads and towns, sold in Malawi or in South Africa. Unita sold off captured diamonds and at times controlled some diamond production areas.[24]

For access to the outside world, Unita used Zaire as well as South African-controlled Namibia. Renamo had Malawi in addition to South Africa. South African influence was very strong in Lilongwe, and signifi-cant in Kinshasa as well, and thus neither link was an entirely in-dependent alternative to Pretoria. But in the case of Unita, Washington's open involvement after 1985 gave the option of playing one patron against the other. For Renamo, contacts through Malawi opened alter-nate channels of international right-wing support.

To what extent did these factors of potential autonomy, as contrasted with South African war aims, influence the course of the wars in Angola and Mozambique? The answers are different for different time periods, as well as for the significantly distinct western and eastern fronts.

Continuity and change on the western front:
Angola and Namibia

After initial failure to install a client regime in Angola, South African leaders generally accepted that reversing that verdict by force was unrealistic.[25] South African war strategy on the western front therefore had more limited objectives. From mid-1976 until the 1988 agreement on Namibian independence, the primary goal was preservation of South African control in Namibia, defined operationally as blocking an independent state dominated by SWAPO.[26] Military operations in Namibia and Angola were aimed primarily at SWAPO. Angola's military and economic infrastructures were secondary targets. Once committed to Unita, the SADF also found itself obliged to defend its client when it was threatened.

The war was thus derivative from the political objective of buying time to construct an alternative to SWAPO. The lesson Pretoria drew from Mugabe's victory in Zimbabwe was that a free election contested by a liberation movement claiming guerrilla credentials could not be manipulated easily. But if SWAPO was sufficiently discredited by military defeats, and Pretoria bargained successfully for sufficient control over the election process, then perhaps South Africa's clients could confine SWAPO to a subordinate role.

The criteria for ending the war, then, were intrinsically ill-defined. A total military defeat of SWAPO was elusive without the impossible corollary of a victory over Angola. Pretoria's political clients in Namibia were repeatedly disappointing. There was little prospect that the South West African Territory Force would be viable without SADF supervision. Buying time could go on indefinitely, as long as the cost was manageable.

How then did the notorious linkage goal of getting the Cubans out of Angola fit into South African war goals? In the American political context the Cuban issue ranked close to top priority. But for South Africa, its significance was indirect and even contradictory. On the one hand, if a Cuban withdrawal from Angola preceded implementation of an independence settlement in Namibia, SWAPO would be weakened both symbolically and materially. The South African government could claim a victory for political benefit with the white electorate, and the potential conventional military challenge in the subcontinent could be discounted. If SWAPO still seemed too formidable an electoral opponent, once the Cubans had crossed the Atlantic, Pretoria could, if necessary, resume stalling on elections. If the war continued, new attacks on Angola would be undeterred by the Cuban protective shield.

Even had Angola been so trusting as to offer such a deal, however, it would have been most attractive only if South African officials were confident of engineering an election victory against SWAPO. Neither

Angolan trust in South Africa, nor good election prospects for SWAPO's opponents, were very likely. Thus, as frequently noted by critics, linkage conveniently served Pretoria's interest in buying time. Keeping the Cubans in Angola consolidated Pretoria's position in Washington by maintaining a common enemy. This provided a justification for Washington to share intelligence data with Pretoria, as well as for opposing sanctions against a military ally.

A Cuban withdrawal that would follow Namibian elections and independence, which Angola and Cuba were ready to consider, was even less attractive to South Africa. It would have little point as long as South Africa refused to abandon or adjust its primary goal of blocking SWAPO. With Namibia independent, South Africa would have little leverage to insist that Angola and Cuba stick to the agreement. South Africa accordingly showed little interest in the joint Angolan-Cuban proposals of 1982 and 1984, which offered gradual Cuban troop withdrawals after the military threat to Angola from Namibia was removed.

Thus the carrot offered by US Assistant Secretary of State Chester Crocker to South Africa for a settlement in Namibia was both unavailable and only mildly attractive. It only became attractive, on terms close to the Angolan–Cuban proposals of 1982 and 1984, once the costs of war became disproportionate and the risks of a SWAPO victory grew less threatening.[27]

Over the twelve years of war (1976–88), there were some constant features. SWAPO kept a low-level guerrilla campaign going in northern Namibia. South African repression inside Namibia and raids into Angola, imposing heavy costs on SWAPO and its supporters, were also continuous. Unita's guerrilla war, benefiting after 1979 from its protected base area in Cuando Cubango, varied in intensity and geographical scope, but was relatively consistent in character: ambushes, laying of mines, and attacks on isolated villages, outposts, and occasionally larger urban centres. South Africa kept the conflict primarily on Angolan soil – a telling indicator of the overall military balance. SWAPO's guerrillas were on their own once they crossed the border. Unita could count on direct South African support and on flanking attacks to distract Angola's defenders.

The cycles of conventional combat, however, showed significant variation. After the limited raids of the 1970s, South Africa was drawn into occupation of south-western Angola and then into defending Unita. Confronted with higher risks and costs, Pretoria had to consider compromises.

During the late 1970s, fighting in both Namibia and Angola was at relatively low levels. During this period intensive Western diplomacy produced agreement on a Namibia independence plan. But South Africa had little incentive to implement it. Western countries threatened sanctions to keep South Africa talking, but refused to use the threat to induce compliance. The process of building up the Democratic Turnhalle Alliance as an alternative to SWAPO was in its infancy. Inside South Africa, the regime had weathered the Soweto uprising, and the threat from the ANC had yet to materialize. The cost of buying time still seemed minimal.

In the period 1980–84, South Africa both occupied Cunene province in south-western Angola and stepped up support to Unita. This caused significant difficulties for SWAPO guerrillas, as well as inflicting damage on Angola. But SWAPO continued and modestly escalated guerrilla actions. By late 1983, there were signs that South Africa was overextending its military reach. Operation Askari met with unexpectedly strong resistance and failed to break the Angolan lines in northern Cunene province. Stepped-up Angolan counterinsurgency efforts imposed significant setbacks on Unita. In August the SADF had to come to Unita's aid at Cangamba in Moxico province.

The 1984 Lusaka agreement was a pause for regrouping, not a piece of a settlement. It resulted in an eighteen-month ceasefire between South African and Angolan forces in south-western Angola, a repeatedly delayed South African withdrawal from that area, and restrictions by Angola on movement of SWAPO guerrillas through the reoccupied zone. But it also marked a shift in the geography and the objectives of South African conventional warfare in Angola. Offensive thrusts in Angola were no longer on the agenda. Routine cross-border raids into Cunene resumed in 1985, but the major South African operations from 1985 on all aimed at rescuing Unita.

From the perspective of South Africa's strategic interests, this became a case of the tail wagging the dog. There were hard-liners who wanted a commitment to put Savimbi in power, and if the goal had been easier the more cautious would also have applauded. But it was Savimbi and his ideological backers in Washington who had that objective at the top of their lists. Pretoria, instead, measured involvement in Angola against the goals of control in Namibia and stability in South Africa, and against the costs in money, matériel and lives of white conscripts.

Supporting Unita's guerrilla campaign had the advantages of winning points with Washington, of harassing SWAPO and the ANC as well as Angola, and of being largely deniable. Victories were a bonus and setbacks did not reflect on the SADF or cause political problems with the white electorate. It cost money but was fairly cost-effective. Much of the weaponry could be supplied from matériel captured in southwestern Angola. But the large-scale Angolan offensives against Unita-controlled areas in 1985 and 1987 drew the South African military into an area of greater risk. The conventional battles in 1987–88 then raised the price to a new order of magnitude.

Citing high Angolan casualties, compared with fairly light SADF losses, South African military accounts reject the claim that they were defeated. They say that political considerations blocked the military efforts needed to wipe out the Angolan–Cuban force which held on at Cuito Cuanavale.[28] There is no reason to doubt their contention that Angolan forces, overextended beyond the Lomba River, were forced to retreat by SADF firepower, and that South Africa was not driven back by force. It might even be that without non-battlefield constraints, the SADF could have thrown enough into the conflict to take Cuito Cuanavale. But the 'political' constraints stressed by South African sources were in fact part of the overall military balance.

South Africa did suffer a serious military setback, if not a battlefield 'defeat'. The cost of escalation grew significantly; South African weaknesses stood exposed. The imperative to avoid casualties among white conscripts restricted the number of troops available for Angola. Conscript units had to be rotated out and replaced with fresh troops. The white electorate was increasingly wary of sacrifices in distant Angola. South African goals included building up Unita's credibility, and avoiding too much embarrassment to the US which also wanted to downplay the South African military role. New conventional troop commitments would have carried a political price.

South Africa also had lost its previous air superiority, increasing risks to equipment that sanctions made difficult and costly to replace. Even the renowned G-5 artillery was short on replacement capacity; over half the units at Cuito Cuanavale were inoperational by the end of 1987. This new balance was even more decisive in the south-west. Once Cuban forces moved south to the border in early 1988, most of north-western Namibia was vulnerable to Angolan and Cuban air power. South African forces suffered twelve losses in a confrontation with Cuban troops near the border, at Calueque, in late June. South Africa faced fighting the next round with territory under its control open to enemy air power, and with the reach of its own air force more restricted than ever.

Shifts on the South African side were of course not the only factors leading to the late 1988 agreements on Namibian independence and Cuban withdrawal. It is a truism that successful negotiated settlements must allow all sides some possibility to claim victory. Other parties too were willing to make concessions. Angolan troops and indeed Angolans at all levels were profoundly war-weary. Despite Cuba's willingness to send reinforcements, Havana was also anxious to reduce its commitments, and had long been sceptical of the prospect of a decisive military conclusion. The Soviet Union, essential for sustaining Angola's conventional war capacity, had already turned to a posture of settling 'regional conflicts' by compromise.[29]

Nonetheless, it was only South Africa that made a fundamental change: accepting the prospect of a SWAPO-led government in an independent Namibia. The reasons lay not only in the military context outlined above, but also in other changes which raised the costs of 'buying more time' and lowered the potential threat from a SWAPO-ruled Namibia.

Inside Namibia in 1988, Pretoria's clients were losing more political ground than ever. Unprecedented general strikes by pro-SWAPO students and labour unions won wide support. The SWATF, envisaged as the security core of an independent Namibia aligned with South Africa, was open to doubt after mutinies in the fighting in Angola. SWAPO had made inroads in dialogue with moderate white Namibians. The cost in aggravation of further delays was going up, and new stratagems for boosting the anti-SWAPO forces were in short supply. The largest worker stay-away in Namibian history came only a week before the key negotiating session in Cairo in late June 1988, which also coincided with the Cuban–South African confrontation at Calueque.

The incentive to compromise in Namibia was enhanced by Pretoria's need to focus on the home front. The contrast with 1984 was dramatic: the United Democratic Front (UDF) and the Congress of South African Trade Unions (COSATU) had emerged as potent internal opposition forces, tacitly allied with the ANC. While township unrest had been largely quelled, this had required a state of emergency and troops permanently stationed in many townships. Sanctions imposed in 1985–86 were beginning to bite; about $1 billion in debt was due in 1988 alone. Many South African leaders were beginning to see the need to concede negotiations with the ANC and try to preserve white power through more subtle manoeuvring. Significantly, the National Party began quiet exploratory talks with the ANC in 1986. A cabinet-appointed committee was entrusted with meeting Mandela in May 1988, just as key decisions were approaching on Namibia.[30]

In this context it became attractive to try out a similar strategy first in Namibia. Polls in mid-1988 showed that 57 per cent of white South Africans believed Botha should negotiate directly with SWAPO, up from 52 per cent in 1986 and 33 per cent in 1982. And 75 per cent opposed increased military spending.[31] The odds of defeating SWAPO in the election were not good, but there was a very good chance that the infant Namibian government would be weak enough to pose little threat. Pretoria was confident that intimidation, covert subsidies to anti-SWAPO parties, disinformation and public relations could keep SWAPO's vote under the two-thirds needed to control drafting of the constitution. With *de facto* control during the election, and reduction of the UN monitoring force to a minimal role, South African planners expected only limited interference with such efforts.

Shifts in Soviet thinking also lessened the potential risk. As confirmed in January 1989 when Washington and Moscow jointly opposed funding for a larger UN force in Namibia, the Soviet Union was disinclined to take a hard line in support of SWAPO. Neither did the Soviets express any interest in providing military aid to a future SWAPO-ruled Namibia.

The risks of a settlement as opposed to the risks of buying more time through military action thus had significantly decreased. The carrots offered through the settlement were also more attractive than before, although total Cuban troop withdrawal was not to take place until more than a year after the independence of Namibia. Withdrawal of Cuban forces from southern Angola, offered as the first step, was urgent now that they were close enough to pose a military threat to northern Namibia. Removal of ANC training camps from Angola was another attractive carrot.

South Africa implemented the major provisions of the 1988 agreement, withdrawing troops from Angola and Namibia and proceeding with Namibian independence. South African officials correctly calculated that they could get away with continued military support for Unita by air.[32] Despite Angolan charges, neither the US nor the disintegrating Soviet Union was interested in making a point of these South African violations of the agreement.

The primary focus of the war in Angola reverted to the north. As noted in earlier chapters, the opposition of Zaire's President Mobutu to the MPLA was one of the factors precipitating the Angolan conflict in 1974-76. Even after the agreements between Mobutu and Neto in 1978, Kinshasa was a frequent stop for Savimbi. Without South African and US involvement, however, the low-level hostility from Zaire would have been only a minor threat to Luanda.

Zaire stood to gain from an end to Unita attacks on the Benguela railway, the cheapest route to the sea for the minerals of Shaba province. South Africa, however, and local Zairian traders with South African connections, gained from the dependence of Shaba on the alternate rail link south to South Africa. Angolan efforts to woo Mobutu with prospects of reopening the Benguela route and of better commercial relations never provided sufficient incentive for Mobutu to curb Unita. Particularly during the decisive phase of Zairian involvement, the interests driving Mobutu's hostility to Angola were not primarily bilateral or regional at all. With the official approval of renewed CIA assistance to Unita at the end of 1985, Kinshasa's Angola policy was even more than before based on pleasing Washington by providing the essential staging base for US military aid.

Luanda's diplomatic strategy of 1989, aimed at achieving a settlement by dealing with Mobutu, might have had some chance of success if the issues had been confined to the African and internal Angolan arenas.

But while the key actor for the Namibian settlement was South Africa, Zaire's involvement in the war could only be discussed seriously in Washington. The party to the 1988 agreements that did not make significant concessions, refusing to accept any limitation of aid to Unita, was the US. Nor was Soviet military aid to the Angolan government addressed in the agreement. The next phase of the Angolan war was played out primarily in the shadow of the Cold War, rather than as part of regional conflict within southern Africa.

Continuity and change on the eastern front: Mozambique

The operative goal of Renamo's primary patrons was never, as far as can be determined, to put it in power in Mozambique. This applies most clearly before Nkomati, but also to the subsequent period. Renamo was designed as an instrument of destruction with limited aims. But the logic of the propaganda supporting it implied more, and those involved in the operation gained wider ambitions as the war continued. Even after peace talks began in 1990, there remained fundamental uncertainties about the goals of Renamo and its largely anonymous outside backers. The roots of these ambiguities lay not only in Renamo, but also in links between South Africa's involvement in Mozambique and the struggle over the future of its own society.

Before Nkomati, the picture was relatively clear. Rhodesia used Renamo simply to punish Mozambique for supporting Zimbabwean guerrillas. Renamo leaders had little scope for independent activity. The same applied after the transition to South African control. Support for Renamo was subordinated to the 'total strategy' of defending the white regime's security. The immediate objective, according to a 1983 memorandum, was to cause the maximum destruction possible.[33] The medium-term objective was to force the Mozambican government to adopt a more favourable attitude to South Africa. Overthrowing the Mozambican government was a remote, long-term objective, unaccompanied by plans to make Renamo a viable political option.

Pretoria's objectives included forcing Mozambique to abandon any kind of support for the ANC and to block use of its territory by ANC guerrillas in transit. Other goals were damaging the ideological appeal of Mozambique, and keeping inland Frontline States dependent on South Africa through destruction of transport alternatives. For the military campaign, it was not necessary to choose among these objectives. Operationally, the task could be simply defined as causing maximum damage while obscuring the South African role. That would ensure both that Mozambique was weakened and that the Mozambican government took the blame.

When forced to decide more specific objectives in the negotiations leading up to Nkomati, Pretoria settled on paper for the limited terms offered by Mozambique. Then came the issue of how seriously to implement the agreement. In this case, there was a *de facto* decision not to decide. Those still committed to punishing Mozambique or hoping to push Renamo into power continued to support Renamo. Those who claimed to support the agreement and to aim at building peaceful economic influence in Mozambique either regarded the remaining military operations as useful leverage with Maputo, or simply did not give priority to stopping them.

The Nkomati Accord achieved the South African objective of blocking ANC military use of Mozambican territory. But Mozambique did not accept Pretoria's demand to abandon political support of the ANC. Botha's symbolic victory did not provide lasting satisfaction. Despite its weakness, Mozambique still participated actively in the Frontline States and in SADCC. The ANC's guerrilla campaign continued, with infiltration principally through Botswana and Swaziland.

Mozambique could not escape the impact of South Africa's unresolved internal crisis. But it was not central enough for Pretoria to ensure much interest in stopping the war. What new incentives Mozambique could offer – opportunities for investment, amnesty and jobs for Renamo leaders, helping out in negotiations on Angola – were of only marginal interest to South African policy-makers. Those supporting Renamo had little reason to abandon the operation.

For those with hard-line ideological views, it was still a way to hammer the communists. For some, profits in ivory smuggling and similar activities provided added incentives. The apparatus set in motion to support Renamo was not dismantled. It is likely that even the so-called doves in the South African state agreed with this as at least a contingency measure. The operation continued without being harnessed to any clear objective.

In 1984 the South African Foreign Ministry brokered talks which might have led to an agreement between Renamo and the Mozambican government. Emboldened by Nkomati, Renamo's leadership evidently saw the possibility of gaining some share of power, while Pik Botha sought to enhance his role as regional power-broker. But the deal offered was limited to amnesty, and Renamo refused to proceed. At the time there was speculation that Renamo's recalcitrance was fuelled by right-wing Portuguese supporters, indicating new Renamo independence of the South African state. Documents captured at Gorongosa the next year, however, showed that Renamo's South African military patrons also regarded the negotiations as presaging a sell-out.

The evidence, including military pledges of undying support for Renamo and the revelation that they had bugged the 1984 talks, showed that there were different perspectives on Renamo within the South African state. While Renamo may have gained new ambitions, as well as other backers, its principal patron – the South African military – remained actively engaged. Despite their embarrassment at the revelations, Pretoria's so-called doves repeatedly dismissed new evidence of ongoing military involvement. If they were not involved with the military in continuing to promote Renamo, they were also not interested in taking an active role to stop it.

How does one interpret South Africa's goals in this confusing period after 1985? One option is to deny continued South African state involvement, accepting the official line that any assistance to Renamo from South Africa was strictly private, on a small scale, and overwhelmingly outweighed by Renamo's internal momentum and new outside contacts. This is not empirically plausible.[34] Another option is to see the division between 'doves' and 'hawks' as purely artificial, an elaborately orchestrated game of 'good cop/bad cop'. This too is unlikely, given the evidence of real differences of opinion at top levels in Pretoria.

More plausible is a complex scenario, involving both divisions among policy-makers and the predominance in practice of the hard-line Renamo backers. After Nkomati, Mozambique became a much less central concern for the South African state. The most important objective – restricting the ANC's access through Maputo – had been achieved. The hot arenas were conflict inside South Africa and the military contest in Angola. Mozambique had no real option of abandoning the Nkomati Accord, nor were Western countries willing to do more than deplore South Africa's violations. Even if they thought Nkomati should be observed faithfully, there was little reason for P.W. Botha, Pik Botha or even de Klerk to pursue peace in Mozambique with any seriousness.

This left Renamo's backers a relatively free hand, armed at least with the official mandate of 'keeping in contact' in order to facilitate future negotiations. Even before Nkomati, the financial scale of the Renamo operation was modest. Although evidence may yet turn up that there was still a separate 'Renamo support' line in the covert budget after 1985, more likely it was moved 'off budget', blurring its official status. Aid coming by land or air directly from South Africa for Renamo units in southern Mozambique, which continued into 1992, most obviously required some official complicity in South Africa.[35] But the sea deliveries along Mozambique's coast are hard to trace to their origin. South Africa's links with aid through Malawi are also still obscure.[36]

The hostility to Frelimo of Malawi President Banda was longstanding. He harboured the dream of an expanded Malawi, taking in most of northern Mozambique. He maintained close relationships with the Portuguese colonial regime, and worked with it in fostering a dissident movement which tried to counter Frelimo with a project of Rombézia (a separate Mozambique from the Rovuma to the Zambezi). Elements of this group carried out small-scale attacks along the border in the late 1970s and early 1980s, independently of Renamo. África Livre, as it was called, was largely destroyed by the Mozambican army, but remnants joined up with Renamo in 1982.

Mozambican leaders tried repeatedly to reach a *détente* with Malawi to block or limit support for Renamo's operations. They argued that Malawi's national interest dictated peace in Mozambique, so that the natural transport routes to Nacala and Beira could serve Malawi. These arguments had weight with some Malawi officials, but the security pacts, in September 1984 and December 1986, were never effective in blocking Renamo's access through Malawi.

In 1986 Mozambique, along with Zimbabwe and Zambia, threatened to cut off Malawi's links to South Africa unless Banda changed his stance. There ensued a massive invasion of Renamo forces from Malawi, aimed at cutting Mozambique in two. This was defeated with the aid of Zimbabwean and Tanzanian troops. In subsequent years Malawi downplayed its support for Renamo, and even sent troops to help defend the Nacala rail line. But the land and air supply routes for arms through Malawi never closed down.

Geographically, this connection was vital, since it supplied the Gorongosa headquarters as well as the northern battle zones. From 1988, it was the channel for links to the Kenyan government, which while ostensibly a mediator began providing arms and military training for Renamo. The significance of the Malawi and Kenya connections, however, depends on whether they were independent rivals to the South African operation, or whether they were part of it.

The most likely hypothesis is that, despite their own independent motives, those in Malawi and Kenya who worked with Renamo did so with the encouragement and help of the South African network. In any case, there is evidence of active South African involvement via Malawi in the period 1982–84 and in the 1986 Renamo offensive in Zambézia. The evidence subsequent to 1986 is more sketchy. Renamo's commercial links with Malawi for sale of loot, and support from right-wing missionaries and others through Malawi, became increasingly important. Ivory sales probably provided access to commercial networks for arms supplies, and this is reputed to be particularly important in facilitating the Kenyan connection.

It is questionable whether ivory sales alone could be sufficient to maintain arms supply levels. But regardless of their quantitative contribution, the ivory networks were linked with the South African operations. SADF personnel and front companies were intimately involved in extracting ivory from Renamo areas throughout the 1980s, the secrecy of covert operations serving as a conducive environment for commercial motives as well.

With South Africa's moves towards greater deniability after Nkomati, the scope for both ideological and commercial entrepreneurship in the Renamo operation was enlarged. Continuity in Renamo's operations, nevertheless, indicates that both the private networks and the connections in Malawi and Kenya built on and intertwined with the ongoing South African operation. Whatever portion of this involvement was privatized, the top levels of the South African government at least tolerated continued support for the war in Mozambique. President Botha renewed a verbal commitment to peace at a meeting with President Chissano in September 1988. Hopes rose further after de Klerk took office in 1989. But Pretoria's rulers never made a serious effort to investigate or restrict Renamo's network of contacts in the South African military and private sector.

As indirect talks between Renamo and the Mozambican government in 1989 were followed by direct negotiations the following year, the timing roughly paralleled the dramatic internal developments in South Africa. The stance on Renamo of South Africa's 'reformers' paralleled their ambivalence on state-sponsored violence in South Africa itself. While disassociating themselves from overt violence, they fostered its continuation by their casual dismissals of security force involvement and by supportive attitudes towards the perpetrators. Whether or not they were actively involved, the signals they gave to the networks of covert action were bright green.

Illustrative of the attitude was a May 1991 visit by a South African Broadcasting Corporation film crew to Renamo territory. The team, including a nephew of President de Klerk as cameraman, not only produced a pro-Renamo propaganda piece, but also flew in uniforms, navigation equipment, AK-47s and other military equipment. The trip was reportedly financed by South Africa's Electricity Supply Commission (ESCOM), and the contribution to Renamo explained as a pay-off to the insurgents for not attacking the Cabora Bassa power lines in Mozambique. But those involved in organizing the mission were all avowed partisans of Renamo.[37]

In comparison with unpublicized links, this mission's quantitative contribution to Renamo's military capacity was probably limited. But it is a telling indicator of the South African stance. The sectors identified as 'doves' on Mozambique openly supplied military equipment to Renamo. Military intelligence and special forces networks could only conclude that sustaining Renamo was still part of their legitimate agenda. The parallel to events inside South Africa was not accidental, since it raised the same issue: how to deal with the South African state's covert involvement in violence. As long as it was unresolved inside South

Africa, it was unlikely to be resolved in the peripheral context of Mozambique.

Summing up the South African intervention

The wars in Angola and Mozambique followed parallel courses in the years of escalation. Limited South African and Rhodesian cross-border raids in the 1970s turned to massive sponsorship of Unita and Renamo in the first half of the 1980s. An apparent turn to *détente* in 1984 soon gave way to escalated conflict. Despite the prominence of South Africa's conventional military involvement in Angola, contrasted with its denial of ongoing ties with Renamo, the trends in both conflicts from 1985 to 1987 reflected the intensified conflict within South Africa itself.

The contrast between the two fronts revealed itself sharply, however, as negotiations took centre stage in 1988. For South Africa, Angola was a conflict at a distance, related to the potentially isolated issue of Namibia and to manoeuvring within the global Cold War arena. Involving far more substantial investment in military matériel than in Mozambique, it nevertheless could more easily be separated from the question of power in South Africa itself. Mozambique, by virtue of its intimate geographic, economic and human integration into the South African sphere of influence, found that ending its war was inextricably caught up in the struggle for South Africa's own soul. After Namibia's independence, South Africa was less central to the issues and the actors in Angola. But the forces involved in the clandestine violence in South Africa were closely interlocked with those in the Mozambican conflict, by both ideological and economic ties. In one country as in the other, it was not just a question of negotiating, but of identifying the shadowy forces with interests in perpetuating the violence. As of early 1994, it seemed likely that Mozambique's prospects for transition to a stable peace would closely parallel those in South Africa itself.

The outcome of South Africa's military involvement in Angola and Mozambique was indecisive. The forces that Pretoria sought to destroy – SWAPO in Namibia and the ANC in South Africa – emerged as the premier political organizations of the majority in each country. Both were forced to compromise with the white power structure in the stage of political transition and in post-transition economic policies. Defenders of South African policy may say that the aggressive total strategy was necessary in order to enforce such compromises, by weakening the liberation movements' military capacity and chastening their radical ambitions. But that is to neglect the historical alternatives: had Pretoria been willing to offer Namibian independence and negotiations with the ANC at the beginning of the 1980s, SWAPO and the ANC would also have had strong incentives to compromise at that time. The violence of the 1980s was a result above all of the South African regime's unwillingness to consider in 1980 what it reluctantly accepted in 1990.

For Angola and Mozambique as well, the outcomes of war were still indecisive at the beginning of the 1990s. What new order would emerge was as yet unpredictable. The ruling parties had abandoned socialist aspirations and had enshrined multi-party political systems in new constitutions; but Pretoria's clients had not yet made the transition to a new order of peace. Only the destruction wrought in the 1980s was clearly visible. South Africa had not installed new regimes, or a new regional order. But it had battered mercilessly the physical and social fabric of the two countries. Given their relative economic backwardness, it is unlikely that Angola and Mozambique would have served as models for a new South Africa in any case. The toll of war clinched the argument – a victory, albeit a negative one, for the 'total warriors'.

Notes

1. *The Christian Science Monitor*, 7 March 1984.
2. Geldenhuys (1984), 41.
3. Geldenhuys (1984), 75–82.
4. See sources cited in Chapter 4, note 19, as well as Stockwell (1978).
5. Martin and Johnson (1981), 241.
6. Steenkamp (1989), 80.
7. Jaster (1985), 21.
8. On the ANC guerrilla campaign, see particularly Barrell (1990).
9. The Lusaka Manifesto is reprinted in Jaster et al. (1992), 141–8.
10. Despite many overview accounts of South African foreign policy, this level of detail is only hinted at to date, even in Chester Crocker's (1992) insider account of diplomatic dealings. For general sources see Chapter 2, note 2.
11. For an account of the nuclear programme, see Walters (1987). In 1993 South Africa formally acknowledged its nuclear efforts, while announcing their abandonment (*New York Times*, 25 March 1993; *Washington Post*, 12 May 1993).
12. On the recruitment of blacks into the military see particularly Grundy (1983).
13. Clayton (1976), 54.
14. Beckett and Pimlott (1985), 175.
15. See Wheeler (1976); Estado Maior do Exército (1988): I, 261.
16. Kitson (1977), 47.
17. See Cilliers (1985), 118–34 on pseudo operations.
18. Breytenbach (1990), 12.
19. Breytenbach (1990), 72.
20. Interview, 12 November 1988.
21. A summary version of Ndimene's story was serialized in *Mediafax* (Maputo), 26 January – 1 February 1993.
22. Sitte (1981, 151) says Savimbi told it to him in 1971; Bridgland (1987, 142) in a 1975 interview.

23. See the discussion in Chapter 3.

24. On ivory see particularly Environmental Investigation Agency (1992).

25. In mid-1983, hawks in the SSC reportedly argued for another advance on Luanda, to install Savimbi in power. But army chief General Geldenhuys argued successfully that the plan was unrealistic, and the Soviet Union issued an unprecedented direct warning to Pretoria that such a move would be countered with escalation. Moorcraft (1990), 193.

26. Jaster (1989), 104-5.

27. Crocker's own account is available in Crocker (1992); US policy is discussed more fully in Chapter 6.

28. See Heitman (1990), Bridgland (1990); Breytenbach (1990), as well my review essay on the three in Minter, 'Glimpses of the War in Angola' (1992).

29. See McFaul (1990), Clough (1992, Chapter 2) and references cited there.

30. Africa Confidential, 20 March 1992.

31. Southscan, 12 August 1988.

32. South African supplies, while less than before 1988, were significant both in the fighting in 1989–90 before the 1991 ceasefire, and in the resurgence of fighting in 1992–93. They included both air shipments direct from South Africa, overflying Namibia or Botswana, and flights to Unita bases in Zaire.

33. Notícias (Maputo), 21 March 1992, citing an interview with Roland Hunter, a South African draftee who worked in the operation before being arrested for passing on information to the ANC.

34. See the discussions of this point in Chapters 3 and 7.

35. See Chapter 7.

36. On the Malawi connection see Hedges (1989), Vines (1991) and Austin (1993).

37. Weekly Mail, 10–16 May 1991.

6

The Cold War Connection:
Crusaders and Conflict
Managers

In September 1985, President Machel of Mozambique was warmly received at the White House by President Reagan in what official releases termed 'a very positive atmosphere'. A Renamo delegation that had attended the World Anti-Communist League conference in Dallas the week before denounced the visit. Right-wing members of Congress attacked the Reagan administration for 'wooing Marxists' and introduced a bill calling for military assistance to Renamo. But the legislation languished without administration support. Renamo stayed off the list of officially approved anti-communist 'freedom fighters'.[1]

On the same day that Machel met Reagan, Unita signed its first contract with the public relations firm of Black, Manafort, Stone and Kelly, paying $600,000 for 'the development and implementation of a strategy to aid in getting US assistance'. The way had been paved for official US assistance by repeal, in July, of the Clark Amendment barring such aid. Christopher Lehman, a National Security Council official and brother of the Navy Secretary, left his White House post to handle the Unita account for Black, Manafort. At the recommendation of CIA Director William Casey, President Reagan approved an initial $13 million aid commitment in November.[2]

These developments in the autumn of 1985 reflect contrasting US relationships to Angola and Mozambique. While both countries were caught up in Washington's late Cold War campaign against Marxist regimes in the Third World, US involvement in Angola was high-profile and in large part official – part of mainstream Washington's consensus. Savimbi was repeatedly welcomed as a guest – no Angolan president was received in Washington until 1992. While Renamo enjoyed some high-level support, for the most part its backers operated in the shadows. By the late 1980s the Mozambican government – not Renamo – was one of the top African recipients of official US aid.

Despite the contrast, there were common elements. As the wars in the two countries escalated in the 1980s, US policy signals most frequently blinked green for war on Angola, and yellow for caution in the case of Mozambique. But there was never a clear red for stop directed at South Africa's war machine. Nor, despite condemnation of Renamo atrocities, were Renamo's supporters at home or abroad ever identified as sponsors of terrorism comparable to those denounced by Washington in other contexts. Although the US anti-apartheid movement forced a reluctant administration to impose sanctions against South Africa on the basis of its domestic repression, the connection to South Africa's regional wars hardly entered the public debate. Although Machel brought dramatic proof to Washington of South African violations of the Nkomati Accord, neither the administration nor Congress followed with significant pressure on Pretoria. Most members of Congress remained oblivious to the end of the irony in imposing sanctions on South Africa while simultaneously joining it on the battlefield in Angola.

The bottom line was that the Reagan and Bush administrations, by their tilt towards South Africa and by the priority given to Cold War concerns, reinforced the onslaught against both Angola and Mozambique. But the different historical contexts of the two countries, combined with the outcome of internal political battles in Washington, made for strikingly greater US involvement in Angola and for different official policies towards the two conflicts. The patterns of the 1980s, moreover, were prefigured long before Reagan's rise to power.

Cold War and national liberation

From 1961 to 1974, as Angolan and Mozambican liberation movements waged war for independence, US policy exhibited its characteristic ambivalence on colonial issues. Generalized pronouncements supporting self-determination were tempered by concerns to maintain good relations with a European ally and to ensure that independence offered no new opportunities for Moscow. Despite initial African hopes that President Kennedy would bring a different vision, Washington focused almost exclusively on fighting the presumed communist threat, above all in the Congo. Portuguese colonialism – and its allies in white Rhodesia and South Africa – were seen as threats only in so far as they might provoke revolutionary radicalization. If that threat were postponed by successful repression, then Washington had no urgent reason to be concerned.

The outbreak of guerrilla war in Angola in 1961 posed an unexpected crisis for the new Kennedy administration. Liberals within the administration won unprecedented public condemnation of Portuguese colonialism in a United Nations vote in March. The US imposed an embargo on arms aid for Portugal's African war. But there was no

serious effort to make the restriction effective, and a policy review in
June 1961 opted for a 'quiet' approach towards criticism of Portugal.
Thereafter the need to cooperate with Portugal for access to the Azores
air and naval bases, along with the established priority given to European ties, consistently overshadowed the occasional calls for Portuguese
reform coming from the State Department's Africa Bureau. Portugal
continued to use US weaponry in the wars in Angola and, later, Guinea-
Bissau and Mozambique.[3]

Thus it was only a limited change when the Nixon administration
opted for relaxation of pressures on the white regimes, including Portugal. Approving recommendations by Henry Kissinger in January 1970,
Nixon decided to 'quietly relax the embargo through liberal treatment
of dual purpose items' having both civilian and military uses. Until the
Portuguese coup caught Washington by surprise, the operative assumption was that Portuguese colonialism, like the other white regimes in
southern Africa, was 'here to stay'.[4]

This stance applied to both Angola and Mozambique. But differences
emerged in the contacts, initiated under Kennedy, with African nationalists of the two countries. In 1961 the CIA began covert funding of
Holden Roberto. The US also offered scholarships to exiled Angolans
and Mozambicans, and Attorney General Robert Kennedy met with
future Frelimo President Eduardo Mondlane on an early 1962 visit to
Washington. Such links, especially with Roberto, enraged the Portuguese. In late 1962 Secretary of State Dean Rusk ordered State Department officials to cease any open contacts. Nevertheless, low-key support
for Roberto continued as a contingency measure for the future and to
bolster him against the MPLA.

Frelimo under Mondlane was rebuffed in efforts to win official US
support. Most significant aid for the Mozambican struggle came from
African countries, the Soviet Union, China, and the Nordic countries.
But benefiting from Mondlane's contacts, Frelimo also gained support
from church and other US groups, which survived even after Mondlane's assassination in 1969. Thus independent Mozambique, despite
tensions with Washington, had a sense of access to US society.

US support for Roberto, however, immediately linked Cold War
tensions with the internal divisions among Angolans. Although MPLA
President Agostinho Neto also had US connections (he was the son of
a Methodist pastor, and had served as secretary to an American Methodist bishop), the MPLA had close political ties with the Portuguese
Communist Party. They felt, not without justification, that the US was
unrelentingly bent on their destruction.

Given this history, it was predictable that after independence Frelimo
and the MPLA would see the Soviet Union and others that had supported them against the Portuguese as 'natural allies', and suspect the

US, which had opted to stick with the Portuguese enemy. But neither had any intention of attacking specific US interests, which were minimal in Mozambique in any case and largely concentrated in the Cabinda oil investments of Gulf Oil in Angola. In 1974, diplomatic professionals such as Assistant Secretary of State for Africa Donald Easum and US Consul-General Tom Killoran in Luanda, as well as the management of Gulf Oil Corporation, were convinced that the US should seek pragmatic relationships with the new governments and not favour one movement over another in Angola. Killoran had reported that the MPLA was the best organized, most competent and most accessible of the three, and Gulf Oil officials shared the assessment.[5]

The primary motives for active US intervention against the MPLA in 1974–75 were not based on Angolan or African realities at all. The Angolan crisis came when US Cold Warriors were feeling particularly vulnerable. The US client state in South Vietnam faced its final collapse. The Watergate scandal in Washington was unseating a president and reinforcing doubts about the reliability of US power. Popular revolution and a Communist Party strongly linked to Moscow posed a threat in Portugal itself, a NATO country. For Henry Kissinger, global considerations were paramount. Washington might have to retreat from Indochina, but closer to home, it had to show the Soviet Union it could still defend its turf. Hard-line tactics had succeeded in overthrowing President Salvador Allende of Chile in 1973, and might work in Angola as well.

The plot failed, despite and in part because of US encouragement of active South African intervention. The level of Soviet and Cuban willingness to support the MPLA was unexpectedly high, forcing the CIA to escalate in turn or to back down. Diplomatic and congressional support for the US and its Angolan clients unravelled as South Africa's involvement was revealed. The US public recoiled at the prospect of another foreign adventure just as the Vietnam nightmare was ending. The result in terms of Washington politics: an embarrassing failure which made Angola a symbol of Cold War retreat, sparked recriminations on the right, and gave birth to an Angola syndrome of unrelenting Washington resentment towards the victorious MPLA.

Although it is difficult to isolate its impact, this revenge factor is fundamental to understanding US policy towards Angola over the next fifteen years. Its potency was enhanced by the linkage to Cuba, resented by Washington because of Castro's defiance of superpower authority since 1960. The parallels between the Angolan fiasco and the abortive Bay of Pigs invasion were keenly felt by the intelligence community and by influential Cuban-American exiles. More broadly, 'Angola' was a symbol of US humiliation and Soviet threat for many Washington politicians who would have had difficulty finding it on a world map.

In late 1976, as the Carter administration took over from the Republicans, the relative consensus on US foreign policy had collapsed in the wake of the Vietnam conflict. Broadly, three alternative views entered the public debate, and to varying degrees influenced administration policy: a liberal accommodationist perspective; the emphasis on *Realpolitik* personified within the administration by National Security Adviser Brzezinski; and the 'roll-back' perspective of the incipient far right who regarded liberals and even *Realpolitik* practitioners as traitorously 'soft'.

For the first group, the Vietnam syndrome counselled caution against any overseas commitment which might involve US troops in combat, and was often linked with optimism that the US could safely accommodate Third World radicalism. The second group, whether in its out-of-office Kissingerian variant or in the person of Brzezinski, stressed instead classic Cold War geopolitics: bilateral competition with the Soviet Union, including the manipulation of the China card as anti-Soviet leverage. The third group, preparing its case for US global resurgence in a host of right-wing think-tanks, action committees, and publications, hoped and planned for global counter-revolution.[6] This far-right coalition took up Unita and Renamo as promising outlets for their roll-back campaign, which found its presidential candidate in Ronald Reagan.

Carter administration State Department officials generally adopted an open stance towards Mozambique and a conciliatory posture towards Angola. The administration took a relatively activist role in pressing negotiations on Zimbabwe and Namibia, and even approved a mandatory UN arms embargo against South Africa in late 1977. But by early 1978 this new thrust was overshadowed by traditional US reluctance to confront South Africa and resurgent Cold War.

When South African commandos killed more than 600 Namibians in a raid in Angola in May 1978, at the same time as rebels in Zaire's Shaba province were rising up against the Mobutu regime, the US focused on defending Mobutu and mistakenly charged Cuba with involvement in Shaba. While Washington subsequently helped broker the *détente* between Mobutu and Angola, the option of recognizing Angola was pushed aside. Instead, Brzezinski lobbied for repeal of the Clark Amendment, and encouraged China, Morocco and Saudi Arabia to provide stepped-up military assistance to Unita. Secretary of State Vance argued that the way to get the Cubans out of Angola was to get South Africa out of Namibia. But his view was never accepted by the President.[7]

Although Mozambique attracted less overt hostility and President Machel met with President Carter at the United Nations in 1978, Mozambique also came under political attack during the Carter years. A strong right-wing coalition in Congress in 1977 imposed a ban on bilateral aid to Mozambique. As Rhodesian planes raided Mozambique, administration liberals barely blocked congressional pressure to recognize the white-backed Muzorewa regime in Rhodesia. Only with the unexpected aid of Margaret Thatcher did they maintain sanctions against Rhodesia until agreement on Zimbabwean independence. US press coverage of Mozambique in the Carter years was almost entirely negative, as correspondents stationed in South Africa and Rhodesia generally reflected the biases of their host countries.

US officials appreciated Mozambique's diplomatic role in promoting the settlement in Zimbabwe in 1979. But this appreciation fell short of promoting friendly relations. The CIA station in Maputo, staffed by traditional Cold Warriors, treated the Mozambican government as hostile, while, unknown to the Carter State Department, US intelligence officials continued their long-established exchanges of information with their South African counterparts.

At the end of the 1970s, the prevailing assumption in Washington was still that these countries – unlike apartheid South Africa – were to be counted among US enemies. The Reagan team moved the policy spectrum sharply to the right, but it did not have to invent new themes. Demonizing Angola and even Mozambique was already an established practice among many Democrats as well as Republicans. International rhetoric implied that South Africa was a pariah state. But in Washington very few policy-makers questioned the assumption that for practical purposes Pretoria was still a Western ally, albeit an embarrassing one.

The curious course of constructive engagement

The story of US policy towards South Africa during the Reagan years is an oft-told one: the dramatic public tilt towards Pretoria, complex and prolonged diplomatic manoeuvring by Assistant Secretary of State Chester Crocker, the rise of the anti-apartheid movement and imposition of sanctions over President Reagan's veto, the settlement in south-western Africa just as Reagan was leaving office. Yet the events allow for radically different interpretations of how that policy – and its continuation by the Bush administration – affected the wars in Angola and Mozambique.[8]

Defenders of the policy point to Namibian independence and the withdrawal of Cuban troops from Angola, along with the 1991 Angolan cease-fire, and see the outcome prefigured in Crocker's initial strategies. Critics from the right say that more wholehearted support for Unita and Renamo could have produced clear-cut victories over the Marxist regimes, and prevented SWAPO and the ANC from becoming the leading political movements in Namibia and South Africa. Liberal and leftist critics note that the Reagan administration's complicity with South African military actions and opposition to imposing sanctions on the apartheid regime gave a green light to more than a decade of war, which might have been prevented or at least restrained by a strong US stand against Pretoria. The advocates of constructive engagement reply that such a judgement exaggerates US influence, and that the wars might have been even longer and more bloody without US diplomatic efforts.

Any evaluation of these claims must reckon not only with multiple 'other factors' external to US policy but also with the fact that US policy itself was not just defined by the strategic vision of constructive engagement. To a degree which varied over time and by issue, US policy was influenced by bureaucratic and domestic politics, as well as by the non-governmental lobbies for Unita and Renamo and the diplomatic efforts of Mozambique, Angola and other governments. The fundamental posture – as embodied in the Africa Bureau of the State Department – was relatively stable. But the 'other factors' varied enormously, assuming particular prominence in the second Reagan term. A short list makes the point quickly – Gorbachev's nomination in early 1985, official CIA aid to Unita and the push for US aid to Renamo, both beginning in 1985, limited sanctions against South Africa in 1985 and 1986 – none a result of State Department initiative and all, with the exception of the Soviet leadership change, contrary to the Africa Bureau's views.

Even from the beginning constructive engagement in practice was defined not only by Crocker's views but also by the need to appease far-right Reagan ideologues who had opposed his nomination, charging him with being suspiciously soft on Marxist regimes, too willing to concede some criticism of Pretoria and insufficiently single-minded in pursuit of the anti-communist crusade. In Reagan's first term the Africa Bureau generally got its way on official expressions of Africa policy. But the far right, unlike moderate liberals or anti-apartheid critics, had its own bases within the administration. At the top of the list was CIA Director William Casey, previously involved in promoting far-right views on southern Africa as Reagan's campaign manager.

The primary initial effect of the Reagan administration was to encourage South Africa to escalate both direct and proxy attacks on Angola and Mozambique. As Crocker stressed in a 'scope paper' for Secretary of State Haig's meeting with Foreign Minister Pik Botha in May 1981, the US and South Africa agreed that 'the chief threat to the realization of this hope [for cooperation, stability and security] is the presence and influence in the region of the Soviet Union and its allies'.[9] Crocker also expressed faith in the Botha regime's commitment to internal reform. In an earlier meeting with Pik Botha, Crocker distinguished between cases in which Cuban troops were present, such as Angola, and governments adopting Marxist policies for other reasons. He also counselled South Africa against going beyond reprisals, commenting that 'putting fear in minds of inferior powers makes them irrational'. But there was no hint of US censure if the South Africans failed to take his advice to be moderate in regional adventures. Although Crocker advised Haig that 'we cannot afford to give [Pretoria] a blank check regionally', and expressed hope for a quick settlement in Namibia, he was unalterably committed to using persuasion rather than pressure on Pretoria.

South Africa's assets included not only the friendly posture of the Africa Bureau, traditionally the agency most ready to criticize Pretoria, but also forces even more sympathetic to South Africa, well-entrenched in the White House, Congress and the intelligence agencies. South Africa could count on virtually unconditional US willingness to blame Moscow and excuse Pretoria, even if some officials entertained private doubts about the scale and timing of South African attacks. After two years in which South Africa's involvement in Angola and Mozambique leaped dramatically in scope and destructiveness, the administration was still eagerly feeding carrots to the Botha regime. Coincidentally, an International Monetary Fund credit of $1.1 billion, approved in November 1982 at US urging, was comparable in size to the increase in South African military expenditures from 1980 to 1982.[10]

From late 1982, bolstered by shifts in administration personnel to more pragmatic professionals such as Secretary of State Shultz and National Security Adviser McFarlane, US diplomats began to balance their tilt towards Pretoria with the beginning of dialogue with Angola and Mozambique. A prominent speech by Under-Secretary of State Eagleburger outlined a more even-handed policy including condemnation of apartheid as 'morally wrong'.

But the administration still left little doubt that it regarded Frontline support for SWAPO and the ANC as a more serious offence than South Africa's occupation of Namibia, its repression of the anti-apartheid movement or its attacks on its neighbours. Angola and Mozambique would have to make concessions because they were weaker and because the US initiative was 'the only game in town'. They were advised to accept US assurances that the South African leaders could be trusted to keep their word and live up to their true nature as pragmatic reformers. All Pretoria needed was reassurance of its own security, by expulsion of Cuban troops from the region and Frontline refusal to give any support to SWAPO or ANC guerrilla campaigns. The US did not seek to intervene in the internal affairs of Angola or Mozambique, US envoys assured them, enraging administration hard-liners who heard reports of such conciliatory gestures.[11]

US diplomats played active roles in brokering both the agreement on limited South African disengagement from Angola in February 1984 and the Nkomati Accord in March 1984, proclaimed in that US election year as victories for 'constructive engagement'. There were, of course, many differences between the two set of negotiations. In the one case, the Mozambican leaders had concluded in mid-1982 that they did not have the resources for a primarily military response to South Africa, and would have to split off Western support for South Africa's war. Maputo was actively seeking a rapprochement with the US and a deal along the lines of Nkomati, so long as it did not entail abandoning political support for the ANC.

In contrast, Angola had the military capability, with Cuban assistance, to mount a significant defence effort. For Angola, Washington was not only the ally of South Africa, but also the independent source of covert aggression aimed at its overthrow. Crocker's assurances that the US recognized Angola's security concerns rang hollow in the face of Casey's efforts to promote support for Unita not only from South Africa but also from Saudi Arabia, Zaire and other countries. The limited character of the Lusaka disengagement agreement, as compared with the Nkomati Accord, reflects these contrasts both in the regional power balance and in Washington's role.

But there is also a notable similarity between these two accomplishments of constructive engagement. It was soon clear that there was no political will in South Africa to keep either agreement and that there was no political will in Washington to punish Pretoria for that failure. The administration's self-imposed ban on strong action against South Africa remained intact. When South African commandos in May 1985 launched an abortive attack on Gulf Oil installations in Cabinda, far from any possible excuse of reprisals against SWAPO, there was only a token response from Washington. When South Africa again moved large numbers of troops into southern Angola, not against SWAPO bases but to defend Unita's Cuando Cubango base area, official Washington looked on with approval. After President Machel presented irrefutable documentation of South African violations of Nkomati, the response was quiet – and ineffective – diplomatic contacts with Pretoria. The most vigorous response, withdrawal of the US ambassador for 'consultations', came in July when South African commandos attacked alleged ANC houses in Botswana, which gave strictly limited asylum to peaceful refugees.

As Reagan began his second term in 1985, moreover, changes in South Africa and in US domestic politics made southern Africa policy a more open field of conflict. Administration policy was buffeted from the right and from the left. Most significantly, the 1983 South African constitution signalled the beginning of unprecedented levels of anti-apartheid resistance and government repression in South Africa. Crocker hailed the new tricameral legislature, which excluded Africans while providing separate chambers for whites, coloureds and Asians, as a step towards reform. As the conflict escalated, media coverage helped to galvanize the international apartheid movement, not least in the US. Although few who joined the anti-apartheid campaign made the link to the regional wars, the pressure to distance the US from Pretoria became a potent political force. Ironically, the far-right campaign to support Unita and Renamo also reached a new pitch of intensity in Reagan's second term, for reasons less related to southern Africa than to the power of Washington lobbies and global ideology.

The Unita lobby: at home in Reagan's Washington

Unita's position in Washington politics, practically unassailable in the 1980s, built on multiple advantages. It could count on hostility to Cuba, resentment at the US defeat in 1976, and on opinion-makers with virtually no independent sources of information about Angola. It could also rely on numerous well-placed friends, both in Washington and among key US allies. They included Democrats and Republicans, as well as intelligence officials and politicians in Zaire, Morocco, Portugal, France and key French-speaking states such as Senegal and Côte d'Ivoire. The counterbalance of more moderate views consisted of some State Department officials, as well as US oil companies and other businesses with interests in Angola. A handful of African-American and other liberal members of Congress, as well as the anti-apartheid groups, were vociferous critics of aid to Unita, but were clearly outsiders to Reagan's Washington.

After the 1976 Clark Amendment barring further US covert aid in Angola, US intelligence officials were determined to find other ways to continue the campaign against the MPLA. They had been convinced, moreover, that Savimbi was a more viable client than Roberto. Despite Mobutu's closer links with Roberto, he was encouraged to provide access in Zaire for Savimbi, which continued even after the *détente* with Angola in 1978. When Western countries brought Moroccan troops to rescue Mobutu in the 1977 Shaba uprising, moreover, it opened a significant new contact for Savimbi. Later that year Savimbi reached agreement with King Hassan on using Morocco for military training, arms supplies and diplomatic contacts.[12]

Both the US and France, which were supporting Morocco's military occupation of the Western Sahara, encouraged the Moroccan king. French intelligence chief de Marenches later recorded in his memoirs the invaluable aid Morocco gave him in channelling military aid to

Unita.[13] By early 1978, an international fund of over $15 million for Unita support was put together, with the involvement of France, Iran (still under the Shah), Saudi Arabia and Morocco.

Kinshasa also allowed Savimbi a less embarrassing context than South African-controlled Namibia for contacts with the outside world. A seven-part special series of articles in the *Washington Post* provided unprecedented publicity. By early 1978 Brzezinski was arguing the case for Savimbi within the Carter administration. In November 1979, Savimbi arrived in New York on a trip hosted by Carl Gershman of Freedom House, who later served with Jeane Kirkpatrick at the United Nations and then as head of the National Endowment for Democracy. Savimbi was accompanied by *Newsweek*'s Arnaud de Borchgrave, a far-right intelligence *aficionado*.[14]

When the Reagan team entered, therefore, Unita was already well-connected. French intelligence chief de Marenches advised Reagan to give priority to supporting Unita, and the new administration was committed to repealing the Clark Amendment. Surprisingly, although the Senate approved repeal in 1981, the House of Representatives did not. Gulf Oil officials lobbied actively against the repeal. Simultaneously the Export-Import Bank approved $85 million in credits for Angolan oil. The *Washington Post* published another seven-part series lauding Savimbi in mid-1981. But to all appearances moderation -- and the Clark Amendment -- prevailed.

On a parallel track, however, CIA Director Casey and other administration officials reportedly arranged means to finance Unita and other resistance groups around the world through secret Saudi accounts. Although the Iran–Contra investigation declined to look into the Angolan connection, and full details are not available, there is evidence that the arrangement began in 1981, as a trade-off for the sale of American AWACS planes to the Saudis.[15] Since aid to the Contras in Nicaragua was not barred by Congress until late 1984, this channel was needed primarily for Angola or for other operations not officially approved even by normal US intelligence procedures. At least one $15 million payment to Unita through Morocco in 1983 has been identified in congressional testimony. Despite the congressional defeat, therefore, Savimbi had no grounds for complaint after a late 1981 visit to the US. The following month he told journalists that 'A great country like the United States has other channels ... the Clark Amendment means nothing.'[16]

In Reagan's second term, buoyed by the President's election landslide and enraged by congressional restrictions on US aid to the Nicaraguan contras, right-wing forces launched a campaign for high-profile US support for insurgents in Nicaragua, Angola, Afghanistan, Cambodia and Mozambique. The President proclaimed what came to be known as the Reagan doctrine in January 1985. The Pentagon made 'low-intensity warfare' a popular catchword, and lobbyists cultivated conservative and moderate Democrats who might vote with the President. Prominent far-right activists, such as Howard Phillips of the Conservative Caucus, attacked Secretary of State Shultz and Assistant Secretary Crocker for undermining the anti-communist cause.[17]

Unita's assets included not only the high-powered lobbying adding up to over a million dollars a year, but also the enthusiastic support of CIA Director Casey and others in the intelligence establishment. The Cuban connection brought in the powerful Cuban–American lobby, with both national influence and concentrated power in Florida. Media bias in favour of Unita was guaranteed by skilful cultivation of both reporters and editors. Representative Claude Pepper of Florida, a prominent Democrat and a liberal on domestic issues, took on leadership of the Unita cause in the House of Representatives. Other Democrats, such as Senator Dennis DeConcini of Arizona, also jumped on the bandwagon, seeing support for Unita as a cheap way to gain credit for anti-communism on an issue they and their constituents knew little about. Peter Kelly, a partner in Unita's principal lobbying firm, was a leading fundraiser for Democratic senators. Other partners included Charles Black, Paul Manafort and Roger Stone, all highly placed in the Republican party.[18]

Such a line-up probably guaranteed the defeat of efforts to block the Unita juggernaut. But the contest was made even more unequal by the failure of the Angolan government to make significant countervailing linkages in the US. Without a diplomatic presence in Washington or regular contacts with US groups, Angolan officials had little understanding of Washington political realities. Even critics of US policy had only infrequent access to usable information from Angola. In most Washington contexts Unita's version of events went unchallenged.

The one advantage the Angolan government had was its good relationship with Gulf Oil and other US businesses. To the extent that Luanda focused on improving its relationship with Washington, it relied on these contacts as well as on direct talks with US officials. In 1984 Gulf Oil was absorbed by Chevron, which took a more passive attitude on US Angola policy and even so came under strong right-wing pressure. By 1986 a coalition of far-right groups was organizing a boycott of Chevron for its involvement in Angola. Crocker, trying to protect himself from right-wing criticism, advised oil companies to be cautious on investment in Angola.[19]

The growing anti-apartheid movement, which with its wide base might have provided a counterweight, was largely ineffective on Angola. Without broader public awareness of even basic geographical background, much less the southern African political context, the conflict in Angola was de-linked from that in South Africa, even for many anti-apartheid activists. If Angola appeared on the average American's mental map at all, it was probably closer to Cuba or to Afghanistan than to South Africa. The media rarely noted South African involvement in Angola. The movement lacked the depth of resources to reach even its own constituency on demands more complex than the basic anti-apartheid message.

The Unita lobby largely had its way with Congress. Gaining swing votes to repeal the Clark Amendment with pledges that the administration was not planning to aid Unita but only to regain its freedom from legislative restrictions, Unita backers moved immediately after the vote into a campaign for military aid to Unita. In October 1985 Representative Pepper introduced a bill calling for humanitarian assistance to Unita, while Republican Mark Siljander pushed military assistance. The lobbying campaign culminated in January with another Washington visit by Savimbi. Covert aid, of approximately $15 million, was officially announced in March.

In subsequent years legislative battles over Angola policy continued. But those opposed to Unita aid were almost always on the defensive. Unita supporters introduced legislation to bar economic links with Angola, succeeding in cutting off Export-Import Bank loans by 1988. Lobbying within the administration forced a US vote against Angolan membership in the International Monetary Fund in 1989. Savimbi made high-profile trips to the US in mid-1988 and again in 1989 and 1990, eventually boosting budgeted aid to an estimated $40 million a year or more. The high point of the lobby's influence was probably a pre-inauguration pledge from President Bush to continue both military and diplomatic support, even after agreement on withdrawal of Cuban troops from Angola. During 1989, as the State Department was pressing Savimbi to rejoin Mobutu-led negotiations, Unita's partisans forced a US pledge to support Unita's position in the talks.

Meanwhile, the Angolan government's first effort to hire high-level lobbyists in Washington went awry, when right-wing pressure forced the well-connected Gray & Company to drop a contract signed in 1986. Initial reports of internal killings in Unita, appearing in the Portuguese press in 1988, were ignored by the major US media that year. In 1989, Unita's image suffered its first major challenge, when Savimbi biographer Fred Bridgland repeated similar charges. On his visit in 1989, Savimbi found Washington audiences somewhat more sceptical. The smooth implementation by Angola and Cuba of the agreements on Namibian independence and Cuban troop withdrawal improved the Angolan government's stock with US diplomats. Angolan government contacts with the Washington milieu became more frequent, although they could not match the access or expertise of Unita's partisans.[20]

As direct peace talks between Unita and the Angolan government began in 1990, the Unita lobby maintained a steady vigil to ensure that US diplomats did not put interest in a settlement over loyalty to Savimbi. By the end of the year, however, unconditional US support was waning. Congress passed the Solarz Amendment, which would restrict aid to Unita once the Angolan government showed itself reasonable on an election timetable. Unita lobbyists and the administration were shocked by their defeat. And Unita felt pressure to reciprocate the concessions made by the Angolan government.

By 1991, Unita's image in Washington was somewhat worn. With Cuban troops gone, the Cold War officially over, and the Angolan government committed to free-market economic policies, the zeal of Unita's backers was dampened. Displaying a new level of professionalism, the Angolan government worked with lobbyists to manage a successful visit to Washington by President dos Santos in September 1991. The Angolan government was allowed to establish a diplomatic office in Washington, inconspicuously accredited as an observer mission to the Organization of American States. Most restrictions on US government support for trade with Angola were removed. Few were eager to speak up openly for Savimbi when new revelations from top Unita defectors confirmed the execution of former Washington representative Tito Chingunji. But despite a letter from Secretary of State Baker to Savimbi calling for a full investigation, there was no enthusiasm for embarrassing a US client.[21]

The final straw that toppled Savimbi from his pedestal in Washington was his reaction to the election in September 1992. During the campaign even formerly pro-Unita US officials at the US Liaison Office in Luanda had begun to question Savimbi's belligerent campaign strategy. After the election was ruled free and fair and Unita's complaints of fraud proved to have little substance, Savimbi's return to war exhausted the patience of all but his most diehard admirers. Although Washington delayed until May 1993 in recognizing the Angolan government, the Unita lobby had relatively little impact on this result. The delay resulted rather from residual hostility to Luanda, disarray in the transition to a new administration and State Department officials insistent to the end that they could use the delay as leverage to broker a new agreement.

Renamo's American connection

Renamo never won prominence in Washington policy circles. Its congressional backers were few in number. Dhlakama never visited Washington or hired a high-powered Washington lobbying firm. Renamo's backers within the intelligence agencies and the military joined with private far-right groups to urge official US support on the Unita model, and seemed in 1986 and 1987 to have some chance of success. But by

1988 Renamo was so linked with atrocities that even many right-wingers thought it wise to seek some public distance. The Mozambican Embassy, established in Washington in 1983, worked tirelessly to neutralize hostility to Mozambique, while Maputo officials gave high priority to diplomatic contacts with Washington.

Despite these differences from the Angolan pattern, there were also similarities. In the first Reagan term the US tilt towards Pretoria encouraged the South African assault against Mozambique. In the negotiations leading up to the Nkomati Accord, the US, not even thinking of using sanctions against South Africa, was nevertheless willing to condition US food aid for famine victims on Mozambican 'moderation'. CIA Director Casey's private operations also reportedly included aid to Renamo. Reagan's second term saw a major escalation in US rightwing lobbying for Renamo as well as Unita. And despite Renamo's failure to win the same level of official approval, private networks with semi-official links significantly added to Renamo's base of external support. State Department officials advocating a more diplomatic line worked to defeat the most extreme proposals, but also used the backing for Renamo as leverage to argue for new concessions by the Mozambican government.

The direct US connection was apparently not a major factor in Renamo's early years as a tightly-controlled military arm of first Rhodesia and then South Africa. Even then, however, there were links. One of the six participants in Renamo's founding meeting in 1977 was African-American Leo Milas, a mysterious figure who had infiltrated Frelimo in the early 1960s pretending to be a Mozambican and later turned up in Nairobi representing Renamo in the mid-1980s. American Robert MacKenzie, a mercenary serving as one of the top commanders of Rhodesia's Special Air Service, was initially in charge of support operations for Renamo, making use of his experience in Vietnam. MacKenzie, back in the US after 1985 as a security consultant and correspondent for *Soldier of Fortune* magazine, became one of the key pro-Renamo activists.[22]

During the first Reagan term, Renamo did little to establish a presence in Washington. Although there were a number of anti-Frelimo Mozambican exiles in the US, they had little close contact with Renamo. One exile, Artur Vilankulu, became Renamo Secretary for External Affairs in 1983, linking up with right-wing European supporters of Renamo. But such activities were marginal, with little connection to the Renamo military command in South Africa or to policy in Washington and in Mozambique. There is still no substantive evidence on support to Renamo in this period as a result of CIA Director Casey's personal efforts, although before his death in 1983, Renamo Secretary-General Cristina bragged to acquaintances of getting money from Saudi Arabia.

Whatever evidence of direct ties may turn up, there is no doubt that they were less significant than the indirect support from the general tilt to Pretoria.

In Reagan's second term, however, while US diplomats courted the government in Maputo and failed to confront South Africa for its violations of Nkomati, the Renamo lobby in the US mobilized energetically. Although they failed to win mainstream approval, they forced the State Department into a defensive stance and activated a network of financial and other support for Renamo among conservative activists in the private sector, in Congress and in the government's intelligence agencies.[23]

The network of supporters included, predictably, extremist members of Congress such as Senator Jesse Helms of North Carolina and Representative Dan Burton of Indiana. The most prominent right-wing think-tank, the Heritage Foundation, highlighted the opportunities for anti-communist resistance in Mozambique in its second *Mandate for Leadership*, its guidelines for administration policy issued in 1984. Adventurer Jack Wheeler wrote pro-Renamo articles for *Soldier of Fortune* and the *Washington Times*.[24] Key figures in the far-right spectrum such as Howard Phillips of the Conservative Caucus and Paul Weyrich of the Committee for Survival of a Free Congress also took up the Renamo cause in early 1985, attacking State Department and AID officials as tools of the Soviet Union. Within the administration, Constantine Menges at the National Security Council and Patrick Buchanan at the White House spoke out for Renamo. They received significant support at the Defense Department and the CIA.

These efforts failed to block President Machel's visit in September 1985, or increases in US aid to the Mozambican government. But the issue was firmly implanted on the right-wing agenda, with groups both coordinating their activities and competing to get in on what they expected to be a 'Reagan doctrine victory'. Howard University professor Luís Serapião, an anti-Frelimo Mozambican in the US since the mid-1960s, became Renamo's Washington representative in 1986. That same year Thomas Schaaf, a right-wing religious activist who had covertly aided Renamo while working as an agricultural adviser in Rhodesia and in Zimbabwe after independence, fled Zimbabwe fearing disclosure and arrest. Largely overshadowing the ineffective Serapião, he became Renamo's most energetic lobbyist. He recruited Robert MacKenzie, recently returned from mercenary service with the South African special forces. After visiting Renamo territory with Schaaf, MacKenzie reported meeting Renamo officers he had trained in the Rhodesian days.[25]

In 1987, the Renamo lobby tried to block the appointment of Melissa Wells as new ambassador to Mozambique. Seeking right-wing support for his presidential campaign, Republican Senator Robert Dole joined with Jesse Helms to stall the nomination for almost six months. But their efforts failed, and in October President Chissano's state visit and cordial meeting with President Reagan confirmed the marginal public position of Renamo. After the State Department-commissioned Gersony report of April 1988, documenting Renamo's brutal record, even many conservatives drew back from public association with the group. Schaaf, MacKenzie and other core supporters largely gave up on high-profile efforts, concentrating instead on winning financial aid and other less visible assistance from the true believers on the right.

This shadowy network, whose activities have only recently and incompletely come to light, was funded in part by obscure but well-connected businessmen, such as James Blanchard of Louisiana and William Ball of Indianapolis. Schaaf and MacKenzie remained active. But the network also drew in highly-placed figures among retired intelligence officials. They included Ray Cline, former Deputy Director of the CIA. Cline's US Global Strategy Council in 1989 published a pro-Renamo pamphlet by his daughter, who subsequently married Robert MacKenzie. Also taking up the Renamo cause were Daniel Graham, former deputy director of the Defense Intelligence Agency, and General John Singlaub of Iran–Contra fame, both members of the World Anti-Communist League and, with Howard Phillips, Jack Wheeler, James Blanchard and William Ball, of the Council on National Policy, a secretive coordinating body for the far right.

This network both cooperated with and competed for influence over Renamo with South African-based supporters of Renamo. Speculation that they supplanted the South African link does not stand up, since it rests on systematically underestimating the evidence of continued South African involvement.[26] But through links in both Malawi and in Kenya, the US-based network provided military supplies as well as other material support. They also provided diplomatic advice and encouraged Renamo and its backers in South Africa, Malawi and Kenya to continue the war while holding out for further concessions or the collapse of the Mozambican government. They also maintained contacts with officials in US intelligence agencies, who showed a notable lack of zeal in investigating evidence of supplies to Renamo from South Africa, Kenya and Malawi.

In a particularly ludicrous coda to the Renamo lobbying saga, Washington lawyer Bruce Fein, formerly of the Heritage Foundation, was paid $145,000 in 1991 to draft a constitution and supporting documents for Renamo's use in the negotiations. The result, a combination of right-wing rhetoric and minimally adapted excerpts from the US Constitution, was never even translated into Portuguese.[27]

The failure of Renamo's public lobbying was due partly to their own clumsiness, and partly to structural factors leading to lesser US hostility to Mozambique than to Angola. But in the political atmosphere of

Reagan's Washington it might still have succeeded were it not for the skilful counter efforts by the Mozambican government. Maputo adopted an open-door policy towards US journalists, non-governmental organizations and business, winning many friends if only a trickle of private foreign investment. Policy guidelines stressed reaching out to diverse sectors of US society, from solidarity groups and the anti-apartheid movement on the one hand to right-wing opponents on the other. Mozambican officials realized the strategic importance of Congress as well as the administration. The objectives: make friends if possible, but at least neutralize opponents, reducing the impetus for US backing to Renamo.

Within its limits, the strategy was highly successful. But it was defensive and had to operate within the basic parameters of the administration position. The power realities meant that Mozambique always had to present itself as a petitioner, a skilful player in the diplomatic game, but with few cards other than the sympathy and respect it could gain from the other players. Thus serious US pressure on South Africa to abide by the Nkomati Accord never became a live option. Nor did the administration ever target for intelligence collection the covert networks of support for Renamo, or try to shut them down. Some Washington officials might be sympathetic to Maputo, but few ever doubted that good relations with Pretoria took priority.

Geopolitics, diplomacy and the Reagan doctrine in Angola

In the wake of successful agreements in 1988 and 1991, Reagan and Bush administration officials legitimately took credit for active and skilful diplomacy in shepherding highly complex negotiations to closure. Virtually all analysts, however, also note the convergence of other factors – distinct from US policy or diplomacy – in ripening the conflict for settlement.[28] Less often considered but no less important were the effects of US policies in delaying the settlements.

The questions are most clearly phrased in hypothetical terms. If the US, beginning in 1981, had refrained from direct or indirect military support for Unita, barred sharing of intelligence with South Africa, strictly enforced the arms embargo against South Africa and strongly condemned any South African moves across the border with Namibia, would Namibia have been independent and the Cuban troops gone sooner or later than actually happened? If Washington in 1981 had supported sanctions as strong as those eventually enacted in 1986, what effect would that have had on South African willingness to settle in Namibia? With reference to the Angolan ceasefire settlement, what might have happened after 1988 if the US had cut off support for

Unita, instead of trying to offset Unita's loss of large-scale South African backing? Would Savimbi, or other leaders within Unita, have conceded to a variant of the power-sharing option offered by Luanda? If so, would such a settlement have been more or less viable than the agreement actually reached?

Definitive answers to such questions are elusive. But they are logically prerequisite to determining the causal effect of US policy. It is a logical fallacy to conclude simply from the historical sequence that US aid to Unita facilitated either the 1988 or the 1991 settlement. Analyst Michael McFaul, for example, argues that the 1988 'settlement between Angola, Cuba and South Africa' was achieved despite, not because of, the Reagan doctrine.[29] Deciding whether he is correct, or whether Crocker's self-congratulatory portrait is more accurate, requires considering how and why the parties shifted their positions to those they accepted in the 1988 and 1991 settlements.

Chapter 5 considered several factors leading to the 1988 settlement, particularly the escalating pressures on South Africa which ultimately outweighed the perceived risks in permitting a free election in Namibia. As witnessed by the similarity between the final agreements in 1988 and the joint Cuban/Angolan position in 1982, the fundamental concessions offered were on the South African side. The Cuban withdrawal from Angola followed rather than preceded Namibia's independence. On the other hand, South Africa and the US gained the firm linkage of the two issues, although laid out in separate documents to avoid the impression that Namibia's right to independence was legally contingent on Cuban/Angolan relations. Angolan and Cuban willingness to be flexible on these issues derived both from war-weariness and from confidence in Angola's military capacity once South African control of Namibia was removed from the picture.

Did US aid to Unita, whether indirect in the first Reagan term or direct in the second, facilitate or hinder this final result? By fuelling the war, it undoubtedly contributed to war-weariness on the Angolan government side. But it also repeatedly stoked Angolan suspicions that the US was aiming not at a compromise settlement but rather the overthrow of the government and its replacement by Unita. Assurances from US officials that this was not the goal had little credibility given *de facto* US cooperation with South Africa and Unita.[30]

Such suspicions were reinforced by US refusal to put pressure on South Africa, endorsed both by Reagan doctrine crusaders and the diplomatic managers of constructive engagement. If the US had truly taken an 'even-handed' stance condemning cross-border violence in proportion to the scale of destruction involved, Angola would have had little reason to feel threatened. The flexible negotiating stance of 1988 could have been adopted in 1981, or certainly in 1985.

But could South Africa's agreement have been gained earlier, without the carrots of reassurance offered by a friendly US administration? That depends on whether it was ultimately reassurance or pressure that most influenced the South African shift in position. If reassurance could have done the job, South African concessions should have followed the blatant tilt to Pretoria in 1981–82, or the step-up in US support for Unita in 1985–86. Instead they came after economic pressure and military setbacks in 1987–88, developments which US policy delayed rather than promoted. If different US policies, aimed at increasing the pressures on Pretoria, had been adopted early in the 1980s, South Africa would have been forced to face the necessity of concessions that much sooner.

Reassurance for South Africa was indeed one factor facilitating the 1988 settlement. But it came not primarily from Washington's friendly stance but rather from Soviet eagerness to resolve regional conflicts, in southern Africa as elsewhere in the world. While advocates of the worldwide Reagan doctrine may claim Soviet changes as a result of Afghanistan in particular, the shifts were not a result of events in southern Africa. Domestic problems in the Soviet Union, interlinked with the costs of high-tech military confrontation with the West, were producing a de-emphasis on regional confrontation even before Gorbachev took office in 1985. Gorbachev's policy, downplaying involvement in the Third World and seeking regional agreements, was manifest in Soviet approaches to the US on southern African issues in mid-1985, before the repeal of the Clark Amendment and resumption of large-scale US assistance to Unita. That assistance, far from promoting a more conciliatory Soviet stance, made it more difficult for Moscow to argue to Luanda the need for compromise, and provoked the investment of additional Soviet military resources.

The Soviet Union in the 1980s, far from pursuing an aggressive expansion of influence in southern Africa, aimed to limit its involvement – without, however, being forced to withdraw or seeing its allies collapse under joint South African and US pressure. If the US had been willing more quickly to distance itself from Pretoria, Moscow was eager for compromises in a region that most Soviet policy-makers saw as marginal. Despite the appearance of close Soviet–Angolan alignment, the mutual commitment was far from unconditional even in the Brezhnev years. The attacks from South Africa, however, combined with the US tilt to Pretoria, forced both into a common front of scepticism about diplomatic solutions, until finally South Africa itself was weak enough to retreat.

The major differences of perspective in analysing this phase of southern African history are not about the details of diplomatic history. Sorting out who said what to whom when – the microdynamics of negotiations – is certainly interesting and important. What is fundamental, however, is what factors, including US policy, accelerated or delayed what is now popularly referred to as ripeness for settlement. And that depends on evaluating the intentions of the parties. If one assumes, with the apologists of constructive engagement, that the Botha regime was fundamentally reformist, simply seeking reassurances in order to allow Namibian independence and reform in South Africa, then it made sense to try to weaken their African opponents. If one judges instead that the South African regime was trying to hold on to as much power as it could as long as possible, stretching out negotiations and making real concessions only when left with no alternative, then it made sense to try to weaken the regime.

African countries, together with the anti-apartheid movement in South Africa and internationally, focused on increasing the pressures on South Africa. Throughout the 1980s both wings of the Reagan administration, the fanatic crusaders and the diplomatic managers, did their best to block such pressures, although they finally lost the legislative sanctions battle in 1986. In contrast, they joined in mounting military and economic pressures directed at undermining the Angolan state. However much US diplomats struck rhetorical postures of even-handed mediation, administration actions served to strengthen one party, the Pretoria regime. This in turn delayed the moment when Pretoria was finally convinced to make the negotiations more than a stalling game.

A parallel question arises on the May 1991 internal Angolan settlement. US and Soviet negotiators assisted Portugal in mediating this settlement. Continued US military support for Unita was used as pressure against the government and as reassurance for Unita, while at key points diplomats urged concessions on both sides. It was obvious, however, that the US was a patron of one side rather than a genuine neutral. Stepped-up US military involvement strengthened Unita just at the crucial moment that it was losing access to supplies over the Namibian border. While occasionally urging compromises on Unita, Washington generally supported Unita demands, insisting on successive concessions by Luanda.

This US posture resulted in settlement terms more favourable to Unita than might otherwise have been the case. Both Unita and US officials expected that Savimbi would win the election and take power, vindicating the war effort. The short time before the election would ensure that the government could not reap the benefits of peace in time to recoup popularity and that, in practice, Unita could retain the threat of returning to war. Even if demobilization and formation of a new national army had been completed on schedule as the settlement prescribed, that new structure would have been untested. As Nicaraguans had seen a vote against the Sandinista government as a vote for peace, so Angolans would oust their government out of fear of renewed war.

The US argued throughout for parity between the government and Unita, denying the legitimacy of the Angolan state. The government's efforts to propose power-sharing solutions which offered Unita a subordinate role rather than parity or a chance for predominant power were dismissed by US negotiators as unrealistic ploys. They were indeed unrealistic, but the primary reason was US determination to reject them and to provide Unita with the support it needed to hold out for better terms.

US officials were convinced from the start, as instanced by Crocker's dismissive remarks on meeting the Angolan foreign minister in Paris in 1982, that Savimbi's claim to an equal or predominant share of power in Angola was legitimate.[31] State Department officials did not share the crusading enthusiasm for Unita of the far-right, but they consistently rejected Angolan government worries about Savimbi as paranoia. They casually dismissed what they saw as moralistic questions based on his ties to South Africa or his internal human rights record.

This may partly be explained by sensitivity to the Unita lobby. But it also reflected their fundamental misjudgements about Angolan society, as well as their personal prejudices. Savimbi was a man who understood power, geopolitics and political games, and was willing to play for the US team. For that they could easily forgive him his personality cult and dismiss human-rights criticism as mud-slinging inspired by Luanda. Without a US diplomatic presence in Angola, there was no opportunity for direct acquaintance with Angolan social reality. Judgements about Angolan government officials apparently were based on how well their personal style meshed with that of their US counterparts, and how skilfully they played the diplomatic game.[32]

US military support for Unita, in the period 1989–91, had a double effect on the negotiations. It sustained Angolan suspicions that Washington supported Savimbi's ambitions to take power, and weakened the arguments for compromise within the ruling party. But by keeping up the military pressure, while developments in the Soviet Union eroded the prospects of long-term military support for the government, it also played on Angolan war-weariness. Luanda ultimately accepted competitive multi-party elections rather than power-sharing, and agreed to eighteen months rather than three years before elections.

The Bicesse agreement also included concessions from Unita, particularly agreement on government sovereignty and on military demobilization before the election. In October 1990 the US Congress approved an amendment suspending military aid to Unita on condition that the Angolan government agree to a ceasefire and a reasonable timetable for elections. The following month Soviet Foreign Minister Eduard

Shevardnadze became actively involved in the talks, in conjunction with Secretary of State James Baker. In retrospect, however, Unita's concessions on these points may have been in full awareness of how easy it would be to stall on implementation.[33]

The abortive Gbadolite agreement, on terms far more favourable to Luanda than Bicesse, would have ensured a subordinate role for Unita personnel in government and in the army, at the expense of the chance to gain dominant power through elections. The US encouraged Savimbi to reject the deal, and gave him the military support necessary to make up for his loss of the supply route through Namibia.[34] Stepped-up supplies for Unita's northern guerrilla front in particular enabled Unita to offset the government's conventional military campaign on Mavinga. Although the volume of US supplies was far less than the Soviet supplies to the government, as US officials never tired of pointing out, the fundamental asymmetry of guerrilla warfare meant that they were sufficient to maintain a military stalemate.

It is unlikely, nevertheless, that the Gbadolite agreement would have held even if the US had cut off supplies and pressured Unita to accept it. The terms were too vaguely defined, Unita had not suffered significant military defeat, Savimbi's ambition would not have been satisfied, and his hold on power within Unita was secure. Another round of fighting in the new circumstances after Namibian independence and the withdrawal of Cuban troops was almost inevitable, for both sides to test their strength. The most that can be said is that without US aid, Unita would have been severely battered in that confrontation and that any subsequent settlement would have reflected to some extent that battlefield balance. Given international political trends and internal Angolan developments, it is likely that such an alternative settlement would still have included some form of competitive elections. But it might have provided a far longer period before elections and interim arrangements for participation of Unita personnel in a national government and army rather than full parity in creation of a new national army.

Putting aside speculation as to whether an alternative settlement might have enhanced the prospects for long-term peace, the question remains whether impartial and firm enforcement of the Bicesse Accord could have averted the return to war in Angola. It is clear in retrospect that Unita's refusal to allow government administration in the territory it controlled, and its success in maintaining its military power intact, gave it the capacity to reject the election result. Yet the Angolan government itself made only low-key protests against these violations, knowing that it would have no international backing for threatening to postpone the elections. Implementation of the accords took place in the context of a one-superpower world. Only Unita's patron still had weight, and incipient US disillusionment with Unita fell far short of willingness to pressure it to comply.

In the wake of renewed war in Angola, observers have cited a wide variety of lessons to be learned. Virtually all acknowledge the need for a larger United Nations military and civilian presence. Regardless of the size of that presence, however, the issue of political direction and mandate remains critical. In the Cold War context which still survived in US Angola policy during this period, partiality towards the party least amenable to democratic rules of the game removed the option of deterring the resort to violence. Previous US sponsorship, together with residual South African support, gave that party the capacity to carry out its threat.

Superpower default and terrorist blackmail in Mozambique

In contrast to Angola, where superpower rivalry both escalated the level of conflict and aided at key points in promoting conflict resolution, the dynamics of conflict and conflict resolution in Mozambique were dominated by regional rather than global geopolitics. Nevertheless, the actions of the US and the contrasting inaction of the Soviet Union had profound implications for prolonging the conflict.

During the 1980s the US moved from intense hostility to the Mozambican government, falling just short of open endorsement of Renamo, to prominence as one of the government's leading aid donors and the indispensable backer of international settlement efforts. The effort to 'woo Marxist Mozambique' upset the far right in Washington, and helped foster the controversial Nkomati pact between Maputo and Pretoria. It also led to increasingly intrusive US influence over Mozambican domestic policies. But Mozambique's gestures of friendship were never rewarded by US willingness to try to curb Renamo's backers in South Africa and elsewhere. That was ruled out by the taboo on coercive pressures against the Pretoria regime.

The Soviet Union, meanwhile, opted out early from serious competition. Despite the mutual security treaty with Moscow signed in 1977, the scale of arms aid and military advice was limited. Enough to cope with the Rhodesian challenge in the late 1970s, it was pitifully inadequate for the 1980s. Moscow rejected the Mozambican bid to join Comecon (Council for Mutual Economic Aid), and made it clear that no substantial increases in economic or military aid would be forthcoming. Soviet officials repeatedly advised Mozambique that Maputo had no choice but to woo Washington.

That was a difficult task. The US had a diplomatic presence in Maputo, and had supplied small quantities of food aid. But there had been no support to compensate Mozambique for damages from Mozambican compliance with United Nations sanctions against Rhodesia. President Machel's meeting with President Carter in 1978, and repeated Mozambican statements that the country was interested in Western investments, never resulted in more than token contacts. Most of the diplomatic credit Maputo gained for facilitating the Lancaster House agreement on Zimbabwe's independence was lost when US diplomats stationed in Maputo were expelled as CIA officers in March 1981. Even US food aid was cut off in reprisal.[35]

Mozambican intelligence officials had been monitoring the espionage activities of personnel in the US embassy, who seemed interested primarily in collecting data on the Mozambican military, on Zimbabwean and South African liberation movements, and on the personal habits and movements of President Machel. But the sudden expulsions were in reaction to South Africa's raid in January, in which commandos killed thirteen ANC members in a suburb of Maputo. The raid followed by days a well-publicized speech by Secretary of State Alexander Haig condemning 'rampant international terrorism'. The Mozambican government suspected that US intelligence being shared with South Africa played a hand in preparation for the attack.

It was quickly apparent, however, that Mozambique could not afford such a public affront to Washington. Although the Soviet Union sent warships on a symbolic visit to Maputo, as a warning against direct South African attacks, they were unwilling and probably unable to provide military support for the massive counterinsurgency efforts that would have been necessary to contain South Africa's support for Renamo. By the time the Soviet Union vetoed Mozambican membership in Comecon in mid-1981, Mozambican envoys were actively exploring openings in Washington. In 1982 the Frelimo Central Committee approved a diplomatic offensive aimed at splitting Western support from South Africa. Mozambique accepted West German conditions recognizing West German authority over Berlin, clearing the way for formal association with the European Economic Community.

In subsequent years, Mozambican diplomacy consistently aimed at isolating Renamo, trying to play on divisions within the South African state and on separating South Africa from its Western partners to maximize pressure on Pretoria. The prize was to win support in Washington, the key both to international economic aid and to pressure on South Africa. But Maputo had only a few cards. One asset was good relations with Margaret Thatcher's Britain, established during the Lancaster House negotiations and sustained in part by British economic interests in the subcontinent. Another was the quiet intermediary role Mozambique could play in contacts with Angola. After the concessions made at Nkomati in denying any sanctuary for ANC military operations,

there was little more to offer in compromise with South Africa. Mozambican adjustments in internal political and economic policy won continued US support and fended off the Renamo boosters in Washington.
But nothing was sufficient to get US officials to deliver the reward of
substantive pressure on South Africa and Renamo's other backers.

The pattern of US diplomacy was constant, both leading up to the
Nkomati Accord and in the subsequent protracted period of South
African violations and Renamo delays in reaching a peace settlement.
Concessions were urged on the Mozambican government, making full
use of the leverage that the promise or the reality of aid supplied. In
dealing with South Africa and Renamo, however, US diplomats pleaded
lack of leverage. Nor did they show much interest in finding ways to
squeeze Renamo's supply lines.

US–Mozambican relations began to improve in the second half of
1982. In January 1983 the State Department sent an important signal
by publicly acknowledging South African sponsorship of Renamo. But
Crocker still firmly believed in no public criticism of Pretoria, and above
all no substantive pressure. The real pressure that year was on Mozambique.[36] The combination of Renamo attacks and severe drought in
southern Mozambique led to the almost complete failure of crops in
some areas. The government issued an emergency appeal for food aid.
The US and other donors committed some assistance, but held back on
major commitments pending more dramatic signs of Mozambican accommodation with South Africa and the West. Total food aid in the
first half of 1983 was actually lower than previous levels. Despite repeated government appeals, aid fell short and an estimated 100,000
people starved to death. Mozambique at the time had an efficient
government system of relief distribution, with very little corruption. The
need was well documented. But aid began to flow in significant quantities only after the Nkomati Accord, and after negotiations for direct
involvement of US and other international agencies in the distribution.

In the wake of Nkomati, US self-congratulation faded as South
African violations surfaced. The State Department proposed a token $1
million of non-lethal military assistance to Mozambique in early 1985,
but the measure was dropped after stiff opposition in the administration
and in Congress. Even if the State Department had been willing to
confront Pretoria over continued supplies to Renamo, it lacked the
detailed information needed to do so. 'Despite our requests, it somehow
was never possible for US intelligence to document Renamo's barbaric
modus operandi or the pattern of continuing South African support',
noted Crocker.[37] The US intelligence agencies, instead, painted a picture
systematically biased towards Renamo.

Even the State Department never identified South African violation
of Nkomati as a key issue. It instead offered continued economic

assistance to Mozambique and sought new concessions which could be used to show success in 'wooing Marxists'. When Machel visited Washington in late 1985, his documentation of South African violations of Nkomati got little attention. He was urged to consider a power-sharing arrangement with Renamo, and to increase cooperation with the World Bank and the International Monetary Fund. Meanwhile many in the US military and intelligence community argued for considering support for Renamo and downgrading ties with Maputo.[38]

South African officials were well aware of the disarray in Washington on Mozambique policy, and had little incentive to respond when State Department officials mildly suggested that Pretoria might do more to curb support for Renamo. Concern for Mozambique was at best third on the State Department's southern Africa agenda, after the escalating crisis in South Africa and the high-profile Angola/Namibia front. Mozambique had no leverage in Washington apart from good will, subject to the fickle fortunes of lobbying. Unlike Angola, where Cuban troop reinforcements could up the ante in 1987–88, Mozambique had no threat. The US did not lose influence because of its failure to deliver South African compliance on Nkomati.

In 1987, despite the failure of pro-Renamo forces to block the nomination of Melissa Wells, pressures from the right continued. President Chissano's 1987 visit to Washington helped hold the line, but again there was no progress in getting the US to target South African support for Renamo. Not even the Gersony report's evidence of Renamo atrocities served to bring Washington to a more pro-active policy in favour of peace. The operative objectives remained wooing Mozambique with aid, while promoting concessions towards Renamo and further liberalization of the Mozambican economy. Curbing Renamo's supply lines was conspicuously uninteresting to US officials.

This pattern continued through the prolonged period of pre-negotiations and negotiations from 1989 through 1992. Although US officials recognized that supplies continued, and several times commented publicly to that effect, they always characterized the evidence as insufficient to justify action. As Kenya became involved in training Renamo troops and supplying arms through Malawi, Washington said it was unable to confirm detailed allegations by the Mozambican government and in press reports. A Renamo attack on the border town of Ressano Garcia in April 1989, in which South African soldiers on the other side of the border cooperated, was characterized by diplomats in Maputo as a 'smoking gun' demonstrating South African military involvement. Back in Washington, not even the Mozambique desk officer at the State Department thought it particularly interesting.[39]

Visiting Washington again in early 1990, President Chissano committed himself to direct talks with Renamo, and President Bush committed his administration to active diplomatic support for the peace process. In keeping that pledge, US diplomats expressed support for the general posture of the Mozambican government and frustration at Renamo's delaying tactics. But just as had the Reagan administration, they rejected any suggestion that the US should put pressure on Renamo through its supply lines. Towards the end of the Bush administration, aid to Kenya and Malawi was suspended as a result of congressional pressure and the rising pro-democracy movements in the two countries. But there was no linkage to the issue of Renamo's support. As late as 1991, the administration was still proposing military aid for both Kenya and Malawi.

Most significantly, the Bush love affair with the de Klerk regime implied that South African security force involvement with violence, whether in South Africa or in neighbouring Mozambique, was a non-issue for Washington officials. Once Mandela was released, and the necessary minimum of apartheid laws repealed, the priority was to reward de Klerk by lifting sanctions. Reasoning with most observers that it was not in de Klerk's own interest to promote violence, the administration played down charges by the African National Congress and others that the regime was pursuing a two-track policy combining covert violence with high-profile reform and negotiations. De Klerk would be strengthened in dealing with his right wing, the argument went, by rewarding him – not by pressuring him. The US should not 'take sides' by allocating blame for the escalating violence in South Africa.

This policy framework had direct implications for Mozambique. If de Klerk would not confront his security forces on internal issues, he would certainly not do so over the relatively unimportant Mozambique question. A probe of one issue would inevitably lead to the other, given the involvement of units like 5 Recce both in supplying Renamo and in train attacks and other violence in the townships. The US stand, on Mozambique as on South Africa, stressed accommodation and negotiation as the solution. In both cases, the option of putting greater international pressure on the party most responsible for violence was ruled out in advance.

As delays added up in implementation of the peace agreement in Mozambique, the international community and the US were still confronted with defining the assumptions behind their involvement. Would the premise be neutrality defined as an intermediate position between the parties regardless of their behaviour, thus leaving the process at the mercy of the party most willing to resort to violence? Or would the relative weakness of the Renamo lobby, as compared with that of Unita, imply greater willingness to insist on implementation of the agreement as signed than in Angola? These questions would be answered in totally different circumstances than the late Cold War context of previous years. But the fate of both the Nkomati Accord and the Bicesse Accord raised ominous questions.

Notes

1. There is as yet no comprehensive study of US relations with Mozambique, and Renamo in particular. But see particularly Nesbitt (1988); Vines (1991), 42–50; Austin (1994), and sources cited there.

2. Again, there is no comprehensive study on US/Angola relations and the Unita lobby. In addition to the administration viewpoint in Crocker (1992), see particularly articles by Bender (1978, 1981, 1985, 1989) and coverage in *Africa News* (Durham, North Carolina).

3. Among other sources, see Minter (1972), Noer (1985).

4. See particularly Antunes (1986), Cohen and El-Khawas (1975) as well as Minter (1972).

5. On the US in Angola in 1974–76, see particularly Stockwell (1978), Marcum (1978), and Bender (1978). A study based on new interview data is expected soon from Phyllis Johnson and David Martin.

6. On the rise of the right wing and US foreign policy see particularly Sanders (1983), Blumenthal (1986) and Ferguson and Rogers (1986). An advocate's view of the crusade is Menges (1988, 1990).

7. See Vance (1983).

8. The official perspective is found in Crocker (1992). My interpretation, based on events through 1985, is spelled out in Minter (1986) and in slightly greater detail in my chapter in Johnson and Martin (1986, 1988). A good summary of developments during the Reagan years is Baker (1989). More comprehensive analyses, particularly of the Bush years, have not yet been written. This chapter relies to a large extent on news coverage during the period, as well as participant observation as a commentator and activist working with anti-apartheid groups opposing administration policy, particularly the Washington Office on Africa.

9. The documents, leaked to the African–American lobby TransAfrica in 1981, are reprinted in Baker (1989).

10. Minter (1986), 319.

11. Some analysts postulate subsequent close cooperation on strategy between the US and South Africa, with explicit division of responsibility to play 'good cop, bad cop' roles in destabilizing the Frontline States (Gervasi and Wong, 1991). Given divisions and rivalries within both US and South African policy-making circles, consistently orchestrated cooperation seems to be unlikely. But it is probable, nonetheless, within the context of convergent goals and perspectives, that there was much *de facto* collaboration and coordination. It is likely to be a long time, however, before sufficient reliable data emerge to reach firm conclusions on this issue.

12. Bridgland (1987), 255ff.

13. Marenches (1988), 156.

14. Louis Wolf, 'UNITA's Savimbi Seeks U.S. Understanding – Again', *Covert Action* (Dec. 1979/Jan. 1980); Bridgland (1987), 273–4, 287ff.

15. *New York Times*, 4 February 1987; 2 July 1987.

16. *Washington Post*, 23 January 1982. Whatever indirect aid from the US reached Unita in this period, however, South African military assistance remained by far Unita's primary external supply.

17. On the Reagan doctrine and debates surrounding its implementation, see Rosenfeld (1986), Menges (1988), Crocker (1992).

18. On the Unita lobby, see particularly *Africa News*, 4 November 1985; 24 February 1986; 24 March 1986; 15 May 1989; November 1989.

19. *Africa News*, 6 February 1986.

20. See sources cited in Chapter 7 on killings in Unita.

21. See particularly Fred Bridgland, 'Angola's Secret Bloodbath', *Washington Post*, 29 March 1992; also *Washington Post*, 7 April and 12 May 1992 and *New York Times*, 7 April 1992.

22. For more information on this private US connection, see particularly Nesbitt (1988) and Austin (1994).

23. See the discussion in Crocker (1992), 147–250, 284–5.

24. See, for example, *Washington Times*, 5 February 1985, where he identified Hama Thai, head of the Mozambican airforce, as a North Vietnamese; the ludicrous error (no one who has met Hama Thai would think he could be Vietnamese rather than African) was picked up and repeated by US Ambassador to the UN Jeane Kirkpatrick.

25. *Soldier of Fortune*, May 1987.

26. See the discussions in Chapters 5 and 7.

27. Foreign Agents registration with U.S. Department of Justice, 22 July 1991.

28. See, on the negotiations, in addition to references already cited in Chapter 5, Gunn (1989, 1990), McCormick (1991), Zartman (1989).

29. McFaul (1989), 100. See also Bender (1989).

30. See particularly Bender (1985).

31. Crocker (1992), 141ff, refers to the meeting and complains about leaks of its contents; the well-informed report in *AfriqueAsie* (1 February 1982) cites Crocker as casually dismissing Angolan concerns about South Africa.

32. Crocker (1992), for example, while venturing comments on individual Angolan negotiators based on his contacts, shows no hint of any understanding of Angolan society going beyond simplistic stereotypes.

33. On details of the negotiations, see McCormick (1991).

34. *Africa News*, 15 May 1989; November 1989.

35. See Mutemba (1982) on the expulsions, Clough (1982) for a review of US/Mozambique relations in the early 1980s.

36. See Hanlon (1991), 28–9, 43–4; Crocker (1992), 232–44.

37. Crocker (1992), 28–85.

38. See Menges (1988), Austin (1994).

39. Personal communication from a Western diplomat who raised the issue with the State Department after receiving urgent messages from their country's embassy in Maputo.

7

How Contra Warfare Works: the Military Component

Sustained guerrilla warfare, according to the conventional wisdom, requires popular support. Revolutionaries, counterinsurgency theorists and social scientists alike cite Mao's remark that guerrillas must be to the people like fish in the water.[1] British counterinsurgency analyst Kitson says that 'no campaign of subversion will make headway unless it is based on a cause with wide popular appeal'.[2] Historian Clarence-Smith, in a recent debate on Mozambique, even claimed that the fish-in-water analogy 'seems axiomatic'.[3]

Likewise, guerrilla recruits are often assumed to be volunteers, motivated by national, ethnic or other causes. In such classic cases as China or Vietnam, a revolutionary party was linked with a highly politicized guerrilla army. Political commitment was seen as essential to military success.[4] More historically-minded analysts caution that guerrilla techniques have no necessary political correlates.[5] Even if there are popular grievances, a guerrilla war may never emerge or be suppressed by superior force. A popular cause is thus not a sufficient condition for guerrilla war. Nor is it a necessary condition. Guerrilla strategies may be used by small groups or by commandos attached to a foreign army. Mao concedes that counter-revolutionaries may use guerrilla warfare against the people, but adds that they are easily defeated.[6] Most analysts concur.

No such sweeping assumptions apply to conventional armies. Few doubt that an oppressive hated regime may maintain itself in power and win military victories. And such a regime may rely in large part on conscripted troops. Political support, legitimacy and ideological hegemony are of course relevant to a conventional army's success or failure. But firepower and terror may easily outweigh such consensual components.

Guerrilla warfare is seen as different, partly because of the best known twentieth-century examples. Although its role may be exaggerated, the political component was indeed at the heart of such conflicts.[7] But generalizing this model assumes certain background conditions. The guerrilla force must rely on political commitment and popular support, it is argued, because the state under attack has the army and police, control of the economy and state revenues, the capacity for repression and the troops to prevail in conventional battles. The guerrillas have none of these. This disparity is why insurgents adopt guerrilla tactics of mobility and surprise in the first place.[8]

These conditions do not, however, hold universally. Before the modern era, the distinction between armies of an established state and other bodies of armed men was not always so clear-cut. Currently, the contra wars of the 1980s raise doubts about this imbalance of force. The states under attack were generally weaker in material terms than the conventional wisdom assumes. And the outside military resources available to the insurgents in Nicaragua, Cambodia, Afghanistan, Angola and Mozambique largely counterbalanced the presumed guerrilla inferiority.[9]

Even if one takes conventional wisdom as 'axiomatic' for the classic cases, it is questionable whether the priority of political mobilization over force applies in the same measure to more recent conflicts. Data from Angola and Mozambique strongly suggest that insurgent armies with sufficient outside support can and do substitute force and technical military capacity for political mobilization. The extent to which this happens and how it works in each case are empirical questions which cannot be answered by invariant axioms of guerrilla warfare.[10]

This chapter and the next look at the functioning of the armies of Renamo and Unita. The data sources include my own interviews with ex-Renamo participants in 1988 and with ex-Unita participants in 1989, as well as other studies based on primary interview and documentary sources. The focus is not technical military questions, but rather the social mechanisms which enable an insurgent army to exist and function. Although there is much more evidence from Mozambique than from Angola, and great variability in the coverage of regions within each country, there is enough for preliminary conclusions on several important topics.[11]

The evidence indicates, for example, that forced recruitment has been an essential component of building the insurgent force. My working hypothesis before interviewing ex-participants was that there would be considerable variety in recruitment, including forced recruitment, ideological or ethnic motives, and material incentives for a young population with many people marginalized by the successive traumas of economic collapse, drought and war. The interviews in Mozambique revealed a far more consistent pattern than expected, with forced recruitment overwhelmingly dominant. The Angolan pattern was mixed,

174 APARTHEID'S CONTRAS

with voluntary recruitment predominant at first and forced recruitment taking on a major role in the 1980s.

Recruitment and control in Mozambique

Of thirty-two interviewees in Mozambique, only three recounted ideological motives for recruitment; two cited material incentives. None of the five was a rank-and-file Renamo soldier. The other twenty-seven said they had been recruited by force. They spoke in very specific terms, many citing the date, most commonly using the word *raptado*, meaning 'abducted' or 'kidnapped'. Three said that soldiers took them in 1978–79, first on foot to the Rhodesian border, and then by truck to Odzi, the Renamo training base in eastern Rhodesia. Each arrived in a group of captives, ranging in number from fifty to seventy. One said his group of seventy were tied to each other during the day of walking.

A similar pattern appeared in the other interviews. The captured recruits were marched to training bases inside Mozambique, some first being forced to carry goods for Renamo soldiers or to serve as guides in their home areas. Some were abducted in their fields, while on the way to visit relatives, or at home. Others were captured in large groups, during attacks on schools, villages, plantations, or small towns. One peasant in Nicoadala district in Zambézia, for example, was taken with 200 other villagers to carry food to the Renamo base in 1985. All the men were selected for military training. Another was a worker at Sena Sugar in August 1985 when 182 workers were abducted. They walked for three days before reaching the base, where he and eighty others were forced to begin military training. Another, a school administrator, was abducted with eighteen others in an attack on the school by 150 Renamo soldiers on Christmas Eve 1985.

I also asked each interviewee about the recruitment of others. Paulo Oliveira, a Mozambican of Portuguese origin and an ideological convert to Renamo, said that of approximately eighty Mozambicans who served with him at Renamo headquarters in South Africa in 1983–84, only three had not been forcibly recruited.[12] Staff for the radio station he directed, and for other office operations, included many former students of a secondary school in Inhambane who were abducted *en masse*.

Of the ex-combatants, fifteen said that all or almost all those who trained with them had also been abducted. One, who had been in Renamo since 1979, added: 'The *matsanga* take you, you can't say no.' Another, in Renamo 1982–87, said: 'In general, all the regular soldiers [*soldados simples*] were abducted.' Twelve others were hesitant about summary judgements, making comments like 'I didn't have a chance to count,' or 'I really didn't talk to everybody'. In follow-up questions I asked whether those abducted were 'many' or 'a few', and they uniformly answered 'many'. When asked about volunteers, their answers ranged from 'a few' to 'very few'.

The highest estimate of voluntary recruitment came from a Zimbabwean who served as a Renamo sector commander near Mavonde. He sent seventy to ninety recruits each six months to the central base for training, he said, including fifteen to twenty volunteers. Even this commander confirmed that 'kidnapping people' (*raptar pessoas*) was a regular task of Renamo military units.

The interviewees as a group showed no common attitude towards the Mozambican government or towards Renamo. The dominant stance seemed to be fatalism, as if the idea of choice was not particularly relevant. And in fact the only common factor which seems to have determined their entry into Renamo was that of being in an area vulnerable to attack, not any commonality in ideology, class position, ethnic group or political attitude.

Although my interviews did not include children, other sources indicate that forced recruitment of children was widespread.[13] Among my interviewees, those captured in large groups said that the captured males selected for military training ranged in age from 12 up to 30 or 40. Several said that those too old or young for actual combat were used for other tasks, such as porterage, servants for the officers, or messengers. The use of children in combat differed significantly by region, with the practice particularly prominent in Gaza and Maputo provinces.

Recruitment by means other than kidnapping did exist. In addition to volunteers, one interviewee recalled fellow recruits who told him they had been seeking jobs in Malawi when offered jobs by whites who took them to Rhodesia, where they found they were in Renamo. Other sources also cite specific credible examples, such as unemployed youth being recruited in Mozambique or among illegal Mozambican immigrants in South Africa. But the predominant role of forced recruitment is confirmed by other studies independent of my interviews.[14]

One study, by anthropologist Christian Geffray, is based on extensive field work in Erati district, Nampula province. Geffray stresses government policies which alienated the local population and produced a welcome for Renamo when it initially arrived in the district. His description of recruitment, however, confirms that kidnapping was the rule, while voluntary enlistment was the exception. He provides several first-hand accounts of kidnapped recruits, who describe being tied and marched to the base for training. Recruits were regarded as captives until after their training and incorporation into the Renamo forces. Geffray mentions the existence of 'numerous' volunteers as well, at least at the beginning, when several chiefs voluntarily adhered to Renamo, and youth loyal to them joined the Renamo ranks. In subsequent years, some recruits were mobilized from zones controlled by Renamo rather than captured in attacks on government zones. But Geffray does not specify how much of this mobilization may have been voluntary.

In over eighty systematic interviews with former Renamo participants in Inhambane, Sofala and Cabo Delgado, Swedish researcher Anders Nilsson observed the same pattern of recruitment by kidnapping. Nilsson, who travelled widely in the Mozambican countryside as a journalist between 1983 and 1988, says the practice of forced recruitment to Renamo was consistent and virtually universal. The crucial test of a recruit's attitudes towards Renamo, he cautions, was not whether or not he was kidnapped, but his subsequent responses. He noted a pattern of rapid turnover, with escapees being replaced regularly by new captives.

Researchers from Mozambique's Arquivo de Patrimônio Cultural, with Canadian anthropologist Otto Roesch, carried out interviews in 1990 in southern Mozambique, and in 1991 in central Mozambique.[15] Even in central Mozambique, the area of greatest Renamo influence and stable control, Roesch noted, 'recruitment of combatants here, as elsewhere in Mozambique, is still primarily by capture'. In the south, Roesch's informants, primarily from southern Mozambique, confirmed that non-Ndau combatants at least were almost all forcibly recruited, although they were less sure about the Ndau commanders. Roesch also confirmed the widespread use of child captives as soldiers in southern Mozambique.

Two national studies provide additional data. Save the Children interviewed 504 children (ages 5 to 15) with direct experience of the war, from forty-nine districts representing seven of Mozambique's ten provinces. Of the total, 323 had been abducted by Renamo. Over one-fourth of those abducted were subsequently forced into military training. An Africa Watch survey, which also includes an account of the government's draft programme and of voluntary recruits to Renamo, provides additional evidence of extensive forced recruitment by Renamo.

Since no research to date is based on a random sample, there can be no precise estimate of just how dominant forced recruitment was. The proportion would vary, presumably, not only by region and by time period but by whether one took as the denominator Renamo's total strength at any one time or all those who, however briefly, were forced into its ranks. Some forced recruits, as Africa Watch cautions, later expressed voluntary support for Renamo. But there can be no doubt that forced recruitment was overwhelmingly the most common entry into Renamo military ranks.

In Angola

Research on the Angolan case is less comprehensive. Published reports based on systematic interviews so far include only my own and two by

Africa Watch.[16] But the evidence does indicate a mixed pattern, in which forced recruitment played a significant but less prominent role than in Mozambique. There was a clear distinction between two generations. The first generation joined voluntarily, primarily in 1974–76 and principally because they saw Unita as the natural movement for their region. The second generation were mostly recruited by force. Some referred to a draft-like conscription in Unita zones, but most described being abducted (*raptado*) by Unita from government-controlled areas.

Among the interviewees, the five who joined Unita voluntarily did so between 1974 and 1976. Apparently, the greatest influx of recruits was in 1974, before open fighting began. One typical case, a 22-year-old draftee in the Portuguese army in Bié, heard about Unita from friends among his fellow troops, who told him 'Savimbi is our man'. Of Umbundu origin, he went to the Unita office in Cuito in August 1974 to join up. Another, a 19-year-old Umbundu from Huambo then working at the docks in Luanda, said he joined because 'the sentiment of the Umbundu was mainly for Unita'. A third went with others from his school to join Unita in January 1975. The students were divided, he said; 'many' joined Unita, but 'many' joined the MPLA instead.

These interviewees' descriptions tally with other accounts of the period. The majority of Unita's present-day leadership probably comes from this generation. Some had previous contact with clandestine Unita networks.[17] The experiences of my informants, however, imply that many recruits had little awareness of any Angolan movement prior to April 1974. Augusta Conchiglia, an Italian journalist who has interviewed ex-Unita soldiers on several occasions, also says the majority from 1974–76 were unaware of Unita before the *coup*.[18] Those months were marked by sudden euphoria, with political discussion opening up for the first time and youth flocking to the first nationalist movement that presented itself. For Umbundu youth and for ethnically diverse Moxico province, Unita was the most prominent and most accessible movement.

Most of the Unita recruits interviewed by Leon Dash in 1976–77 gave similar reasons for joining.[19] Many were former members of the Portuguese army who, according to Dash, 'joined voluntarily because of ... an emotional attachment to kinship, tribe and the Angolan south, and an almost mystical allegiance to Unita's charismatic guerrilla leader'. Unita's military recruits in this period also included a significant number of whites and *mestiços*, according to Dash[20] and Sitte.[21] But the majority were Umbundu-speaking youth.

Evidence of forced recruitment appeared both in the cases of the remaining eleven interviewees and in descriptions of later years given by the voluntary recruits. Nine of the eleven described being forcibly abducted by soldiers, using such words as *ataque* (attack) or *raptado* (kidnapped). The other two said they were *levados* (taken) along with others in their school or village.

Only two forced recruits were from the 1974–76 period. The first said that Unita soldiers took seventy-nine students from his school in Huambo province in May 1975 – all those of military age. They were told it was their duty, he said. The other, a hospital nurse, who said he did not support any political group at the time, was abducted at night from his mother's home in Bié province. Dash tells of a Unita officer who said he and his friends were invited to a party in Cuito in April 1975, loaded into trucks and taken to join the Unita army.[22]

The interviewees with knowledge of this period said such incidents were exceptional at that time, but that forced recruitment became widespread in the 1980s. In 1977 Unita decided to expand its military from a guerrilla army to one with semi-regular and regular forces, to implement what Savimbi termed the 'theory of large numbers'.[23] As one interviewee explained, when local commanders could not meet their quotas for recruits, they received orders 'from higher up' to begin abductions in government-controlled areas.

None of the interviewees entered Unita in 1977–81. But all nine who entered after 1982 said they had been recruited by force. One, of Ganguela origin, said that between 1975 and 1982 some men from his village left voluntarily to join the MPLA, while others left to join Unita. In 1982, when he was 28 years old, Unita carried out a recruitment raid (*rusga*) in the area and took him along with ten other villagers. He volunteered a distinction among *voluntários* (volunteers), those taken in *rusgas* (drafted), and *raptados* (abducted), saying there were 'a lot' (*muitos*) of each among his fellows. Another, a Cuanhama speaker, said his whole village was captured in mid-1983 and taken first to Namibia and then in trucks to a Unita base near Jamba. He said everyone he knew from Cunene province had been forcibly recruited, but that he didn't know about other provinces.

The remaining seven were abducted from rural areas of Huambo or northern Huíla, five in attacks on villages, two in road ambushes. All were taken in large groups on foot to bases in the bush, after which those of military age were sent to Jamba for training. Asked about the proportion of forced or voluntary recruits among their fellow soldiers, several interviewees said they didn't discuss the subject except with close friends. One said all those from his village at least were abducted. Another said that those abducted like himself were few in comparison with 'those they took from the population they already controlled'. Two others distinguished those abducted in combat from those taken in areas controlled by Unita. One of the better-educated interviewees said that in general officers were volunteers, but that among ordinary soldiers volunteers were rare after 1980.

With the exception of Dash in 1976–77, journalists who travelled with Unita appear not to have spoken with Unita soldiers about their recruitment. Angolan press interviews with ex-Unita soldiers also rarely give such details. But there are independent accounts referring to kidnapping of Unita recruits, including several from Africa Watch, three interviews by Conchiglia, and other brief press reports.[24] Together with my interviews, these suffice to establish the existence of forced recruitment on a significant scale in the 1980s. The evidence is insufficient to estimate the proportion, but the trend is clear: from predominantly voluntary recruitment at the start to greater use of forced recruitment (both draft and abduction) as the war grew. Such a trend makes sense, given both war-weariness and the need for large numbers for conventional warfare.

Control and assimilation

How then are young men recruited by force moulded into soldiers in guerrilla armies that actually work? The question is not entirely different from that for a conventional conscripted army, common to Angola and Mozambique, and indeed most modern armies. Countries with a draft rely both on force (threat of prison for draft evaders and deserters) and on claims of legitimacy to keep recruits. Military training is designed not only to impart technical skills but to incorporate recruits into a new social order (the army) and instil a sense of inevitability and pride in their new status.

Military conscription by governments, enacted into law, is acknowledged as legitimate despite abuses in practice (such as raids for draft evaders in Angola and Mozambique). Insurgent recruitment by abduction in enemy territory is apparently devoid of any such justification, although conscription in territory controlled by the groups may be legitimized by customary authority or the group's political mobilization. With legitimation playing a lesser role, other mechanisms must assume greater importance. For Renamo and Unita these included the threat of execution, transfer of recruits away from their home areas, fear of punishment by government forces, and training and assimilation into the soldiers' way of life.

Threat of execution

In both Renamo and Unita new recruits and soldiers faced the credible threat of execution for trying to desert. Some escape attempts resulted in less severe punishment, but the death penalty was frequent enough to serve as a powerful deterrent.

In Mozambique thirteen of the interviewees said they had personal knowledge of executions of soldiers who tried to escape, that their commanders had threatened them with execution, and that they believed this was the normal penalty. Six said the usual punishment was not so severe, instead citing ninety days in prison (in a hut or hole in the ground), beatings or torture. Second-hand reports in Maputo often referred to executions for demonstration purposes among abducted Renamo recruits, to discourage the others from resisting. None of the thirty-two interviewees gave specific examples of this. Colopes Sitoi, however, describing his abduction with some 200 others from Manjacaze on 10 August 1987, said several who could not keep up the pace were killed during the first night, and sixteen Muslims who protested that they wanted to return to town were executed the next day.[23]

Although the evidence is insufficient to determine the frequency, Unita also often executed attempted deserters. One interviewee in Angola said that four people abducted with him, including his primary school teacher, tried to flee shortly after being captured. Unita recaptured and executed them. Others said they witnessed executions of attempted deserters on several occasions. Several independently noted that this was one of the themes of the graduation speech Savimbi gave each group of recruits when they finished their training.

Transfer

Transferring recruits served both to separate them from their home communities and to make it physically difficult to escape. In Mozambique, almost all the interviewees described marches of at least two days from capture to the training base. Geffray and Nilsson report a similar pattern. With few exceptions, Renamo recruits were posted as soldiers in districts other than their own, and some to other provinces. They all described their military units as mixed in origin, and said they were not with people whom they had known at home or who had trained with them. One commander in Manica province said the policy was to transfer soldiers in order to make it harder for them to run away.

This strategy seems to have been particularly effective in areas such as Zambézia province, where there is little tradition of long-distance migration. Having to learn both the geography and the local language before attempting escape was a major obstacle. This difficulty was less significant in the south, where the migratory tradition and common language led to familiarity with a wider range of territory. Most transfers appeared to be within the same region of the country (south, centre and north). But the interviewees in each region also reported the presence of soldiers from other regions, with the Gorongosa headquarters bringing recruits from all over the country.

Unita also made it difficult for recruits to desert by moving them weeks or months of walking time from their home areas. In contrast to

Mozambique, however, the initial transfers were all in one direction, to the Jamba area. This was far from the homes of most recruits, who in the 1980s were generally taken there in trucks. Those among the interviewees who did desert all said it was virtually impossible to do so from Jamba, remote as it was from populated areas of the country. The risks, they said, were not only recapture but also starvation or attacks by wild animals.

Fear of government forces

Apart from the fear of execution by Renamo or Unita, the reason most frequently given for not deserting was that the soldiers were told by their commanders that if they did succeed in escaping, the government would kill them. In neither country was this official government policy. Particularly since 1988, both governments strongly stressed amnesty programmes which implied trying to attract deserters rather than punishing them. But such incidents happened often enough to serve as a real threat.

In Mozambique, several interviewees reported speeches by Renamo President Dhlakama in 1988 saying that the government's amnesty programme was a lie, and that if they turned themselves in they would first be interviewed on the radio and then shot. One, a prisoner, said that he knew of Renamo soldiers who had fled and then been killed by government forces. Mozambican government officials confirmed that, particularly in earlier years, there had been cases of mob violence against Renamo soldiers and summary executions by local commanders. With the amnesty programme, such incidents diminished, but some continued to be reported.[76]

The rank-and-file Renamo soldier was thus faced with a difficult choice: if he tried to escape and failed, he might well be executed, and, as far as he knew, if he succeeded he might then be killed by the government. One of those I interviewed said he had debated with himself for months which side was most likely to be lying before he finally decided to try to desert.

In Angola as well the interviewees mentioned fear of punishment by the government, including execution, as a deterrent to desertion. According to the interviewees, Unita told recruits that the government executed former Unita soldiers whether deserters or prisoners. Several described their surprise at finding alive acquaintances that Unita told them had been killed.

The available evidence does not confirm the extent to which such fears were justified. By 1989, after a widely publicized amnesty and the release of numerous prisoners, the government programme for dealing with prisoners and deserters seemed relatively well organized, and aimed at reintegrating the ex-Unita soldiers into society. The personal experiences of several interviewees, both prisoners and deserters, show that this programme was also functioning earlier in the 1980s. The dominant thrust of government policy, with programmes to reunite such people with their families and to find jobs (successful in some cases), was to attract deserters rather than to exact vengeance.

Angolan press accounts in earlier years, however, as well as other sources, report the death penalty applied by military tribunals to Unita prisoners. Amnesty International also regularly reported allegations of extra-judicial executions.[27] Regardless of official policy, it is clear that there was much indiscriminate retaliation in some locations on both sides. The potential Unita deserter did have credible fears of what government forces might do.

Attrition

Despite such obstacles large numbers of recruits managed to escape, at least in Mozambique (comparable data is not available for Angola). Mozambique reported 3,000 formally accepting amnesty in 1988, probably a minimum figure since many who deserted Renamo preferred not to report to the government. No total estimates for earlier years are available. But radio message logs from a Renamo commander in Maputo province, captured in 1984, referred to sixty-nine desertions from his forces over seven months, out of an estimated strength of 425 men.[28]

Nilsson attributes particular importance to this process of attrition. Those most opposed to Renamo were more likely to escape or to be killed for trying. Those remaining, therefore, were precisely those most available, willingly or unwillingly, for assimilation into its ranks.[29]

Initiation and training

For one group of recruits – young children recruited in southern Mozambique – there is evidence of initiation into violence by forcing them to commit violent acts against civilians. Such extreme violence, however, does not appear to have been the general rule throughout Mozambique or for all recruits.[30] Nor does it appear to apply to Angola. Unita clearly differed from Renamo in that the interviewees reported no pattern of forced recruitment of young children for military training. With the exception of one, who said he was involved in training 'children' (*crianças*) in 1986, all the interviewees said that recruits were not sent for military training until they were adults – minimum ages mentioned ranged from 17 to 19. Two had themselves attended school after joining Unita before being sent for military training.

Well-organized basic training was essential to both insurgent armies.

While foreigners, primarily Rhodesians and South Africans, were involved, Mozambican and Angolan instructors recruited from the ranks carried the major responsibility. The three Mozambicans trained in Rhodesia said the course took six months. For those trained later in Mozambique basic training was two to three months. The content of the training was mostly weapons-handling, and on completion of the course they were given an AK-47. Some received additional training, in artillery, anti-aircraft, communications or first aid. With few exceptions the instructors in the courses inside Mozambique were Mozambicans, identified by the interviewees as 'veterans' with greater experience.

The Angolan pattern was somewhat different. The early recruits were trained at Unita camps in Moxico province, before the fighting began in 1975. Their instructors included a few of Unita's pre-1974 guerrillas, but most were veterans of the Portuguese colonial army. In the 1980s, the principal training camps were located near the Zambian and Namibian borders, in the most remote south-eastern triangle of Angola. Basic training was three months, after which the recruits qualified as 'semi-regular' troops. Some recruits took specialized courses of six months; a few received only minimal guerrilla training.

There were two notable differences from the Renamo pattern. In the Renamo case, some troops were trained by South African instructors, but by the early 1980s most were trained by Renamo instructors at provincial bases inside Mozambique. The Unita system was centralized in the Jamba area and jointly run by South African and Angolan officers. Two or three of each were responsible for training one company, with the Angolans doubling as instructors and as translators.

Regardless of the means of recruitment, integration into a military unit and completion of basic training is likely to ensure some degree of group solidarity. Research on conventional armies has indicated that loyalty to one's comrades in arms is one of the most potent motives for soldiers in combat, often more significant than patriotism or other abstract loyalties. It is plausible that this factor would apply to insurgent groups as well.[31] Only those with the strongest loyalties to the other side would be likely to resist such pressure.

Political mobilization and assimilation

For Renamo, political mobilization even within the army seems to have been minimal. None of the interviewees referred to regular political meetings, discussions or courses. They regarded themselves as part of an army, not a political movement. Only two said there were regular political meetings with the civilian population.

The nine interviewees who did refer to political meetings said these were occasional gatherings of soldiers to hear speeches by President

Dhlakama or other commanders. All said the speakers stressed themes such as 'we are against communism, we are against socialism, we are for capitalism, we are against [communal] villages and want to live individually in the bush'. They were promised that the war would be over soon and they would go to live in the city. Nevertheless, the loyalty many Renamo recruits developed probably resulted more from the social dynamics of the group than from political arguments. There is still little evidence to refute Geffray's characterization of the group as a purely military organization existing for the sake of war itself.[32]

Except for a core group, ethnicity was apparently not a major barrier to assimilation into Renamo. The interviewees said the majority of the commanders were Shona-speakers, but they also stressed that the soldiers came from all parts of Mozambique, and that men from any ethnic group could move up the command ladder. In many cases soldiers had to learn Shona, but the language spoken in a unit depended on the ratio of different groups. On this issue, notably, both Shona and non-Shona speakers made similar comments. Nevertheless, there is also good evidence that Ndau identity was significant for coherence within Renamo's core military leadership, affecting their attitudes both to lower ranks and to the civilian population.[33]

In terms of both political mobilization and ethnicity, assimilation into Unita contrasted with Renamo. Most officers and many soldiers were volunteers, and the social context into which forced recruits entered was highly politicized. Savimbi and his subordinates devoted time to justifying their cause; the military structure was embedded in a political context. The sanction of force was in the background should the recruit not be convinced, but Savimbi's personal persuasiveness was a powerful influence, as was the cadre of devoted followers.

Unita's ethnic homogeneity facilitated political assimilation. The interviewees agreed that within Unita the overwhelming majority of both soldiers and civilians were of Umbundu origin. Other ethnic groups in Angola were also represented, but in relatively small numbers. The interviewees noted the presence of a few non-Umbundu speakers in the top leadership, as well as in the officer corps. Unita used both Portuguese and Umbundu as linguae francae, but in practice everyone was required to speak Umbundu. While this *de facto* ethnic hegemony may have hindered integration of non-Umbundu speakers, it facilitated the incorporation of Umbundu-speaking recruits, to whom allegiance to Unita was presented as a natural loyalty.

Rewards

Even for those forcibly recruited, the rewards of military life may have provided some positive incentive. Geffray stresses the limited opportunities for youth in Nampula province in the early 1980s, and the prospects of independence from family and access to food, loot and women given by possession of a gun. It seems reasonable that this explanation would apply in some measure elsewhere in Mozambique and in Angola.[34] Such benefits, however, were significant only for a fraction of the insurgent force. Conditions for the rank-and-file, according to my interviews, were often extremely harsh.

For Unita, there was opportunity for advancement within the army, and the expectation of power after the expected victory. For some there was overseas training, such as military courses in Morocco and other countries, and civilian scholarships primarily to Portugal. In short, for the Unita recruit, military service could be an opportunity as well as a political obligation. The rewards for Renamo soldiers were more limited. Commanders in some areas, particularly on the borders with Malawi or South Africa, profited from sale across the border of looted goods. Mozambicans from Renamo being trained in South Africa sometimes received regular salaries as members of the South African Defence Force, with Renamo officials receiving 500 to 750 rand a month in the early 1980s.[35]

A final benefit, apparently well-organized in Renamo as well as Unita, was the system of first aid and other medical care for the soldiers, including possible evacuation to South Africa for the most serious cases. While this did not entirely compensate for the risks of combat, it probably served as one of the most important measures for maintaining morale.

In summary, there are alternative mechanisms available to mould an insurgent force into a workable military machine. In Unita, these mechanisms included systematic political mobilization. But even with minimal political mobilization, as in Renamo, the combination of continued threat and of assimilation into the social structures of the army served to keep the machine working.

The logistics of military operations

Sustained guerrilla warfare relies on logistics. Despite the myths, successful insurgency without regular access to outside supplies is rare. Renamo and Unita had an added advantage: organization of the supply operation by an outside power with sophisticated planning and transport. Guerrillas fighting the Portuguese were able to use adjacent African territories. But they relied on irregular shipments from a variety of foreign powers, underdeveloped transport networks in the neighbouring countries, and exclusively head porterage once across the border. Renamo and Unita, in contrast, used head porterage only at the far end of the supply line.

Mozambique

The interviewees in Mozambique described a coherent pattern of supply of arms, ammunition and medicines. All who served in combat areas made some reference to captured matériel, but none claimed it was the basic source of supplies. The supply operation encompassed deliveries over land borders, by parachute drop, by landings of Dakota DC-3 aircraft, and by sea, as well as transport by head porterage within and between provinces.

Two interviewees, in Renamo less than six months, said the arms came 'from the warehouse' in the base. Others in subsidiary bases said that when supplies were running low, the base commander would radio to the provincial base and send carriers to pick up the resupply. Interviewees with no experience in a provincial base consistently said they were uncertain how the weapons arrived there, but that they had been told by other combatants it was from South Africa.

Those with experience in provincial bases or near the Renamo headquarters described a strict need-to-know system in which only elite groups of soldiers met airplanes or ships. Several who were involved both before and after 1984 said that secrecy intensified after the Nkomati agreement. Afterwards, said a commander who spent nine years with Renamo in central Mozambique, the Dakota aircraft came only at night, to sites kept secret from most soldiers.

The pattern differed significantly by region. One interviewee, in a base near the Mozambique, Swaziland and South African borders during 1984–88, said that some matériel came over land from South Africa, by head porterage. He added that South African helicopters came at two-month intervals, bringing supplies, doctors, instructors for special courses, or other visitors.

Interviewees in central Mozambique cited parachute drops and airplane landings, both before and after the Nkomati Accord. One, stationed near Espungabera in 1979–82, said planes came every three months, making two drops in the same night. Afterwards, as a commander near Mavonde (1982–88), he normally received supplies by parachute drop once a year. The quantity was generally enough for one year; he was also expected to maintain the arms he captured as a reserve supply. One year, 1987, the expected shipment did not arrive, he said. Others similarly described annual shipments, with more frequent deliveries to some areas. Central Mozambique at least received regular shipments in several different locations.

In Zambézia, the interviewees cited both air landings and porterage across the river from Gorongosa. One who spent December 1986 to June 1988 in the provincial base at Alfazema said an airplane landed on two occasions during this period, in April 1987 and April 1988. He did not see it, since it was at night, but he heard the noise and saw the special troops sent out to get the matériel. Another, in the Maringue area in 1985–86, helped prepare fires to mark the airstrip. A special unit of sixty soldiers met the airplane. After he was transferred to a company-level base in another area in 1987, forty to sixty porters were sent back to Maringue each year for supplies.

Interviewees who recognized specific airplanes referred most frequently to Dakotas. Two with experience in Renamo bases in South Africa before Nkomati referred to the use of DC-3s (Dakota) and C-130s. Fernando Machia, in Renamo 1981–88, told a Mozambican journalist after deserting that he had seen four-engine Dakotas (DC-4s) drop supplies in Gorongosa.[36]

The interview data matches documentary evidence captured at the Renamo central base at Garágua in Manica province in December 1981, and at the successor headquarters in Gorongosa in August 1985.[37] Minutes from a 1980 meeting between Renamo representatives and South African officers noted difficulties in maintaining a high level of supplies by parachute drop, and indicated that 'the South Africans showed willingness to send monthly supplies as from 1981 but by sea'. In another 1980 meeting with Renamo, Colonel Charles van Niekerk 'spoke of the difficulty of restocks as the aircraft cannot carry too much weight'. He also asked for 'two places where they can make the supply because it cannot be always made at the same place'.

The Gorongosa documents, dated December 1983 to September 1984, provide particularly revealing details in the diary of Dhlakama's secretary.[38] An entry on 16 January 1984 noted: 'Because of the commitment which the South Africans will make to Machel, the resupply for the first six months of 1984 will all be delivered in the first few months: 500 pallets in 25 flights in addition to the resupply for January 1984.' A marginal note indicated five drop zones in the south, seven in the centre, and three in the north. Other entries listed sixteen additional scheduled drops.

These supplies only lasted about six months. In June 1984 Renamo President Dhlakama wrote to 'Friend Commander Charles' that 'we no longer have war matériel, mainly in the central and southern areas of our country. We appreciate that we received that last consignment but as soon as we unloaded we had to relieve all the regions in the central area. ... So we want to remind our friends of the pledge they gave us of keeping up support to us clandestinely.' Van Niekerk asked Renamo to conserve matériel and promised to consult his superiors. A month later he radioed a promise to supply 26 tons beginning 1 August in 'the drop zone to the east of Inhaminga.'

A Renamo delegation was taken to South Africa by sea later in August to discuss the supply situation. South African military officials cited fourteen air deliveries made in May, June and July, but added, 'at this moment we have transport difficulties because we can't now use the C-130s, which are controlled by the Air Force, and we can't use the Navy because the information might leak'. They suggested that Renamo prepare airstrips for civilian aircraft. A diary entry for 29 August listed six air deliveries for September and October 1984.

The interviews, together with press accounts from Mozambican eye-witnesses, document a similar supply pattern at least until late 1988. With the entry into office of President de Klerk in late 1989, supplies diminished but did not stop, according to Mozambican government sources. A higher proportion of deliveries reportedly came overland from South Africa or Malawi rather than by air, a pattern consistent with greater involvement of semi-private clandestine networks. There are no systematic interview data for the later period on this topic, but there are indications that supplies continued to flow until the 1992 ceasefire.[39]

Thus a US military attaché, on the basis of detailed interviews with a Renamo prisoner, concluded that South African supplies were arriving regularly by helicopter at a Renamo base in Maputo province as late as February 1991. A South African reporter who visited a Renamo camp across the border immediately after the ceasefire was told by its commander that SADF vehicles had been supplying the camp with food and water three times a week. The commander refused to confirm but did not deny that he also received military supplies.[40]

By the war's end, in fact, the traffic in arms between South Africa and southern Mozambique went both ways. A surplus of AK-47s in Mozambique and the escalation of violence in South Africa led to a booming smuggling trade to South African townships, including supply of AK-47s to Inkatha. Renamo still needed, however, regular restocks of ammunition, selected weaponry and other supplies in the south as well as the centre and north. Press reports on resupplies to central Mozambique mentioned both Malawi and ships sailing from Kenya as well as South Africa.

Angola

In contrast to Renamo support, the scale of military operations in Angola and the wish to gain publicity for Unita made consistent deni-ability impractical. Instead the strategy was to keep the details secret and minimize the significance of South African support.

At times, Savimbi denied that South Africa provided aid, saying that Unita paid for all supplies. He portrayed the period before 1980 as one in which the South Africans gave Unita no help at all.[41] The presence of South African troops was rarely acknowledged publicly, either by Unita or by South Africa. Despite these efforts, which affected media coverage, few analysts doubted massive and sustained South African military support for Unita, at least from 1980 to 1988. The data are not sufficient to estimate reliably how significant that aid was, in proportional terms. But they are enough to show how the system worked.

Supplies from South Africa continued on a small scale during 1976–79. Some aid also came from other sources, including France, Zaire, Morocco and Saudi Arabia. According to Savimbi, South Africa made the decision to aid Unita in 1980, when it established a regular system for Unita to submit requests three months in advance.[42] In fact, the shift to regular large-scale South African supplies probably came in late 1978 or early 1979. One of the interviewees said he helped transfer Unita's central base south to Jamba in April 1979. The move was not only to flee government attacks but to establish a secure supply base, about six hours by truck through the bush from Namibia. By mid-1980, when Austrian journalist Fritz Sitte visited the area, Unita commanded a fleet of fifty supply trucks.[43] Three impeccably-uniformed battalions were on parade at Unita headquarters, a striking contrast to Sitte's visit three years earlier.

Jamba has been described in numerous newspaper reports, and the description does not warrant repetition here. Several points are worth mentioning, however. First, the area was accessible by land from South African-controlled northern Namibia. Although journalists in the 1980s were invariably flown to an airstrip near Jamba, most supplies came in overland. According to the interviewees, South African and Unita personnel regularly moved back and forth across the border. One interviewee, in Savimbi's personal entourage in the early 1980s, said Savimbi often spent weekends at a base assigned to Unita in Namibia. This land route was critical in reducing the cost of supplying military operations, making southern Cuando Cubango in effect an extension of Namibia. South Africa's official designation of northern Namibia and southern Angola as one 'Operational Zone' was more than a figure of speech.

Secondly, the area was previously very sparsely populated. In colonial times most of southern Cuando Cubango was game park, roughly the size of the US state of South Carolina and only slightly smaller than Portugal. The population of Jamba was estimated by several interviewees at roughly 8,000 to 10,000 in the mid-1980s, with perhaps ten times that number in the surrounding area. The vast majority were brought by Unita from other parts of Angola.[44]

Unita expanded this area in the early 1980s by picking off isolated government outposts in eastern Angola. Thus their fleet of trucks could deliver ammunition and troops to the edge of the densely populated central plateau. In the second half of the 1980s, conflict centred on control of these supply routes north from Licua, the Unita supply base in the Jamba area.

By 1983, Unita's heavy trucks, numbering about 250 to 300, regularly transported journalists as well as matériel and troops north of Jamba, to Mavinga and on to Munhango on the Benguela railway. Diesel fuel and spare parts made up a significant portion of the supplies received from South Africa. Captured vehicles were converted from petrol to diesel to use the South African-supplied fuel. Unita mechanics told a Portuguese journalist that motors only lasted eight to ten months under bush conditions, requiring regular replacements.[45]

Supplies reached the bush camps by a mixture of transport. Sometimes carriers were sent on foot to Licua, on trips as long as two or three months each way. At other times carriers picked up supplies at transfer points from trucks or from airdrops. The airdrops were regular, at least in the mid-1980s. One interviewee, responsible for receiving matériel near the Huíla/Huambo provincial border, said two South African C-130s dropped supplies every six months. Another interviewee, who had been in Kuanza Sul province, said three C-130s arrived every six months. In a revealing comment to an Italian journalist, a Unita prisoner whose unit received airdrops in the Lunda–Malanje border area said they 'had a right to four aircraft a quarter'.[46]

In early 1988, Savimbi told French journalist Jean Larteguy that Unita paid for South African military aid, and that only medical aid was provided for free.[47] The statement, undoubtedly an exaggeration, was later denied after it provoked controversy in South Africa, but it called attention to another aspect of Unita's war economy, cited in several first-hand reports. Although currency and private enterprise were not permitted in Unita-controlled territory, the organization exported teak and other valuable hardwoods, diamonds and ivory.

Both interviewees and some journalists also noted that Jamba received a substantial portion of its food supplies and other goods from South Africa. Unita's semi-regular and regular troops also relied partly on such rations. Very few outside food supplies, however, were passed on to guerrillas or civilians in the bush.

From 1979 until the Namibian peace process in 1989–90, therefore, Unita's logistics depended on a motorized transport network from South African-controlled Namibia. Namibian independence in March 1990 removed this option. The Jamba area had to be supplied by airlift, in part from South Africa, but more importantly by CIA flights from Kamina in Zaire's Shaba province. By mid-1990, the major focus of Unita offensive operations had shifted to north-western Angola, adjacent to the CIA supply lines close to Zaire's port of Matadi.

In the aftermath of the abortive Gbadolite agreement, tension between Mobutu and Unita led to the temporary suspension of CIA supply flights from Zaire's Kamina airbase. When flights resumed in November 1989, the first supply flight crashed. In violation of the 1988 accords, however, South Africa maintained supply flights to Unita during this period, enabling Unita to resist government attacks on Mavinga until new US supplies arrived. Most significantly, Unita was able to launch new guerrilla offensives in northern Angola with supplies over the Zaire border, which were not affected by the suspension of the Kamina airlift.

Strategy and organization

Angola and Mozambique fit closely the classic conditions for guerrilla warfare, favourable in geography and balance of forces to guerrilla attack rather than to defence.[48] Both countries are huge territories with low population densities and vast expanses of bush unintegrated into a modern transportation grid. Mozambique, with some 800,000 sq. km., is twice the size of California; Angola is 55 per cent larger, twice the size of Texas. Mozambique has a population of only some 15 million; Angola about 10 million. Railways run inland on east–west axes; north–south connections are minimally developed road networks. Blocking one trunk road can paralyse communication among major centres. In the interior there are no viable north–south land links at all.

Size estimates for the armies are not exact, but in the mid-1980s security forces in Angola (including the Cubans) probably ranged between 100,000 and 150,000; in Mozambique the total (including the Zimbabweans) was probably under 70,000.[49] Whatever the exact figures, such numbers are manifestly inadequate for a comprehensive defensive grid for such large countries, even if the guerrilla attackers were as weak as the classic image implies. In fact, by the late 1980s estimates of Unita guerrillas (not including regular troops) went as high as 35,000, while Renamo was generally estimated at about 20,000.

Commentators have often noted facilely that the Angolan and Mozambican armies failed to retain the lessons of their pre-independence guerrilla struggles, and were therefore unequipped to match Unita and Renamo's strategies. This is only a half truth, because insurgency and counterinsurgency require totally different strategies. Defence of fixed installations and settled populations, inherently more difficult than sabotage and guerrilla attack, requires a different kind of army. Angola and Mozambique had to prepare for conventional attacks and to build forces capable simultaneously of static defence and mobile action against guerrillas.

Their efforts fell far short. The Angolan military with Cuban aid grew to a relatively well-trained, well-equipped force. But it never had adequate resources to mount both conventional and counter-guerrilla actions on all necessary fronts. The Mozambican army, with the exception of a few units, never had adequate levels of equipment or trained personnel. It was unable to be effective militarily in more than one geographical area at a time. In both cases the fundamental weakness was that the attackers could choose from many targets to attack; the defenders had no such luxury.

As significant as military weakness was the more general fragility of the states under attack. The guerrilla strategy of attrition reinforced other crippling blows, including loss of the Portuguese settlers, damage from direct South African and Rhodesian attacks, and recurrent droughts. In Angola damage to the transportation infrastructure from the 1975–76 war was severe, with destruction of 128 bridges and only 6,000 out of 28,000 heavy trucks left on the road.[50] In Mozambique much infrastructure in Gaza, Manica and Tete province was destroyed by Rhodesian raids. South African economic sanctions against Mozambican migrant labour and transport services crippled Mozambique's traditional sources of revenue.

In short, since the insurgents' principal military task was to destroy, while the governments had to build and defend, Unita and Renamo started with an enormous initial military advantage. To the extent that they were willing to risk alienating popular support by attacks on dispersed civilians, the defensive task became even more unmanageable.

Mozambique

Renamo's war strategy can be clearly discerned in its selection of targets. High on the list were the transport networks. Mozambique's railways, key sources of foreign exchange, were also strategic for the regional landlocked states. Between 1982 and 1988 almost 500 railway workers and passengers were killed in Renamo attacks. Material losses over the same period were estimated at $898 million, equivalent to six times yearly export earnings in the late 1980s. By 1987 even routes still open – Beira to Zimbabwe and Maputo to South Africa – were only operating at 40 per cent of capacity. International traffic to Malawi was entirely cut; the railway to Mozambique's coal mines at Moatize was shut down in 1985.[51]

Road traffic within the country suffered even more drastically. Passenger buses and cars as well as trucks with trade goods, food relief supplies or peasant produce were consistent targets of ambush. What was not looted was burned. Killings of civilians in such attacks were common; in other cases, the victims were kidnapped and used to carry booty to Renamo bases.

Another strategic target was the Cabora Bassa power line, constructed to carry electricity to South Africa from the hydroelectric project on the Zambezi. With 890 km. running for the most part through sparsely settled bush country, it was an easy target. It was forced to close in 1982. A captured order from a South African liaison officer to Renamo in 1980 read: 'DESTROY THE CABORA BASSA POWER LINES TO SOUTH AFRICA TO COVER THE IDEA OF SOUTH AFRICAN SUPPORT.' Although South Africa lost surplus electricity capacity, it gained almost $500 million in revenues from supplying electricity to southern Mozambique. Without offsetting Cabora Bassa revenues, Mozambique had to pay hard currency.

Adequate defence of such targets as the power line, railways and roads would have been physically impossible even with a large and efficient counterinsurgency force. In practice, protection extended only to a few corridors, while other routes were travelled only at serious risk or in large military convoys.

Other economic targets included sugar and tea plantations and other commercial farms, many of which were totally destroyed. Direct attacks on urban industrial plants were relatively minor, and sabotage in the ports was confined to a few attacks by Rhodesian and South African commandos. The effect of the war on industry was generally indirect: cement production was crippled, for example, by sabotage against the rail line from the quarry to the factory, and then by an attack on the quarry. In 1986 Renamo occupied several district capitals, particularly in Zambézia and Sofala provinces. By 1988 most had been recovered, but whatever could be looted had been taken away; few buildings were left standing.

Assaults on district capitals were exceptional, but attacks on smaller settlements were common throughout the 1980s. Typically, an attacking force of company or battalion size confronted a much smaller defensive garrison, and Renamo killed government officials, destroyed buildings and carried off loot. Sometimes other local residents were killed; more often they were used to carry the loot. Those not recruited by force were sometimes allowed to return home, but were more frequently kept near the Renamo base in the bush. A few attacks stand out in scale and brutality. Sometimes there were only a few killed. But the pattern was consistent.

Education and health, the most prominent benefits brought by the government to rural areas, were particularly significant targets. Between 1983 and 1987, for example, 45 per cent of the existing 5,886 primary schools were closed by Renamo attacks and over 400 teachers were killed or wounded. By the end of 1988, 191 rural health posts had been destroyed and another 687 looted or forced to close – 46 per cent of the primary health network. New building and repairs averted an aggregate decline until 1986, but from 1986 to 1988 the number of functioning posts fell from 1,326 to 1,143.

Another Renamo objective was capturing civilians not only for military recruits, but also to provide food and head porterage for Renamo.

Settled in a protective shield around the Renamo base, they also enabled Renamo soldiers to escape from government attacks leaving them behind. Such *recuperados* were then taken, also by force, to government-controlled areas.

The size of the countryside ensured that despite successful government offensives in specific areas, Renamo bases could move to another undefended zone or even return to the original location once government troops departed. The result was a shifting patchwork quilt war, with insecurity even in many areas not subject to Renamo attack at a particular time. This pervasive insecurity continuously undermined the government.

Angola

Unita used a wider array of strategies than did Renamo. A guerrilla-type strategy predominated before 1980, and in most of the country in the 1980s. But Unita/South African occupation of south-eastern Angola in the 1980s entailed conventional combat, with artillery and aircraft on both sides of the battlefield. Although Unita relied entirely on South Africa for airpower, it had its own artillery.

Early in the war, Savimbi described his strategy as one of bringing the Angolan economy to its knees.[52] One key target, running both through Unita's area of greatest ethnic support and through sparsely populated eastern Angola, was the Benguela railway. According to railway figures, 198 railway workers were killed by mines or attacks between 1976 and 1987. Suspension of international traffic led to annual revenue losses of some $89 million.[53] Attacks on economic targets also included several successful raids on diamond mines in the mid-1980s, and less successful efforts against oil installations. The latter were carried out by South African commandos, with little direct Unita involvement. Unita claimed responsibility in any case, except for an unsuccessful raid on Cabinda in which Angolan troops captured a South African saboteur.

Other Unita actions aimed at disrupting transport in the rural areas, targeting civilian as well as military vehicles. In the early years of the war, according to Unita officers cited by Dash, peasants in areas Unita claimed were divided politically, and Unita attacked villages whose residents refused to leave government-controlled zones to join Unita in the bush. Unita carried out several large-scale massacres of villagers, but the incidents were not as prominent as in the Mozambican case. Far more than Renamo, however, Unita made extensive use of land-mines, occasionally resorted to urban bombings, and captured hundreds of foreign hostages.

Land-mines were used not only along roads but also to deprive government-controlled areas of food supplies. In many areas, Unita systematically planted mines in fields. According to the interviewees, mining was normally carried out by specialized units. One, with a note of pride in Unita's military capacity, bragged that the government side was not really experienced in the use of mines; Unita had many more well-trained explosives experts. An extensive post-war study by Africa Watch, based on their own interviews together with a survey by the International Red Cross, concluded that the majority of mines were laid by Unita.[54]

The use of bombs in urban terrorist attacks was most frequent in Huambo, where Unita was able to set up clandestine networks. The targets were sometimes buildings where government officials or foreign advisers lived, but the attacks were also designed to cause general civilian insecurity. In 1990, with increased US aid through Zaire, there were several such incidents in Luanda.

Taking foreign hostages was aimed at paralysing the economy and attracting international attention. Savimbi repeatedly warned that foreigners in Angola were at risk, and released hostages were required to pledge they would not return to Angola.[55] Some hostages were taken in the course of other military actions, but other attacks specifically targeted foreign workers. More than eighty Czechs and Portuguese, for example, were taken from a hydroelectric site in Benguela province in 1983.[56] In 1984 three English workers, two Americans, seventeen Filipinos and four Portuguese were captured at a diamond mine.[57] Almost 200 foreigners, mostly Portuguese and Filipinos, were taken in an attack on the diamond-mining town of Andrada in 1986.[58]

One extraordinary effect of Unita's hostage-taking was relatively favourable publicity, in a decade when the media were highly sensitized to threats of international terrorism. Unita skilfully exploited media bias towards a 'pro-Western' group.[59] Only a few of the hostages were from major powers such as the US or Great Britain; instead the victims were Portuguese, Filipinos, Brazilians, Czechs or Swedes. The captives were not abused beyond the wounds they sometimes received in the initial attacks, and the experience of being forced to march hundreds of miles through the bush. A few died, but most were eventually released in press conferences hosted by Savimbi.

Unita built up its troop strength for conventional war, growing from some 15,000 mainly guerrilla soldiers in 1981 to as many as 65,000, including 28,000 regulars, in 1988.[60] This force was supplemented throughout the 1980s by South African troops. Of the large-scale South African invasions of Angola in 1981, 1983, 1985 and 1987, the first two aided in expanding Unita's area of control, and the latter two served to block Unita defeats. With the exception of 1987-88, Unita's conventional army played the most active role in the south-east and east, while South African forces were concentrated in the south-west, north of Ovamboland. Between 1980 and 1984 Unita took control of much of eastern Angola, including the Cazombo salient near Zaire and several towns on the Benguela railway. Mavinga came under Unita control in 1980, Cangamba in 1983. In 1985 and again in 1987–88, Unita conventional forces lost ground to government counter-offensives, and were saved from defeat by South African air power and ground troops.

These battles were confrontations of conventional armies, the outcomes dependent on logistics, technology, balance of forces and battlefield tactics. In this arena, at least, issues particular to guerrilla warfare were moot. The relatively few civilians in the area were bystanders or victims, in no way resembling the water for the guerrilla fish in Mao's metaphor. The existence of the Unita enclave was the result primarily of conventional geographic and military factors.

Organization and communications

In both countries the coordination of war over large areas, and in Angola the integration of conventional with guerrilla actions, required centralized organization that fits better the image of a conventional military force than of under-equipped guerrillas. In both cases this was made possible largely by good radio communications.

Given its strong conventional component, and the number of officers trained in Morocco and South Africa, it is no surprise that Unita military structure followed conventional models, with a full range of officer ranks and units up to brigade strength. Renamo has sometimes been portrayed as a loose collection of warlords and roving bands. According to the interviewees, however, Renamo was also an army with a clear hierarchical structure and good command, control, communications and intelligence. This picture was confirmed when, contrary to many observers' predictions, the Renamo command was able to enforce a consistent ceasefire policy after the 1992 accord.[61]

The basic operational unit was the company, composed of approximately 100 to 150 men, generally grouped in one main base with satellite bases for special functions such as security and reconnaissance. Each company, with apparently few exceptions, was equipped with radio-transmission facilities and a communications officer in regular touch with the provincial base and indirectly with Gorongosa headquarters. Two or three companies made up a battalion. A provincial base had two or more battalions in its immediate vicinity, sometimes dispersed a few hours' march away. Recruits were kept in separate training bases.

Efficient radio communications made it possible to coordinate this army dispersed over rural Mozambique. One interviewee, for example, had been a sector communications officer in 1982–83, responsible for the area between the Save and Buzi rivers in Manica and Sofala provinces. He had twenty-one radios in his sector, with orders to check in with each five times a day and to transmit a summary report to Gorongosa over a separate radio link. Another interviewee, in a Renamo group occupying Caia in early 1987, said they received advance notice by radio that Zimbabwean and Mozambican troops were to attack the town. Renamo headquarters then instructed them to burn it down. This indicates sophisticated radio-monitoring capability, consistent with Oliveira's statement that South Africa monitored Mozambican radio communications and passed useful information on the Renamo headquarters.[62]

The interviewees in Angola did not include Unita specialists in radio communications. But the detail and rapidity of Unita military communiqués, appearing in South Africa and Washington very quickly after military actions, pointed to an effective network. So did the coordination between South African and Unita military actions.

In Mozambique Renamo's access to radio communications and timely intelligence was often superior to the government's. In Angola Unita and the government, with their respective allies, were more equally matched. But in neither case did the balance resemble the presumed overwhelming superiority of an established state over a guerrilla force.

The operational role of external sponsors

In addition to supply and training, South African personnel were also directly involved in military operations with Unita and Renamo. Some aspects of this involvement are still cloaked in secrecy, but the general outlines reveal expected contrasts between Angola and Mozambique.

The best documented are the open South African operations in southern Angola.[63] The attacks in the south-west were distinct from support operations for Unita, but affected Unita's prospects since Angola had to allocate resources to defend both areas. The involvement of regular South African forces, including draftees, made these operations particularly visible. Often South Africa did not seek deniability, instead justifying them as retaliation for SWAPO attacks. The actions of 32 Battalion were, in contrast, almost always kept away from publicity. The unit operated regularly in both south-western and south-eastern Angola, and, according to one early defector, was responsible for a number of battles claimed by Unita.[64]

Most obscure of all are details of the role played by small South African special forces units, which reportedly served in operations as well as in training Unita. Some sabotage operations by South African commandos were carried out separately, such as the unsuccessful raid on Gulf Oil in 1985. But references to those who accompanied Unita are short on details.

South African direct attacks on Mozambique were limited to occasional commando raids. But South Africa's role in Renamo operations, at least in the early 1980s, was more direct than with Unita.
Renamo headquarters was located in South Africa from 1980 through
early 1984.[65] The general lines of strategy were planned by South
African officials in conjunction with Renamo Secretary-General Cristina
until his death in April 1983. The day-to-day command was also in the
hands of South African officers. President Dhlakama, dividing his time
between South Africa and Gorongosa, participated in the planning but
generally deferred to the South Africans.

In preparation for the Nkomati Accord the headquarters staff was
divided into south, centre and north and sent into Mozambique. HQ
south and north were mobile, while HQ centre, at Gorongosa, also
served as national headquarters. Six Renamo communications officers
remained in South Africa to handle communications between Gorongosa and the special forces at Phalaborwa.

The presence of South African troops or advisers with Renamo inside
Mozambique was episodic rather than constant. The standard pattern,
according to one special forces member, was to send in a five-man
group for two to three months, for special training courses, intelligence
gathering or participation in specific actions. This group would normally
be composed of two Afrikaners (the commander and a doctor) and
three Africans, one of Angolan origin, one of Zimbabwean origin and
one of Mozambican origin. A diary entry in the Gorongosa documents
for 16 January 1984 fits this pattern, speaking of a 'team' of South
Africans to go to Zambézia at the end of January to train 100 instructors
and 200 infantrymen.

One interviewee, in Maputo province, spoke of regular arrival of
South African 'visitors' by helicopter in the base until he escaped in
mid-1988. Other reports refer to occasional presence of small groups of
South African soldiers as late as 1989. Only during the 1986 Renamo
offensive in the Zambezi Valley were larger numbers apparently involved. One interviewee said he was in a base in Zambézia in 1985–
86 where there were black Malawian and South African as well as
white South African instructors, and a separate unit of black South
African soldiers.

The systematic character of South African involvement probably
diminished in the late 1980s. But the radio link between Gorongosa
and Phalaborwa was operational through 1988 at least, and reports in
the South African press refer to Renamo bases in the Transvaal and
northern Natal at that time.[66] Details of the connection in the final
years of the war await further revelations of the links between the South
African security forces and private right-wing forces.

The operations of South African special forces and military intel-

ligence are insufficiently documented as yet to provide reliable details.
A semi-official book on *South Africa's Border War*, for example, gave only
a few paragraphs to the Recces, although the section was headlined
'Unseen, unheard but always there'.[67] A full picture of the interaction
between South Africa, Unita and Renamo will only be possible when
and if reliable inside information emerges on these elite, multiracial
and multinational forces.

Notes

1. The quote from Mao is from Mao Tse Tung (1961), 93. It is also used by
Giap (1962), 56. It shows up in Valeriano and Bohannan, (1962), 7, and in Kitson
(1971), 49. Bell (1971), 31, quotes it and so does Laqueur (1976), 267.

2. Kitson (1971), 29.

3. Clarence-Smith (1989), 22.

4. An early Rand Corporation study of prisoners and defectors in Vietnam,
for example, stressed the strong political component in guerrilla morale. Donnell,
Pauker and Zasloff (1965).

5. See especially Chapter 1 of Laqueur (1976) and the editor's introduction
in Chaliand (1982)

6. Mao Tse Tung (1961), 47.

7. This is clear not only from the works cited above by Mao Tse Tung and
Vo Nguyen Giap, but also from the prominence given to political issues in Mao
Tse Tung (1968) and from analyses of these wars by scholars of a wide variety
of perspectives. See the works by Bell and Laqueur cited above, as well as Rice
(1988), by a former US diplomat with extensive experience in Asia. Studies based
on interviews with prisoners of war, including Donnell, Pauker and Zasloff (1965),
Henderson (1979) and Bradbury, Meyers and Biderman (1968), note a variety of
methods of recruitment to the Vietnamese and Chinese armies, including forced
conscription even in the guerrilla phase. But they agree in stressing the importance of political motivation for the core of the revolutionary armies, and of
political indoctrination for both willing and unwilling recruits.

8. Rice (1988), 52–78, is particularly clear and concise in expounding the
conceptual framework of the distinctiveness of guerrilla strategy.

9. An anthology covering the Reagan doctrine insurgencies is Radu (1990).
On the Reagan doctrine see Rosenfeld (1986). Sarkesian (1986) gives an advocate's overview of US involvement in 'low-intensity conflict'. Klare and Kornbluh
(1987) is an anthology from a critical perspective.

10. 'Guerrilla warfare' is the term most commonly used in the literature,
referring to the actions by small units making use of mobility and deception
against larger conventional forces. Most authors also recognize that the ideal
type is rarely found in its pure form, and, as in China and Vietnam, may be
combined with actions by larger-scale units and more conventional military
strategies. Using the term 'guerrilla' stresses the tactical and strategic use of the
methods of the weak against a superior force. This overlaps but does not coincide
with the term 'insurgent', referring to a military force fighting to overthrow an
established government. The term 'contra warfare' deriving from the conflict

against the Sandinista government in Nicaragua, is used in this essay in a generic sense, to refer to an externally-backed insurgency against a left-wing government, relying primarily but not necessarily exclusively on guerrilla strategies and tactics.

11. Results from interviews in Mozambique and Angola are reported in Minter (1989) and Minter (1990). Other major sources, cited specifically later in this chapter and the next, include the work of Gersony, Geffray, Roesch, and Wilson. Anders Nilsson has also conducted extensive interviews with ex-Renamo participants, but the results are not yet published. There are also a significant number of first-hand reports scattered through other published sources on the war, including Finnegan (1992), Africa Watch's *Conspicuous Destruction* (1992), and many shorter accounts by journalists and non-governmental organizations.

12. Oliveira repeats this observation, with details of several individuals, in a 121-page unpublished manuscript, Oliveira (1990), 19, 36.

13. See Boothby, Sultan and Upton (1991); Africa Watch, *Conspicuous Destruction* (1992), 95–8; also Richman, Ratilala and Aly (1990), and McCallin and Fozzard (1990).

14. Gersony (1988). Geffray (1990), 96–113. Source of data on Nilsson interviews, personal communication. Dutch journalist Wim Bossema also interviewed a significant number of ex-Renamo combatants in several provinces (*De Volkskrant*, 24 June 1989).

15. The results of this research are in Roesch, 'Renamo and the Peasantry in Southern Mozambique' (1992), and Roesch, 'Mozambique Unravels' (1992), and in as yet unpublished conference papers: 'A Paradigm Shift? Rethinking Renamo's War' (1992) and 'Peasants, War and "Tradition" in Central Mozambique' (1993). The quote is from p. 11 of the 1993 conference paper.

16. Africa Watch, *Angola* (1989), *Angola* (1991).

17. Linda Heywood, in an article citing Unita leader Tito Chingunji, says that such clandestine support was widespread, especially among Umbundu Protestants. Heywood (1989), 53–4.

18. Augusta Conchiglia, 'Les Hommes de l'U.N.I.T.A. Parlent', *Afrique-Asie* (February 1987).

19. Dash (1977), 41–7.

20. Dash (1977), 84–7.

21. Sitte (1981), 82–91.

22. Dash (1977), 42–3.

23. Savimbi (1979), 8–9; Savimbi, 'The War against Soviet Colonialism' (1986), 13–14; Dash (1977), 100.

24. Africa Watch (1989, 1991); Conchiglia, 'Les Hommes'. Other press reports are cited in Minter, *Unita*.

25. Author's notes from viewing of unedited videotape of interview by Mozambican journalists.

26. Geffray, for example, reports that troops killed several people who turned themselves in in Erati district, despite disapproval by other government officials (Geffray, 1990, 195ff.).

27. See annual reports of Amnesty International, as well as Amnesty International (1982). Although not directly applicable to the time-period under discussion here, and undocumented in detail, it should be noted that reports on the renewed conflict in 1992–93 included numerous cases of indiscriminate action

against both civilians and enemy combatants by troops on both sides, as well as by armed civilians.

28. *Tempo* (28 April 1985). A captured internal Renamo report from Nhamagodoa, dated 6 May 1988, cited the flight of seventy-four recruits from one battalion, leaving 159, with an average of five fleeing a day, because 'they are from here'. The report then proposed sending the recruits to another province (Africa Watch, *Conspicuous Destruction*, 1992, 87).

29. Personal communication.

30. See the reports cited in note 13 above. On this general issue see K.B. Wilson, 'Cults of Violence and Counter-Violence in Mozambique' (1992).

31. See, for example, Janowitz (1959), 44–82, and references cited there, including Stouffer et al. (1949).

32. Geffray (1990), 154.

33. Research on Shona language and ethnic identity in Mozambique is very limited, but this point is clearly important (see Roesch on central Mozambique, as well as Vines, *Renamo* (1991), 84–5 and Vines, 'Diary' (1991). Careful research on this point would have to consider both the possibility of assimilation (becoming 'Ndau' by learning the language) and the fact that the term itself means different things to different people. Among my interviewees, those from central Mozambique distinguished between different Shona dialects, such as Ndau and Manica, but those from elsewhere in the country referred to all Shona-speakers as Ndau. And non-Ndau Shona speakers sometimes refer to Ndau as Changana (Shangaan), reflecting the fact that they were part of the nineteenth-century Gaza Nguni state; but southern Mozambicans normally referred to as Changana would not think of the Ndau as included in their number (Roesch, personal communication).

34. See also comments by Roesch, 'Renamo and the Peasantry' (1992) and in Finnegan (1992), 70–1.

35. Constantino Reis, 'The MNR from Within', an interview by the Mozambican News Agency, supplement to *AIM Bulletin* (January, 1985). Compare Oliveira (1990), 18, who cites a salary of 720 rand for Renamo president Dhlakama in 1983.

36. *Notícias* (17 October 1988); translated in Minter (1989), 16.

37. Photocopies of documents in author's possession. Selections from the Gorongosa documents were translated and distributed by the Mozambican government in 1985.

38. Confirmed as genuine by South African Foreign Minister Pik Botha in *Hansard*, 6 February 1986.

39. In January 1989, extrapolating from the pattern revealed by my interviews, I estimated the flow of supplies to Renamo to be at least 148 tons a year. Given the speculative nature of the calculation I did not include it in my 1989 report. The minimum character of this estimate was confirmed when two years later I spoke with an officer who had handled the paperwork for supply flights in the early 1980s. The DC-3 flights, at the rate of four per month, added up to approximately 180 tons. Even if the actual volume, including sea and land deliveries, were twice that in the mid-1980s, it would be a relatively low volume to maintain even with private aircraft and helicopter or overland deliveries.

40. Cable, Maputo to Washington, Defence Intelligence Agency, 1 April 1991; *Weekly Mail*, 9–15 October 1992.

41. See the descriptions of this period in Bridgland (1986) and in Loiseau and de Roux (1987).

42. Loiseau and de Roux (1987), 226.

43. Sitte (1981), 40.

44. Philippe Chatenay, 'Dans la brousse angolaise avec les maquisards de Savimbi', *Le Point* (19 December 1983): 75–81. Christopher S. Wren, 'Angolan Rebels Look to Life after South Africa', *The New York Times* (30 October 1988). There were 113,000 registered for the 1992 election in Cuando Cubango province, including both Unita and government-controlled areas.

45. Paulo Camacho, 'Unita: A Angola Proibida', *Expresso* (26 September 1987).

46. Augusta Conchiglia, 'Récit d'un Prisonnier', *Afrique-Asie* (21 December 1985).

47. Jean Larteguy, 'Jonas Savimbi: Comment J'ai Vaincu les Russes d'Angola', *Paris-Match* (18 March 1988).

48. See the discussion in Chapter 3. Also Laqueur (1976), 275 and Beckett and Pimlott (1985), 9. Rice (1988), 90–118, provides a good summary of concepts of counterinsurgency.

49. At the end of the war, Angolan government troops were estimated at 110,000 for the purpose of demobilization; the number of Cuban troops withdrawn, after major reinforcements in 1988, totalled 50,000. In Mozambique the number of Zimbabwean troops may have reached a height of over 15,000 in the late 1980s. The total number of Mozambican troops to be demobilized was variously estimated from 50,000 to 150,000, with 92,000 said to be on the military payroll while some foreign military attachés suggested that there were less than 50,000 active troops.

50. Hodges (1987), 31.

51. Data on destruction is summarized in United Nations (1989) and in Johnson and Martin, *Apartheid Terrorism* (1989).

52. Luís Rodrigues, '2400 km com a Unita no centro e no Sul de Angola', *Expresso* (24 March and 15 April 1977).

53. Johnson and Martin, *Apartheid Terrorism* (1989), 130–1.

54. Africa Watch, *Land-Mines in Angola* (1993), especially 34–5.

55. Savimbi, *Por um Futuro Melhor* (1986), 48, 132.

56. Mário de Oliveira and Joaquim Vieira, 'Relato de um Refém da Unita', *Expresso* (6–27 August 1983).

57. Dixon (1986).

58. J.L., 'Portugueses Repatriados Falam da Unita', *O Diabo* (27 March 1986).

59. See Windrich (1992).

60. Western intelligence sources put the figure at about 40,000, while Angolan government estimates were lower, but all sources agreed that a significant proportion of the total were conventional troops. Just before the Bicesse Accord Unita claimed a force of 75,000, but only estimated 50,000 in September 1991 to be demobilized. It is still not verified whether Unita deliberately held back large numbers from the official count.

61. Unorganized banditry and criminality undoubtedly existed during the war years, increasing as conditions of economic as well as physical insecurity became increasingly apparent. And local Renamo commanders undoubtedly also had a certain degree of autonomy. But in the absence of systematic numerical data,

anecdotal evidence, over-generalization and rumour almost certainly exaggerated the proportion of this disorganized violence in the perceptions of both urban Mozambicans and foreign observers.

62. Oliveira (1990), 19, says that Renamo headquarters received regular reports from a South African military communications team of twenty-four persons assigned to monitor communications in Mozambique. Roland Hunter, an aide to Colonel van Niekerk at the time, recalls receiving transcripts of these intercepts regularly (personal communication).

63. See the summary accounts in Hanlon (1986) and Cawthra (1986), Steenkamp (1989) and other sources cited in Chapter 3.

64. See Minter (1988), 106–9, and references cited there. After the agreement on independence of Namibia, 32 Battalion was withdrawn to South Africa. There it played a controversial role in South Africa's internal violence, amidst unconfirmed reports of veterans returning to Angola, to serve either with Unita or with government forces. Also see the recent book by former 32 Battalion commander Breytenbach (1990), which claims that 32 Battalion members constantly posed as Unita. Breytenbach's book is thin on detail, and a more informative report of the unit's history has not yet surfaced.

65. See, for example, the account in Oliveira (1990).

66. Among other sources, see the detailed information given in Oliveira (1990) and Weekly Mail (18 August 1989; 30 March 1990; 27 July 1990).

67. Steenkamp (1989), 7, 230; Hamann (1990). For a summary description of the special forces units, see Weekly Mail (20–26 September 1991).

8

How Contra Warfare Works: The Military/Civilian Relationship

The military operations described in the previous chapter require civilian cooperation, but not to the extent of the classic fish-in-water analogy and not necessarily voluntarily. With military supplies from outside, forcible recruitment if necessary, and much countryside left undefended, guerrillas are just as capable of imposing themselves on civilians as is a conventional force. They need to prevent the population from serving as government informers, to collect information about government troops, to get food for the soldiers and porters for transport. This cooperation may be obtained by persuasion or by force; the precise mix of incentives is not predetermined.

If the population is strongly mobilized in favour of the government, the insurgents' task is more difficult. But if the government cannot provide protection, even pro-government civilians may be forced to collaborate. If civilians are favourable to the insurgent cause, that makes it easier for the insurgents. But if civilians have no strong sentiments either way, insurgents as well as counterinsurgents can impose themselves. Overly politicized interpretations probably underestimate the extent to which ordinary people respond not from political conviction but in order to survive and preserve their livelihood in the midst of conflict.

The enormous regional diversity within both Angola and Mozambique implies that nationwide generalizations about civilian attitudes must build both on local studies and on national surveys with interviews from all regions. The number of such studies is still limited, and the data is fragmentary. Nevertheless, there is a significant body of work on Mozambique.[1] On Angola there are no local studies and only a few national studies, with limited coverage. The 1992 election results are, it can be argued, a relevant indicator of regional variation. But they supply neither reasons for the votes nor any guarantee that attitudes in 1992 corresponded precisely with those during the earlier war period. This gap in systematic data can only partially be remedied by systematic analysis of reports by journalists and other scattered testimony.[2]

The data do, however, justify several conclusions on the relationship between civilian support and military success in guerrilla warfare. Comparison between the two countries, and among regions within them, shows that high levels of civilian support were not a necessary condition for guerrilla success. The levels of such support were only one factor, and probably not the most important one, in determining the prospects of guerrilla action.

In some parts of Mozambique, Renamo received voluntary cooperation from some chiefs and others alienated from the government, particularly when first entering a given zone. But even in those areas subsequent collaboration was imposed by force after civilians became disillusioned. There was little apparent correlation between Renamo's political appeal in an area and its military effectiveness in that area. In Angola, voluntary collaboration with Unita by Umbundu-speakers in particular was common in the early years of the war, although even then coercion was also used. Unita maintained a system of political mobilization and provided some benefits for its rural adherents. Voluntary support diminished, however, with escalation of the war and Unita actions against civilians. Unita's fortunes at different times and places, moreover, varied less by levels of political support than in accord with more narrowly military factors.

In both countries, despite voluntary support for the insurgents from some portion of the population under their control, loyalty was enforced by brutally effective use of force and threats of force against civilians, which continued into the post-ceasefire period. The political freedoms called for by peace treaties were in practice largely confined to areas under government administration. Treaty provisions mandating extension of central state administration to insurgent-controlled areas were never implemented in Angola, and had not yet been implemented in Mozambique over a year after the October 1992 ceasefire.[3]

Mozambique: force, persuasion and indirect rule

There are several features of Renamo's relationship with civilians on which different researchers converge despite their contrasting methodologies and perspectives. These include: 1) the systematic resort to violence and threats of violence; 2) initial support for Renamo from some rural groups due to the impact of government policies or to ethnoregional affinities, generally followed by disillusionment; 3) the use of traditional authorities and religious practices to apply a variant of indirect rule; 4) the largely coercive extraction of resources for food and porterage; and 5) regional variations based on ethnic affinity, local conditions and the changing fortunes of war.

Inside Mozambique the systematic nature of Renamo attacks on civilians, reflected in journalistic and word-of-mouth accounts, was common knowledge. But the first formal research on the issue was by a US State Department consultant, engaged to assess the rapid increase in Mozambican refugees and displaced persons. Robert Gersony's April 1988 report was based on interviews with nearly 200 refugees and displaced persons in Mozambique and four border countries, including South Africa. The report showed a pattern of extraordinary abuse of civilians. He concluded that 'the relationship between Renamo and the civilian population ... revolves almost exclusively around a harsh extraction of labor and food. ... It appears that the only reciprocity provided by Renamo for the efforts of the civilians is the possibility of remaining alive.'[4]

The Gersony interviews included numerous cases of eyewitnesses to murder, torture, kidnapping and forced porterage. While he distinguished 'tax areas' with less use of force from 'control areas' of tighter administration, civilians living under Renamo administration were consistently portrayed as captives, consisting both of original residents and of others abducted from government-held zones. There were also 'destruction areas' in which Renamo did not try to gain control, instead maximizing damage to property and civilians. Although Gersony did not identify these zones, later studies noted that much of southern Mozambique corresponded to 'destruction areas', with the less clearly distinguished 'tax' and 'control' areas located farther north.

Gersony also reported abuses by government forces, but in much smaller numbers and not systematic. Of 600 murders they witnessed, his informants attributed 94 per cent to Renamo, 3 per cent to the government, and 3 per cent to unknown parties. The Gersony report was vehemently criticized by Renamo, and questioned by some others, who alleged deficiencies ranging from fabrication of stories by Mozambican secret police to systematic distortion in the final report.[5] Critics noted that the report was a tool in the bureaucratic infighting between Renamo supporters and constructive engagement advocates in Washington. Despite legitimate questions over projecting the results to reliable numerical estimates, however, the range of the interviews and their consistency with what journalists and relief workers were hearing helped the report stand up under criticism.

Gersony admitted that his interviewees were not a random sample of the entire country. But they were chosen by a random process in the refugee camps, and they represented a wide range of geographical areas.

Even allowing for a probable bias against inclusion of strong Renamo supporters, who would presumably stay in Renamo areas, the conclusion of extensive use of coercion by Renamo was inescapable.

In 1988 French anthropologist Christian Geffray carried out the first detailed study of Renamo and local communities, in Nampula province, at the request of Mozambican officials. Geffray and a colleague, Mögens Pedersen, had published a widely discussed paper noting the possibility of widespread support for Renamo by peasants disaffected by Frelimo's rural policies. From his 1988 field research in Erati district, Geffray challenged the unrelievedly negative picture of Renamo's relationship to civilians.[6] But he also confirmed its character as an apolitical military force imposing its will ultimately by force. In including both aspects, Geffray's later work differed from the earlier essay which described the war as 'transforming latent internal conflicts of the peasantry into an open conflict between a fraction of the peasantry and the state'.[7]

Geffray's thesis was that the government, by excluding traditional authorities from power, giving authority to non-traditional village officials and ultimately forcing peasants to leave their land and regroup in villages, aroused hostility which translated into support for Renamo when Renamo soldiers arrived. He hypothesized that the pattern he described for Erati district probably applied to other parts of Nampula province and elsewhere in Mozambique as well.

Geffray portrays the Mozambican state as a rigidly modernizing institution imposed from the outside in disregard of local traditions and authority structures. The installation of the state is symbolized by the imposition of 'villagization' with new authority structures and by displacement of the population from their ancestral lands. The peasantry and the chiefs, wrongly stereotyped by the government as discredited collaborators with colonial rule, resent the state, and therefore welcome arriving Renamo forces as potential liberators. Thus Geffray sees the paradigm applying even in areas such as Zambézia, where villagization was never of major significance. Apart from the issue of generalizing the paradigm, however, one of the virtues of Geffray's work is that it provides substantial detail, which on some points significantly qualifies his general thesis, even with respect to Erati district itself.

He describes the pre-1984 alienation of traditional authorities and peasants by Frelimo policies, but acknowledges this almost certainly would not have developed into armed warfare without the arrival of Renamo from the outside. Although he makes no explicit distinction between villagization imposed for ideological or for military motives, his description makes clear that it was military actions which precipitated the alliance of some chiefs with Renamo. The population of remote areas in Erati district was forcibly regrouped for defence against Renamo in early 1984, in response to rumours that Renamo soldiers were nearing the district. A number of chiefs, particularly the Macuane, then led their followers in welcoming Renamo. Among the Erati, however, most chiefs opted for the government side, despite their differences with the government. Geffray notes that the Macuane were marginalized relative to the Erati in both the colonial and independence periods, and that rivalries dated to pre-colonial times. He describes how government soldiers killed a suspect Macuane chief in 1984, setting off armed conflict between villages before Renamo arrived.

Thus, if the attitude of the state towards traditional society in general was the key factor making Erati district vulnerable to Renamo penetration, it remains to be explained why some sectors and not others moved in that direction once conflict began. Was it military considerations that led Renamo to enter more remote areas, and the government military forces to concentrate their forced resettlement on those same areas? Or was it, as Geffray hypothesizes, divisions going back to pre-colonial times? And what about the later period when, as Geffray describes it, the state took a much more low-key attitude towards traditional authority, while disillusionment with Renamo's abuses grew in areas under their control? To what extent did traditional rivalries rather than concerns with survival affect peasant behaviour? Geffray's account is nuanced enough to raise such questions, but his reticence in attaching numbers to any of his descriptions makes the answers elusive. He gives no estimate of what proportion of the population welcomed Renamo initially, or how quickly how many of them became disillusioned.

According to Geffray, the implicit contract between Renamo and the chiefs who invited Renamo to set up bases on their land was that Renamo would block government interference with their way of life and enable them to remain on their land. In return, the chiefs would serve as administrators for Renamo, taking the Renamo title of *mambos* and mobilizing the population to provide food and collaborators to serve as police (*madjiba*).

Geffray noted that youth who joined Renamo as *madjiba*, at least at the beginning, did so with enthusiasm, although in contrast to other sections of the work he cited no specific testimony on this point. His tendency to romanticize traditional authority and to stress government abuses he feels other researchers have neglected probably led to some exaggeration here, but there is no reason to doubt that many people did welcome Renamo. Given his general position, it is notable that Geffray went on to say that this welcome, even by the chiefs, was based on a 'misunderstanding' and was followed by 'disillusionment'. His description of mechanisms used by Renamo to maintain control corresponded closely with those by Gersony of 'control areas'.

Geffray's description of the Renamo base of Mariri notes a rigid separation between soldiers and civilians. None of the Renamo commanders spoke Macua, the local language, and even the Renamo soldiers spoke other dialects of Macua. Renamo organized the captive and volunteer population by making use of their own traditional leaders. But it was 'a foreign body ... ruling over a closed world where no inhabitant of the region could enter'.[8] The local communities were free to live under their own leaders, but they had to suffer the extraction of resources and forced recruitment of auxiliaries to enforce order. They were grouped at some distance around the Renamo base, providing a civilian barrier to penetration by government attack.

Geffray also gives a richly descriptive account of the subsequent pattern of settlement and survival in the war zones of Erati. It was characterized by a low profile for government administrators, few direct confrontations between Renamo and government troops, and deferential attitudes by government administrators towards many of the traditional community leaders. Symbolically deferring to the state at officially designated villages, local people nevertheless made a *de facto* return to traditional lands, with temporary or more permanent habitations depending on the security situation. Disenchantment with Renamo and the cut-off from market contact experienced under Renamo was matched by only sporadically effective government efforts to protect the populations nominally under its control. Overall, when one considers the likelihood of significant regional variation in the degree of Renamo's reliance on force, his account of this period is more consistent with Gersony's overview than their contrasting perspectives would suggest.

In my interviews with ex-combatants of Renamo in 1988, I deliberately refrained from questions about their treatment of civilians. Given previous reports of atrocities, I thought it unlikely that the combatants themselves would speak frankly about this during a short interview, and that pressing these questions would make them less likely to talk freely about other subjects. The interviews, together with other data from that research trip, however, provided data overlapping with the results of both Gersony and Geffray. In conversation with local government officials in Zambézia province, for example, I was told that in some areas people had at first welcomed Renamo, because of their disenchantment with the economic and political policies of the government. Within a few months, they said, the same people were criticizing Renamo as no more than thieves and murderers.

More generally, the interviews with ex-combatants provided confirmation both for the general picture derived from Gersony and for Geffray's description of the situation after the initial welcome for Renamo. The interviewees typically described a situation in which certain local chiefs and traditional healers cooperated with Renamo. They were clear, however, that both chiefs and healers belonged to the subject civilian population rather than the Renamo structure. Several said that the Renamo soldiers 'went to the healers' for treatment just as the civilians did. Several commented that most of the chiefs had no choice about collaborating when Renamo came into an area. One interviewee, who had been a prominent farmer and elder in his village, had been appointed by Renamo to direct the village as chief *mudjiba* (policeman). He said they occupied his house, sleeping on the veranda, several times tied up his wife when she objected to giving them food, and killed his brother-in-law after an escape attempt.

All the interviewees agreed that there was a strict separation between the Renamo military structure and civilians, and that very rarely was any civilian permitted closer to a Renamo base than a control point 100 to 200 metres distant. They described the relationship with civilians as centred around obtaining food for the Renamo soldiers and transporting looted goods.

In some areas, soldiers were sent out to collect food, or *madjiba* organized the people to bring food to a control point near the base. Some mentioned that groups of women or old men were specifically assigned to cultivate fields for the base. Three who had been in Renamo since 1979 said the people had enough food and gave voluntarily. Another, with Renamo 1984–88, said the people gave voluntarily at first, but not later. All four were from Manica province or Zimbabwe, including three Shona speakers and one Sena speaker.

The majority, however, described the food contributions as involuntary. As one described it, 'There was a team to go ask for food from the people. They arrive, ask for it; if the people refuse they take it by force, maybe all their food.' Most said the food situation in the bases was adequate but not good, and many said the commanders ate the same food as they did. Several complained that the commanders got better food, canned goods from Malawi or South Africa, or beef from slaughtered cattle. One, stationed where local peasants owned many cattle, said there was never a problem. They sent out a group every few days to kill a cow, and there was always meat on the grill for everyone. But others complained of repeated food shortages for both soldiers and civilians.

A few interviewees, with experience in the Gorongosa area, said Renamo male nurses and first-aid orderlies sometimes treated civilians as well as soldiers. One said the women soldiers 'went to school'. One said that material from South African parachutes was given to people for clothes, and another that clothes captured in raids were distributed to civilians as well as soldiers. But there was virtually no other reference to benefits for Mozambican civilians.

Since 1989 there have been several additional studies with data from interviews with direct participants.[9] *Children of Mozambique* reported on interviews in 1989–90 with 504 children directly 'affected' by the war, between the ages of 6 and 15. Although not randomly selected, the group represented forty-nine districts and seven provinces. Their experiences mirrored those of Gersony's adult interviewees: all had witnessed or been personally subjected to violent abuses by Renamo; about 9 per cent had also witnessed or been personally subjected to abuses by government forces. Among the children, over 300 had been abducted; ninety were subsequently put into military training.

The report noted a strict hierarchy with Renamo presiding over captive civilian population, indirectly through chiefs in control zones, directly inside the camps, where children were used for porterage, domestic service and, in the case of girls, sexual servitude. The relationship between base camps and civilian population varied according to security. In less secure areas, civilians were forced to reside just outside the base, rather than dispersed under control of their chiefs as in the pattern Geffray noted. When imminent attack was threatened, civilians were kept inside the bases themselves. The threat of force – beatings and ultimately execution – to deter escape was constant; many killings the children reported were examples intended to establish an atmosphere of terror.

Mozambique: regional variations

Africa Watch's *Conspicuous Destruction*, based on fieldwork by journalist Karl Maier, with supplementary material by Alex Vines, attributed the 'vast majority of gross abuses' to Renamo.[10] It was also highly critical of a number of government actions, including forced relocation and scorched-earth tactics contributing to famine conditions.[11] Assembling substantial evidence confirming the overwhelmingly disproportionate use of violence by Renamo, they also noted that most large-scale massacres occurred in southern Mozambique, in zones regarded as under government control. In Renamo-controlled zones, by contrast, Renamo had a policy restraining some abuses. Chiefs could appeal to commanders against actions by individual Renamo soldiers, and disciplinary measures could be taken. The report also cited Renamo's indirect rule of civilians through a hierarchy of *mambos* and *madjiba*.

The extent of repression and extraction of resources varied considerably depending on military and logistical pressure on Renamo. Extractions were the least and voluntary support the greatest, the researchers noted, in areas under relatively firm Renamo control in central Mozambique. More detailed regional studies, added to Geffray's earlier work, subsequently provided significant confirmatory evidence of these variations.

Anthropologist Otto Roesch, who had previously done extensive research on agricultural policies in southern Mozambique, hypothesized that: 'if Geffray and Pedersen's work showed anything it was that Renamo's relative success in exploiting popular disenchantment with Frelimo was the result of specific social and cultural-historical conditions prevailing in Nampula.'[12] In successive fieldwork in 1990–91, with researchers from the Ministry of Culture's Arquivo do Patrimônio Cultural, Roesch investigated first Gaza province and then central Mozambique. In Gaza they conducted over a hundred interviews with peasants in affected areas, as well as with a former Renamo commander and others who had spent substantial time on Renamo bases. In Manica and Sofala the team interviewed more than 200 displaced persons and former Renamo combatants.

In Gaza, in contrast to Nampula, most villagization came in the wake of Limpopo Valley floods in early 1977. While the resettlement was organized from the top, and justified by ideology as well as by pragmatic reasons, it was unconnected with military counterinsurgency considerations and generally accepted by the population. Only a few villages were created in the 1980s, mainly in remote, sparsely populated areas, either in efforts to resettle drought-affected populations or for military reasons. In Gaza the state's disregard for local traditional culture caused some resentment, but it was outweighed by high levels of enthusiasm for Frelimo, particularly in the early years. By 1983, when the war began to spread seriously in Gaza, the government had already ceased actively promoting villagization in the province and was allowing people to return to their lands. But the majority declined to do so: 'most communal villages stabilized as forms of human settlement and have now become a fixed part of the rural landscape in the province.'[13]

Traditional authority structures in Gaza had lost much more legitimacy during colonial times than in Nampula. Labour migration to the mines in South Africa left peasant populations less totally dependent on agricultural production, and those resettled in villages were for the most part valley-dwellers already accustomed to centralized forms of settlement. For all these reasons, Roesch argues, Renamo found less social space for penetration than in Nampula. The vast majority of civilians living on Renamo bases or under their control were kidnapped, and the only civilian social sector that apparently showed some voluntary adherence to Renamo was marginalized male youth. Roesch links this support not with Renamo's initial approach – as did Geffray – but with later economic marginalization of youth following both the escalation of war and the structural adjustment programmes beginning in 1987.

Like Geffray, Roesch noted Renamo's appeals to traditional religious beliefs and its 'neo-traditionalist' ideology. But in Gaza it did not result even initially in significant levels of popular support. In southern Mozambique Renamo was seen as an Ndau project, with the predominantly Ndau composition of its military leadership confirming its 'foreign' character. The prominence of southern Mozambicans in Frelimo encouraged both Renamo brutality and resistance by local people to Renamo's message, whatever their disillusionment with government policies.

According to Roesch, Renamo was effective in inspiring fear, both through force and through belief in the magical potency of Ndau and the local spirits they were presumed to command. Despite government suspicions to the contrary, even traditional political and religious authorities often performed ceremonies for Renamo out of fear rather than voluntary commitment. Roesch's Gaza informants estimated that as many as 50 per cent of the captive population on Renamo bases eventually came to accept their fate as preferable to returning to the insecurity of their home areas. But this would be a small proportion of the total kidnapped, many of whom eventually escaped.

For southern Mozambique, then, Roesch's data make a strong case that what limited civilian support for Renamo came to exist resulted from war rather than contributing to its outbreak. Yet Renamo's military efforts there – benefiting from easy access to South Africa, large sparsely populated areas into which to retreat, and the government's weak defensive capacity – were as effective as anywhere in the country, and almost certainly more brutal and deadly.

Central Mozambique, according to Roesch, was significantly different. In Gaza mobile bases, small administered populations and an economy of plunder prevailed. In Renamo areas of Manica and Sofala, there were fairly permanent bases, taxation of the peasantry, and relatively large areas under administration.[14] Despite the large areas under its control, however, Roesch estimated that Renamo controlled no more than 20 per cent of the 1.7 million population of the two provinces. New arrivals in government-controlled areas included a minority forcibly displaced by the government, but the majority voluntarily opted to flee Renamo and the insecurity of the countryside.

The area of most stable Renamo control appeared to be the Ndau-speaking area in southern Sofala and Manica provinces, where, according to Ndau-speaking refugees, Renamo rule was relatively benign. Outside these areas, Renamo relied more on plunder, and the administration of taxes was more harsh. Even in the control areas, support for Renamo was largely involuntary, and related to whether or not a family had male members who had been recruited into Renamo. Although most recruitment was forced, this was offset by Ndau leadership in military ranks and the consequent identification of Renamo commanders as 'our sons'.

At the time the war began in central Mozambique, support for Frelimo there was still widespread, although shallow. After 1977, however, government resettlement plans seriously affected the livelihood of much of the peasantry. Although some peasants joined the villages voluntarily, poorly-planned settlements put peasants at unsustainable distances from fields and fruit trees. Imposition of sanctions on Rhodesia cut both migrant labour to Rhodesia and wage employment in the Beira corridor, previously a significant source of peasant income.

As in Nampula, Roesch found that the villagization programme was implemented inconsistently in the early years, with many peasants continuing to live in their home areas while maintaining nominal residence in the new villages. Roesch does not venture an estimate on what proportion may have been resettled for military reasons. But other data show that during the Rhodesian phase of the war, only a small proportion of the rural population were grouped into villages, for whatever motives. In late 1980, 8 per cent of Sofala's rural population and 6 per cent of Manica's was in villages – far less than Gaza's 37 per cent.[15]

The major thrust towards villagization in these two provinces came after 1980, in response both to the escalation of the war and to the ten-year plan mandating ambitious rural development. Roesch agrees that as in Nampula, these measures contributed to peasant disillusionment and a willingness by some to welcome Renamo. His account of which sectors were more likely to collaborate with Renamo, however, differs from Geffray's picture of Erati.

Instead of stressing traditional rivalries between communities, which Geffray saw as influencing the line-up once Renamo arrived, Roesch emphasizes the contradictory reactions of different social strata. While many chiefs retained religious respect from villagers, this was complicated by resentment of their exploitative role as 'collaborators and material beneficiaries' of the colonial system.[16] Ordinary peasants were not necessarily inclined automatically to follow the chiefs' leadership. In general the more educated and affluent sectors of the peasantry welcomed the communal village project, as did many women and youth. Once confronted with war, moreover, many traditional leaders as well as ordinary peasants opted for survival strategies dependent on location and the fortunes of war, with little allegiance to either army.

Ironically, 'the rural commercial, craft and capitalist agricultural sectors of central Mozambique were either basically supportive of the communal village programme or indifferent to it, and though perhaps critical of Frelimo policies generally, rarely felt sufficiently aggrieved to pass over into active rebellion against the state in support of Renamo.'[17] Renamo's predatory actions represented a greater threat to their livelihood than did state policies.

The interviews reported by Roesch cited significant resentment of onerous Renamo taxation, 'random' abuses by individual Renamo soldiers, and abduction of youth for sexual purposes, porterage or military training. 'By following Renamo's orders to abandon the communal

villages and return to their former homes, many peasants expected to
be freed of Renamo abuses and violence. When this did not prove to
be the case, levels of peasant disillusionment and distrust of Renamo
mounted steadily, even in Ndau-speaking areas.[18] Renamo rule was
particularly harsh, moreover, in non-Ndau and particularly in Sena-
speaking areas of central Mozambique, although not approaching the
levels in southern Mozambique.

In research beginning in 1990, Kenneth Wilson collected extensive
interview data, in Malawi, Zambia, and later in Mozambique, on Renamo activities in western Zambézia and portions of Tete province.
Wilson's studies to date provide both additional confirmation for major
features of the relationship between Renamo and the civilian population,
and evidence of further variations by local context. Wilson's major
sources included Jehovah's Witnesses, whose history of resistance both
to state authority and to Renamo gives their testimony particular
weight.[19]

Wilson noted that the level of violence by Renamo in Zambézia was
low by comparison with southern Mozambique. One possible reason
was that there was a previous history of armed opposition to Frelimo
in Zambézia with local roots. It apparently operated initially in only
loose coordination with Renamo, but was formally merged by 1982 in
time for the first major Renamo offensive in Zambézia. With this background, Renamo apparently opted for greater use of persuasion in its
approach to Zambézia.[20]

Nevertheless, Wilson's interviews led him to stress the importance
for Renamo of a 'cult of violence'. Despite few cases of large-scale
massacres (he refers to Renamo killing 'only ten' Jehovah's Witnesses in
a 1984 incident), exemplary killings, sometimes with ritualistic brutality,
were used to inspire fear. Combined with Renamo's reputation for
magical potency, this often resulted in compliance without the need for
additional killings. In the case of determined non-violent resistance,
such as by the Jehovah's Witnesses, Renamo sometimes accepted a *modus
vivendi*. Wilson's informants reported systematic use of rape by Renamo
soldiers, despite official prohibitions by Renamo commanders. But they
added that there was generally greater restraint with respect to under-
age girls or married women. In a number of cases, Renamo imposed
penalties on offenders after protests by local communities.

The pattern of administration described by Wilson replicated that in
other parts of Mozambique: at the top was the Renamo military command, with top officers predominantly Ndau-speaking, then local chiefs,
some recruited voluntarily and others forcibly, with local *madjiba* serving
as enforcers. Wilson, however, describes the chieftancy structure as of
questionable local legitimacy, instead placing it into the context of
colonial and precolonial structures of tribute collection and labour

mobilization. In contrast to Geffray, Wilson says that the chiefs appointed by Renamo were for the most part those who had collaborated with the Portuguese as *régulos*. Renamo thus became the latest of a long series of outside conquerors.

Mobilization of the peasantry against the state in Zambézia, to the extent that local people joined in or applauded Renamo attacks, appears in Wilson's account not as loyalty to traditional authorities or as resentment at villagization, which was of little significance in Zambézia. Rather, it reflected the fact that previous 'modernizing' sectors of Zambézian society – those families with some educational or commercial standing in the regional economy – had by and large successfully maintained their status under and as a part of the Frelimo state apparatus. Despite economic decline, they managed to retain relative affluence compared to estate workers or peasants, and were thus principal targets of Renamo's economy of pillage.

Wilson stressed the complexity of interaction between Renamo and the local context, with significant variation even within small geographical areas and over time. He also highlighted the importance of the varying economic base for Renamo's activities in western Zambézia. The looting of small towns, with resale of the goods in Malawi, was at its height during the mid-1980s, following major Renamo military advances, but could not be sustained. Extraction of food from the peasantry was hindered by drought, and generally became more difficult over time as peasants in Renamo areas suffered increasingly from lack of purchased tools. Wilson identified this lack of access to the market as one of the major sources of discontent with Renamo.

Despite the overall environment of coercion, Wilson reported that in western Zambézia during the second half of the 1980s Renamo made efforts to establish educational and, to a secondary extent, health infrastructures. The schools were close replicas of the government system, and indeed were largely staffed by former government teachers who had come under Renamo control. These services, started in Zambézia in 1984–85, functioned on a substantial scale only for a few years. Elsewhere in the country, Wilson notes, there is no evidence of similar structures apart from the area around the Renamo headquarters in Gorongosa.

New research after the October 1992 ceasefire is likely to show additional local variations, but it is likely they will confirm the main features of research to date. The major contrast is between the fairly consistent rejection of Renamo in the south, with Renamo's reliance on the most extreme forms of violence there, and a much more complicated patchwork pattern in the centre and north of the country. Despite modifying factors, however, Renamo remained fundamentally a coercive organization imposed on the civilian population. As shown by its record in the south, significant levels of civilian support were not a prerequisite for success at the military task of destruction.

Angola: ethnic loyalty, political organization and violent dictatorship

There is very little detailed research on life in Unita-controlled areas during the war, despite the steady flow of foreign visitors to Jamba. Data for analysis of regional variation are practically non-existent.[21] The conclusions that can be drawn are therefore very general. On the critical question of the extent of Unita's use of persuasion and/or force to mobilize civilians, my research showed that both elements were involved, and that there were variations, both by location and by time period. Other research confirms the initial voluntary adherence to Unita of a significant portion of Umbundu-speakers, the building of a fanatical core of loyalists, and the systematic use of force to ensure compliance in Unita areas as well as to punish the population in government areas.

As with recruitment, Unita's approach to civilians before March 1976 was based primarily on political persuasion and social pressure. On the central plateau in particular, Unita made systematic use of contact with traditional chiefs and with young educated Umbundu, as well as with conservative whites. The dominant themes were nationalist and ethnoregional. People from the south (i.e., primarily Umbundu) should support their movement (Unita). Since southerners were the largest group, Unita implied, their party had the right to a dominant share in power.

The evidence on response to Unita's appeal is ambiguous. There were no systematic polls taken at the time. It is clear that the majority of Umbundu-speaking Angolans with political views adhered to Unita, particularly in the provinces of Huambo and Bié. But it is also clear that there was no unanimity. The extent of Unita's majority in the central plateau is unknown, and support was significantly less towards the coast and in non-Umbundu-speaking areas of the south and east.

One of the most articulate of my informants, from Huambo province, estimated support for Unita among Umbundu in 1974–76 as about 80 per cent. He noted that support for the MPLA rather than Unita increased closer to the cities, as well as closer to the coast. Another, also from Huambo, said that in Huambo and Bié there was more support for Unita, in Benguela province more for the MPLA. He added that some families were divided by the conflict. Further south, in the Lubango area, another interviewee noted, Unita had comparatively little support.

These judgements overlap with an evaluation at the time by MPLA President Agostinho Neto, in a private interview with US consul Tom

Killoran in May 1975. Neto told him that MPLA political mobilization had eroded Unita support in the south over the previous six months, and that MPLA support was strongest on the coast, diminishing towards the interior. In the Huambo area, they were about equal, Neto claimed.[22]

As conventional combat ended in 1976, Savimbi called on his supporters to retreat into the bush to begin a guerrilla struggle. MPLA sources acknowledge that significant numbers responded to that appeal. Huambo provincial commissioner Santana André Pitra, noting in mid-1980 that as many as 800,000 people had come out of the bush to government areas over the previous six months, explained that 'initially Unita told the people that we were all northerners and city people who would destroy their traditions and their culture'.[23]

One interviewee described this period as one of indiscriminate reprisals on both sides. Dash relates several first-hand accounts, including killings of civilians by government troops in the northern Huíla town of Kavanga in October 1976, and killings of civilians by Unita in an attack on Ringoma in Bié in November 1976.[24] A Unita officer told Dash that he had to attack the village of Chitembo, in Bié province, seven times 'before the peasants would leave [the village] and live with us in the bush'.[25] His unit attacked peasants in the fields, and killed both civilians and government troops in attacks on the town, he explained, until finally the villagers joined Unita in the bush because they no longer felt safe.

Unita Major Mateus Katalayo told Dash that the war was particularly complicated because in the villages there were both Unita and government supporters.[26] One interviewee explained that villagers were classified by their expected reliability. Those thought to be loyal to Unita were allowed to live near government zones, he said. Those suspected of loyalty to the government were transferred deeper in the bush, where it was more difficult to flee to government zones.

The proportion of genuine support for Unita in the contested rural areas is impossible to estimate from the fragmentary data. Some journalists, such as Dash and Fernandes, talked to chiefs and villagers who were clearly part of a civilian support base. Others who visited outside the Jamba area saw few civilians.[27] Some caught glimpses of civilian hostility: a Portuguese hostage held by Unita described how villagers fled from them; Sitte described passing through an Ovambo area in southern Angola and finding most peasants closed and silent.[28]

Although the interviewees gave no general estimate of the level of civilian support, those present during both periods agreed it was greater before 1979–80 than afterwards. The earlier period was one of great hardship, they said, caused not only by government attacks but even more by the struggle to survive food shortages and disease in the bush. But these hardships were tolerable for many because of the hopes raised by Unita leaders for an eventual victory. Later, they said, many people simply became tired and discouraged.

The option of becoming a refugee was more restricted in Angola than in Mozambique, since the most densely populated and contested regions were far from international borders. Many fled to urban or peri-urban areas inside Angola.[29] But, as one interviewee explained, some people did not want to leave their home areas under any conditions. Several commented that local people, having little choice, adapted to the control of whatever troops were around them. Several added that there were local groups of armed men, associated with neither Unita nor the government.

The interviewees generally agreed that in contested areas Unita's food came from two sources: taxed contributions from civilians under Unita control and raids on villages under government control. The Jamba area, they said, was relatively privileged, with food and other goods from Namibia distributed free. One interviewee commented that much of the area was not good for agriculture, although there was some production on Unita farms. Renaud Giraud, in an article in the Portuguese weekly *Tempo*, noted that Unita imported large quantities of maize, wheat and rice from South Africa.[30]

Judging by visitors' reports, a significant portion of the population in the Jamba area was loyal – even fanatically so – to Unita and to Savimbi. While some visitors privately described this allegiance as cult-like, most were impressed or even inspired by the organization and communal spirit they saw. They tended to assume that those they talked with were representative of Unita's presence elsewhere in the country.

Several interviewees said that in areas under Unita control, political activists were assigned to mobilize the civilian population, in conjunction with traditional village chiefs deemed loyal to Unita. The activists spoke against the Soviet and Cuban presence in Angola and attributed the difficulties of the Angolan economy to the MPLA government. The interviewees described the political activists and local authorities as subordinate to the Unita military command.

Positive incentives for loyalty offered by Unita to civilians varied by time period and location, according to the interviewees. In the first few years, there was relatively little organization of Unita services. If there happened to be a nurse or a teacher in a given area, health services or schools were organized. But there was little support from Unita headquarters. After the establishment of Jamba, however, organization improved. While the Jamba area had priority, there was a sustained effort to provide rudimentary health and education services for civilians in all military regions. This was in addition to the military medical services.

Jamba housed a central hospital with as many as thirty nurses in

1980, one interviewee said; others mentioned the later presence of a small number of Angolan and European doctors. Other settlements in the Jamba area also had clinics, according to both the interviewees and visiting journalists. The regional hospital in the Benguela/Huambo area in the early 1980s had six trained nurses, one interviewee said. Another said that the Kuanza Sul region in the early 1980s had 180 military health personnel and 200 civilian health personnel, numbers which seem high even if untrained personnel are included.

In 1988, a report produced by Unita's health secretariat stated that the Jamba central hospital had 100 workers.[31] The total number of nurses in Unita's military health services was estimated at 3,000, with 3,800 in civilian health services, one nurse for each twenty-three of Unita's claimed 70,000 soldiers. One interviewee, however, said that each battalion (of several hundred men) normally had three nurses, a ratio only about one-fourth that figure. From the interviewees' fragmentary data, however, it is impossible to estimate to what extent the report's figures might be exaggerated.

There was clearly a sustained effort at education in Portuguese, although reliable numerical estimates are lacking. Both interviewees and foreign journalists spoke of schools in the Jamba area, including a secondary school (Instituto Polivalente) which had about 600 students when one interviewee attended it in the mid-1980s. Outside the Jamba area the reports were inconsistent, some saying there were very few schools in areas they knew, others saying each community controlled by Unita had a school. Statistics given by Unita officials and in a report from the Unita Secretariat for Education and Culture claimed over 200,000 students in Unita schools, over 2,000 of them secondary students (5th grade and up). But the figures given showed dramatic shifts from year to year, raising doubts about their accuracy.[32]

With the exception of the Cuanhama interviewee, the informants denied that there was any discrimination between Angolans of different ethnic origins within Unita. The idea that Unita aimed at separatist goals for Umbundu or for southerners, occasionally voiced by outside observers, was not supported by any of the interviewees. In practice, however, participation in Unita remained overwhelmingly Umbundu, with a secondary contribution from the sparsely populated north-east and south-east, and, for some time, from Cuanhama. From 1976 to 1984, many Cuanhamas under their traditional leader António Vakulakuta participated in Unita on a voluntary basis. Thereafter, conflict between Vakulakuta and Savimbi eventually led to Vakulakuta's death. Subsequent Cuanhama participation was reduced and apparently more grudging.

Further investigation of the balance of voluntary and forced support for Unita, either in control zones or contested areas, must await new systematic research, now made unlikely by Angola's return to war. Before 1991, foreign journalists, non-governmental organizations, embassy staff and businessmen had some access to government-controlled areas, but their travel in disputed areas of the countryside was highly restricted. Independent access to Unita-controlled areas was even more restricted, with few foreign residents other than military advisers. Journalists visiting Unita areas, except for a few such as Dash in 1977, did little to investigate the official line presented on their tours.[33] In the ceasefire and election period, many foreign observers had extensive contact with Unita-controlled areas, despite continued restrictions by Unita. But to date there are only scattered accounts and no systematic research reports published.[34]

Despite uncertainty about many details, one feature that stands out is the dominant role of Jonas Savimbi. Both admirers and critics agree that Savimbi's personality stamped the character of the organization. 'Savimbi is the chief', Unita officer Jaka Jamba told Dash in 1977. 'If he were killed, I don't know what would happen to Unita.'[35] Among the central issues in the peace talks of 1989–91 were the position of Savimbi, and the credibility of his commitment to an agreement. The return to war in 1992 indicated that the concern was well-founded.

Before 1991 commentators often focused on the multiple contradictions in Savimbi's ideological stances and external alliances. According to Dash: 'Savimbi is an enigma, a man on whom many labels can stick – brilliant, charismatic, affable, unyielding, forgiving, temporizing, Machiavellian, opportunistic, lying, nationalistic, Marxist, Maoist, pro-Western and socialist'.[36] There were, however, several consistent threads in his record.

One was Savimbi's conviction that he was destined to be the leader of Angola and his intense personal hostility to those he saw as his chief rivals. As early as 1961, according to an American diplomat cited by Gerald Bender: 'Savimbi showed much more hostility toward other rebel groups in Angola than he did against the Portuguese.'[37] He had introduced himself at the US Embassy in Switzerland as the 'future president of Angola', and denounced the MPLA, accusing its leaders of being mulattos disliked by most Angolans. Whether voiced as black against mulatto, southerner against northerner, Umbundu against Kimbundu, rural against urban, or 'genuine Angolan' against deracinated Luandan, hostility to other Angolans was a constant theme of Savimbi's rhetoric. In his eyes, and those of his followers, this is what justified any strategy or outside alliance.[38]

Another thread was Savimbi's capacity to maintain a cohesive second-rank leadership around him, without any publicly visible dissent or challenge to his authority until recently. This second echelon included Savimbi's contemporaries such as Nzau Puna and Tony Fernandes, as well as others from the 1974–76 generation, such as Tito Chingunji and Jeremias Chitunda. Below the leadership level as well, dissent was restrained both by loyalty and fear. Until recently only the official version of Unita reached the outside world.

Savimbi excelled at presenting different images to different audiences. In the early 1970s he presented a 'black-power' face to visiting black nationalists from the US and an 'anti-revisionist' Maoist image to white radicals. In the African context he portrayed Unita as a purely independent guerrilla movement, surviving alone in the bush with no outside aid. Visiting journalists had no hint of his covert military alliance with the Portuguese authorities. In the 1980s, Savimbi received visitors in Jamba with consummate public relations skills. Although his *licence* from Switzerland was roughly equivalent to a US master's degree, few journalists could resist the easy paragraph profiling the bearded and charismatic guerrilla leader with a beret, an ivory-handled pistol and a Ph.D. Savimbi's interviews invariably produced quotable material, and showed awareness of the national and political context of the interviewer. The image was sustained by talented young aides who could also converse convincingly with journalists in English or French.

None of my interviewees were members of Unita's inner leadership group, but a few did spend significant time in Jamba and had the opportunity to observe Savimbi and his colleagues. Their observations provide confirmation for some of the allegations by Angolan exiles which appeared in the press and in Amnesty International reports in 1988 and 1989. Further confirmation emerged with the first defections of prominent Unita leaders in 1992.

The first public hint of specific charges against Savimbi came in May 1988 from three dissident Unita students in Portugal. Expressing their continued confidence in the movement as a whole, they denounced Savimbi for lack of democracy within Unita, and cited the disappearance or punishment of several rivals to Savimbi. One of the three, Ermelindo Kanjungu, said he had been an eyewitness to several incidents of abuses.[39]

Kanjungu said that three Unita leaders (Tony Fernandes, Samuel Chiwale, and Colonel Kanjungu) were accused of being 'reactionaries' and severely beaten in a public session of Unita's Fifth Congress in 1982, which he attended. The students also said that Dr Jorge Sangumba, formerly Unita's foreign secretary, was decreed a reactionary and had 'disappeared' after 1981. They added that Savimbi had also had other leaders killed, including Brigadier Xandovava, Colonel Vakulakuta, and Valdemar Chindondo, Unita chief of staff from 1975 to 1979.[40] Kanjungu said he witnessed, on 7 September 1983, the incineration of a number of people at Jamba, accused of being witches and executed in a public ceremony directed by Savimbi. Among those killed, he said, were six members of the Kalitangue family, the widow of Mateus Katalaio, and her two children.

The charges attracted little international attention until March 1989, when Savimbi biographer Fred Bridgland repeated similar allegations.[41] Sousa Jamba and Dinho Chingunji, who spoke on the record to Bridgland, were both relatives of prominent Unita leaders. Neither claimed to have witnessed specific incidents, but said their information was based on conversations with many others who had. They said they still opposed the Angolan government and supported the ideals of Unita, but had finally decided to speak out against Savimbi.

Dinho Chingunji, a member of one of Unita's most prominent families, ascribed the death in 1974 of his father Samuel, Unita's first chief of staff and a celebrated Unita hero, to Savimbi. He said family members also believed that three other brothers had been killed by Unita instead of dying natural deaths as Unita claimed. Such rumours, although they at the least indicated mistrust between Savimbi and the Chingunji family, could be retrospective explanations of genuine natural deaths. Chingunji added, however, that when his grandfather Jonatão expressed his suspicions to Savimbi in 1979, he and his wife Violeta were beaten to death for witchcraft, within hearing range of one of their daughters. And, Chingunji said, his aunt Chica had been accused of witchcraft in 1983 and subsequently killed.

Writer Sousa Jamba, younger brother of Unita Education Secretary Jaka Jamba, reiterated in published articles that he had talked with numerous eyewitnesses to the September 1983 public burning of witches in Jamba, attended by 'hundreds'.[42] He said that his nieces and nephews were part of the crowd of witnesses and that the witches were identified by a healer (curandeiro) named Mariano whom he had known in Huambo in 1973. Amnesty International told Bridgland that three reliable sources had provided evidence that Jonatão and Violeta Chingunji were clubbed with rifle butts, kicked and then run over by a truck. In Amnesty International's 1989 annual report, two specific witch-burning incidents were reported: three women in March 1982, and at least twelve people in September 1983, including the Kalitangue family.

Five of my interviewees said they knew about the killing of rivals to Savimbi. One was a direct eyewitness, while the others were present in Jamba at the time and talked with others who were eyewitnesses.[43] Two said they were in Jamba when a Colonel Sabino Lumumba was killed, allegedly for indiscipline, after the Fifth Congress in July 1982. The cases most frequently mentioned, by four interviewees who attended the Fifth Congress, as well as by another who was not in Jamba at the time but afterwards heard about the incidents, were those of Sangumba, Chindondo, Chiwale and Fernandes. Sangumba and Chindondo were executed in 1982, beaten to death in public around the time of the congress, the interviewees said. One said he witnessed the killings. Several others referred specifically to Savimbi's announcement in the congress of the deaths, in which he accused Sangumba and Chindondo of wanting to betray him. Chiwale and Fernandes were under suspicion at the time, the interviewees said, and were demoted and beaten in public. They survived, however, and later returned to leadership positions.

Three referred to the Cuanhama leader Vakulakuta, but none had much detail. One interviewee, of Cuanhama origin, said there was a conflict in 1984 in Cunene province. The Umbundus were killing the Cuanhamas, he said, and Vakulakuta fled to Namibia after this. Vakulakuta died later, he added, but said he was not in Cunene at this period and did not know any details. Another said Savimbi had accused Vakulakuta of wanting to form a separate tribal movement, that the South Africans captured him in Namibia and handed him over to Unita, where he was severely beaten. Yet another said he saw Vakulakuta in a hospital in Licua in 1986, but didn't know what was wrong with him or how long he survived.[44]

The existence of punishment for witchcraft in rural Angolan society, in times of intense social tension, is not disputed. And there is even some evidence that Unita sought to moderate the practice.[45] But the evidence is also strong that Savimbi himself used this tactic against dissidents on at least one occasion. Three of my interviewees said they knew of such incidents. One saw a woman accused of being a government infiltrator burned as a witch, on the order of a regional commander in the Benguela/Huambo area. He had heard of but not witnessed such incidents in Jamba. Another said he was present in Jamba in 1983 when people were burned as witches, and along with others was required to gather wood for the fires. Savimbi, he recalled, summoned the people together and read the condemnation. He said a total of twenty-seven people were killed on two separate occasions within a month, including Katalaio's widow and a Chingunji daughter. He said that as far as he knew 1983 was the only time something like that happened in Jamba.

A third person said he did not witness the event, but arrived in Jamba in October 1983 to find the community 'traumatized' by it. He also said he knew of no incidents after that. He added that there had been cases of witch-burning in 1976–77 initiated by local commanders, and that in some cases it was used for personal revenge on women. But this shocked the people, and Savimbi gave orders to stop it, he said. The only time he heard of such a punishment being authorized after that was in Jamba in 1983.

Initially, Unita responded to all allegations by defectors with blanket denials, charging that they were involved in a government disinformation campaign. There is no doubt that the Angolan government was eager to make political capital from the revelations, and that some allegations, such as a generalized campaign of witch-burning, were exaggerated. But confirmation of the pattern of intense internal repression continued to emerge in subsequent years.

Chingunji and Bridgland, for example, alleged in 1989 that Dinho's uncle Tito Chingunji, formerly Unita foreign secretary, was being held in Jamba and had been tortured. They warned that his life was in danger. Some Unita supporters visiting Jamba met Chingunji and were reassured, but the fears were later confirmed. Chingunji, Wilson dos Santos and members of their families were killed in November 1991. High-level Unita defectors Nzau Puna and Tony Fernandes, who fled early in 1992, charged Savimbi with responsibility; Unita in turn alleged that security chief Puna had ordered the killings without authorization. Confirmation of Chingunji's death made it difficult for any but the most adamant Unita supporter to deny the pattern.[46]

The internal history of Unita has yet to be written. But when it is, it will certainly have all the complex ambiguity of the diaries of Unita vice-president Jeremias Chitunda, killed by pro-MPLA attackers in fighting in Luanda in November 1992. Chitunda, a loyal follower of Jonas Savimbi to the end, nevertheless feared for his life when rebuked by O Mais Velho (the 'Oldest One'). Returning to Jamba in May 1989, he recorded abject apologies for being deceived by Chingunji and rejoiced in a presidential pardon. The mix of genuine loyalty to a movement many identified with, together with fear of the consequences should they show doubt or disloyalty, is an apt paradigm for the relationship between Unita and the constituency it claimed among rank-and-file soldiers and civilians alike.[47]

Unita, Renamo and political pluralism

Ironically, in the ceasefire and election periods, it was Unita and Renamo that had greatest difficulty in adapting to their rhetorical objective of multi-party democratic competition. Sympathizers attributed the flaws to lack of resources and experience, while critics said it simply confirmed the hypocrisy of their democratic pretensions. But both agreed that the phenomenon was a significant feature of the post-settlement political environment.

It is too early to venture an analytical account of this period. As this is written, renewed war rages on in Angola. A shaky ceasefire holds in Mozambique, despite repeated postponements in the election and demobilization timetables. The internal, regional and international dynamics of the post-1991 period are profoundly different from the earlier years of war, and require consideration on their own terms. There is ample reason for caution in reading current realities back into the earlier period. Nevertheless, events to date – particularly the election in Angola – shed some light on the relationship with civilian constituencies, and warrant at least brief comment here.

First of all, the scope for party competition, free movement and debate was greatest in urban areas, somewhat less in rural areas under government control, and least of all in zones which, in violation of the peace accords, remained under *de facto* control of the insurgents. Secondly, both disillusionment with government and fear of the insurgents proved significant themes in electoral sentiment, leading to a pattern of negative voting. But third parties, despite their proliferation, apparently failed to offset electoral polarization between the two battlefield opponents. Thirdly, relative support for government and insurgents was affected by the patterns of regional disparity discussed earlier in this chapter and in Chapter 4. But the link between ethno-regional divisions and political allegiance fell far short of an exact correlation. And finally, overwhelming popular sentiment in favour of peace did not prevent the Unita leadership from returning to war or Renamo from repeatedly stalling on demobilizing its troops.

The Angolan election process revealed all these features. The days of the elections were calm, the procedures certified as fair both by international observers and, although Unita later challenged the outcome, by both government and Unita poll watchers at every polling station.[48] The context, however, still reflected the history of the war. The government enjoyed – and used – the patronage and other advantages of an incumbent administration. But it also paid the penalty of the incumbent, taking the blame for the disastrous state of the country. Third parties, having neither armies nor developed organizational structures, were at a disadvantage, despite free media access that put them in a better position than their counterparts in the US. Despite effective procedures to ensure ballot secrecy, it is likely that many rural voters followed the directions of the party in effective military control in their area.

Evaluating public sentiment during the election was an ambiguous exercise at best. A popular and much-quoted slogan on Luanda walls succinctly summed up the choice as 'MPLA thieves, Unita murderers'. At first many observers thought that Unita was a sure winner, because of public disillusionment with the government and a sentiment that both sides were to blame for the war. But MPLA's image as a party of peace was given a strong boost by the bellicose tenor of Savimbi's campaign. On election day each side expected a win. The verdict of the voters was a 54 per cent to 34 per cent margin for the MPLA in the legislative contest, and 49.6 per cent to 40.1 per cent in the presidential race, just short of the majority needed to avoid a runoff.

The regional voting pattern broadly reflected the historical constituencies of the two major contenders. Savimbi racked up over 80 per cent majorities in the plateau provinces of Huambo and Bié, 76 per cent in Cuando Cubango. The MPLA took 86 per cent in Kuanza North and just over 70 per cent in Luanda, Bengo and Kuanza South. Even in these core provinces, however, this indicates substantial minorities opposed to the presumed natural allegiance, in far greater numbers than could be accounted for by migration between provinces. Third parties took upwards of 8 per cent in almost every province, rising to 43 per cent for the FNLA in Zaire province and 42 per cent for the Partido de Renovação Social (PRS) in Lunda South. The legislative results, with proportional representation pegged to both national and regional returns, gave 129 seats to the MPLA, seventy to Unita and twenty-one to other parties.

The high participation in the election and virtually unanimous popular sentiment during the campaign clearly indicated a profound desire for peace among the constituencies on both sides, including rank-and-file soldiers as well as civilians. But the potential for renewed war was implicit in the failure to complete the agreed formation of a new national army. There is much debate as to what the international community could have done to avert this tragedy. But there is no doubt that it was Unita that was best prepared for a new war. That decision reflected the ambitions and preoccupation with military force of the Unita leadership, not the demands of its constituency. And in the subsequent ebb-and-flow of battle, civilians were victims or bystanders. The new war was more destructive and just as bitter as before. But it fitted neither the pattern of guerrilla war nor of external invasion, but civil war of a more classic variety featuring the clash of conventional armies.

Notes

1. National studies include Gersony (1988), Boothby, Sultan and Upton (1991), and Africa Watch, *Conspicuous Destruction* (1992). Local studies, cited later, include Geffray in Nampula province, Wilson in Zambézia and Tete and Roesch on Gaza and central Mozambique.

2. For a somewhat more complete list of sources than can be included here, see Minter (1990). Sources surveyed on Angola as well as Mozambique included press reports from a wide range of sources, in Portuguese, French, German and Dutch as well as English, and radio transcripts from the BBC Summary of World Broadcasts.

3. On Angola, see particularly the Eduardo Mondlane Foundation (1992, 1993), Vines (1993) and reports by Victoria Brittain in the *Guardian*; on Mozambique *Mozambique Peace Process Bulletin* from AWEPAA (European Parliamentarians for Southern Africa, Amsterdam).

4. Gersony (1988), 25.

5. The strongest critique was by Renamo supporters, such as Hoile (1989)

and Cline (1989). But others also questioned whether the emphasis in the results may have been tilted. The question of representativity is a serious one; it is likely that a purely random sample would have elicited more critiques of the Mozambican government. But none of the critics have presented any alternate research based on systematic interviews, or any anecdotal evidence that is inconsistent with Gersony's overall summary for his informants' story of 17 per cent negative comments about government abuses as compared with 96 per cent negative comments about Renamo abuses.

6. Geffray (1990). Geffray's book deservedly won much favourable commentary. But his overall perspectives did not go unchallenged. For an incisive and nuanced review which criticizes his view of the peasantry as undifferentiated and oversimplified, see O'Laughlin (1992).

7. Geffray and Pedersen (1986), 315.

8. Geffray (1990), 117–18.

9. The studies considered here, only a small fraction of the voluminous writing about Renamo, are selected because each is based on extensive primary interview data. There are a few others in the same category, such as Legrand (1991), which I have not been able to consult. Other studies not examined systematically here range in quality from excellent to superficial. Several demand at least brief mention. Hall (1990) is a summary article by one of the most careful and well-informed analysts. Vines' study (1991) is very well-informed and has the widest range of sources, but is weaker on analysis and has little grass-roots level primary interview data (Vines also collaborated, however, on the Africa Watch 1992 study which does contain much such information). Finnegan's work (1992) is unsurpassed for its vivid descriptions, but the book is marred by lapses into exoticism and a tendency to stretch a casual remark or observation into questionable generalizations. For incisive reviews of both Vines and Finnegan, see Kathleen Sheldon in *Africa Today* (1992: #1–2), 139–44.

10. Africa Watch had extensive access to visit prisoners and interview detainees, a level of access which it called 'unprecedented in Africa Watch's dealings with African governments' (Africa Watch, *Conspicuous Destruction*, 1992, 1).

11. Africa Watch, *Conspicuous Destruction* (1992), especially pp. 115–21.

12. Roesch, 'Gaza' (1992).

13. Roesch, 'Gaza' (1992).

14. Roesch, 'Central Mozambique' (1993), 11.

15. See sources in Chapter 10, note 21, as well as the letter by Paul Fauvet in *Southern African Review of Books* (August/September 1989).

16. Roesch, 'Central Mozambique' (1993), 7.

17. Roesch, 'Central Mozambique' (1993), 9.

18. Roesch, 'Central Mozambique' (1993), 12.

19. With the exception of Wilson, 'Cults of Violence' (1992), most of Wilson's research to date has been reported in conference papers and drafts as yet unpublished. For a listing to mid-1992 see Wilson, *Deslocados Internos* (1992).

20. See Chapter 5. More on the Malawi background can be found in Vines (1991), 38–53, as well as Wilson's papers.

21. Africa Watch, *Angola* (1989), *Angola* (1991) and to a lesser extent, *Angola* (1993), which concentrates on land-mines, all provide some data from interviews with civilians. My 1990 report relied on interviews with ex-Unita combatants

and on distilling data from published reports, but did not include systematic interviews with affected civilians. Since the 1991 ceasefire, new accounts by defectors from Unita have surfaced, and there is scattered journalistic coverage of the areas under Unita control.

22. Cable released under Freedom of Information Act, Luanda to State Department, 10 May 1975. See the discussion on election results later in this chapter.

23. *Guardian*, London (1 August 1980).

24. Dash (1977), 29–33.

25. Dash (1977), 25-7.

26. Dash (1977), 32.

27. Jason Laure, for example, saw only 200 civilians during an eighteen-day stay in 1981. *Sunday Nation*, Kenya (23 August 1981).

28. Sitte (1977), 161.

29. See Sogge (1992), 5–16.

30. *Tempo*, Lisbon (15 November 1985).

31. Unita, Secretariado da Saúde, *Informação Sanitária* (Jamba, 1988).

32. Savimbi, 'The War against Soviet Colonialism' (1986), 19; Unita, Secretariado da Educação e Cultura, *Sistema de Ensino* (Jamba, 1989). In 1986, for example, Savimbi said Unita had 6,951 primary schools; a table in Unita's own education report said there were 976 primary schools in 1987, and 3,139 in 1988. The number of primary teachers went from 7,127 in 1986 to 3,003 in 1987 and 8,611 in 1988 according to the education report. The data provided by the interviewees make the largest of these numbers unlikely, but provide no basis for an alternative numerical estimate.

33. Radek Sikorski, a journalist for the conservative *National Review* who spent three months with Unita in 1989, charged that his hosts were 'compulsive liars', who had prepared a series of Potemkin villages for him. Radek Sikorski, 'The Mystique of Savimbi', *National Review* (18 August 1989).

34. An important exception was Sogge (1992), who worked with Angolan researchers and provides a great deal of data about the economic and social situation around the country. But this report did not focus on political issues or implementation of the peace accord.

35. Dash (1977), 113.

36. Dash (1977), 113.

37. Bender (1981), 59.

38. See Minter (1988) for documentation on the 1971-74 period of collaboration with the Portuguese military; also a 1969 letter from Savimbi to the Portuguese authorities in Angola cited by Conchiglia (1990), 10-11.

39. *Africa*, 11 May 1988; *Expresso*, 7 May 1988.

40. *Expresso*, 30 April 1988.

41. *Sunday Telegraph*, 12 March 1989.

42. *The Spectator*, 18 March 1989; *Expresso*, 6 May 1989.

43. See Minter (1990), 12-14 for interview material on this topic, and press references through early 1990. Other key articles include Leon Dash, 'Blood and Fire: Savimbi's War Against His Unita Rivals', *The Washington Post*, 30 September 1990; Fred Bridgland, 'Angola's Secret Bloodbath', *The Washington Post*, 19 March 1992.

44. Nzau Puna, after deserting, said that Vakulakuta was indeed sick, but that he had been executed on Savimbi's orders (*Expresso*, 25 April 1992).

45. Dash (1977, 79–81) describes a case presented to Unita guerrillas by villagers in Bié province. In this case, the guerrilla leader ordered two accused women to be released. Journalist Ferreira Fernandes (*O Jornal Ilustrado*, 8 July 1988), for example, visited a village which his Unita guides told him was set up in 1984 for people accused of witchcraft, who could not stay in their own villages. The settlement, with sixty-nine women and fourteen men when he visited in 1988, was just to the north of Mavinga.

46. The US government officially reacted with an inconclusive investigation after the public confirmation of Chingunji's death. But the typical attitude of indifference was reflected in remarks by administration officials, such as one official's response to a question on the topic in a discussion in 1989 ('For God's sake, why bring that up when we are engaged in delicate negotiations?'). In May 1993, in a radio debate with the author, Chester Crocker responded to mention of this aspect of Savimbi's record with 'Well, if you want to get into mud-slinging …'

47. Diary of Jeremias Chitunda, excerpted in *Domingo* (Maputo), 17 January 24, 1993).

48. For a report focusing on the election itself, see Bayer (1993). Vines (1993) raises some of the broader issues.

9

The State Under Siege:
Military and
Political Vulnerabilities

'The mobilizations into communist villages and for a new war against a theoretical and external enemy, and the collectivization of the economy', writes Renamo spokesman Jorge Correia, obliged Mozambicans to rise up 'against the new tyrant.'[1] 'The people of Mozambique rejected Marxism,' according to Afonso Dhlakama, 'leading to the formation of Renamo to fight for a just and democratic pluralist system.'[2] In a 1991 interview Dhlakama said the alleged Rhodesian role in forming Renamo was 'all a lie', and claimed never to have heard of Rhodesian intelligence chief Ken Flower.[3] The Renamo explanation of the war's origin, in short, squarely blames Frelimo.

The Renamo account does not stand up against the historical record, since the evidence for Rhodesian initiative in formation of Renamo is compelling. Dhlakama, Matsangaiza, Cristina and a handful of others had their own reasons to join with the Rhodesians in attacking Mozambique. But it is doubtful they could have started a war without the Rhodesian initiative.

Most analysts agree that it is highly unlikely that those policies alone would have provoked armed resistance on any significant scale. Whether one rates opposition to Frelimo's policies as marginal or massive, the opposing forces lacked organizational coherence. The most likely responses by peasants to abuse or neglect by the state would have been accommodation or other forms of resistance, as in many other African states. The real question is not whether Marxist policies precipitated war, but how government policies and structures affected an ongoing war. In what ways did such factors weaken the state or increase support for insurgency? And to what extent could regime weaknesses have been remedied by different policies, as contrasted with structural vulnerabilities inherent in the post-colonial states?

In Angola the origin of the war clearly predated independence. Even for Unita, the war in Angola was thus linked not to the policies of the Angolan government, but to its very existence. 'In 1974, Neto claimed to be the only one speaking in the name of the Angolan people, and he is still claiming the same thing', wrote Jonas Savimbi. 'That is the reason for war in Angola.'[4] 'Unita knew, a priori, that it would be the winner of any elections,' he added, but the MPLA, fearing to lose, initiated the arms race and brought in Cuban troops.[5] Unita blamed the war on Soviet interference – 'a cause not an effect' – and denounced the 'minority, petty-bourgeois regime' of Luanda.[6] This viewpoint was reflected in what US envoy Crocker called 'the principled American rejection of the MPLA's victory and the manner in which it took place'.[7] And it was echoed in Savimbi's pre-election announcement in 1992 that Unita's loss would automatically be proof of election fraud.[8]

Whatever the relative weight of internal and external factors in 1975–76 (see Chapter 4), the time sequence alone rules out attributing the origin of war to the post-independence policies of the Angolan government. The relevant question for Angola, as for Mozambique, is therefore to what extent those policies contributed to escalation of war in 1980 and to its continuation thereafter.

At one level these questions pertain to the justifications for war cited by Unita or Renamo. But the answers are also relevant to current policy choices. Will elections and/or power-sharing result in stable national unity, for example? Will economic liberalization provide opportunities for peasant advance that were denied by previous agricultural policies? The general 'lesson' of the war years is that the states' vulnerability led both to loss of faith in the hopes for societal transformation and to peace agreements granting significant concessions if not victory to the insurgents. It is easy to say that 'errors' were made. But it is more difficult to determine what lessons to draw; misidentifying errors may simply lead to making new ones.

Practically every realm of policy had some relevance to the wars. A full survey would be impossible here even if sources of empirical data were much richer. But looking at particular policy areas can suggest which lessons are likely to be misleading and which are more likely to stand up under further investigation. This chapter considers first the legacy of the Portuguese colonial state, then military counterinsurgency efforts and finally several political aspects of the post-colonial state. The next chapter takes up economic policies and their social consequences. In each the focus is on the effects of government structures and policies on popular sentiment, and the extent to which possible alternatives might have decreased vulnerability to war.[9]

The legacy of the colonial state

The post-colonial African state, analysts of diverse political tendencies agree, has been beset by multiple structural weaknesses. With few exceptions, authoritarian colonial rule was succeeded not by popular and effective democratic institutions, but by centralization of power, elite privilege and overall disappointing returns to the wider society. Despite enormous diversity in ideology, in extravagance, in degree of repression, and in economic success, a similar diagnosis applied almost across the board.[10] Almost every African state would have been vulnerable to the kind of externally supported insurgency experienced by Angola and Mozambique.

What then were the distinctive vulnerabilities of these two countries? Using labels of 'Afro-Communism' or 'Afro-Marxism,' some analysts have stressed ideological factors distinguishing Angola and Mozambique, together with Ethiopia and sometimes other explicitly Marxist regimes, from other African states. Later sections in this chapter will examine how specific components of Marxist ideology may have affected the state's capacity. But first one must factor in the colonial legacy. An observer in mid-1980s Angola or Mozambique, for example, might blame the cumbersome bureaucracy primarily on socialist influences, thus missing the essential fact that much of the frustrating red tape was already embodied in colonial-era practices.

The ex-Portuguese colonies were doubly afflicted: first by the relatively backward structures of state and civil society the Portuguese left, and then by the withdrawal of almost all the skilled personnel who had managed those structures. Both factors are commonly noted in passing. Yet their continued structural relevance is less often appreciated, as if both critical and sympathetic commentators shared the initial confidence of Angolans and Mozambicans that new societies could be created virtually overnight.

Like other colonial powers, Portugal imposed a top-down administrative structure. In the 1960s, however, the administrative and legal structure of the Portuguese state still lagged significantly behind the rest of Europe. Portuguese underdevelopment was also reflected in the persistence of forced labour in Angola and Mozambique. Before the 1974 *coup*, the Portuguese political system had no tolerance for democratic opposition at home, much less for building representative institutions overseas. The educational system was adapted neither to modern teaching techniques nor to African realities. Secondary education for Africans was minimal and higher education virtually non-existent; even the expansion of primary education in the 1960s and 1970s left both countries with illiteracy rates among Africans in excess of 90 per cent.

In the fifteen years before independence, in response to the colonial wars and to the changing Portuguese economy, significant economic and social modernization took place in Angola and Mozambique. Although growth still relied in large part on non-Portuguese capital, Portuguese capitalists made significant investments in manufacturing and construction, particularly in Luanda and Maputo. As in the extractive agricultural economy, however, Portuguese settlers occupied virtually all the skilled and even semi-skilled positions. Between 1960 and 1970 the number of whites in Angola jumped from 172,000 to 290,000; in Mozambique from 97,000 to 163,000. Both new consumer goods manufacturing and construction were directed to the settler market. Asians (in Mozambique) and *mestiços* (in both countries) were represented in the middle ranks of state- and private-sector employment. But Africans were almost entirely relegated to unskilled labour.

The vacuum produced by the settler departure included the administrative apparatus of the state, urban commerce and almost all the small merchants who, together with coercive state administrators, had formed the link between peasant production and the market. It also included virtually all the owners and managers of medium-sized commercial farms. Even had the new states not discouraged private entrepreneurs and farmers, there were very few Africans ready to step into the shoes of the departed Portuguese. It was by default as much as ideology that the post-colonial state took on management of much of the modern economy.

The state assumed both colonial state responsibilities and new administrative burdens. At the top there were a handful of committed revolutionaries and trained personnel. But despite the symbolic significance of the liberation struggle, those with experience of leadership in that struggle were few. It was easy to adopt revolutionary rhetoric, out of conviction or of opportunism. But in practice the primary administrative model remained the one inherited from the colonial state.

The model was being implemented, moreover, by persons with much less education than their Portuguese predecessors, themselves relatively backward in European terms. In 1983, for example, less than 6,000 individuals in Luanda (2.8 per cent of the total labour force) had secondary education; less than 200 were university graduates. Outside the capital the percentages were lower. In 1989, only 300 of the 1,500 high-level Mozambican civil servants had a university education, 600 had secondary education and the rest only primary school or less.[11]

While in former French and British colonies smaller gaps in skilled personnel were normally filled by citizens of the respective European power, the expatriates in Luanda and Maputo were diverse in origin. Most were new arrivals unfamiliar with Portuguese language, culture and administrative practices. Although in some sectors (health in Mozambique, for example, and the military in Angola) the results were relatively fruitful, problems of coordination, turnover and lack of familiarity with local conditions were constant impediments to effective state action. While in many other African countries the multiplicity of international donor agencies led to similar problems, in Angola and Mozambique language barriers and the small number of trained local personnel raised these difficulties to massive proportions.

The mix of foreign personnel in the two countries differed somewhat. In addition to Cuban troops in Angola and Zimbabwean troops in Mozambique, expatriate workers included substantial contingents of Soviets, East Germans and other eastern Europeans in both countries. Portuguese nationals included both previous residents and new arrivals on technical contracts. Sweden and other Nordic countries, with large aid programmes, sent technical personnel. Cubans and Brazilians were in both countries, but in much larger numbers in Angola. There was a sprinkling of expatriates from Africa, Latin America and Asia, and larger numbers from Western Europe and North America. In Angola Westerners were mostly management and technical personnel in the oil industry and some other sectors. In Mozambique they were, in the early years, predominantly 'cooperantes', recruited through solidarity networks and often supported by non-governmental organizations and aid agencies in Canada, the Netherlands and other European countries.

The diversity of languages, backgrounds and motives made for working environments that were sometimes stimulating and creative, but also often beset with miscommunication. The results differed dramatically from sector to sector, depending on the quality both of local leadership and of foreign personnel. Ideology was only one factor determining policy advice that was given or taken. Just as significant, if not more so, were the operational models Angolans, Mozambicans and foreigners drew on from previous experiences.

In almost all state sectors, continuity with colonial precedents was substantial. But the extent of this influence, as compared with new models from the liberation struggle or other national experiences, varied. Ironically, the break in tradition was probably greatest in the area where previous technical experience might have been most useful: the military.

The intractable dilemmas of counterinsurgency

In most African countries, the nucleus of the post-colonial security forces was the colonial army and police. In many cases, military advisers stayed on for years in operational as well as training capacities. In Angola and Mozambique, however, the army was new, without experience in either conventional or counterinsurgency warfare. Frelimo's army numbered not much more than 10,000 when the Portuguese left. The MPLA had probably only about 3,000 guerrillas in late 1974. The post-colonial army was recruited hastily as conflict escalated in 1975, including some veterans of the Portuguese army but large numbers with no military training at all. Systematic training with Cuban assistance only got under way after independence.

Until 1980, the new armies coped passably with the limited threats from cross-border raids and guerrilla action. But the challenges they faced in the 1980s were overwhelming. Once Renamo and Unita were equipped and trained by South Africa in numbers exceeding 10,000 each, with secure sanctuaries, adequate logistics, and back-up support from SADF commando units, even the numerical prerequisites for successful defence were beyond reach. General Maxwell Taylor's 25-to-1 guideline would imply some 250,000 counterinsurgency troops in each territory, even if the insurgent numbers did not increase. Portuguese forces in Angola before independence had peaked at about 66,000, and in Mozambique at about 52,000. Even the most expansive estimates of defensive troop strength in post-colonial Angola or Mozambique never went much above 150,000.

Successful counterinsurgency is not just a matter of numbers. But the qualitative requirements were even more daunting. If Mozambique or Angola had retained guerrilla traditions of forces close to the people, able to move quickly on foot through the countryside and to fight the insurgents on their own ground, that would have at most provided one component of a successful defence. Simultaneously, they had to prepare for ground incursions or air raids by conventional South African forces, and to build capacity for other standard counterinsurgency measures. Such measures include interdiction of supply lines, protection of key targets and population, rapid mobility, supply of food, arms and ammunition both to defensive garrisons and to assault forces, and C³I (Command, Control, Communications and Intelligence). And that is without mentioning maintenance of good relations with civilians and provision of social services, commonly referred to as winning hearts and minds.

In each sector the obstacles were significant. Interdiction of supply routes with retaliatory cross-border raids was barred by South Africa's overwhelming conventional military superiority. Such raids were inadvisable even to curb supplies from Zaire or Malawi, since they might provoke those countries to greater involvement and aggravate the problem of maintaining both southern and northern defensive fronts. Western opinion, moreover, relatively tolerant of South African cross-border attacks, would have reacted harshly to parallel action by Angola or Mozambique.

Protection of key targets and population, given the attacker's advantage of choosing the location to attack, required immobilizing large numbers of troops in defensive positions. Even then, geography made it impossible to defend more than a small fraction of connecting roads, rail corridors and power lines, much less dispersed rural population. Attempting to reduce this difficulty by regrouping population, despite all its negative effects, was probably an inevitable component of counter-insurgency strategy.

Aggressive pursuit of guerrilla forces, in turn, needed the ability to move troops quickly and in sufficient numbers to confront guerrillas before they dispersed or moved to another location. This required adequate air capacity, particularly helicopters and paratroops, as well as good communications and intelligence. Given the insurgents' radio communications capacity and access to intelligence from South African radio monitoring of government communications, government forces needed to match South Africa's technical intelligence capacity, as well as to process local intelligence from civilians quickly enough for operational use.

Some minimal level of success at these military tasks was a prerequisite for the broader politico-military imperative of winning hearts and minds. If government agents providing political leadership, education and health services, or foreign nationals engaged in development projects, could not be protected, the wisdom or deficiencies of their policies became a moot point. Good or bad, authoritarian or participatory, practical or misguided, no meaningful policies could be implemented without military protection. If the state could not provide at least a minimum of security, it would lose credibility regardless of prior civilian sentiments.

Despite the heroic and dedicated efforts of many government officers and soldiers, and victories in particular campaigns or battles, these defensive efforts were unable to block the objective of the insurgents: to destroy systematically the economic and social viability of the societies and regimes. In retrospect, it is relatively easy to identify points of military vulnerability. But it is difficult to conceive alternative policy choices that might have produced significantly better results.

Foreign troops were a decisive addition to the defensive capacity of both countries; without them the military advantages of the South African-backed insurgents would have been even more overwhelming. Most important, of course, were the Cuban contingent in Angola and the Zimbabwean troops in Mozambique, but limited contributions also came from ANC and SWAPO forces in Angola, and from Tanzanians and even a small contingent from Malawi in Mozambique. With the additional troops came all the normal problems of coordination between armies with different levels of capacity: stereotypes of superiority on the part of Cubans and Zimbabweans, mutual recriminations in the face of battlefield defeats, differences on strategy and failures to exchange vital information, doubts on the home front in Cuba and Zimbabwe, denunciation of foreign occupation by Renamo, Unita and their supporters.

It is notable, however, that these real problems, contrary to the propaganda, did not approach in comparative terms the experience of the US in Vietnam or the Soviet Union in Afghanistan. The foreign troops were in well-defined primarily defensive roles and limited to specific geographical areas. Zimbabwean troops concentrated on defending the Beira corridor and, secondarily, the Limpopo route. Attacks on Renamo base areas, such as the Gorongosa headquarters just north of the Beira corridor, were the exception rather than the rule. Cuban troops provided defensive garrisons for major urban centres and transport routes in Angola, rarely ventured on campaigns against Unita areas, and played a decisive role in conventional combat only in 1975–76 and again in 1987–88. There was no overcommitment that might have turned the wars into Cuban rather than Angolan, or Zimbabwean rather than Mozambican wars.

The restraint was probably wise; it is doubtful that even doubling the outside troop commitment would have compensated for the inherent advantage of attack for the insurgents in such large territories. And such escalation would have possibly boosted rumblings of discontent at home beyond manageable proportions. There were good reasons of ideology, national prestige and national security for supporting Angola and Mozambique. Many Cubans and Zimbabweans proudly and patriotically supported the military engagements. But the costs were by no means popular; higher costs might have been unbearable.

Coordination was a problem in both countries. In Mozambique there was a generally accepted geographical division of responsibilities between Mozambican and Zimbabwean troops. In Angola coordination was further complicated by divergences between Soviet and Cuban advice. Particularly for the conventional offensives against Unita, Soviet supplies were critical. Both Western and Cuban accounts fault Soviet strategic advice for significant errors in these campaigns, in which there was a repeated tendency for Angolan troops to overrun their supply lines, leaving them vulnerable to South African and Unita counterattacks.[12]

Even with foreign assistance, moreover, the government armies never approached the capability for significant interdiction of the Unita or Renamo supply lines. Malawi and Zaire as well as South Africa and Namibia were secure sanctuaries for supplies over land for the insurgents. Only Angola's anti-aircraft capacity had much technical sophistication, and that in limited areas, inadequate to block supply flights. The idea that the minuscule Mozambican navy could patrol a coastline equivalent to Western Europe's from the Netherlands to Spain was not even a joke.

What, then, about blocking the insurgents' access to the local population, on which they depended for voluntary or involuntary contributions of food, head porterage and other services? Even if there were resources to train and arm local militia, in addition to regular troops on stand-by for rapid response, such a massive military task for populations dispersed over remote rural areas would have required levels of coordination, communication and transport that were inconceivable under Angolan or Mozambican conditions. The Angolan and Mozambican armies, like both successful and unsuccessful counterinsurgency forces in other wars, accordingly resorted to forcible as well as voluntary regroupment of people, with results that were at best ambiguous.[13]

Such measures, despite human rights abuses, sometimes succeed in military terms.[14] But for the positive military effects to outweigh the resentment built up by forcible relocation, several supplementary conditions are required, none of which was adequately met in Mozambique or Angola. The displaced population must be provided with security from attack in the new location. It must have interim relief supplies and, eventually, the opportunity to make an equivalent or better living than before. With inadequate resources to defend locations close to arable land, and inability to provide employment in the cities or small garrison towns, neither government could cope even with the massive unorganized voluntary flow of people fleeing the countryside seeking greater security – much less the additional number displaced by force.

People displaced by the military did usually receive some relief supplies. Unlike the insurgents, who extracted resources, the governments and international agencies operating in government territory put in resources. Nor, despite documented abuses, did government forces match the systematic assault on the peasantry perpetrated in contested areas by Renamo and, to a lesser extent, Unita. The bottom line, however, was that, for a large proportion of those voluntarily or involuntarily subject to their administration in rural areas, the governments did not provide the benefits of adequate security or a viable livelihood. Security was somewhat better in urban centres, but at the price, for most, of lack of access to land or employment.

None of the local studies to date, even including Geffray's and Wilson's, is fine-grained enough to trace the complex pattern of voluntary and involuntary relocation as rural people sought to survive, insurgents attacked and kidnapped villagers, and government troops recuperated escapees from Renamo and Unita or took unwilling families from their land in the ebb and flow of military operations. But given the acknowledged defects in government actions, it is notable that discontent seems to have been translated primarily into political apathy and personal survival strategies rather than into active support for insurgency. Instead, most rural people seem to have concluded that the insurgents were worse, or that such judgements were irrelevant to practical survival strategies of adjusting to whichever force happened to be in the area.

In a militarily and politically successful counterinsurgency, necessary relocation of population would have been minimized, accompanied by social services, and followed up by mobile search-and-destroy missions aimed at the insurgent forces. Well-armed and well-trained militia would replace regular troops in defending the rural population, ideally in locations of their own choosing. Particularly gross human rights abuses by particular officers or soldiers would be followed by judicial action against those responsible.

Sufficient military force might bring military success even without political success. But the scale of the defensive task was enormous, and chances of success made even more elusive by institutional weaknesses. Both armies had virtually no officers with experience of managing a national army, and relatively small numbers with any war experience at all before 1975. The gross educational deficiencies of society were carried over into the military. Draining skilled personnel from the civilian sector could improve the situation only to a limited extent. And it had the effect of weakening government capacity to provide other services that would be essential components of comprehensive counterinsurgency strategy. Both armies relied on the draft for most recruitment. Legally legitimate, its implementation was nevertheless often abusive and disorganized, with a substantial portion of recruits being youth caught up in draft raids. Morale problems were accentuated by frequent failures to provide adequate supplies for troops in the field.

In Angola such weaknesses were alleviated in part by the involvement of Cuban advisers, but even more by foreign exchange from oil sales. Defence purchases, not only from the Soviet Union but from Western suppliers, provided transport and communications equipment, food, uniforms and other necessary goods. During the course of the war the officer corps gained experience and upped its educational level significantly; a merit system included educational achievements as a prerequisite for advance to higher ranks.

The Mozambican army too improved its officer training significantly during the war, with the aid first of the Soviet bloc and then of British and other Western advisers. But the pool of officer recruits with secondary education was even smaller than in Angola. Guerrilla veterans with little education who had been early promoted to high ranks feared possible younger or better-educated rivals. The government acceded to their fears by not recruiting significant numbers of whites, Asians or *mestiços* into the military.[15] The Mozambican government lacked the financial resources to provide its army with expensive equipment, adequate air and ground transport, or even basic supplies such as ammunition, food, boots and uniforms. Government communications equipment was notoriously inferior to that of Renamo, and troops often could not respond to emergencies because of lack of ammunition, fuel or even radio batteries. As the war and economic hardship continued, corruption in the officer corps advanced apace, accelerating demoralization in lower ranks.

The insurgent armies of Renamo and Unita faced some of the same difficulties. But they had the guerrilla option of concentrating on attack while paying relatively little attention to the multiple other tasks of a defensive army. Guerrilla logistics were secured by South Africa and other outside suppliers, and by extraction of basic food supplies from the rural population. Particularly in the case of Renamo, they could concentrate on war, undistracted by managing an economy, maintaining infrastructure or providing social services to civilians.[16]

In both Angola and Mozambique the security forces' incapacity to control the situation increased the likelihood of abuses against civilians presumed to sympathize with the insurgents or simply slow to respond to orders. Mechanisms to control or limit these abuses were largely ineffective. The Mozambican government's response to the threat included the reintroduction in 1979 of the death penalty that had been banned at independence, and of flogging in 1983. Even supporters of the governments in both countries at times feared arbitrary or uncontrolled military action.

When the detailed military histories are written, there will no doubt be ample material for a critique of particular strategies and tactics. But it is unlikely that the fundamental counterinsurgency weaknesses could have been corrected by alternative choices at that level. They instead reflected the vulnerability of the overstretched state itself, in which success at one time in one sector almost always implied neglecting other problems elsewhere.

State, party and participation

In the euphoric atmosphere at independence, it seemed that popular enthusiasm and mobilization might overcome immense obstacles. The Portuguese state had been forced to withdraw, and even the mighty South African army had been beaten back short of Luanda. Reliance on those excluded from participation by the colonial order had sustained an expanding guerrilla war in Mozambique, and had defended Luanda until Cuban troops helped turn the tide. The slogan 'people's power' expressed the hope and provided the justification for a new post-colonial order. It was assumed, as in the struggle against colonialism, that realization of this hope required guidance from the liberation movement, now transformed into ruling party.

'People's power' was a critique not only of the colonial model, but also of the first generation of African states. With elites groomed for neo-colonial cooperation by the colonial powers, these states were seen as tending to replace white elites with black, without other significant changes in the social order. The need for a 'second independence' was blatant in the Zairian kleptocracy which had joined with the US and South Africa in targeting Angola. The dependence of most of francophone Africa on French direction was notorious. Even the populist socialisms of Tanzania and Zambia were seen by MPLA and Frelimo leaders as insufficiently aware of the dangers of growth of a new privileged class. Unless the working people (both peasants and workers) were actively engaged in building a radically new order, the natural tendency would be for the colonial legacy and the international capitalist order to swallow up revolutionary hopes, leaving African leaders as privileged neo-colonial intermediaries. In contrast, revolutionary rhetoric implied the necessity to 'smash the colonial state apparatus'. The movement, building on its links with the people established during the anti-colonial struggle, would forge the institutions by which the people would build a state serving their own interests.

Some critics charge that this goal was never more than cynical rhetoric. Other analysts contend that the model was inherently flawed by the contradiction between participation and centralized party leadership. And yet others say that it never had a proper chance to be tried before war pounded idealistic hopes out of leaders and followers alike. Whatever the reason, the historical outcome is clear. In both Angola and Mozambique, significant numbers of the 'people', as well as others ambiguously classified as petty bourgeois, did move into positions of party and state leadership. For a few years grass-roots mobilization was substantial in scale, particularly in Mozambique. But the ruling party, instead of institutionalizing participatory patterns and serving as an effective check on state bureaucracy, became in practice a part of that bureaucracy.[17]

Socialism in Angola, President dos Santos reflected in a 1992 interview, hardly left the drawing board, 'a system of good intentions'.[18] The new models of the state, whether in the vaguer version of 'people's power' or in more orthodox Marxist-Leninist terms, were never more than sporadically implemented. A brief examination of some of the reasons shows that alternative models might have changed the balance of who was included or excluded from access to power. More accommodation of leaders with traditional legitimacy or other local bases of power might have strengthened the state significantly. Even had alternative models been adopted, however, implementation would have faced many of the same problems and still left the state overstretched and vulnerable to insurgency.

Frelimo and the MPLA drew on different images of people's power. In Mozambique the primary model was the experience of the liberated areas during the armed struggle. Samora Machel's speeches summed up success in that period as derived from reliance on the masses, with a leadership that both learned from and gave direction to the people's interests. The ideal party militant was one who was self-sacrificing, willing to put commitment to the revolution over personal ambition, simultaneously disciplined and engaged in constructive criticism. People's power was in stark contrast to the power of the exploiters, both the colonial rulers and those who sought independence simply to change the colour of the faces at the top.[19]

The construct, in part myth, also had roots in lived experience of interaction with the rural population. But however consistently implemented, it applied at most to a few hundred thousand people for a few years in the late 1960s and early 1970s.[20] The MPLA's experience of administering liberated areas was even more fragmentary. The most vivid images of popular initiative were from 1974–75, when urban supporters of the MPLA organized spontaneously and mounted resistance to attacks on Luanda.[21] In either case, applying such models at the national level was a task of a different order. Bonds between leaders and followers forged in intense moments of confrontation and enthusiasm were more likely to erode than to be sustained on their own. Relatively direct dialogue between top leaders and masses – a fragile prospect at any time – became even more difficult when mediated through layers of bureaucracy.

As a model to implement people's power, both Frelimo and the MPLA opted formally by 1977 for a Marxist-Leninist approach. The liberation movement become Marxist-Leninist party, the theory went, would apply affirmative action for workers and peasants within its ranks, and bind itself together with ideological commitment. The party, operating through control over the state and guidance of mass organizations such as women's groups, youth groups, trade unions and peasant associations, would ensure that the state really served the people rather than minority interests. Elected people's assemblies, under party guidance but not restricted to party members, would provide an additional check. Actual or aspiring petty-bourgeois tendencies inherent in the state apparatus would be overcome. Development would build up the industrial working class and raise peasant productivity, providing new resources for equitably distributed gains.

In the wake of the global collapse of the Soviet-type model, few would claim that such a scheme could satisfy popular aspirations for democratic participation. In successfully institutionalized revolutions before the late 1970s, however, it could be credibly claimed that the model greatly increased popular participation for previously subordinate classes. Moreover, the model had a record of establishing a 'hard state', successfully resisting counter-revolutionary onslaught through both military might and tight party supervision of society.

In practice, neither the Marxist-Leninist model nor an alternative, less centralized model of people's power provides a reliable guide to analysing the reality of post-colonial Angola and Mozambique. Neither the party nor the organs of people's power became powerful parallel structures directing or checking the state apparatus. Instead, party leaders at the top became primarily directors of states under siege. Almost all party officials at middle levels, serving simultaneously as state administrators, operated as agents of a top-down bureaucracy. The theme of democracy and popular participation was expressed repeatedly in campaigns of popular discussion and criticism of administrative abuses. But such checks on the state never became effectively institutionalized realities.

Had the vanguard party model been successfully implanted, with ideologically mobilized members directing the state and mass organizations, it would doubtless have produced a new entrenched elite common to state socialist societies on other continents. But it would also probably have been more effective in repressing subversion. As it happened, in transforming themselves from liberation movements into vanguard parties, Frelimo and the MPLA reaped the disadvantages of restricting party membership and losing potential sources of support from excluded social sectors. In the mid-1980s, Frelimo members numbered only 110,000, and MPLA members fewer than 50,000. They failed to fully exploit the potential for new models of governance in their traditions. Yet they did not gain the compensating security advantages of a 'hard state'.

In Mozambique the experience of the *grupos dinamizadores* in the transition period before independence and the first few years thereafter demonstrated Frelimo's capacity to stimulate popular creativity and involvement. The achievements in education, health and women's rights of this period depended on extraordinary levels of participation by previously disenfranchised Mozambicans, including rural as well as urban and small-town residents. The class origins and interests of those who became leaders have not been investigated in detail, but they were undoubtedly diverse, including many with a background of relative privilege under colonialism.

Frelimo's ideological winnowing, from the *grupos dinamizadores* to the vanguard party, was designed to mould this process in the direction of a new revolutionary society.[22] Collaborators with the colonial regime, polygamists and religious leaders were excluded from political leadership. The 'masses' were encouraged to identify opportunists who abused their power for personal gain. Candidates for party membership were supposed to be judged by their co-workers or neighbours on their fitness for leadership. And the party, once formed, was supposed to elicit public criticism to ensure responsiveness to mass interests.

In 1983, just over half the 110,000 party members were classified as peasants, one-fifth as workers. One-fourth of the total were women. The same concern for representativity appeared in indirect elections for people's assemblies in 1977 and 1980, with candidates nominated by the party, and subject to popular veto in the local assemblies. At the district level in 1980, for example, 43 per cent of assembly members were peasants and 13 per cent were workers; women members accounted for 17 per cent. On several occasions, including campaigns in 1980 and in preparation for the Fourth Party Congress in 1983, the party did stimulate popular criticism. Afterwards it acknowledged 'an incontestable trend of growing elitism, bureaucratism and formal isolation from the people'.[23]

This kind of debate aroused hopes that the trend would eventually be corrected. Instead, whether out of self-interest, bureaucratic inertia, or the pressures of war which were already overwhelming by 1982, it became more deeply entrenched. By the mid-1980s, political changes were being driven not by efforts to implement a model of participation, Marxist or other, but by the diplomatic and practical concerns of survival and peace. Ironically, when Frelimo again elicited significant public debate, this time on a new constitutional order, and found that the majority in rural areas favoured continued one-party rule, the party leadership decided that it still had to opt for a multi-party system. The concept of democratic participation shifted to the combination of multi-party competition and opening up space for civil society.

In Angola, the context of political institution-building was significantly different. The initial atmosphere was not national unity, but open conflict. The MPLA itself had a history of internal disputes. The initial people's power institutions, particularly strong in the neighbourhoods of Luanda, soon became the terrain for turf wars between party factions. Less than two years after independence, when this erupted in the violent *coup* attempt headed by Nito Alves, there were significant casualties on both sides. When the MPLA constituted a vanguard party later the same year, it was preoccupied with maintaining control and loyalty.[24]

The 'rectification' campaign by which members of the movement were screened for party membership focused on identifying exemplary workers, based on opinions of their workplace colleagues, both movement militants and ordinary workers. As in Mozambique, the explicit criteria centred on demonstrated commitment to popular interests, in contrast to pursuit of individual ambition. The party composition by

1980 was 49 per cent workers, 2 per cent peasants, 17 per cent white-collar employees and 22 per cent state office-holders. While many of the office-holders were of peasant family background, peasants were clearly underrepresented. In 1985, although the percentage of peasant background was increased, President dos Santos frankly stated that 'the virtual abandonment of the countryside ... prevented us from organizing the peasants'.[25] People's assemblies at provincial and national level were not established until 1980.

Mass organizations in the two countries (women's movements, youth movements, trade unions) were another avenue for popular participation. The Organization of Angolan Women (OMA) and the Organization of Mozambican Women (OMM) in particular provided scope for creativity that had been consistently denied under the colonial order. But like the other mass organizations, their structure was fundamentally top-down and their power to check or influence the state apparatus was marginal.

Despite the formal subordination of state to ruling party, the party too found control over the state elusive. As the Economist Intelligence Unit put it, the Angolan state 'is a vast, ponderous body, most of whose employees are not party members and do not necessarily share the party's goals'.[26] Also applicable to Mozambique, this meant that party members who were not simultaneously state officials were not necessarily more effective than ordinary citizens in influencing bureaucratic actions. Party members who were state officials often found their actions constrained more by bureaucratic procedures than by ideological guidelines. At provincial and district levels, the top party official was almost invariably the top state official, leaving little scope for checking the centralizing tendency of officialdom.

For the ordinary Angolan or Mozambican, the promise of a responsive state was, more often than not, unfulfilled. Popular mobilization for defence was thus a waning asset, even though the insurgents' strategy of destruction impeded large-scale transfer of allegiance to the other side. But, given the background at independence and conditions of war, could different models of governance have done significantly better? What would have been the prospects for one-party socialism with a mass rather than a vanguard party, on the Tanzanian model? Or a patrimonial order like most other African states, based on patron–client relationships between national leaders and local elites? Or the attempt to build a multi-party electoral system, as in Botswana or Senegal?

The record of such models in building participation or a strong state in other African countries gives little support for optimistic answers. The African Party for the Independence of Guinea-Bissau and Cape Verde (PAIGC) refrained from adopting a Marxist-Leninist model, instead retaining the broader formulation of liberation movement days.

And it was not subjected to war. Nevertheless, analysts agree that the post-colonial government effectively cut itself off from its rural roots.[27] The ruling party in Tanzania incorporated more than 10 per cent of the population as members, but still confronted the dilemmas of top-down administration and weak popular support once economic setbacks offset the social gains of independence. Patrimonial systems based on patronage to local communities through traditional or newly emergent elites fostered corruption, inequality, and rapid disillusionment once the limits of trickle-down became apparent. The most cited success story, Botswana, had multiple advantages – relative ethnic homogeneity, small population size, abundant income from diamonds, and an inherited bureaucracy with relatively high levels of education and competence.[28]

One might trace out an 'ideal' pattern, in which the ruling parties relied at local levels on leaders respected by their communities, including traditional leaders and aspiring capitalists. That would have been better, no doubt, than rigidly ruling out participation by such forces in the party on grounds of their incompatibility with revolutionary theory. But the catch is that such a solution could not be implemented by rote. Many traditional leaders and others claiming local prominence in fact lacked legitimacy, by virtue of their past collaboration with the colonial system. An open-door policy for such local elites, with no affirmative action in favour of workers, peasants and 'revolutionary intellectuals', would have changed the local power-base of the parties. But it also would have restricted avenues of participation for women, youth and others.

Whether the net result proved marginally better than the policies actually adopted would have depended, above all, on implementation. By the late 1980s, both states had in fact shifted to pragmatic approaches along these lines. But the weaknesses of implementation, accentuated by the cumulative toll of war and economic adjustment, were still dramatic. Any alternative model of participation or governance, even if adopted early on, would have faced the same fundamental questions: who would implement it, given the lack of political, administrative and technical personnel at middle levels to translate national policy into local realities, and to provide reliable reports to national leadership? And what long-term benefits would participation bring, if the state proved unable to deliver concrete results?

State, bureaucracy and 'administrative measures'

Despite Marxist-Leninist symbolism, the state in Mozambique and Angola was not much larger proportionally than other African states. Mozambique's 105,000 civil servants (including teachers) and 122,000 parastatal employees added up to 14 civilian public-sector employees per 1,000 people. That was considerably lower than Zambia's 43/1,000, and below Nigeria's 19/1,000 ratio. Mozambique's civil service accounted for only about 10 per cent of formal sector employment, among the lowest in Africa. Angola's figures, bolstered by oil revenue, were higher at 36 per 1,000 population (160,000 civil servants and 184,000 parastatal employees), but still less than Zambia's.[29]

As mentioned earlier, these personnel included scarcely more than a thousand in each country with even a full secondary-school education. Yet they were responsible for administering states to which nationalization had added the tasks of managing the majority of commercial enterprises. Although most of these businesses fell into the hands of the state as settlers fled, ideology reinforced the determination to maintain centralized control. Despite theoretical openness to both local and foreign private investment, bureaucratic disincentives combined with war insecurity to limit large-scale involvement to particularly profitable sectors such as oil.

Both provision of services and maintenance of control outside the capital depended on reliable communications and transportation. That would have been a difficult proposition even without war. As one descended the administrative hierarchy from the capital to the provincial capitals, then the district capitals and finally local rural areas, communication links became progressively more remote. Telephone links were irregular at best even in provincial capitals, and almost nonexistent further into the countryside. With low educational levels in the civil service, written reports and instructions were of limited value. Effective management required visits from higher officials; local officials could not count on responses from higher-ups without lobbying visits to the next level up. While such conditions may be endemic to bureaucracies, particularly in the Third World, Angola and Mozambique experienced them at extraordinarily high levels.

Attacks on transportation multiplied these difficulties many times over. Flight of settlers with their vehicles was followed by insurgent tactics which included targeting civilian travellers. The resultant damage to the effectiveness of state action proved, as intended, an ongoing vicious circle. Whatever policies were adopted, military or civilian, their implementation in the countryside depended on accessibility. With many locations only accessible by air, the cost of providing relief or other services escalated uncontrollably. Provincial and district capitals became islands connected by air flights or military convoy.

Within the state administration, education and health workers were the largest civilian component, reflecting the most immediate benefits the post-colonial state had to offer. In Mozambique 51,000 employees in education and 25,000 in health far outnumbered the employees of any other ministry; over 90 per cent were deployed in the provinces rather than central administration. In Angola more than 36,000 in education and 19,000 in health accounted for over one-third of government employees, a lower percentage than in Mozambique but still substantial. Government budgets, until cuts in the late 1980s, gave high priority to these sectors despite the burden of military expense. But maintaining popular support depended on delivery of the services, which was slashed by direct war damage to schools and clinics as well as by transportation difficulties.

Increasingly, then, and from the start in areas initially affected by war, the population's experience of the state was concentrated on its control functions, which easily overbalanced its capacity to deliver needed services. The capacity to promote economic advance (to be discussed in the next chapter) was very limited. It was easy for military officials or for insecure civilian administrators to adopt what were labelled 'administrative measures' (i.e., giving orders). Exceptionally competent and self-assured local officials, with sufficient connections in higher circles to protect them from bureaucratic reprisals, might avoid this tendency. Individual leaders might instil a different working style in a particular ministry or a particular province for a time, but hierarchical habits were generally seen as the safest path.

The factors that made for effective state action, in particular campaigns or locations, were difficult to generalize. When top leaders concentrated on a well-defined plan for a limited time period, such as Mozambique's early public health and literacy campaigns, the results could be extraordinary. Health and education lent themselves to replicable implementation packages that could be fairly effective as long as basic security was assured. But most political, military or economic programmes required flexible adaptation to enormously diverse and changing local realities. Rigid implementation of top-down guidelines, even ones that were generally appropriate, was a recipe for increasing the chances of failure. Yet there were few officials with the technical skills and political confidence to act flexibly and to provide informative reports on failed policies up the ladder.

There is no more than impressionistic data on variations in government effectiveness by state sector or geographical area, but there can be no doubt that the range was enormous. An effective provincial governor, district administrator, local commander or provincial director in a particular ministry could break through the normal inertia, adapt general guidelines to local conditions and win the confidence of local constituencies even when the war and other external conditions limited the fruits of success. There were structural as well as personal factors that raised the chances of ineffective or abusive administration: distance from the capital, the extent of the cultural gap between administrators and local people, the geographical vulnerability of a particular area to military disruption, and the extent to which *de facto* local policy was being made by military or civilian leaders. All these factors differed significantly by region and even by district within each country. Any serious study of the state's impact on rural areas must delve more deeply into these variations, a task which has barely begun.

Fundamental to understanding the post-colonial state's relationship to the rural population, however, is the fact that, in contrast to the colonial state, it did not establish effective mechanisms for extraction of resources from the countryside. Despite occasional speeches by frustra-ted administrators recalling the forced labour and forced cultivation policies of colonial times, neither state farms nor peasants produced the profits they had provided to the colonial system. The old exploitative mechanisms were gone, but functioning new ones, exploitative or other-wise, were not institutionalized. As a result the state primarily related to the rural population, other than in military terms, as a promised provider of services, all too frequently undelivered.[30]

With agricultural production reduced to minor significance as a provider of surplus, the state relied on other sources. In Angola, oil moved from being the primary source of revenue to virtually the only one. In Mozambique, after reduction of income from the labour and transport sectors serving other countries, taxes on consumption and import trade made up the bulk of government revenue, massively sup-plemented in the late 1980s by grants from international donors. The issue became how much of this revenue trickled down into services, and how much simply maintained those who lived by state employment or by other ways of tapping into state revenues.

Despite the images of the post-colonial state as intrusively omni-present – and the elements of reality on which the images were based – it was the insurgents who imposed the tightest controls on rural popu-lations, extracting food, loot and forced porterage at gunpoint. The greatest flaws of the states, in contrast, probably came not so much from what they did as from what they failed to do.

Were there other non-state resources in Angolan and Mozambican society which, with a less rigid approach, might have been brought into alliance with the state to provide more effective resistance to externally-backed insurgency? Was accommodating or fostering civil society an option that could have compensated for the weaknesses of the state? The most plausible answer is yes, but only to a limited degree, because civil society in both countries suffered from weaknesses paralleling those of the state itself.

State and civil society

In current usage civil society most commonly refers to non-state organ-izations and networks that can, ideally, serve both to check the power of a state elite and to provide the glue integrating the public realm. Economic interest groups, professional groups, independent media, local community organizations, cultural and religious associations, social welfare, human rights and other non-governmental organizations interlock in a complex pattern that takes many burdens from the state and promotes a common civic coexistence contributing to peaceful resolution of differences. Multiple networks link the national context with regional and local counterparts, providing back-and-forth contacts that prevent the state from being too far removed from its constituencies.

Yet the thinness and fragmentary reach of such networks, even as compared to other African countries, was one of the distinctive characteristics of post-colonial society in Angola and Mozambique. Even within regional zones of broad cultural unity, there were few established unifying institutions apart from the coercive Portuguese state. The Portuguese colonial model deliberately cut wider links among traditional elites, making chiefs subordinate to local Portuguese officials. Even within small local units there was no clarity as to which traditional authorities were legitimate or which more prestigious. There were few organized improvement associations of communities or of specific segments of society and almost no trade unions. Even the mass organizations affiliated to the liberation movements were at independence mostly organizational shells waiting to be filled, rather than broad-based groups with a local institutional life of their own.

Intermediary institutions, to the extent that they existed prior to independence, were overwhelmingly colonial institutions, most based in the settler community. There were, without doubt, other seeds that could have been cultivated more assiduously. But who would do the cultivating, and with what resources? And, most significantly for our topic here, what difference would it have made to strengthening resistance to insurgency?

In practice, even in the early years, informal local networks of leadership and prestige often interacted with and penetrated local party and state structures. In Geffray's study of Erati district, for example, he notes that the 'structures' were filled with the segment of society that had gained education under the Portuguese, the Erati, while the Macuane, marginalized by the colonial state, provided the terrain of Renamo control. Heimer, in the southern Mozambican area of Vundiça, noted the connections between local Frelimo leadership and traditional authority.[31] Local officials in both Angola and Mozambique dealt with local power structures, whether traditional or emergent, to whom they were in many cases related by kinship or personal acquaintance. If there had been no orientations from above mandating revolutionary hostility to traditional authority, collaborators with colonialism and the aspirant petty bourgeoisie, such penetration of the state by local civil society would have been more open and unrestrained. But it existed never-theless. By the mid-1980s pragmatism from the top mandated an open door to any sector of society that could provide resources, material or symbolic, for defence against the insurgents. In some cases, of leaders with particularly high local prestige, this could provide exemption from attack for specific areas.[32]

The catch was that to generalize such policies successfully would have required precisely the capacity to make local judgements that the state lacked. A policy of respect for local power structures probably would have avoided many offences to local sensitivities, but it probably would also have reinforced many local structures that were themselves abusive of large segments of the population. Competition to fill the vacuum of authority left by the Portuguese would have provided multiple opportunities for conflict for insurgents to take advantage of.

The option of retaining much of the structure of the settler society, overseen by an Africanized state, as in Kenya or in Zimbabwe, would have been much more difficult in the ex-Portuguese context. Slots filled by Portuguese settlers extended much lower down in the social order and in the state than in Kenya or Zimbabwe. Even if the settlers who fled could be enticed back, or could have been persuaded not to leave, the consequences for vulnerability of the state would have been un-certain. In this scenario, the new states would have gained from less discontinuity, retained many functioning institutions and reduced the threat from discontented exiles allying themselves with insurgency. But they would also have forfeited much enthusiasm and participation, and faced paralysis in state programmes trying to better the welfare of the majority.

Leaving aside this speculative option of wholesale retention of colo-nial institutions, the foremost non-state institutions at the national level which might have aided in fostering civil society were the churches, followed, perhaps, by specific economic interest groups. The states did pursue such ties, with increasing urgency as the wars intensified and restrictions based on ideological fervour faded. The courtship was im-peded, however, not only by the ideologies and radical policies of the early post-colonial state, but also by other incompatibilities, derived from history or external conflicts, not subject to alteration by one side alone.

The hostility of the ruling parties to institutional religion came in part from Marxist dogma, but also from the Iberian anti-clerical tradi-tion, and from the close identification of the Catholic Church in par-ticular with the colonial order. The most intense conflict came not with the churches as such, but with an unreformed Catholic Church resentful of loss of its previous privileges as state church. Conflict was at its height in the late 1970s, as the state moved to restrict religion to the sphere of private devotion, removing the prominent church role in education, denying party membership to overt believers and reacting angrily to church denunciations of the revolution. Despite an uneasy *détente* in the early 1980s, and restoration of church properties at the end of the decade, relations between church and state remained clouded by suspicion.[33]

Indeed, the Portuguese Catholic hierarchy had identified almost without exception and without question with the colonial state. Dissent and criticism of colonial abuses came from a small minority of priests and missionaries, mostly non-Portuguese Europeans along with a few Portuguese and Africans. In Angola a number of African priests, including several with personal ties to MPLA leaders, were imprisoned by the Portuguese. But in Mozambique African priests were conspicuous by their small numbers and by their abstention from anti-colonial protests. In both countries the cohort who became bishops as the church rapidly Africanized its ranks at independence were above all religious bureaucrats. In comparison with Latin America, South Africa or Zimbabwe, they had little exposure to or sympathy with liberation theology.

Their opposition to the new order stopped short of providing direct support for insurgency. And as the wars wound on, their pastoral letters shifted from sharp attacks on the governments to more even-handed appeals for peace. But it is notable that they rarely condemned Rhodesian or South African involvement in the wars, and even argued with their fellow southern African bishops against condemnation of South Africa's apartheid policies. The ruling parties, for their part, found it easy to dismiss as hypocritical the critical comments on abuses of the post-colonial state, from an institution which even in retrospect failed to acknowledge its own complicity in colonial human rights abuses.[34]

Some degree of rivalry with the Catholic Church was probably inevitable, given both the institutional background and the enormous gulf in visions of a future social order. But a more conciliatory, less dogmatic stance in the early years by the post-colonial state could have eased some of the conflict. Specific concessions, such as allowing a subordinate role for church schools rather than wholesale nationalization, might have given the Catholic Church a greater stake in the post-colonial social order. But given the insurgents' demonstrated willingness to target both African and foreign religious personnel in government zones, it is not clear how much such church participation would have decreased the society's vulnerability to attack.

Other religious groups, primarily Protestant but also Muslim in Mozambique, lacked the Catholic handicap of identification with the colonial state. Despite official government policies favouring anti-religious Marxist ideologies, non-Catholic groups found their freedom far less restricted after independence than previously under the Catholic state church. Most religious groups experienced rapid growth. After government decisions in the early 1980s to seek closer cooperation, church councils in both countries took significant roles in relief work. Church members and leaders participated in the elected assemblies and in mass organizations. Even among party members, opposition to religious belief was not consistently enforced. Many Protestant church leaders had access through personal or family ties to government leaders.

But in terms of providing resources for national-level civil society, and for restraining division exacerbating the war, the non-Catholic groups were regionally restricted in a pattern paralleling the political arena. In Angola the Methodist connection to the MPLA had helped mould the social milieu of Luanda and its hinterland. The Congregational connection to Unita was even more intimate: while part of the church adapted to life in government-controlled zones, Unita supporters from this church maintained a separate institutional structure based in Jamba, and were prominent in the Unita hierarchy. In Mozambique, the concentration of Protestant churches in the south was one of the factors that had moulded the Maputo-centred environment prominent in the personal history of many of Frelimo's top leaders. No Protestant church in either country had a nationwide network comparable to that of the Catholics. The Muslim community in Mozambique, although significant numerically with upwards of 10 per cent of the population, had only a rudimentary organizational network at the national level.

In general, relations between the state and religious institutions in both Mozambique and Angola were most sharply conflictual in the late 1970s, before the South African-inspired escalation of conflict in the 1980s. The shift to a more cooperative stance, on the side of the state, was signalled by a well-publicized dialogue with religious groups in 1982 in Mozambique. A parallel although more gradual process in Angola also led to reduced tension. In the subsequent course of war, Catholic Church calls for peace and eventual participation in negotiations in Mozambique were bedevilled by suspicions of partiality against the ruling parties. But even the Catholic Church avoided identification with insurgency, instead reflecting, as the wars wound on, the popular insistence on peace regardless of the relative virtues or defects of the warring parties.

One may speculate that a more open stance by the ruling parties, without the initial confrontations, might have enabled the churches to play a more effective and earlier role in national reconciliation. But that would have required not only shifts in state policy but also profound changes in the churches. Religious institutions unwilling to criticize their heritage of collaboration with colonialism, still divided among themselves, often indifferent to the drama of liberation of remaining white-minority-ruled Africa, and largely concerned with institutional self-preservation, were ill-equipped to play a major role in compensating for the weaknesses of the post-colonial state. Better relations between church and state would surely have closed some breaches in vulnerability to insurgency. But it is unlikely that this would have made more than a modest difference in the outcome.

What then about the other major potential source of non-state societal resources? What if the states had fostered rather than feared a nascent petty bourgeoisie or bourgeoisie, to replace the departed Portuguese in key economic sectors? What were the prospects of promoting a prosperous market-oriented peasantry to serve as a shield against insurgent infiltration? In short, what if the free-market policies adopted under pressure at the end of the 1980s had been pursued from the start? Would Angola and Mozambique have then proved much more resistant to the escalation of South African-sponsored insurgency in the 1980s? The answers require, first of all, a look at the reality as well as the rhetoric of post-colonial economic policies.

Notes

1. Correia (1989), 13.

2. President Afonso Dhlakama In Interview 1988–90, *Mozambique Political Notes No. 1* (1991), 9. For other sources representing the official Renamo perspective see Hoile (1989) and Cline (1989).

3. *Expresso*, 16 November 1991. The Rhodesian connection is fully documented, with testimony by former Rhodesian officials, in Johnson and Martin (1986, 1988), Flower (1987), Cole (1985) and Ellert (1989).

4. Savimbi (1979), 32.

5. Savimbi (1979), 56.

6. Savimbi (1979), 203–7.

7. Crocker (1992), 53.

8. Report of rally in Kuito by Karl Maier, *The Independent*, 23 September 1992.

9. The issue of villagization, critical for Renamo's self-justification, is taken up in two different sections (counterinsurgency and agrarian policy), since there were multiple reasons for the policy.

10. Among many sources on this topic, see Young (1982), Young (1988), Hyden and Bratton (1992) and Davidson (1992).

11. World Bank, *Angola* (1991), 106. The figures on Mozambique are from an internal World Bank survey.

12. See the descriptions in Jaster (1990), Crocker (1992) and Deutschmann (1989).

13. See particularly Africa Watch reports on both Angola and Mozambique. It is clear from these and other sources that in both countries resettlement was primarily a military policy, with developmental and ideological goals secondary or marginal.

14. On the classic British experience in Malaya, for example, see Stubbs (1989).

15. In later years, this was sometimes popularly interpreted as special exemption for non-blacks. But Mozambican officials acknowledge that this exception from the principles of non-racialism was originally adopted because of fears of racial rivalry in the officer corps.

16. This is fundamentally different from the renewed Angolan war after 1992. Then Unita took control of much more area, including provincial capitals, which it had great difficulty in administering.

17. For a sampling of the abundant general literature on Marxist-oriented states in Africa, see Ottaway and Ottaway (1986), Young (1982), Keller and Rothschild (1987), Lopes and Rudebeck (1988). The references on the debate in Mozambique are too numerous to cite here, but one convenient place to follow the discussion is the periodical *Southern Africa Report* (Toronto). A highly critical account by a French scholar is Cahen (1987). O'Meara (1991) summarizes the debate. On Angola the literature is much less comprehensive, but see the article by Christine Messiant in Eduardo Mondlane Foundation (1993). For some additional references see Minter (1992). The question left unanswered in the text – i.e. the reasons for the insensitivity of the state to popular concerns – is fundamental. But the fact that it is common to other African states, of different ethnic and class compositions and different ideologies, makes me sceptical that it can be explained primarily by looking at the social origins of state personnel (south/north; urban/rural; etc.). In any case there is as yet no empirical research that goes beyond very general impressions on that issue for post-colonial Angola and Mozambique. As suggested by the discussion in Chapter 4, such background factors as ethno-regional disparities are indeed relevant. As an explanation for unresponsiveness of the post-colonial state, however, it seems to me more promising to start from the position that given the state's heritage, lack of responsiveness is by far the most likely outcome, whatever the ideological or social composition of new incumbents. Unless, that is, new mechanisms of accountability to society are developed. The focus then shifts to the conditions under which such mechanisms might develop: level of education of the population, strength of institutions of civil society, and others.

18. *Expresso*, 18 July 1992.

19. See Munslow (1985), particularly 1–33.

20. Adam (1988), 68, notes that 158,000 out of the total 400,000 population in Cabo Delgado were out of Portuguese control.

21. On Luanda in 1975–76 see Gjerstad (1976).

22. See particularly Egerö (1990), chapter 7.

23. Egerö (1990), 117.

24. See the general discussions in Wolfers and Bergerol (1983), Somerville (1986). On the 1977 *coup* attempt see Birmingham (1978).

25. Somerville (1986), 104.

26. Hodges (1986), 13.

27. On Guinea-Bissau see Galli and Jones (1987), Lopes (1987) and Forrest (1992).

28. See the sources in note 10 above. Even Botswana, however, was characterized by high inequality and *de facto* concentration of power in one ruling party (Parson, 1984).

29. Figures from internal World Bank document.

30. This general idea is laid out clearly by Kenneth Hermele. See, for example, on Mozambique, Chapters 1 and 2 in Brochmann and Ofstad (1990) and, on Angola, Hermele, *Angola* (1988). More detailed references on the economy are found in the next chapter.

31. Geffray (1990); Heimer and da Silva (1988). For a particularly incisive critique of Geffray's view of traditional Mozambican society see O'Laughlin (1992).

32. See, for examples, Heimer and da Silva (1988), Wilson (1992), Maier (1991) as well as numerous shorter newspaper articles.

33. On churches in Angola see particularly Henderson (1992), and Nederlandse Missieraad (1979); on Mozambique see particularly Instituto de Estudios Politicos (1979), Bertulli (1974) and Nederlandse Missieraad (1976).

34. See particularly the critique in Instituto de Estudios Politicos (1979), which features an extended dialogue of Mozambican government officials with Catholic bishops.

The State Under Siege:
Economic Failures
and Social Consequences

A special *Economic Report* of Mozambique's National Planning Commission summed it up in January 1984. After growing a modest 3 per cent a year between 1975 and 1981, the economy had plummeted almost 7 per cent in one year. Losses since 1975 due to natural disaster, increase in world oil prices, and regional conflict added up to US$5.5 billion, more than ten times annual earnings from exports and services.[1] The report, designed for external donors and investors, was the first of many attempts to quantify the economic impact of the regional wars and other external factors on Mozambique and other Frontline States.[2]

In the 1990s the focus shifted to internal policy. Mozambique and Angola prepared reports to show how they were implementing World Bank and IMF structural adjustment programmes. Post-independence economic failures were chalked up to unrealistic state planning and ideological refusal to let the market work. But the stubborn reality was that neither market mechanisms nor state-directed projects could make much headway against the destructive impact of war. Policies – realistic or misguided – had their own independent effect. But for the decade of the 1980s, and extending into the 1990s, the impact of destruction so far outweighed 'normal' economic mechanisms that survival took priority over development of any kind.

Acknowledging the overwhelming effects of war, it is still useful to ask to what extent different economic policies might have lessened support for insurgency or strengthened the state's capacity to resist. In what ways did pre-existing structural constraints and policies actually implemented affect the relative strength of insurgents and the state? Did the imposition of socialized production on the countryside provoke a peasant reaction? Did frustrated private businessmen and commercial farmers join or lead the revolt against the state?

To anticipate, despite significant differences between Angola and Mozambique, the answers were clearly no. Aspiring entrepreneurs were far more threatened by insurgent attacks than by government restrictions. Peasant families in both countries suffered primarily from systematic neglect rather than from imposition of collective agricultural production. That neglect was fostered by failure to replace the exploitative colonial structures of agricultural production with new functioning structures, either state or non-state. Both macroeconomic trends and state revenue depended primarily on oil in Angola and on services and then donor support in Mozambique. The abandonment of socialist ideology in the late 1980s did not change these fundamental realities. During the war, however, Unita and Renamo attacks directly threatened the livelihood and possible capital accumulation of both ordinary peasants and aspiring rural entrepreneurs. Economic failures attributed to the regimes therefore primarily led to disillusionment and disengagement rather than to active support for insurgency.

The economic reform packages of the late 1980s, accepted under war conditions and under the direction of external creditors and donors, had some positive macroeconomic effects. But they had little impact on rural communities isolated by war and previous neglect, and they drastically widened already significant inequalities. The retreat from socialism, since it did not deliver benefits to the majority, added new levels of disenchantment with the incumbent parties. Apart from the negative virtue of not being incumbents, however, not even Unita, much less Renamo or the multiple new parties in both countries, inspired much confidence as future economic managers.

In looking at economic policy in the two countries, one can see the cumulative impact of initial structural problems, compounded by policy failures and by war. Without war, development after independence would have been difficult. Socialist aspirations would probably have given way to structural adjustment programmes in any case. With war, the negative impact of every policy error was multiplied many times over. The rural economy lacked the fundamental prerequisites for progress in any ideological model – security and transport links. Alternate policy decisions or ideological guidelines might have averted some failures. But it is unlikely they could have had decisive effects on the course of the wars.

Angola's enclave economy

In 1973, the last and best year for Angola's colonial economy, oil and coffee contributed 30 per cent and 27 per cent respectively to export earnings.[3] One-third of the coffee production came from African farmers. Maize production was over 700,000 tons, including over 100,000 tons for export. Diamonds and iron ore also provided significant export earnings. But this system, which showed almost 8 per cent growth rates between 1960 and 1974, still depended on administrative force for most agricultural production, and on Portuguese manpower for key economic functions in every sector except oil. Production on Portuguese-run farms provided 86 per cent of agricultural production. Portuguese bush traders provided the commercial link tying peasants to markets. Settlers provided both markets and manpower for a growing industrial sector.

Once this economic structure collapsed, in the wake of the settler exodus and war of 1975–76, it was never restored or replaced on more than a piecemeal basis. Efforts to do so were impeded by the war and by ineffective policies, but also because there was an easily available alternative that was not affected by the settler departure. Oil production, which began in 1968 and grew rapidly, was under the control of large multinational companies – not the Portuguese. Independent Angola worked closely and cooperatively with the global oil industry, and oil revenues provided the essential resources both for defence and for feeding the burgeoning urban population. By the mid-1980s oil consistently provided over 90 per cent of export earnings and over 50 per cent of state revenues. Much of the rest of the economy, with the exception of diamond production, fed indirectly from oil revenues. The countryside sank into neglect.

It is an oft-remarked irony that the economy of an allegedly Marxist state should depend almost entirely on Western big business. And there was nothing uniquely socialist about the national oil company Sonangol, which took charge of the country's oil resources in 1976. The petroleum law of 1978 established joint ventures with private companies and production-sharing agreements by which foreign companies served as contractors to Sonangol. Advised by the US consulting firm Arthur D. Little, Angola's agreements included a 'price cap' which ensured that Sonangol rather than foreign contractors would receive the lion's share of windfall profits from unexpected price increases. Nevertheless, foreign companies found the terms attractive. More than twenty companies, including American, French, Italian, Japanese and Brazilian, were involved by the mid-1980s. The largest was still Cabinda Gulf, which became a subsidiary of Chevron in 1984.

The largest oil fields were off Cabinda, but other sites, mostly offshore, extended south of the Zaire River and down the Angolan coast to the Namibian border. Oil production rose steadily, from under 200,000 barrels a day in 1980 to more than 500,000 barrels a day in the early 1990s. New oil investment averaged over $400 million a year in the 1980s, and even after the return to war in 1992 oil companies were bidding actively for exploration permits. Angola had 'an excellent track record for exploration drilling successes and amicable industry-government relations'.[4]

The easy money from expanding oil production was enough to compensate for falling world oil prices. While oil prices dropped from a high of almost $39 a barrel in January 1981 to $26 a barrel in 1985, Angolan oil revenues still grew from $1.3 billion to $1.9 billion in the same period. Even when prices dropped below $20 a barrel after 1985, revenues continued to climb. But with rising payments due on earlier debt, balance of payments deficits mounted, and available funds for imports dropped drastically. The shock led both to internal plans to move in a free market direction and to accelerated efforts to reach agreement on membership in the World Bank and IMF.

The pattern, however, had been set. Under ideal conditions, perhaps, much of the oil revenue would have been invested in rehabilitating the shattered transport infrastructure, and in providing tools and consumer goods for sale to peasant farmers in exchange for food supplies for the cities. Instead, revenues were used overwhelmingly for defence and to import food and other consumer goods for the urban population. Despite high defence expenditures, secure land transport to rural areas became ever more elusive as conflict mounted in the 1980s. The most productive areas for grain were in the central plateau and further south in Huíla. But urban population was concentrated in Luanda, linked to provincial capitals mainly by expensive air transport.

The difficulties were real: war damage (both initial and recurrent), the lack of commercial networks, the inefficiency of state structures set up to fill the gap. But the failure was compounded by the fact that money for imports was available. Feeding the cities with imports, arguably a necessary short-term expedient, became a structural feature of the economy. The countryside became no more than an afterthought. The enclave effect of the oil sector, in some measure common to any less developed oil-producing country, was multiplied both by the disappearance of the colonial trading networks and by insurgent attacks aimed precisely at breaking the remaining links between city and countryside. Nor was there any strong countervailing force within the government to campaign against the path of least resistance: imports paid for with oil money. Little was left over for productive investment in development of any kind.

As a result, the vast majority of rural dwellers reverted to subsistence production. State farms, along with a handful of private commercial farms, continued to produce export crops but at drastically lower production levels. Abandoned Portuguese farms fell to state control, but in practice much of their land was appropriated by individual peasant families. Commercialized production of domestic staples stagnated at less than 10 per cent of pre-independence levels. For most peasants, there was no opportunity to sell a surplus, and few goods to buy if they did sell. The state had only a fraction of the capacity needed to administer the enterprises, and only about 3 per cent of the government budget was allocated to agriculture.

As long as they were not directly touched by war, peasant families were largely left to their own devices. But they had little access to outside goods, hampering even subsistence production. In the mid-1980s maize seed inputs were less than 10 per cent of the quantity required. The supply of hoes also consistently fell short. Families increasingly turned to more resilient crops such as cassava, millet and sorghum. Tens of thousands fled war and sought opportunities for survival in the cities. The urban population grew from 18 per cent of the total in 1975 to 31 per cent in 1986. By 1990 over half Angola's population was estimated to be living in urban areas.

Although only about half of industrial enterprises came under state control, leaving a substantial private sector, industrial production also plummeted at independence. Output in 1977 was only 18 per cent of that in 1973. By 1985 output had recovered, but only to 54 per cent of the 1973 total, constrained by lack of management and shortage of raw materials. Urban consumers therefore not only lacked domestic agricultural supplies, but faced shortages of manufactured goods. Even light industries such as textiles and shoes fell significantly short of recovering 1973 production levels.

Oil monies were sufficient to maintain a minimum level of imports for towns, but little more. Urban consumer demand was not satisfied, there was only a trickle left over for rural areas, and essential inputs for both agriculture and industry were in short supply. There was no hope of addressing the fundamental issues unless the link between city and countryside was restored, so that the food deficit would be met by domestic production and peasants would have income and goods to purchase from the market. State policies did not cut the link initially – that was the result of the first stage of war in 1975–76 and the Portuguese exodus. Nor is it clear that alternate free-market policies could have restored the links under war conditions. But there is no doubt that state policies failed to address the crisis. The survival mode of dependence on oil-bought imports, allocated by an inefficient bureaucracy, was one with no ready exit.

Price-controlled goods sold in state shops provided only minimal supplies to the urban population, with access pegged to employment. Salaried employees (*responsáveis*) had access to somewhat better supplies, and a small number of top officials enjoyed comfortable living standards and official rations. But, in the words of the Economist Intelligence Unit, the price control system was 'so extensive and rigid, yet also so disorganized and incoherent, that it produced extreme distortions of relative values'.[5] The result was a burgeoning parallel economy, illegal and unregulated but tolerated by the state, where free enterprise and corruption ran rampant. Average citizens had to resort to the parallel economy for survival, and entrepreneurs in and out of state employment found opportunities for large profits. The goods came from resale at higher prices of purchases from state shops, from products allocated to workers at their place of work and, increasingly, from theft and fraud. Everyone had to have an *esquema* (scheme) for combining complex barter of goods and favours with transactions in Angolan kwanzas and hard currency.

Behind the facade of a state-run economy, therefore, existed another economy highly responsive to market forces. But it was only partially related to production, as peasants and rural traders found transport possible and urban vendors hawked small-scale crafts. Intead it consisted for the most part of recirculating imported goods, while draining off the energies of the workforce from their formal employment. Those who made money in this free-wheeling environment included not only those with political clout but also significant numbers of Kikongo-speaking entrepreneurs returned from Zaire and Umbundu-speaking merchants from the central plateau.[6]

The social order that resulted was one that generated significant disillusionment. As the incumbent, the government took the blame for economic failure and social deficiencies; harsh criticism was widespread even among loyalists who never considered abandoning the MPLA. But only a small minority among aspiring entrepreneurs were attracted to Unita's war in the bush or the Cold War slogans of Unita's sponsors; most simply sought what opportunities they could in the economy spun off from oil revenues. In both urban and rural contexts, the preferred alternatives were individual survival strategies rather than active support for insurgency – with the significant exception of those already inclined on grounds of ethno-regional loyalties to support Unita. The peasantry were never given much incentive to support the government. But Unita also offered few benefits, even for its regional constituency. The decision to seek a precarious survival in the war-ravaged countryside or to pursue uncertain prospects in the urban shanty-towns was thus driven by practical concerns and only rarely accompanied by political motives.

Oil both saved the economy from total collapse and postponed the search for other solutions. But even when lower oil prices and rising costs forced a turn to new policies, structural adjustments would not address the unresolved issue of the relationship between city and countryside. The social consequences of an enclave economy paralleled those of other countries dependent on oil or minerals. Without war, Angola's economic and social problems would probably have had many points of comparison with Nigeria's. With war, the danger was that the social order would instead move in the direction of Zaire's extreme kleptocracy.

Mozambique's service economy

Like Angola's, Mozambique's colonial economy depended on forced agricultural labour and on Portuguese domination of both skilled employment and internal commerce. Industrial production, boosted by the increase in settler population and by openness to South African as well as other foreign investment, grew almost 7 per cent a year between 1957 and 1970. Mozambique's crops, produced both on plantations and by peasants, provided the bulk of exports. While grain production did not create an export surplus, the urban market was primarily supplied by rice and maize produced inside the country.

Declines in all sectors marked the transition to independence, a result above all of the settler exodus. In the period 1973–75 agricultural production dropped 11 per cent, industrial output 38 per cent and services 28 per cent; the overall decline was 21 per cent. Mozambique differed in several important respects from Angola, however. Mozambique did not suffer the initial war which hastened the schism between city and countryside in Angola. And the sector on which it was structurally dependent was totally different from Angola's oil enclave. Mozambique's foreign exchange earnings in 1973 were roughly equally balanced between exports, primarily agricultural goods, and services. Transport and migrant labour services were tied not to a world commodity market, but to neighbouring countries. Their economic prospects depended on regional conflict as well as economic factors.[7]

The Mozambican service sector – including rail and port services for all the interior countries as well as migrant labour to South Africa and Rhodesia – was highly vulnerable to bilateral political tensions and to loss of business confidence among exporters, importers and employers. Unlike offshore or coastal oil sites, the sector was at the mercy of sabotage attacks. It had direct impact on the agricultural economy since, unlike oil, it provided significant employment which under normal conditions provided families with income to invest in agriculture. Cuts to the service economy had distinct social consequences in different parts of the country. Drastic reductions in these sources of income in the late 1970s and early 1980s, on top of cuts in agricultural production, left the country with no major source of foreign exchange save the goodwill of international donors.

There is no doubt that cuts in service income were primarily a result of external factors, and that political decisions by the South African state played the major role. But it is over-simple to see them as an orchestrated application of economic pressures by Pretoria. Initial cuts in income resulted from applying UN sanctions against Rhodesia. Other reductions resulted from commercial decisions by businessmen as well as from South African state policies. Labour flows and trade levels depended on negotiation and administration of agreements which suffered from lack of management capacity in Mozambique as well as from South African hostility. Sabotage of transport facilities, in addition to the direct destruction, had spin-off effects in overloading management capacity and in reducing confidence of potential customers.

Mozambique decided to comply with UN sanctions against Rhodesia and to renew active support for guerrilla war there after the failure of talks in 1975–76. Between March 1976, when the border was closed, and the Lancaster House agreement at the end of 1979, damage to the Mozambican economy was estimated at $556 million, equal to more than two years of export earnings.[8] The policy made a critical contribution to Zimbabwean independence. As a result, Mozambique had an ally rather than an enemy on a 1,200 km. border, and Zimbabwean–Mozambican economic cooperation was the backbone of SADCC plans to restore the regional transport grid.

But the initial impact was a tremendous burden. It hit particularly the central provinces, cutting off migrant labour to Rhodesia and curtailing Beira's transport-dependent economy. Regional suspicions of the south were reinforced. With Rhodesian intelligence networks in place from the colonial period, it was a conducive environment for Renamo.

South African cutbacks in migrant labour also began in 1976 and the number of Mozambican miners dropped from 118,000 in 1975 to 41,000 in 1977. The reduction was primarily the result of a mining industry decision to decrease dependence on foreign labour in order to reduce vulnerability to political change.[9] With the rise in the gold price in the 1970s, the mines could afford to raise wages and recruit more labour from South Africa's rural areas; the proportion of South African miners rose from lows of 25 per cent in the early 1970s to around 60 per cent in the 1980s, with most of the remaining foreign workers coming from Lesotho. The sharp drop in Mozambican recruitment in 1976 was also facilitated, inadvertently, by Mozambican administrative decisions requiring the South African recruiters to close down seventeen of their twenty-one offices in Mozambique.[10]

The cutbacks severely restricted opportunities for wage employment in rural southern Mozambique, long dependent on migration to the mines. But the Ndau-speaking area of southern Manica and Sofala provinces was also hard hit. Recruitment from the south was reduced but the flow from central Mozambique, on the edge of the recruitment zone, practically disappeared.[11] In subsequent negotiations with the Chamber of Mines, Mozambique gained slight increases in recruitment.[12] But in 1986, coinciding with Renamo's invasion of central Mozambique and the death of President Machel, the South African government announced expulsion of all remaining mineworkers at the end of their contracts. The mining industry, which needed the experienced Mozambican workers, succesfully lobbied to retain some 40,000 in upper skill levels.

Mozambique's international transport services, which accounted for most surplus foreign exchange before independence, were vulnerable to external forces and easily sabotaged. South African exports through Maputo dropped by 20 per cent between 1973 and 1975, and continued a gradual decline until 1980. Sharp drops then took the volume down to only 7 per cent of the 1973 total in 1988. Some of the drop was due to commercial decisions, as customers opted for more secure or better-managed ports in South Africa. But there were also political pressures to redirect trade. Sabotage played a major role, reducing capacity by over 60 per cent on Maputo's rail connections to South Africa and Swaziland by 1987, and shutting down the Limpopo line from Maputo to Zimbabwe from 1984. Zimbabwe's trade through Maputo harbour was forced to transit South Africa, producing income for South Africa's state-owned railways.

Direct traffic through Beira from Zimbabwe recovered significantly after Zimbabwe's independence, despite the war. Zimbabwean troops and international investment in port and rail rehabilitation through SADCC's transport sector made it possible to transport more than a million tons a year by 1987. But sabotage sharply cut traffic on the line north from Beira to the coal-mines of Tete province and to Malawi. By 1986 that line was totally out of commission after sabotage of a rail bridge over the Zambezi River. In the late 1980s total freight traffic via Beira was still no more than 10 per cent of pre-independence levels. The northern railway link from the port of Nacala to Malawi declined only gradually until 1983, but afterwards international traffic was totally cut, and domestic traffic as far as Nampula slowed to a trickle.

Thus transport, which provided over $100 million in foreign exchange surplus before independence, balancing the trade deficit, produced only a $67 million surplus in 1980. The surplus dropped to less than $1 million in 1985 and had only recovered to $36 million by 1990. Like Angola's oil industry, Mozambique's international transport sector depended both on state management and on cooperation with foreign business. But many of the foreign interests had economic and political reasons to hinder rather than foster Mozambique's recovery efforts. To cite only one example, 75 per cent of freight handling through Mozambican ports was controlled by South African-owned Manica Freight Services. In 1983 Dion Hamilton, director of Manica's Beira office, was exposed as the chief of a network supplying arms and information to Renamo.[13]

A similar contradiction was visible in the fate of the giant Cabora Bassa hydroelectric scheme, constructed under the Portuguese to supply power to South Africa over a powerline stretching 890 km. inside

Mozambique.[14] It was a potentially significant earner of foreign exchange. The line was first sabotaged on South African orders in 1982. In 1984 and 1988, each time following new meetings among Portuguese, South African and Mozambican partners on resuming operation, hundreds of additional pylons were blown up. The apparent damage to South African interests was deceptive, since at the time South Africa's electricity grid had surplus capacity. Instead of selling Cabora Bassa power to South Africa, Mozambique was forced to spend almost $500 million for electricity from South Africa for southern Mozambique.

Failure to restore service revenues and decline in agricultural exports was reflected in the escalating balance of payments crisis. In 1975 service income still made up for the trade deficit, leaving a $37 million surplus. But the deficit on current account rose to $235 million by 1977; by 1980 it was $561 million, and by the late 1980s it was consistently running over $1 billion a year. This desperate financial situation set the context for all government policies. In contrast with Angola, there was little available either for defence or for importing food. Mozambique thus avoided the trap of neglecting the task of rural development. But its resources as well as its policies fell short, and soon it had to turn to external donors to supply both.

Neither Mozambique's problems nor its policies in the service sector were particularly linked to its choice of socialist ideology. Instead they derived primarily from the context of regional conflict and secondarily from lack of management capability. They affected the war fundamentally by the resources that were unavailable rather than by specific initiatives that went awry. The failure on the agrarian front was much more complicated.

Mozambique's agrarian economy

As in Angola, Mozambique's agrarian economy was devastated by the settler exodus. Unlike Angola, however, destruction of infrastructure by war only came later, and until 1980 was largely confined to areas bordering Rhodesia. There was no easy foreign exchange to import food. And Frelimo's history gave it a strong ideological emphasis on serving rural interests. In the first eight years of independence, then, rural development ranked high on the agenda. Investment in agriculture did well in government budget plans, rising as high as 34 per cent, ranking first or second to construction and water, which also had a substantial rural component. The party congress of 1977, which declared Frelimo a Marxist-Leninist party, highlighted agriculture as 'the principal source of accumulation' for the country's first phase of development.[15]

Before the turn towards market-oriented development which began in 1983, agricultural policy was seen as promoting both the socialization and the modernization of the countryside. It was expected that state farms and cooperative peasant production would eventually outweigh private commercial farms and peasant family production. There was vigorous debate between advocates of state farms and those favouring peasant-based approaches. But only the state-farm approach was seriously implemented, and it proved a fairly consistent economic failure. The rural development budget had little left over, either to promote cooperative peasant production or to support the vast majority of peasants who continued individual family production. There were villages with cooperatives which tried to improve peasants' lives by increasing collective agricultural production. But they were a minority in comparison to others created for military or administrative purposes; an even smaller group, favoured by good leadership or access to outside funding, gained significant support from the state.[16]

In the colonial system marketed agricultural production was divided almost evenly between peasant production, settler farms, and plantations owned primarily by non-Portuguese foreign companies. But the division differed significantly by region and by crop.[17] In the south settler farms accounted for 76 per cent of marketed production, peasants for 20 per cent and plantations for 4 per cent. The south, moreover, produced most of the food crops – maize, rice and vegetables – to serve the major urban market Maputo. In the central provinces, including Zambézia as well as Tete, Manica and Sofala, plantations dominated with 57 per cent of marketed output, while settler farms had 24 per cent and peasants 19 per cent. These plantations produced the largest portion of export crops such as copra, sisal, tea and sugar. Only in the far north (Nampula, Niassa and Cabo Delgado) did peasant cash crop production predominate, with 65 per cent of the market compared with 30 per cent from settler farms and 5 per cent from plantations. The major cash crops in the north were cotton and cashew. In all areas most peasant agriculture took the form of subsistence production, concentrating on maize, sorghum and cassava.

The 1977 party congress mandated the organization of peasants into 'communal villages' and called for priority attention to both cooperatives and state farms.[18] But the *de facto* policy of agricultural development included only the state-farm component. As the 1983 party congress complained, only 2 per cent of investments in agriculture between 1977 and 1981 went to cooperatives. Support for the family sector (small peasants) 'was virtually non-existent'.[19] Yet state farms failed to produce as hoped, afflicted with lack of management skills, inappropriate technological imports and problems in directing a work force that had previously been controlled by coercion.

The reasons for this bias, seen by critics of both left and right as a strategic error, were multiple. It was the settler farms of the south, abandoned by the settlers, which had provided the essential foodstuffs for the capital city. The decision to continue to rely on these same farms implied investments in keeping them running. Naïve faith of much of the leadership in technology and economies of scale promoted the generalization and expansion of this policy. Foreign advisers, both Eastern European and others, reinforced the bias. But its persistence, in the face of internal party criticism, was also a result of bureaucratic inertia and patterns of access derived from the colonial period. Settler farms and plantations had privileged access to the state under the colonial system; those same enterprises, under state management, could lobby the bureaucracy for the inputs they needed. To provide services to cooperatives or peasant families required creating entirely new structures. It should be no surprise that the bureaucracy resisted.[20]

The programme of 'socialization of the countryside' never happened. Individual families maintained over 90 per cent of the cultivated area, and provided the livelihood of more than 80 per cent of the population. Cooperative and collective production in communal villages accounted for only a minute fraction of agricultural production. The mass villagization in the 1980s was primarily war-related resettlement (both voluntary and involuntary), secondarily an administrative action by officials seeking to meet quotas, and least of all a rural development strategy.

The colonial state had not only served the settler farms and plantations by compelling peasants to work. It had also supported the settler rural trading network and imposed fixed low prices on the peasants. The post-colonial state had serious management problems in dealing with the farms that came under its control. But it had even less capacity to create new institutions for maintaining the peasants' link to the market.

Initial efforts to replace the rural Portuguese traders with *lojas do povo* (people's shops) were quickly abandoned in favour of encouraging private traders and consumer cooperatives, supplemented by state purchases of crops as buyer of last resort. A 1979 law formalized the legitimate status of private traders. By 1981 the agricultural marketing network numbered 3,600 private traders and 740 consumer coops, as compared with about 240 state purchasing posts and mobile brigades. The state continued to control prices, a colonial practice rather than an innovation.

The entire structure was hampered by the lack of commercial skills on the part of the state and many of the private traders, by severe shortages of transport and storage facilities, by a cumbersome system of price setting, and, above all, by the lack of consumer goods for peasants to buy. The shortage of goods, in turn, resulted both from lack of foreign exchange and from the decline in domestic industrial production.

Investment in large projects took first call on the scarce foreign exchange resources that were available. Adding the lack of significant state investment in extension or inputs for peasant agriculture (seeds, hoes, machetes), the overall picture was one of neglect. For many officials, this was rationalized by the assumption that peasant agriculture, requiring no advanced technology, could simply take care of itself until the state farms developed sufficiently to serve as poles of attraction and technical support for the rest of the rural population.

This fundamental reality was common to all of rural Mozambique. By the 1983 party congress, which mandated a shift towards greater support of peasants, war had already taken over from policy decisions as the primary determinant of agricultural results in most of the country. But there was also substantial regional variation based on previous agricultural patterns, on natural disaster and on the spread of war.

Priority investment in state farms was concentrated in the fertile Limpopo valley of Gaza province, where irrigated land had been occupied by Portuguese farms which supplied the essential foodstuffs for Maputo. Income from migrant labour to South Africa was a fundamental component of peasant income in this area, supplemented both by family plots and by wage labour on farms. At independence many peasants hoped to occupy the irrigated lands occupied by settler farms. Instead, the state retained control, and took the opportunity of floods in 1977 to resettle peasant families in communal villages away from the river, suitable for rain-fed agriculture. In theory, the state farms were intended to absorb surplus labour and serve as nuclei of development.

The peasants went along, if often reluctantly. Many decided to take advantage of the opportunities offered by the villages, actively participating in the *grupos dinamizadores* and cooperatives. But as in the colonial period, the irrigated farms (now state-run) and peasant production were in direct competition. The farms needed labour, especially seasonal labour for the rice harvest. Seasonal labour did not provide enough income to live on throughout the year, and it interfered with household production. The colonial state had forced peasants to work on farms; the post-colonial state exhorted them to do so, occasionally using coercion, and consistently experienced labour shortages during peak periods of the agricultural year.

State farm investments in capital-intensive technology, moreover, used up foreign exchange without providing much more permanent employment. The communal villages, without significant new investment from the state or adequate marketing networks, could not absorb the surplus labour. The drift to Maputo, as well as illegal migration to South Africa, accelerated. In the Gaza countryside settlement in communal villages grew rapidly, from 20 per cent of the provincial population in 1978 to over 60 per cent in 1982.[21] Movement into these villages came partly from administrative pressures and even coercion, but many entered in hopes that this was indeed, as Frelimo promised, the way to a more prosperous future.

Although those hopes were disappointed, Gaza, as noted earlier, proved resistant to Renamo penetration. The war spread significantly in Gaza only in late 1983. That was after the government had ceased actively promoting villagization and allowed people to return to their previous homes. Subsequent movement into villages consisted largely of refugees fleeing Renamo attacks.[22]

Ironically, nowhere else in the country was the conflict between state farms and peasant livelihood so direct as in Gaza, where both wanted access to valuable and scarce irrigated lands. Villagization was earlier and more extensive than in any area except Cabo Delgado, where it preceded independence. Yet evidence of resentment of villagization serving as an entrée for Renamo comes primarily from central Mozambique and from Nampula.[23] The province with least villagization as of 1982, with only 2 per cent in communal villages, was Zambézia. Yet in the mid-1980s Zambézia saw perhaps the most significant Renamo military gains. There was clearly no simple link between villagization and support for Renamo.

Teasing out more complex relationships would require comprehensive studies of the timing and character of villagization, in relation to the war, in different provinces. On the basis of data available now, however, it seems plausible that the differences may be related not only to ethnic differences or to the different economic base of the peasantry in different areas, but also to the timing and motivation for resettlement. Before 1978, and even as late as 1980, new communal villages established outside the south were few in number and largely resulted from voluntary mobilization.[24] The impulse towards greater compulsion in resettlement came largely as the war accelerated, most intensively and earliest in central Mozambique, subsequently in Nampula. Both in Manica and in Nampula, reports indicate that administrators blindly following guidelines to promote communal villages also played a significant role.[25] But even there, the rush to villagize – and the use of force – was primarily a military response to the guerrilla threat. In any case, by late 1982 national policy was changing.

The National Commission for Communal Villages was closed down in 1983, a sign that subsequent population flows into villages – more massive in numbers – were reactive rather than part of development efforts. By then, the crisis in foreign exchange had imposed even tighter restraints on new policy efforts to support peasant agriculture. Simultaneously came escalation of the war and the worst drought in living memory, particularly affecting south and central areas.

The drought began in late 1981 and grew steadily worse.[26] Government relief efforts, which had coped with an earlier drought in 1979, were targeted for attack by Renamo. Meanwhile export earnings dropped from $281 million in 1981 to $96 million in 1984. In 1983 debt service of $384 million outpaced new loans of $339 million. Mozambique appealed for an increase in international food aid, but significant response was delayed until the next year, after Mozambique had convinced the US that its foreign policy shift to the West was genuine. By then the drought was ebbing, but an estimated 100,000 people had died.

Frelimo's fourth party congress in April 1983 saw vigorous internal debate, acknowledgement of the errors made in neglecting the peasants, and resolution to seek a new course. That new course would be shaped, however, less by Mozambican initiatives than by overwhelming dependence on foreign donors.

Structural adjustments and aid dependence

By the early 1980s, even before formal structural adjustment programmes, top leaders in Angola and Mozambique were aware of multiple weaknesses of the state-directed economies. They called for greater openness to private traders, greater attention to peasants' needs, and more efficient use of market mechanisms. There was concern that the state retain overall control, and the free-market boosterism that marked the end of the decade was not yet evident. But the failure of the state to restore the economy to pre-independence levels was obvious. State enterprises that were not losing money were exceptional. Official exchange rates were so far out of line with the black market that it was impossible to ignore. Shortages of commodities produced empty shelves in the shops, while parallel unregulated markets burgeoned, with sky-high prices. The goods shortage further reduced peasant incentives to produce food or export crops.

It was foreign exchange that seemed decisive in determining significantly different responses in the two countries. With falling world oil prices, Angola introduced a series of economic adjustment plans between 1983 and 1990. The plans envisaged adjustments in exchange rates and prices, curbs on imports, encouragement for rural producers, scaled-back government payrolls and a reduced role for state planning. But only the 1990 programme, a year after Angola joined the World Bank, was implemented in more than a fragmentary way. Angola's balance of payments turned consistently negative beginning in 1986, with a $300 million deficit, and was running an annual deficit of over $900 million by 1989.[27]

Resistance to implementation of the adjustment plans came from bureaucrats and from the large vested interests that had built up in operation of parallel markets. The fixed exchange rates, for example, meant that air tickets for overseas travel could be purchased in local currency for little more than the price of a few cases of beer. Market traders flew regularly to Portugal and to Brazil to stock up on consumer goods, which were taken back as excess luggage and then sold on the parallel market. Other less visible deals made even larger profits.[28]

The bottom line was that adjustment in economic policies in Angola – with devaluations, decontrol of prices, and lay-offs of government workers – got under way only in the last year before the May 1991 peace accord. The negative effects came in time to erode government credibility further before the 1992 elections, but the positive effects in increased production were only beginning to be felt when war began again.

Mozambique was a different story. There the shift in policies in 1983 resulted both from recognition of internal failures and from the rising war burden. The foreign exchange crisis came abruptly and earlier; policies in the aftermath were largely determined by the donors whose grants and loans filled the gap.

There has been extensive research on the structural adjustment programmes in Mozambique, leading to consensus on several points despite significant differences between advocates and opponents of the standard World Bank package.[29] Liberalization of prices, successive devaluations and significant input of new grants and concessionary loans checked the precipitous macroeconomic decline. The growth rate in GDP turned positive at 1 per cent in 1986, and averaged over 4.5 per cent for the next three years. But growth declined again in 1990, and turned negative in 1992 as a result of renewed drought. Although part of the new aid was in grants, the debt burden continued to rise uncontrollably, from $2.7 billion in 1985 to $4.7 billion in 1991. The deficit on trade and services ran over $500 million a year. Even in macroeconomic terms, sustaining the growth rate depended on ending the war and continued international aid, as well as getting the prices right.

In the meantime, cutbacks in government budgets for health and education, removal of price controls on basic consumer goods, and other similar measures had the predicted effect of squeezing the urban poor. According to a UNICEF report in 1989, more than a quarter of urban residents and one-half of peri-urban dwellers were living in absolute poverty.[30] Urban real wages declined significantly with inflation, particularly after subsidized urban food rations were phased out. Steep cuts in health and education budgets further crippled services in rural areas as well. Education and health, at 17 per cent and 7 per cent of the budget respectively in 1986, dropped to only 3.2 per cent combined in 1991.[31]

In theory, such difficulties would be temporary, and compensated for by improved rural production in response to higher prices. This would eventually produce both more food for the cities and export earnings to finance further growth, the argument went. In practice, such positive results are debatable even for African countries in more favourable circumstances. In Mozambique at war, still burdened with the post-colonial skills deficit, the result was increased hardship without significant recovery. World Bank reports soon echoed the government's concern that cuts in social services and state capacity could push the economy below the minimum levels needed for recovery.

Large inflows of foreign aid, accompanied by expensive foreign personnel, staved off total collapse but rarely operated to build Mozambican capacity. The life-support package even eroded Mozambique's capacity to chart an effective development policy. Especially in rural areas, improvements in income were largely limited to a small minority with access to markets and agricultural inputs. The government, in response to previous failures, laid a strong emphasis on providing support for peasant farmers through restoring the rural trading networks. But these programmes gained little funding from donors, who were preoccupied either with supporting commercial farms or with their own individual programmes of emergency relief.

Lessening of the state's role was in part the explicit objective of ideologically driven assistance programmes, particularly USAID's.[32] But the standard adjustment package and massive aid presence also had indirect outcomes that alarmed many donors.[33] Particularly damaging was the effect of growing corruption and competition for scarce skilled Mozambican personnel.

Until the mid-1980s, Mozambique's leadership and state administration - whatever their faults - had a well-deserved reputation for honesty and hard work. After structural adjustment, Mozambicans at all levels found it practically impossible to make ends meet on official wages. Meanwhile, even a driver working for an international organization in Maputo earned more in dollar terms than a senior administrative civil servant. The wage bill for some 3,000 foreign personnel added up to about $180 million, three times the total wages for the 100,000 Mozambicans in the civil service (including education and health personnel).[34] Even the most honest state workers found it necessary to cut corners; a significant number, entering enthusiastically into the spirit of the free market, engaged in large-scale corruption. More and more, including many of the most competent, decided to take attractive offers to work for international aid agencies or the private sector.

Another indirect consequence was the shift in policy-making influence to external donors. This was no doubt inevitable, given that external assistance was by far the largest component of foreign exchange, virtually the only source of government capital investment and even a substantial portion of recurrent expenditure in many ministries. But the consequences were enormous.[35] In 1990 there were no less than thirty-two multilateral agencies, forty-four bilateral donors from thirty-five countries and 143 external non-governmental organizations from twenty-three countries working in Mozambique.[36] A high proportion of their personnel served on short-term contracts, and had little knowledge of local conditions. Parallel reporting structures, contradictory external advice, organizational rivalries, and the frequent necessity for Mozambican staff to train their foreign counterparts further stretched Mozambique's limited management capacity.

The net result was policies which, instead of alleviating the neglect of the peasantry, provided market opportunities only for a small minority while leaving the majority untouched or dependent on food aid. Without ending the war, of course, no conceivable economic policies could be more than partially effective. But many promising directions suggested by Mozambican policy-makers were hardly explored because they did not coincide with donors' priorities. Most fundamental of all, few donors were willing to help with the basic need for security. Britain provided training for Mozambican troops, but most others refused even to provide non-lethal military aid, such as armoured vehicles for relief convoys, communications equipment for the army, or uniforms for soldiers. Private businesses deciding to invest in Mozambique built the cost of protection into their estimates, but few donors responded to repeated pleas to provide security support to accompany development projects or even relief efforts.

The Mozambican government consistently urged that relief efforts be linked to rehabilitation and development, by providing hand tools and seeds, restoring social services, ensuring consumer goods to encourage new production of food for the market, and similar measures.[37] Yet the politics of aid meant that imported food aid was the easiest item on the list to cover; other elements of the appeals consistently fell far short. Mozambican arguments in favour of local procurement of supplies when possible fell foul of tied aid requirements to rely on imported products. Funds for development of the internal transport network were in short supply, even when the government sought support for private haulers and traders. Within agricultural programmes as such, resources were most easily available for commercial farmers rather than for peasants; USAID, for example, specifically limited its support to commercial farmers.

The optimum mix of policies was by no means obvious, to either Mozambicans or foreign advisers. Implementation would have been a problem whatever the policies adopted. But the structural adjustment package, of questionable effectiveness in peacetime, left little promise for a country at war other than continued aid dependence. The institutional base for an independent economy remained to be built. Neither Mozambique's initial efforts after independence nor subsequent donor-driven policies of the 1980s established a viable economic framework to replace the coercion-based colonial system. The margin for success was limited both by the colonial legacy and by war. But to the extent that errors of policy and implementation were responsible, donors as well as Mozambicans should take the blame.

Social disintegration and the struggle for survival

How then can one sum up the interaction between post-colonial economic policies and the wars? To what extent might alternative policies have made a difference? Most obviously, every economic failure deprived the state of resources with which to fight the war, and of public support that would have come from providing prosperity. Yet even the most enlightened policies would hardly have created sufficient resources for comprehensive defence. Nor could they have established a new productive framework linking city and countryside when those links were the most vulnerable targets in a war aimed precisely at crippling the civilian infrastructure. As development agencies rapidly learned, a new project providing resources to a local community could easily become a magnet for insurgent attacks.

If the major negative impact of economic policies on the war came from 'socialist' policies offending constituencies such as peasants or aspiring entrepreneurs, then it could have been corrected simply by stopping those policies and letting the market function in the private sector. But such cases were the exception rather than the rule. Neither Angola nor Mozambique remotely resembled the image of a Stalinist-type state extracting surplus from the peasantry and aggressively repressing private enterprise. The fundamental issue was rather the failure to create national institutional structures capable of supporting either public or private economic initiatives. That task, difficult under the best of circumstances, was rendered practically impossible by war. Relatively successful sectors – Mozambique's early social programmes, Angola's oil industry – fell far short of compensating for the vicious circle of war and policy failures.

The result for both society and state was to accelerate social disintegration and reliance on immediate survival strategies. The state lost capacity and legitimacy, but without any proportionate transfer of allegiance to the insurgents. The predominant response from almost all sectors of society was to seek physical and economic security wherever it could be found.

In the countryside the vast population movement in search of survival far exceeded the numbers moved in government resettlement campaigns or taken forcibly by insurgents. By the early 1990s, up to 1.9 million Mozambicans – more than 10 per cent of the population – were refugees in neighbouring countries. Some 4 million more, almost 25 per cent of the population, were displaced within the country.[38] Some 425,000 Angolan refugees lived in Zaire or Zambia; an estimated 800,000 rural people were displaced at the time of the 1991 ceasefire, in a total population of almost 11 million.[39]

The pattern of movement was complex, but the general directions were clear: out of war zones to areas that were safer and offered some chance of securing a livelihood. Food aid was an incentive, but wherever possible refugees and displaced people sought the opportunity to begin farming again or find employment. Many sought ways to stay on their own land, finding hiding places from insurgent attack and government sweeps or making accommodations with whatever army was most visible. Hundreds of thousands walked long distances to their fields during the day, returning to garrison towns or hiding places in the bush at night. The decision to stay or flee was influenced not only by 'traditional' attachments to particular places and by war, but by practical economic reasons such as the extent of investment in fruit trees and knowledge of local agricultural conditions. Even when peasants were largely reduced to subsistence production, finding some market access for supplies such as hoes and cloth was a high priority. And that was available, if at all, in government-controlled rather than insurgent zones.

Fleeing to the cities, before structural adjustment, might mean the opportunity to get on the rolls for subsidized rations, or to find a relative who was. But with urban economic activity still far below pre-independence levels, the opportunity for viable formal-sector employment for newcomers was very small. The result was a burgeoning informal economy shading over into criminal activity. Officially repressed black-market transactions soon were outweighed by generally tolerated parallel market trade. Both were free-for-all competitive environments in which success depended on wits, entrepreneurial talent and lack of scruple as well as the complicity or tolerance of key officials. In Angola, fed by oil wealth and the more profound break between city and countryside, this sector grew earlier and larger. But it was present in both countries.

Inequality within the urban environment was partly a result of the formal state economy. A relatively small number of officials had access to additional goods, special shops or foreign exchange as a result of their position. These relative privileges, however, provided only modest levels of consumption. Even in Angola, a well-informed observer in the early 1980s noted that top officials 'live comfortably, with access to modest consumer durables that one would find in any middle-class home in the west'.[40] In Mozambique, in the early years of independence,

Frelimo officials enjoyed a reputation for relatively modest life-styles. Even as hardships increased, there was still a popular sense that the leaders too were making sacrifices.

The informal economy that operated in the shadows of the state-controlled system, however, as well as the free-market environment that followed structural adjustment, operated on different principles. Especially in rich Angola, gaps grew between those in both the private sector and the state who knew how to work the system for personal benefit and those who, lacking opportunity and skills or having more scruples, failed to do so. There was a fine line between adjustments necessary for survival and explicit corruption based on greed – but there was no doubt that the number crossing that line continued to grow.

Access to profits in the informal economy was clearly facilitated by kinship, personal and ethnic ties to party and state officials. But it was also open to energetic opportunists of any background. No group could credibly claim to be excluded or to be left with no outlet for ambition other than joining the insurgency. With the shift to market economies, both legitimate and illegitimate business opportunities opened to private entrepreneurs of diverse backgrounds. Those opportunities varied with access to the state, as well as with the racial and regional disparities inherited from colonialism. State inefficiency hampered the prospects for private entrepreneurs of all groups, but outside the major cities insurgent attacks posed a more substantial obstacle to trade.

Despite ostensible commitments to free enterprise and peasant welfare, the insurgents failed to offer attractive alternative models or practical options for either rural or urban dwellers. The logic of their war strategy instead dictated destruction of both state property and private enterprise in government-controlled zones. And their own economic efforts focused on sustaining their military machines. The peasants were taxed for produce and labour. What profits ensued from insurgent trade in ivory or diamonds went to the organization and its leaders or to middlemen in neighbouring countries, with only minimal benefits for civilians except, perhaps, in the Jamba area.

Thus defections of government supporters to join the insurgents in the bush or to offer clandestine support were extraordinarily few, and in no way proportional to the governments' loss of support due to economic failures. As incumbents, Frelimo and the MPLA inevitably took most of the blame for economic disaster. But ordinary Angolans and Mozambicans well knew that the primary threat to their livelihood was the war. For that the blame was allocated primarily to the insurgents or, increasingly, to both sides.

By the time of the peace accords of 1991–92, it was difficult for either potential voters or outside observers to find plausible policy or ideological differences between incumbents and challengers. At the grass-roots level, an overwhelming desire for peace and the chance to get on with life was accompanied by generalized scepticism about political leaders. Effective economic solutions, it was generally agreed, depended on a stable peace. But the threat to peace was not the social and economic demands of constituencies voting for the insurgents from ethnic loyalty or anti-incumbent sentiment, or resistance by incumbents to reforms proposed by challengers. Peace was instead hostage to the ambitions of insurgent leaders with no more lofty platform than substituting themselves for the residents in the halls of power.

Notes

1. People's Republic of Mozambique (1984), 41–2.

2. See sources cited in Introduction, note 6.

3. Major general sources consulted on the Angolan economy include Hodges (1987, 1993), World Bank, *Angola* (1991), Hermele, *Angola* (1988), Sogge (1992).

4. Economist Intelligence Unit, *Country Report, Angola* (1993, 3rd Quarter), 22.

5. Hodges (1987), 40.

6. See especially Birmingham (1992), 96–101.

7. Major general sources consulted on the Mozambican economy include Isaacman and Isaacman (1983), Brochmann and Ofstad (1990), Hermele, *Mozambique* (1988), as well as recent Mozambique government and World Bank documents.

8. People's Republic of Mozambique (1984), 30.

9. Roesch, *Central Mozambique* (1993), 4; Crush, Jeeves and Yudelman (1991), 108ff.

10. Foreign exchange earnings from the migrant labour was further cut in 1978 when the Chamber of Mines unilaterally renounced the previous agreement with the Portuguese by which the portion of miners' wages paid after return to Mozambique was transferred in gold at official prices. The Portuguese government had thus earned a premium on the differential between the official and world market price of gold.

11. Roesch, *Central Mozambique* (1993).

12. Crush, Jeeves and Yudelman (1991), 111ff.

13. *Tempo*, 2 February 1983; also Hanlon (1986), 138–9.

14. Johnson and Martin (1989), 14–17. Also see Chapter 7.

15. Frelimo, *Directivas Económicas e Sociais* (Maputo, 1977), 20.

16. There has been much research done on agricultural development policies, particularly in southern Mozambique. Major sources based on primary research include Roesch (1986), Bowen (1986, 1989), Hermele, *Land Struggles* (1988), and subsequent articles by all three researchers.

17. Wuyts (1978).

18. Frelimo, *Relatório do Comité Central ao 3e Congresso* (Maputo, 1977), 124–5. The emphasis was reiterated by the Central Committee meeting in 1978, when it was noted that support for cooperatives and the family sector was not being implemented.

19. Frelimo, *Out of Underdevelopment to Socialism: IV Congress* (Maputo, 1983), 28.

20. For analyses of this phenomenon, see, in addition to the sources cited in note 16, O'Laughlin (1981), Raikes (1984), Galli (1987).

21. Summary statistics on communal villages in 1982 are in Isaacman and Isaacman (1983), 155; Egerö (1990), 96) gives figures for 1978 as well. Additional sources include Araújo (1986, 1988), Geffray and Pedersen (1985) and Raposo (1991).

22. See Roesch, 'Gaza' (1992); also Chapter 8.

23. See Chapter 8.

24. In 1978 communal villages accounted for only 0.1 per cent of the population in Manica, 1.3 per cent in Sofala and 2.6 per cent in Nampula; in 1980 the percentages had risen to 5.9 per cent in Manica, 8 per cent in Sofala and 4.3 per cent in Nampula. By 1982 they were up to 25.4 per cent in Manica, 12.6 per cent in Sofala and 7 per cent in Nampula. Detailed figures are not available for the subsequent period, a result of the abolition of the National Commission for Communal Villages in 1983.

25. Hanlon (1984), 129; Araújo (1988), 13.

26. Hanlon (1991), 20ff.

27. See Aguilar and Zejan (1990), 31–2. World Bank, *Angola* (1991), 51ff; Hodges (1993), 50–2.

28. See the good description by Allister Sparks in an article in the *Washington Post*, 9 October 1989.

29. See the extended discussions and sources cited in Brochmann and Ofstad (1990) and Hanlon (1991). Major articles include Hermele (1990), Bowen (1992), Marshall (1990, 'Structural Adjustment'), Mittelman (1991), Tickner (1992), and Marshall and Roesch (1993).

30. Cited in Brochmann and Ofstad (1990), 166.

31. Bowen (1992), 267.

32. In an unusually explicit statement, reacting to criticism of failure to build local capacity and other technical problems in USAID for relief transport, USAID Maputo head Julius Schlotthauer told Swedish researchers: 'We are fully aware of the mentioned shortcomings. However, it has never been the USA's political and aid-related intention to go in and strengthen Mozambican public administration by helping to establish a national, state organization to counteract emergencies. Quite the opposite; the faster such attempts erode, the easier it will be for private interests and non-governmental organizations to assume responsibility for the distribution of emergency aid and to reach targeted groups.' Abrahmsson and Nilsson (1992), 19.

33. World Bank documents in the early 1990s, such as a review of public sector pay in 1991 which described the flight to the private sector, often contained carefully worded or implicit critiques of earlier policies.

34. Mozambican Finance Minister Abdul Magid Osman, quoted in Mozambique Information Office Bulletin, 21 February 1991.

35. This general conclusion is comprehensively documented in Hanlon (1991). Despite a tendency to overstatement, and possible errors and biased conclusions on some particulars, Hanlon's overall case for the negative effects of donor policies is devastating, well-documented and difficult to refute. Whether those effects were so overwhelming that in net terms Mozambique would have been

better off without the aid is, however, another question on which both donors and Mozambican officials legitimately doubt his conclusions. For a balanced review affirming the importance of Hanlon's work see Ken Wilson in *Southern African Review of Books* (July/October 1991). Also see, on the same topic, Abrahamsson and Nilsson (1992), a careful study of CARE and USAID's role in transport for emergency food distribution, and, more broadly on the new socio-economic context, Bowen (1992).

36. *Mozambique: Out of the Ruins of War* (Africa Recovery Briefing Paper, May 1993), 20.

37. See Ratilal (1990), Hanlon (1991), 79–81.

38. *Africa Recovery* (May 1993), 1.

39. Hodges (1993), 31.

40. Bhagavan (1986), 25.

11

Concluding Reflections

Southern Africa's wars and historical responsibility

When wars are won unconditionally, the victors may judge and punish the defeated for their conduct. The victors' faults are left to historians and writers of memoirs. In southern Africa's wars – whether in Zimbabwe, Namibia, South Africa, Angola or Mozambique – the post-war imperative has been and will be reconciliation. Outsiders have marvelled at the capacity of ordinary southern Africans to live, work and even govern jointly with former enemies guilty of atrocities. The process – both necessary and admirable – requires a bracketing out of the war period as one in which ordinary people found themselves in a position to commit inhuman crimes, for which they are subsequently not held responsible.

Yet human rights groups also rightly protest that the blank slate of amnesty may perpetuate human rights abuses. Those granted immunity for abusive practices during wartime may not easily abandon these precedents. If criminal prosecution is ruled out by the necessity for political compromise, then at minimum what happened should be exposed to public scrutiny. That is the rationale for open inquiries such as the Truth Commission in El Salvador, internal investigations undertaken by the ANC, and calls – as yet unanswered – for a similar accounting by the outgoing South African regime.

One implication of the present study is that many of those guilty of atrocities committed them as part of military machines they entered under duress. There will be no Nuremberg trials in Angola or Mozambique, or formal Truth Commissions with the impossible task of tracking down responsibility for hundreds of poorly recorded or undocumented incidents stretching over almost two decades of war. The individual truths will emerge, if they do, piecemeal. Historical reflection, however imperative, cannot and will not take priority over the difficult struggle for individual survival and national reconstruction.

Amnesty and reconciliation, however, should not imply amnesia. The credibility of political actors in the post-war period should have some relationship to their record during years of conflict. Responsibility for reconstruction should have some link to responsibility for destruction, whether or not this is recognized in formal tribunals or agreements. Unresolved or misidentified causes of conflict may reappear even after agreements have pronounced them settled.

This inquiry underscores the complexity of the determinants of war and the variations of local circumstance; it leads to no blanket judgements about individual culpability. Such judgements, it should be clear, require much more fine-grained examination, resembling a judicial inquest or a biography. But broader conclusions are possible. The reader must decide how well the data in this book – and new information yet to emerge – support the following summary conclusions.

If one considers Angola and Mozambique at the time of the Portuguese coup in 1974 – imagining away both the regional southern African and Cold War conflicts – what kind of wars, if any, might have resulted from internal factors alone, with an external environment similar to those of other African states? The most likely answer: no war in Mozambique and a war in Angola both shorter and more decisive than the one which occurred. The post-colonial states would still have suffered the effects of ethno-regional disparities; policy failures and ideological conflicts would still have led to disillusionment. The societies would have experienced conflict, possibly violent at times. But it is unlikely that these factors alone could have engendered the prolonged and destructive wars of the 1980s. Neither country was structurally divided on the order of a Sudan, Chad or Ethiopia. The most likely historical parallels – despite obvious differences beginning with different colonial rulers – would be Tanzania with Mozambique, and Nigeria with Angola.

In Mozambique it is simply not plausible that a coherent military organization such as Renamo would have emerged without external initiative. Without the Rhodesians and the South Africans, it is likely that those involved in Renamo would have resembled the leaders of the factious 'third parties' now emerging. Peasants or traditional leaders neglected, sidelined or abused by the post-colonial state might well have engaged in isolated protests. The political and economic policies of the state would have led to disillusionment as promises fell short of expectations, even without the war's wholesale destruction. Almost certainly there would have been pragmatic policy changes under the impact of economic pressures and rising education levels.

Instead, the war came from outside. Once it started, a variety of internal factors fed into the conflict, but they did not become the driving forces responsible for continuing the war. Ethnic and regional tensions, while they existed, did not divide Mozambicans so deeply as to have sustained a war on these grounds. Nor were the policies towards peasants, economic ideology or the one-party state what the war was about. These were real issues, of course, but it is a bizarre misreading to see Renamo as fighting for a better deal for peasants or as speaking for the emergent civil society. When policy shifts away from socialist ideology and policies began, it was people from Frelimo's rather than Renamo's milieu who were best situated to adapt to economic or political competition. Renamo seemed alarmed, rather than pleased, by the prospect of that competition.

What sustained the insurgency, in addition to the essential if diminishing external sponsorship, was on one hand the organizational and personal self-interest of Renamo's leadership, and on the other hand the incapacity of the state to maintain fundamental state structures for much of the country, beginning with the basic responsibility of any state to provide security. This analysis corresponds with the popular perception in Mozambique – the more widespread the longer the war continued – of a war between the two armies, with neither of them 'representing' the people despite the overwhelmingly more abusive behaviour of one side. It fits the empirical data on Renamo as a military organization imposing itself on the civilian population, as well as the waning support for the government as military and economic disaster stretched on year after year.

For Angola – if one puts aside the possibly decisive influence of the external environment in promoting nationalist disunity before independence, as well as subsequent Cold War and South African intervention – a purely non-violent resolution of nationalist rivalries in 1974–76 would still have been improbable. Nevertheless it is likely that the MPLA, with its implantation in the capital, the widest national outreach across ethnic lines and its edge in skilled personnel, would have gained military victory and international recognition. And there is a good chance that Unita, with few military prospects, would have succumbed to marginalization and defections as did the FNLA.

Without significant external involvement, Unita might have maintained a small-scale insurgency. But it is unlikely that it could have posed a major threat, much less made the transition to conventional combat. It had a record of ineffectiveness before independence, and of declining military fortunes after 1976 until the new Botha regime made it a favoured client. Control of oil revenues would have given the Angolan government the capacity to purchase ample military resources on commercial terms, even without politically based support from Cold War allies.

This could conceivably have led to peace, with Unita supporters incorporated in a subordinate role into national unity schemes of a victorious MPLA. But such a scenario becomes plausible only if one envisages Unita without Savimbi. In that case, both government willingness to be flexible in sharing power and Unita willingness to accept a subordinate role become plausible. Despite the majority support of Umbundu-speakers for Unita, crystallized by the events of 1975–76, the ethno-regional rivalries were not so entrenched that they were bound to prevail over national unity. Even in military weakness, however, the prospect of Savimbi accepting a subordinate role or voluntarily relinquishing his dictatorial powers over his organization seems remote. The disappearance of Savimbi's internal rivals was repeatedly linked to their alleged willingness to pursue compromise with the government. If *O Mais Velho* had been removed from the scene, Unita would undoubtedly have been both militarily weaker and more open to concessions.

Internal factors, above all Savimbi's hegemony over Unita, would probably have promoted continuation of war, albeit on a much smaller scale, even without external intervention. In the event, external involvement did help transform Unita into a powerful military machine, reinforcing its previous political base with enhanced capacity for repressive control over the constituency it claimed. As in Mozambique, the organizational interests of the insurgent army, together with the institutional weaknesses of the state, produced a scenario in which millions of war-weary Angolans saw themselves as victimized by rather than represented by the contending forces.

Even in the most peaceful scenario – imagining away Cold War, regional conflict and the ambitious Savimbi – Angola would most likely have seen conflict over sharing of power and oil revenues. Internal struggles and plots, with or without party affiliation, might have provoked eruptions of violence. The disparity between the oil-export political economy and the interests of peasants in the interior would have been an ongoing structural issue. But the destructive and prolonged war of the 1980s, and the capacity of Unita to restart the war after the 1992 election, are necessarily linked to external rather than internal factors.

In sum, Angolans and Mozambicans had their own internal reasons for disagreement, and perhaps even for some measure of violent conflict. But the wars of the 1980s attained their deadly height as a result of external forces which raised destruction to levels far beyond the capacity of the societies to resist. It was, above all, the intertwined pacing of apartheid's death struggle and the end-game of the Cold War that determined their rhythm and intensity.

In the late 1970s, the liberation struggle had yet to pose a direct challenge to the South African state. The 'total strategists' were just beginning to build the special operations components of their war machine. Fresh from defeat in Vietnam, the US was exploring accommodation rather than confrontation with Third World revolution. The international component of war in Angola and Mozambique was significant but manageable. Then came the 1980s. As threats to the regime multiplied, Botha's national security state responded with aggression directed most intensively at the most vulnerable targets. The rightward shift in Washington added fuel to the military campaign against Marxist countries, while minimizing international restraint on Pretoria.

The relative weight of regional and global involvement in sponsorship of Renamo and Unita was significantly different in the two halves of the decade, as well as between the two conflicts. In the first phase, South Africa tended to monopolize the operational role, with Washington alternating cheers and cautions in the background. Later the picture was complicated by direct US military aid to Unita and international right-wing support for Renamo. Towards the end of the decade both regional and global trends inclined towards peacemaking rather than escalation. But the bottom line was that Washington alternately bolstered and winked at Pretoria's surrogate war strategy. And that strategy deliberately targeted not only the regimes in Luanda and Maputo but also the lives and livelihoods of hundreds of thousands of civilians. Despite all the nuances, all the excuses, and all the sophistry of self-congratulatory peacemakers, US as well as South African policymakers stand condemned by their callous willingness to sacrifice these lives to their strategic objectives.

The fortunes of the internal contenders were decisively influenced by the scale of external intervention. Whatever may have been the grievances or goals of Unita and Renamo leaders, their capacity to build powerful military machines was dependent both on clientship to the apartheid state and on enrolment in the global Cold War crusade. They took advantage of existing social cleavages and regime policy failures. But the fundamental course they and their patrons laid out for the insurgent armies was to weaken the state by destroying the economic and human infrastructure of society and maximizing civilian suffering. The military advantage they gained by fostering insecurity more than made up for the potential popular support they lost by abusing civilians.

The post-colonial rulers, for their part, underestimated the fury of the apartheid state and held unrealistic hopes for overcoming their own weaknesses through revolutionary voluntarism. They overestimated both the potential support from the Soviet bloc and the willingness of the international community to restrain Pretoria. If the costs had been known, and they had been as cautious as Botswana or Zimbabwe in providing practical support to Namibian and South African liberation, could they have avoided Pretoria's and Washington's sponsorship of insurgency, or deflected the assault elsewhere? Perhaps to some extent. But the post-Nkomati record makes it more likely that both Angola and

Mozambique would have still suffered disproportionately as long as Pretoria fought to preserve minority rule and ideologues in Washington sought cheap Third World victories over Marxism.

As the Cold War rushed to its conclusion and South Africa's rulers finally opted for negotiations over belligerence, peace settlements became plausible in Angola and Mozambique. Outside powers shifted from being explicit partisans to new roles as patrons and supporters of the 'peace process'. But the years of war had profoundly altered the social and political landscape. The peace settlements concluded in wars without winners – with rival armies in place, governments weakened both materially and morally, and insurgents accustomed to relying on force disconcerted by the prospect of the democratic competition their slogans had called for.

In the wake of the Angolan fiasco, analysts who had previously touted democratic elections suggested that perhaps the settlements should have been based on 'power-sharing' rather than 'winner-take-all' elections.[1] But power-sharing was an ambiguous term, leaving unspecified how much power, on whose terms, and within what framework. The internationally endorsed settlements of Bicesse and Rome implied that the vote would determine national leadership, while integration of the incumbent and insurgent armies would ensure that the coercive apparatus of the state was not used against losing parties. If there were to be a guaranteed share of power for electoral losers, the question was how much.

In Angola and Mozambique – as in South Africa and other countries exploring simultaneously how to institutionalize democracy and resolve conflict – there were indeed unresolved questions about the best constitutional order. Such concerns include the balance of central and regional institutions; the form of proportional representation; the relative powers of executive and legislative branches; and the institutional protections for human rights and the civil society. But beyond formal institutions, there remained the fundamental question of to what extent power would be determined by some form of democratic accountability and to what extent it would depend on the demands of military formations with ambition exceeding their peaceful political potential.

The systematically destructive intersection of global, regional and national factors that existed in the 1980s is no more. But neither the national nor the regional bases for stability and peace are in place. The record of the international community in post-election Angola is not encouraging. The unanswered question for the entire region: is Angola the last violent conflict of the old era of apartheid and Cold War, or is it the first of a new era also destined to be symbolized by the gun rather than by the ballot box?

Unconventional warfare from Cold War
to new world disorder

The general lessons from these two cases are sobering. The success of guerrilla armies, as that of conventional armies, does not necessarily depend on extensive voluntary mobilization of civilians. Both material weaknesses of an incumbent state and high levels of external support for insurgency may strengthen the relative advantage of guerrillas. With modern automatic weapons and good radio communications, their destructive capacity may be just as disproportionate to their popular support as that of any repressive regime. This creates the option of greater reliance on force by guerrillas, both within their own ranks and in their relations with civilians.

The availability of this option depends on the military balance between insurgent and counterinsurgent forces. But the extent to which it is used depends, in insurgent as in conventional armies, on social context and political leadership. The use of force does not preclude a parallel political appeal to civilian support. And the mix of force and persuasion – by insurgents or incumbent regimes – undoubtedly varies not only from one war to another but also by area and by time period within a single conflict. This reinforces the increasing recognition by human rights groups of the need to investigate the record of insurgent groups as well as regimes. There is still, however, a vacuum of relevant criteria for investigating the conduct of outside forces whose intervention may be of decisive importance, even if it falls short of invasion or occupation.

Further generalization on the factors influencing guerrilla warfare is impossible without study of a wide range of cases, but a quick review suggests some hypotheses. The prominent contra-type wars of the 1980s – Nicaragua, Afghanistan and Cambodia, as well as Angola and Mozambique – show a wide range of variation in the social bases of both regime and insurgency. Foreign intervention in support of the regime ranged from massive Soviet involvement in Afghanistan and the Vietnamese invasion of Cambodia through the more limited Cuban involvement in Angola and even more limited outside support received by Mozambique and Nicaragua. Foreign initiative in creating rather than just supporting an insurgent army was a notable feature only in Mozambique and Nicaragua. The ideology of the principal insurgent force ranged from Marxist in Cambodia to Muslim in Afghanistan to anti-communist in Nicaragua.

The three non-African insurgencies nevertheless showed some features in common with Angola and Mozambique. The target Marxist regimes were particularly vulnerable. All were recently established; the attacks against them followed the classic counter-revolutionary maxim to try to kill the infant before it grows up. All had small populations –

Afghanistan, with 16 million people, had the most. All had fragile economies. The insurgents all received large-scale logistical, communications and other support from major powers. Mines littered the landscape. Destruction far surpassed what internal conflicts alone would have been able to generate.

The outcomes were varied and all precarious, but in each case the military capacity of the insurgents exceeded their readiness for constructive participation in a post-war order. In each case, the powers that had fuelled the insurgencies showed only moderate interest at most in the more difficult task of reconstruction. Despite new United Nations involvement in Cambodia, Angola and Mozambique, each country faced not only economic and social disaster but also unresolved issues of the structures of political accountability and control over the warriors of the 1980s.

Beyond these historically specific cases, the results of this inquiry do suggest some modifications to the classic images of guerrilla war and revolution. A weakened incumbent regime and the existence of a rival organizational contender for sovereignty, as outlined in Chapter 3, seem to be constants. But there is no guarantee that regimes rely more on force while guerrillas necessarily turn more to voluntary participation. Whether the issue is recruitment or the relationship to civilians, the mix of force and persuasion is a variable to be investigated.

The entirely reasonable argument in the classic model is that guerrillas cannot systematically use terror against their own constituency and recruitment base because it will deprive them of an indispensable weapon against a materially superior opponent. Outside support is not seen as sufficient to compensate for that. Many cases – perhaps most – may generally conform to this model. The international state system implied a *de facto* bias in favour of established recognized regimes, and it is difficult to name other insurgencies that have had outside support as massive in relation to their target as the contra-type wars of the 1980s. During the Cold War, outside support for leftist insurgencies was never as generous or as adventurist as the sponsors of contra-type wars.

Nevertheless most guerrilla forces – even those accepted during or after a conflict as representative or patriotic – probably relied to some extent on intimidation and forced recruitment.[2] Few observers, whether sympathetic or hostile to a particular insurgency, would totally deny the existence of such phenomena. The questions are how much is enough to be analytically significant, and whether it casts doubt on the legitimacy of an organization or the nobility of a cause. To what extent, in other words, does firepower and the willingness to use it outpace the values and the constituencies the warriors claim to represent?

During the Cold War there was a deceiving simplicity in distinguishing legitimate from illegitimate regimes and contenders for power, although of course the choices of different parties might be mirror images of each other. In the post-Cold War era of disorder, even the distinction between states and insurgents is increasingly up for grabs. No global crusade mandates international military intervention to shore up a certain set of regimes or bring others to their knees. But the international community, and major powers in particular, now have even more weight in tipping the balance of military force or legitimacy one way or the other in a host of conflicts.

Participants in these new conflicts may be labelled warlord or indispensable negotiating partner, war criminal or statesman, a force for stability or for disorder, freedom fighter or terrorist. Each label has practical implications for arms sales or embargos, sending or setting guidelines for multinational forces, representation in international forums, bilateral or multilateral assistance. International action or inaction in turn may be decisive in determining which party to a conflict gains greater advantages, and in some cases whether or not the conflict continues. The question becomes who decides on the character of the international involvement, and on the basis of what criteria. If, as seems likely, the input into decision-making is pegged to the politics of big powers able to contribute the most military resources, and to the vagaries of international bureaucracy, domestic civilian opinion runs the risk of being marginalized.

If the popular watchword of democratic accountability is to apply to territories contested by rival armies, it must apply across the board. Minimum standards of respect for human rights and consultation with those affected by the conflict must apply to incumbents, insurgents, individual outside powers and the international community alike. It is a tall order, with low odds for consistent implementation. But it is the only course that reflects the fact that the sources of conflict – as of conflict resolution – may lie outside as well as inside the borders of the country where the battles are raging.

Notes

1. See, for example, the US State Department document *Conflict Resolution in Africa: Lessons from Angola* (6 April 1993).
2. See particularly Kriger (1992), which sharply questioned the role of voluntary peasant support for the war in Zimbabwe and added another strand to the rich research tradition on that war. For other references see Chapter 3, note 15.

Bibliography

Abbreviations: *JSAS = Journal of Southern African Studies; ROAPE = Review of African Political Economy.*

Abrahamsson, Hans, and Anders Nilsson, 1992, *Power and Powerlessness in a Starving Mozambique*, Gothenburg, Sweden: Institute for Peace and Development Research.

Adam, Yussuf, 1988, 'Kollektive Ländliche Entwicklung und Genossenschaften in Mozambique: Die Lage in den alten "Befreiten Gebieten" von Cabo Delgado', in Peter Meyns, ed., *Agrargesellschaften im portugiesich-sprachigen Afrika*, Saarbrücken: Verlag Breitenbach.

Africa Watch, 1989, *Angola: The Violations of the Laws of War by Both Sides*, New York: Africa Watch.

— 1991, *Angola: Civilians Devastated by 15-Year War*, New York: Africa Watch.

— 1992, *Accountability in Namibia*, New York: Africa Watch.

— 1992, *Conspicuous Destruction: War, Famine and the Reform Process in Mozambique*, New York: Human Rights Watch.

— 1993, *Land Mines in Angola*, New York: Africa Watch.

Aguilar, Renato, and Mario Zejan, 1990, *Angola*, Stockholm: SIDA.

Alpers, Edward, 1984, 'To Seek a Better Life: The Implications of Migration from Mozambique to Tanzania for Class Formation and Political Behavior', in *Canadian Journal of African Studies*, 18: 367–88.

Amnesty International, 1982, *People's Republic of Angola: Background Briefing*, London: Amnesty International.

Anderson, Benedict, 1991, *Imagined Communities* (2nd edn), London: Verso.

Antunes, José Freire, 1980, *O Império com Pés de Barro: Colonização e Descolonização, as Ideologias em Portugal*, Lisbon: Publicações Dom Quixote.

— 1986, *Os Americanos e Portugal, Vol. I: Os Anos de Richard Nixon*, Lisbon: Publicações Dom Quixote.

— 1990, *O Factor Africano, 1890–1990*, Lisbon: Bertrand Editora.

Araújo, Manuel, 1986, 'Seis Aldeias Comunais da província de Inhambane', in *Garcia de Orta (Lisbon)*, 11: 1–2: 69–81.

— 1988, 'Dinámica das Novas Formas de Redistribuição da População Rural em Moçambique,' in *Gazeta Demográfica (Maputo)*, December: 3–26.

Austin, Kathi, 1994, *Invisible Crimes: U.S. Private Intervention in the War in Mozambique*, Washington: Africa Policy Information Center.

291

Baker, Pauline H., 1989, *The United States and South Africa: The Reagan Years*, New York: Ford Foundation.

Barker, Carol, 1985, 'Bringing Health Care to the People', in John S. Saul, *A Difficult Road: The Transition to Socialism in Mozambique*, New York: Monthly Review Press.

Barrell, Howard, 1990, *MK: The ANC's Armed Struggle*, London: Penguin.

Bayer, Tom, 1993, *Angola, Presidential and Legislative Elections, September 29–30, 1992: Report of the IFES Observation Mission*, Washington: International Foundation for Electoral Systems.

Beckett, Ian F.W., and John Pimlott, eds, 1985, *Armed Forces and Modern Counter-Insurgency*, New York: St. Martin's Press.

Bell, J. Bowyer, 1971, *The Myth of the Guerrilla*, New York: Knopf.

Bender, Gerald J., 1978, *Angola under the Portuguese: The Myth and the Reality*, Berkeley: University of California Press.

— 1978, 'Kissinger in Angola: Anatomy of Failure', in René Lemarchand, ed., *American Policy in Southern Africa*, Washington: University Press of America.

— 1981, 'Angola: Left, Right and Wrong', in *Foreign Policy*, 43 (Summer): 53–69.

— 1985, 'American Policy Toward Angola: A History of Linkage', in Bender et al., eds.

— 1989, 'Peacemaking in Southern Africa: The Luanda–Pretoria Tug-of-War', in *Third World Quarterly*, 11 (April): 15–30.

Bender, Gerald J., James S. Coleman and Richard L. Sklar, eds, 1985, *African Crisis Areas and U.S. Foreign Policy*, Berkeley: University of California Press.

Benguela Railways and the Development of Southern Africa, 1987, Luanda: Editorial Vanguarda.

Berridge, G.R., 1989, 'Diplomacy and the Angola/Namibia Accords', in *International Affairs*, 65: 3 (Summer): 463–79.

Bertulli, Cesare, 1974, *Croce e Spada in Mozambico*, Rome: Loines.

Bhagavan, M.R., 1986, *Angola's Political Economy 1975–1985*, Uppsala: Scandinavian Institute of African Studies.

Birmingham, David, 1978, 'The Twenty-Seventh of May: An Historical Note on the Abortive 1977 Coup in Angola', in *African Affairs*, 309 (Oct.): 554–64.

— 1992, *Frontline Nationalism in Angola and Mozambique*, Trenton, NJ: Africa World Press.

Bloomfield, Richard J., ed., 1988, *Regional Conflict and U.S. Policy: Angola and Mozambique*, Algonac, MI: Reference Publications.

Blumenthal, Sidney, 1986, *The Rise of the Counter-Establishment*, New York: Times Books.

Boothby, Neil, Abubacar Sultan and Peter Upton, 1991, *Children of Mozambique*, Washington: U.S. Committee for Refugees.

Borges Coelho, João Paulo, 1989, *O Início da Luta Armada em Tete*, Maputo: Arquivo Histórico de Moçambique.

Bowen, Merle L., 1986, *Socialist Agricultural Development Strategy in Mozambique, 1975–1983*, Toronto: Ph.D. University of Toronto.

— 1989, 'Peasant Agriculture in Mozambique: The Case of Chokwe, Gaza Province,' in *Canadian Journal of African Studies*, 23: 3: 355–80.

— 1992, 'Beyond Reform: Adjustment and Political Power in Contemporary Mozambique,' in *Journal of Modern African Studies*, 30:2: 25–79.

Bradbury, William C., Samuel M. Meyers and Albert D. Biderman, eds, 1968, *Mass Behavior in Battle and Captivity*, Chicago: University of Chicago Press.

Bragança, Aquino de, and Jacques Depelchin, 1988, 'From the Idealization of Frelimo to the Understanding of the Recent History of Mozambique,' in *Review*, 11 (Winter): 95–117.

Breytenbach, Jan, 1990, *They Live by the Sword: 32 'Buffalo' Battalion – South Africa's Foreign Legion*, Alberton, South Africa: Lemur.

Bridgland, Fred, 1987, *Jonas Savimbi: A Key to Africa*, New York: Paragon House.

—— 1990, *The War for Africa*, Gibraltar: Ashanti Publishing.

Brito, Luís de, 1988, 'Une Relecture Nécessaire: La Genèse du Parti-Etat FRELIMO,' in *Politique Africaine*, 29 (Mars): 15–27.

Brochmann, Grete, and Arve Ofstad, 1990, *Mozambique: Norwegian Assistance in a Context of Crisis*, Bergen: Chr. Michelsen Institute.

Cahen, Michel, 1987, *Mozambique: La Revolution Implosée*. Paris: L'Harmattan.

Castro, Armando, 1978, *O Sistema Colonial Português em Africa (meados do século XX)*, Lisbon: Editorial Caminho.

Cawthra, Gavin, 1986, *Brutal Force: The Apartheid War Machine*, London: IDAFSA.

Chaliand, Gérard, ed., 1982, *Guerrilla Strategies: An Historical Anthology from the Long March to Afghanistan*, Berkeley: University of California Press.

Christie, Iain, 1988, *Machel of Mozambique*, Harare: Zimbabwe Publishing House.

Cilliers, J.K., 1985, *Counter-Insurgency in Rhodesia*, London: Croom Helm.

Clarence-Smith, Gervase, 1980, 'Review Article: Class Structure and Class Struggles in Angola in the 1970s', in *JSAS*, 7:1 (October): 109–26.

—— 1989, 'The Roots of the Mozambican Counter-Revolution,' in *Southern African Review of Books*, April/May.

Clayton, Anthony, 1976, *Counter-Insurgency in Kenya*, Nairobi: Transafrica.

Cline, Sibyl, 1989, *Renamo, Anti-Communist Insurgents in Mozambique*, Washington: U.S. Global Strategy Council.

Clough, Michael, 1982, 'Mozambique: American Policy Options', in *Africa Report*, Nov./Dec.: 14–17.

—— 1992, *Free at Last? U.S. Policy Toward Africa and the End of the Cold War*, New York: Council on Foreign Relations.

Cock, Jacklyn, and Laurie Nathan, eds, 1989, *War and Society: The Militarization of South Africa*, Cape Town: David Philip.

Cohen, Barry, and Mohamed A. El-Khawas, 1975, *The Kissinger Study of Southern Africa*. Nottingham: Spokesman Books.

Coker, Christopher, 1987, *South Africa's Security Dilemmas*, New York: Praeger.

Cole, Barbara, 1985, *The Elite: The Story of the Rhodesian Air Service*, Transkei, South Africa: Three Knights.

Conchiglia, Augusta, 1990, *UNITA, Myth and Reality*, London: European Campaign against S.A. Aggression on Mozambique and Angola.

Correia, Jorge, 1989, *RENAMO: Resistência Nacional Moçambicana*, Lisbon: Forum Moçambicano.

Crocker, Chester, 1992, *High Noon in Southern Africa: Making Peace in a Rough Neighborhood*, New York: W.W. Norton.

Crush, Jonathan, Alan Jeeves and David Yudelman, 1991, *South Africa's Labor Empire: A History of Black Migrancy to the Gold Mines*. Boulder: Westview Press.

Dash, Jr., Leon De Costa, 1977, *Savimbi's 1977 Campaign against the Cubans and the MPLA*, Pasadena: Munger Africana Notes.

Davidson, Basil, 1973, *In the Eye of the Storm: Angola's People*, Garden City, NY: Anchor/Doubleday.

—— 1992, *The Black Man's Burden: Africa and the Curse of the Nation-State*, New York: Times Books.

Davies, Robert, and Dan O'Meara, 1985, 'Total Strategy in Southern Africa: An Analysis of South African Regional Policy since 1978', in *JSAS*, 11:2 (April): 183–211.

De Saavedra, Ricardo, 1975, *Aqui Moçambique Livre*, Johannesburg: Livraria Moderna.

DeLancey, Mark W., ed., 1992, *Handbook of Political Science Research on Sub-Saharan Africa*, Westport, CT: Greenwood Press.

Deutschmann, David, 1989, *Changing the History of Africa: Angola and Namibia*, Melbourne, Australia: Ocean Press.

Dhada, Mustafah, 1993, *Warriors at Work: How Guinea was Really Set Free*, Niwot, CO: University Press of Colorado.

Dias, Jill, 1984, 'Uma Questão de Identidade Respostas: Intelectuais às Transformações Económicas no Seio da Elite Crioula da Angola Português', in *Revista Internacional de Estudos Africanos*, 1: 61–94.

Dixon, Glen, 1986, *Hostage*, London: Columbus Books.

Donnell, John C., Guy J. Pauker and Joseph J. Zasloff, 1965, *Viet Cong Motivation and Morale*, Santa Monica: Rand Corporation.

Eduardo Mondlane Foundation, 1992, *Democratization in Angola: Seminar Readings*, Leiden: Eduardo Mondlane Foundation, KZA and African Studies Center, Leiden.

—— 1993, *Democratization in Angola: Seminar Proceedings*, Leiden: Eduardo Mondlane Foundation, KZA and African Studies Center, Leiden.

Egerö, Bertil, 1990, *Mozambique: A Dream Undone, The Political Economy of Democracy, 1975–84* (2nd edn), Uppsala: Nordiska Afrikainstitutet.

Ellert, H., 1989, *The Rhodesian Front War: Counter-Insurgency and Guerrilla Warfare, 1961–1980*, Gweru, Zimbabwe: Mambo Press.

Environmental Investigation Agency, 1992, *Under Fire: Elephants in the Front Line*, London: Environmental Investigation Agency.

Estado Maior do Exército, 1988, *Resenha Histórico-Militar das Campanhas de África*, V.1, Lisbon: EME.

Ferguson, Thomas, and Joel Rogers, 1986, *Right Turn*, New York: Hill & Wang.

Ferreira, Manuel, 1986, *Literaturas Africanas de Expressão Portuguesa*, Lisbon: Livraria Bertrand.

Finnegan, William, 1992, *A Complicated War: The Harrowing of Mozambique*, Berkeley: University of California Press.

Flower, Ken, 1987, *Serving Secretly*, London: John Murray.

Forrest, Joshua, 1992, *Guinea-Bissau: Power, Conflict and Renewal in a West African Nation*, Boulder: Westview Press.

Frankel, P.H., 1984, *Pretoria's Praetorians*, Cambridge: Cambridge University Press.

Freeman, Jr., Chas. W., 1989, 'The Angola/Namibia Accords,' in *Foreign Affairs*, 68:3 (Summer): 126–41.

Galli, Rosemary E., 1987, 'The Food Crisis and the Socialist State in Lusophone Africa', in *African Studies Review*, 30:1 (March): 19–44.

Galli, Rosemary and Jocelyn Jones, 1987, *Guinea-Bissau: Politics, Economics and Society*. Boulder: Lynne Rienner Publishers.

Gaspar, Carlos, 1988, 'Incomplete Failure: Portugal's Policies Toward Angola and Mozambique Since Independence', in Bloomfield, ed.

Geffray, Christian, 1990, *La Cause des Armes: Anthropologie de la Guerre Contemporaine au Mozambique*, Paris: Editions Karthala.

Geffray, Christian, and Mögens Pedersen, 1985, *Transformação da Organização Social e do Sistema Agrário do Campesinato no Distrito de Erati*, Maputo: Universidade Eduardo Mondlane.

— 1986, 'Sobre a Guerra na Província de Nampula', in *Revista Internacional de Estudos Africanos*, 4–5: 303–20.

Geldenhuys, Deon, 1984, *The Diplomacy of Isolation: South African Foreign Policy Making*, New York: St. Martin's Press.

Gellner, Ernest, 1983, *Nations and Nationalism*, Ithaca, NY: Cornell University Press.

Gersony, Robert, 1988, *Summary of Mozambican Refugee Accounts of Principally Conflict-Related Experience in Mozambique*, Washington: U.S. State Department.

Gerth, Hans, and C. Wright Mills, eds, 1946, *From Max Weber: Essays in Sociology*, New York: Oxford University Press.

Gervasi, Sean, and Sybil Wong, 1991, 'The Reagan Doctrine and the Destabilization of Southern Africa', in Alexander George, *Western State Terrorism*, New York: Routledge.

Giap, Vo Nguyen, 1962, *People's War, People's Army*, New York: Praeger.

Gifford, Prosser, and Wm. Roger Louis, 1988, *Decolonization and African Independence*, New Haven: Yale University Press.

Gjerstad, Ole, 1976, *The People in Power: An Account from Angola's Second War of Liberation*, Richmond, Canada: LSM Information Center.

Goldstone, Jack A., 1991, *Revolution and Rebellion in the Early Modern World*, Berkeley: University of California Press.

Grundy, Kenneth W., 1983, *Soldiers without Politics: Blacks in the South African Armed Forces*, Berkeley: University of California Press.

— 1986, *The Militarization of South African Politics*, Bloomington: Indiana University Press.

Gunn, Gillian, 1989, 'A Guide to the Intricacies of the Angola-Namibia Negotiations', in *CSIS Africa Notes*, 23 October.

— 1990, 'Unfulfilled Expectations in Angola', in *Current History*, May: 213–34.

Hall, Margaret, 1990, 'The Mozambican National Resistance (Renamo): A Study in the Destruction of an African Country', in *Africa*, 60: 1: 39–68.

Hamann, Hilton, 1990, 'Recce Commandos', in *Soldier of Fortune*, February/March.

Hamilton, Russell G., 1975, *Voices from an Empire*, Minneapolis: University of Minnesota Press.

Hanlon, Joseph, 1984, *Mozambique: The Revolution under Fire*, London: Zed Press.

— 1986, *Beggar Your Neighbors: Apartheid Power in Southern Africa*, Bloomington, IN: Indiana University Press.

— 1991, *Mozambique: Who Calls the Shots?*, London: James Currey.

Harries, Patrick, 1988, 'The Roots of Ethnicity: Discourse and the Politics of Language Construction in South-east Africa', in *African Affairs*, January: 25–52.

Hedges, David, 1989, 'Notes on Malawi–Mozambique Relations, 1961–1987', in *JSAS*, October: 617–44.

Heimer, Franz-Wilhelm, 1979, *The Decolonization Conflict in Angola, 1974–76, An Essay in Political Sociology*, Geneva: Institut Universitaire de Hautes Études Internationales.

—— 1979, *Der Entkoloniesierungskonflikt in Angola*, Munich: Weltforum Verlag.

Heimer, Franz-Wilhelm, and Elisete Marques da Silva, 1988, 'Vundiça: Wandel und Kontinuität in Reproduktion und Inkorporation eines Ländlichen Gesellschaftssegments in Mozambique', in Peter Meyns, ed., *Agrargesellschaften im portugiesich-sprachigen Afrika*, Saarbrücken: Verlag Breitenbach.

Heitman, Helmoed-Römer, 1985, *South African War Machine*, Novato, CA: Presidio Publishing.

—— 1990, *War in Angola: The Final South African Phase*, Gibraltar: Ashanti Publishing.

Henderson, Lawrence W., 1979, *Angola: Five Centuries of Conflict*, Ithaca: Cornell University Press.

—— 1992, *The Church in Angola: A River of Many Currents*, Cleveland, OH: Pilgrim Press.

Henderson, William D., 1979, *Why the Vietcong Fought*, Westport, CT: Greenwood Press.

Hermele, Kenneth, 1988, *Country Report: Mozambique*, Stockholm: SIDA.

—— 1988, *Land Struggles and Social Differentiation in Southern Mozambique: A Case Study of Chokwe, Limpopo 1950–1987*, Uppsala: Scandinavian Institute of African Studies.

—— 1988, *Landrapport Angola*, Stockholm: SIDA.

—— 1990, *Mozambican Crossroads: Economics and Politics in the Era of Structural Adjustment*, Bergen: Chr. Michelsen Institute.

Herrick, Allison B. et al., 1967, *Area Handbook for Angola*, Washington: U.S. Government Printing Office.

Heywood, Linda, 1989, 'UNITA and Ethnic Nationalism in Angola', in *Journal of Modern African Studies*, 27:1: 47–66.

Hobsbawm, E.J., 1990, *Nations and Nationalism since 1780*, Cambridge: Cambridge University Press.

Hodges, Tony, 1987, *Angola to the 1990s: The Potential for Recovery*, London: Economist Intelligence Unit.

—— 1993, *Angola to 2000: Prospects for Recovery*, London: Economist Intelligence Unit.

Hoile, David, 1989, *Mozambique: A Nation in Crisis*, London: Claridge Press.

Honwana, Raúl, 1988, *The Life History of Raúl Honwana, edit. and with an introduction by Allen F. Isaacman*, Boulder: Lynne Rienner.

Human Rights Watch and Physicians for Human Rights, 1993, *Landmines: A Deadly Legacy*, New York: Human Rights Watch.

Hyden, Goran and Michael Bratton, eds, 1992, *Governance and Politics in Africa*, Boulder: Lynne Rienner.

Instituto de Estudios Políticos para América Latina y Africa, 1979, *La Iglesia en Mozambique Hoy: Entre El Colonialismo y La Revolucion*, Madrid: IEPALA.

International Defence and Aid Fund, 1980, *The Apartheid War Machine*, London: IDAFSA.

—— 1981, *Remember Kassinga*, London: International Defence and Aid Fund.

Isaacman, Allen F., 1985, 'Mozambique: Tugging at the Chains of Dependency', in Bender et al., eds.

Isaacman, Allen, and Barbara Isaacman, 1976, *The Tradition of Resistance in*

Mozambique: Anti-Colonial Activity in the Zambesi Valley, 1850–1921, London: Heinemann.

—— 1983, *Mozambique: From Colonialism to Revolution, 1900–1982*, Boulder: Westview Press.

Jamba, Sousa, 1990, *Patriots*, New York: Viking.

James, W. Martin, 1992, *A Political History of the Civil War in Angola, 1974–1990*, New Brunswick, NJ: Transaction Publishers.

Janowitz, Morris, 1959, *Sociology and the Military Establishment*, New York: Russell Sage.

Jaster, Robert S., Moeletsi Mbeki, Morley Nkosi and Michael Clough, 1992, *Changing Fortunes: War, Diplomacy and Economics in Southern Africa*, New York: Ford Foundation.

Jaster, Robert S., 1985, *South Africa in Namibia: The Botha Strategy*, Lanham: University Press of America.

—— 1989, *The Defense of White Power: South African Foreign Policy under Pressure*, New York: St. Martin's Press.

—— 1990, *The 1988 Peace Accords and the Future of Southwestern Africa (Adelphi Papers No. 253)*, London: International Institute of Strategic Studies.

Johnson, Phyllis and David Martin, 1986, *Destructive Engagement: Southern Africa at War*, Harare: Zimbabwe Publishing House.

—— 1988, *Frontline Southern Africa: Destructive Engagement*, New York: Four Walls Eight Windows.

—— 1989, *Apartheid Terrorism: A Report for the Commonwealth Committee of Foreign Ministers on Southern Africa*, London: James Currey.

Johnston, Anton, 1984, *Education in Mozambique 1975–1984*, Stockholm: SIDA.

Kapuscinski, Ryszard, 1987, *Another Day of Life: A Haunting Eyewitness Account of Civil War in Angola*, New York: Viking Penguin.

Keller, Edmond J. and Donald Rothschild, eds, 1987, *Afro-Marxist Regimes: Ideology and Public Policy*, Boulder: Lynne Rienner Publishers.

Kitson, Frank, 1977, *Bunch of Five*, London: Faber & Faber.

—— 1971, *Low Intensity Operations*, London: Faber & Faber.

Klare, Michael T. and Peter Kornbluh, eds, 1988, *Low-Intensity Warfare*, New York: Pantheon Books.

Klinghoffer, Arthur Jay, 1980, *The Angolan War*, Boulder: Westview.

Kriger, Norma, 1992, *Zimbabwe's Guerrilla War*, Cambridge: Cambridge University Press.

Lan, David, 1985, *Guns and Rain: Guerrillas and Spirit Mediums in Zimbabwe*, London: James Currey.

Laqueur, Walter, 1976, *Guerrilla: A Historical and Critical Study*, Boston: Little Brown.

Legrand, Jean-Claude, 1991, 'Logique de Guerre et Dynamique de la Violence en Zambezia', unpublished paper.

Legum, Colin, 1988, *The Battlefronts of Southern Africa*, New York: Africana.

Legum, Colin, and Tony Hodges, 1976, *After Angola: The War Over Southern Africa*, New York: Africana.

Lind, Agneta, 1988, *Adult Literacy Lessons and Promises: Mozambican Literacy Campaigns, 1978–1982*, Stockholm: Institute of International Education.

Loiseau, Yves and Pierre Guillaume de Roux, 1987, *Portrait d'un Révolutionnaire et Général*, Paris: La Table Ronde.

Lopes, Carlos, 1987, *Guinea-Bissau: From Liberation Struggle to Independent Statehood*, Boulder: Westview Press.

Lopes, Carlos and Lars Rudebeck, 1988, *The Socialist Ideal in Africa: A Debate*, Uppsala: Scandinavian Institute of African Studies.

Magaia, Lina, 1988, *Dumba Nengue: Run for Your Life*, Trenton, NJ: Africa World Press.

Maier, Karl, 1991, 'A Traditional Revival', in *Africa Report*, July–August: 64–7.

Mao Tse Tung, ed. Samuel B. Griffith, 1961, *On Guerrilla Warfare*, New York: Praeger.

Mao Tse Tung, 1968, *Selected Military Writings*, Peking: Foreign Languages Press.

Marcum, John, 1969, *The Angolan Revolution, Vol. I: The Anatomy of an Explosion, 1950–1962*. Cambridge: MIT Press.

— 1978, *The Angolan Revolution, Vol. II: Exile Politics and Guerrilla Warfare, 1962–1976*, Cambridge: MIT Press.

Marenches, Conde de, 1988, *No Segredo dos Deuses*, Lisbon: Ediçōs Referendo.

Marques, Alvaro B., 1987, *Quem Matou Samora Machel?*, Lisbon: Ulmeiro.

Marshall, Judith, 1990, *Literacy, State Formation and People's Power*, Bellville: University of the Western Cape.

— 1990, 'Structural Adjustment and Social Policy in Mozambique', in *ROAPE*, Spring: 28–43.

Marshall, Judith and Otto Roesch, 1993, 'The "Green Zones" Agricultural Cooperatives of Nampula City', in *JSAS*, June: 240–72.

Maré, Gerhard, 1993, *Ethnicity and Politics in South Africa*, London: Zed Books.

Martin, David and Phyllis Johnson, 1981, *The Struggle for Zimbabwe*, New York: Monthly Review Press.

Maxwell, David J., 1993, 'Local Politics and the War of Liberation in North-east Zimbabwe', in *JSAS*, September: 361–86.

Maxwell, Kenneth, 1982, 'Portugal and Africa: The Last Empire', in Prosser Gifford and and Wm. Roger Louis, *The Transfer of Power in Africa: Decolonization 1940–1960*, New Haven: Yale University Press.

Mayer, Arno J., 1971, *Dynamics of Counterrevolution in Europe, 1870–1956*, New York: Harper & Row.

McCallin, Margaret and Shirley Fozzard, 1990, *The Impact of Traumatic Events on the Psychological Well-Being of Mozambican Refugee Women and Children*, Geneva: International Catholic Child Bureau.

McCormick, Shawn, 1991, 'Angola: The Road to Peace', in *CSIS Africa Notes*, 6 June.

McFaul, Michael, 1989, 'Rethinking the "Reagan Doctrine" in Angola', in *International Security*, 14:3: 99–135.

— 1990, 'The Demise of the World Revolutionary Process: Soviet-Angolan Relations under Gorbachev', in *JSAS*, March: 165–89.

Menges, Constantine, 1988, *Inside the National Security Council*, New York: Simon and Schuster.

— 1990, *The Twilight Struggle*, Washington: AEI Press.

Mesquitela, Colthilde, 1976, *Moçambique: Sete de Setembro*, Lisbon: Livraria Editora Pax.

Miller, Joseph C., 1988, *Way of Death: Merchant Capitalism and the Angolan Slave Trade, 1730–1830*, Madison: University of Wisconsin Press.

Minter, William, 1972, *Portuguese Africa and the West*, Harmondsworth: Penguin Books.

— 1986, *King Solomon's Mines Revisited: Western Interests and the Burdened History of Southern Africa*, New York: Basic Books.

— 1988, *Operation Timber: Pages from the Savimbi Dossier*, Trenton, NJ: Africa World Press.

— 1989, *The Mozambican National Resistance (Renamo) as Described by Ex-participants*, Washington: Research Report.

— 1990, *The National Union for the Total Independence of Angola (UNITA) as Described by Ex-participants and Foreign Visitors*, Washington: Research Report.

— 1992, 'Glimpses of the War in Angola: Three South African Accounts', in *Africa Today*, 39: 1–2: 130–34.

— 1992, 'Lusophone Africa', in DeLancey (ed.).

Mittelman, James H., 1991, 'Marginalization and the International Division of Labor: Mozambique's Strategy of Opening the Market', in *African Studies Review*, December: 89–106.

Mondlane, Eduardo, 1969, *The Struggle for Mozambique*. Baltimore: Penguin Books.

Moorcraft, Paul L., 1990, *African Nemesis: War and Revolution in Southern Africa (1945–2010)*, London: Brassey's.

Munslow, Barry, 1983, *Mozambique: The Revolution and Its Orgins*, London: Longman.

— ed., 1985, *Samora Machel: An African Revolutionary, Selected Speeches and Writings*, London: Zed Books.

Mutemba, Abel, 1982, *Operação 6° Anniversário: Como uma Rede da CIA foi Desmantelada em Moçambique*, Maputo: Notícias.

Nederlandse Missieraad, 1976, *Moçambique: Een Nieuw Volk, Een Nieuw Kerk?*, s'Hertogenbosch, Holland: Nederlandse Missieraad.

— 1979, *Angola: Een Nieuw Volk, Een Nieuw Kerk?*, s'Hertogenbosch, Holland: Nederlandse Missieraad.

Nesbitt, Prexy, 1988, 'Terminators, Crusaders and Gladiators: Western (private and public) Support for Renamo and Unita', in *ROAPE*, No. 43: 111–23.

Noer, Thomas J., 1985, *Cold War and Black Liberation: The United States and White Rule in Africa, 1948–1968*. Columbia, MO: University of Missouri Press.

Noormahomed, Abdul and Julie Cliff, 1990, *The Impact on Health in Mozambique of South African Destabilization* (3rd edn), Maputo: Ministry of Health.

O'Laughlin, Bridget, 1981, 'A Questão Agrária em Mocambique,' in *Estudos Moçambicanos*, 3: 9–32.

— 1992, 'Interpretations Matter: Evaluating the War in Mozambique', in *Southern Africa Report*, January: 23–33.

Oliveira, Paulo, 1990, 'Os Donos da "RENAMO"', Maputo: unpublished manuscript.

O'Meara, Dan, 1991, 'The Collapse of Mozambican Socialism', in *Transformation*, 14: 82–103.

Opello, Jr., Walter C., 1975, 'Pluralism and Elite Conflict in an Independence Movement: FRELIMO in the 1960s', in *JSAS*, 2:1 (October): 66–82.

Ottaway, Marina and David, 1986, *Afro-Communism* (2nd edn), New York: Africana (Holmes & Meier).

Paige, Jeffery M., 1975, *Agrarian Revolution: Social Movements and Export Agriculture in the Underdeveloped World*, New York: Free Press.

Parson, Jack, 1984, *Botswana: Liberal Democracy and the Labor Reserve in Southern Africa*, Boulder: Westview.

Pélissier, René, 1986, *História das Campanhas de Angola*. Lisbon: Editorial Estampa.

— 1987, *História de Moçambique*, Lisbon: Editorial Estampa.

Penvenne, Jeanne, 1989, '"We are all Portuguese!" Challenging the Political Economy of Assimilation: Lourenço Marques, 1870–1933', in Leroy Vail, ed., *The Creation of Tribalism in Southern Africa*, London: James Currey.

People's Republic of Mozambique, 1984, *Economic Report*, Maputo: People's Republic of Mozambique.

Pepetela, 1983, *Mayombe*, London: Heinemann.

Pereira da Rosa, Victor and Salvato Trigo, 1986, *Portugueses e Moçambicanos no Apartheid*, Porto: Secretaria de Estado das Comunidades Portuguesas.

Pezarat Correia, Pedro, 1991, *Descolonização de Angola*, Luanda: Ler & Escrever.

Pires, R. Pena et al., 1984, *Os Retornados: Um Estudo Sociográfico*, Lisbon: Instituto de Estudos para o Desenvolvimento.

Radu, Michael, ed., 1990, *The New Insurgencies: Anticommunist Guerrillas in the Third World*, New Brunswick, NJ: Transaction.

Ragin, Charles, 1987, *The Comparative Method*, Berkeley: University of California Press.

Raikes, Philip, 1984, 'Food Policy and Production in Mozambique since Independence', in *ROAPE*, 29: 95–107.

Ranger, Terence, 1977, 'The People in African Resistance: A Review', in *JSAS*, October: 361–86.

— 1985, *Peasant Consciousness and Guerrilla War in Zimbabwe*, London: James Currey.

— 1989, 'Missionaries, Migrants and the Manyika: The Invention of Ethnicity in Zimbabwe', in Leroy Vail, ed., *The Creation of Tribalism in Southern Africa*, London: James Currey.

Raposo, Isabel, 1991, *O Viver de Hoje e de Ontem: Aldeia e Musha*, Maputo: Universidade Eduardo Mondlane, Faculdade de Arquitectura.

Ratilal, Prakash, 1990, *Enfrentar o Desafio: Utilizar a Ajuda para Terminar a Emergência*, Maputo: Editora Globo.

Riaúzova, Elena, 1986, *Dez Anos de Literatura Africana*, Luanda: União dos Escritores Angolanos.

Rice, Edward E., 1988, *Wars of the Third Kind: Conflict in Underdeveloped Countries*, Berkeley: University of California Press.

Richman, Naomi, Anabela Ratilala and Aires Aly, 1990, *The Effects of War on Mozambican Children: Preliminary Findings*, Maputo: Ministry of Education.

Roesch, Otto, 1986, *Socialism and Rural Development in Mozambique: The Case of Aldeia Comunal 24 de Julho*, Toronto: Ph.D. University of Toronto.

— 1988, 'Rural Mozambique Since the Frelimo Party Fourth Congress: The Situation in the Baixo Limpopo', in *ROAPE*, 41 (Sept.): 73–91.

— 1992, 'Mozambique Unravels? The Retreat to Tradition', in *Southern Africa Report*, May: 27–30.

— 1992, 'Renamo and the Peasantry in Southern Mozambique: A View from Gaza,' in *Canadian Journal of African Studies*, 26: 3.

— 1993, 'Peasants, War and 'Tradition' in Central Mozambique' (conference paper).

Rosa, Victor Pereira da and Salvato Trigo, 1986, *Portugueses e Moçambicanos no Apartheid*, Porto: Secretaria de Estado das Comunidades Portuguesas.

Rosenfeld, Stephen S., 1986, 'The Guns of July', in *Foreign Affairs*, Spring: 698–714.

Sanders, Jerry W., 1983, *Peddlers of Crisis*, Boston: South End Press.

Sarkesian, Sam, 1986, *The New Battlefield: The United States and Unconventional Conflicts*, New York: Greenwood.

Saul, John S., ed., 1985, *A Difficult Road: The Transition to Socialism in Mozambique*, New York: Monthly Review Press.

Savimbi, Jonas, 1979, *A Resistência em Busca de uma Nova Nação*, Lisbon: Agência Portuguesa de Revistas,

— 1986, *Por um Futuro Melhor*, Lisbon: Editora Nova Nórdica.

— 1986, 'The War against Soviet Colonialism', in *Policy Review*, Winter.

Shultz, Jr., Richard H. et al., eds, 1989, *Guerrilla War and Counterinsurgency*, Lexington, MA: Lexington Books.

Sitte, Fritz, 1977, *Inferno Schwarzafrica*, Vienna: Kremayr & Scheriau.

— 1981, *Flug in die Angola-Hölle: Der Vergessene Krieg*, Graz, Austria: Verlag Styria.

Skocpol, Theda, 1979, *States & Social Revolutions*, Cambridge: Cambridge University Press.

Skocpol, Theda and Margaret Somers, 1980, 'The Uses of Comparative History in Macrosocial Inquiry', in *Comparative Studies in Society and History*: 174–97.

Smith, Anthony D., 1986, *The Ethnic Origin of Nations*, Oxford: Blackwell.

Sogge, David, compiler, 1992, *Sustainable Peace: Angola's Recovery*, Harare: SARDC.

Somerville, Keith, 1986, *Angola: Politics, Economics and Society*, Boulder: Lynne Rienner.

Steenkamp, Willem, 1983, *Borderstrike!: South Africa into Angola*, Durban: Butterworths.

— 1989, *South Africa's Border War, 1966–1989*, Gibraltar: Ashanti Publishing.

Stockwell, John, 1978, *In Search of Enemies: A CIA Story*, New York: W.W. Norton.

Stouffer, Samuel A. et al., 1949, *The American Soldier*, Princeton: Princeton University Press.

Stubbs, Richard, 1989, *Hearts and Minds in Guerrilla Warfare: The Malayan Emergency*, Singapore: Oxford University Press.

Tickner, Vincent, 1992, 'Structural Adjustment and Agricultural Pricing in Mozambique', in *ROAPE*, No. 53: 25–42.

Tilly, Charles, 1964, *The Vendée*, Cambridge: Harvard University Press.

— 1978, *From Mobilization to Revolution*, Reading, MA: Addison-Wesley.

— 1984, *Big Structures, Large Processes, Huge Comparisons*, New York: Russell Sage Foundation.

UNICEF, 1989, *Children on the Front Line: The Impact of Destabilization on Children in southern and South Africa* (3rd edn), New York: UNICEF.

United Nations Inter-Agency Task Force, 1989, *South African Destabilization: The Economic Cost of Frontline Resistance to Apartheid*, New York: Economic Commission for Africa.

Vail, Leroy, ed., 1989, *The Creation of Tribalism in Southern Africa*, London: James Currey.

Valeriano, Napoleon D. and Charles T. R. Bohannan, 1962, *Counter-Guerrilla Operations: The Philippine Experience*, New York: Praeger.

Vance, Cyrus, 1983, *Hard Choices*, New York: Simon and Schuster.

Verschuur, Christine, M. Correa Lima, P. Lamy and German Velasquez, 1986, *Mozambique, Dix Ans de Solitude*, Paris: L'Harmattan.

Vines, Alex, 1991, 'Diary', in *Southern African Review of Books*, July/October.

— 1991, *Renamo: Terrorism in Mozambique*, London: James Currey.

— 1993, *One Hand Tied: Angola and the UN*, London: Catholic Institute of International Relations.

Wallerstein, Immanuel, 1989, *The Capitalist World-Economy*, Cambridge: Cambridge University Press.

Walters, Ronald W., 1987, *South Africa and the Bomb*, Lexington, MA: Lexington Books.

Weber, Max, 1949, *The Methodology of the Social Sciences*, New York: Free Press.

Wheeler, Douglas, 1976, 'African Elements in Portugal's Armies in Africa', in *Armed Forces and Society*, 2: 233–50.

White, Landeg, 1985, 'The Revolutions Ten Years On: Review Article', in *JSAS*, 11:2 (April): 320–32.

Wickham-Crowley, Timothy P., 1991, *Guerrillas and Revolution in Latin America*, Princeton: Princeton University Press.

Wilson, K.B., 1992, 'Cults of Violence and Counter-Violence in Mozambique', in *JSAS*, September: 527–82.

— 1992, *Deslocados Internos, Refugiados e Repatriados de e para Moçambique*, Stockholm: SIDA.

Windrich, Elaine, 1992, *The Cold War Guerrilla: Jonas Savimbi, the U.S. Media, and the Angolan War*, New York: Greenwood Press.

Wolf, Eric R., 1969, *Peasant Wars of the Twentieth Century*, New York: Harper & Row.

Wolfers, Michael and Jane Bergerol, 1983, *Angola in the Front Line*, London: Zed Books.

Wood, Brian, 1991, 'Preventing the Vacuum: Determinants of the Namibia Settlement', in *JSAS*, December: 742–69.

World Bank, 1991, *Angola: An Introductory Economic Review*, Washington: World Bank.

Wuyts, Marc, 1978, *Peasants and Rural Economy in Mozambique*, Maputo: African Studies Center.

— 1989, *Economic Management and Adjustment Policies in Mozambique*, Kingston, Jamaica: Conference Paper.

Young, Crawford, 1976, *The Politics of Cultural Pluralism*, Madison: University of Wisconsin Press.

— 1982, *Ideology and Development in Africa*, New Haven: Yale University Press.

— 1986, 'Nationalism, Ethnicity and Class in Africa', in *Cahiers d'Études Africaines*, v. 103: 421–95.

— 1988, 'The Colonial State and Post-Colonial Crisis', in Gifford and Louis.

Zartman, I. William, 1989, *Ripe for Resolution: Conflict and Intervention in Africa* (2nd edn), New York: Oxford University Press.

Index